RUSSIAN
INFORMATION
WARFARE

RUSSIAN INFORMATION WARFARE

Assault on Democracies in the Cyber Wild West

BILYANA LILLY

NAVAL INSTITUTE PRESS
Annapolis, Maryland

Naval Institute Press
291 Wood Road
Annapolis, MD 21402

Library of Congress Cataloging-in-Publication Data
Names: Lilly, Bilyana, author.
Title: Russian information warfare : assault on democracies in the cyber wild west /
   Bilyana Lilly.
Description: Annapolis, Maryland : Naval Institute Press, [2022] | Includes
   bibliographical references and index.
Identifiers: LCCN 2022006406 (print) | LCCN 2022006407 (ebook) |
   ISBN 9781682477199 (hardcover) | ISBN 9781682477472 (ebook)
Subjects: LCSH: Information warfare—Russia (Federation)—History—21st century.
   | Cyberspace operations (Military science)—Russia (Federation) | Hacking—Russia
   (Federation)—Political aspects. | Disinformation—Russia (Federation) | Western
   countries—Foreign relations—Russia (Federation) | Russia (Federation)—Foreign
   relations—Western countries. | BISAC: HISTORY / Military / Strategy | COMPUTERS
   / Security / General
Classification: LCC UA770 .L48 2022 (print) | LCC UA770 (ebook) |
   DDC 355/.033547—dc23/eng/20220223
LC record available at https://lccn.loc.gov/2022006406
LC ebook record available at https://lccn.loc.gov/2022006407

30 29 28 27 26 25 24 23 22   9 8 7 6 5 4 3 2 1
First printing

To Laura Survant and Fiona Hill

who showed me how to lead with grace

CONTENTS

ILLUSTRATIONS

Figures

Tables

PREFACE

This research examines how Moscow tries to trample the very principles on which democracies are founded and what we can do to stop it.[1] In particular, the book analyzes why and how the Russian government uses cyber operations, disinformation, protests, assassinations, coup d'états, and perhaps even explosions to destroy democracies from within, and what policies the United States and other NATO countries can introduce to defend themselves from Russia's onslaught.

The Kremlin has been using cyber operations as a tool of foreign policy against the political infrastructure of NATO member states for over a decade. Alongside these cyber operations, the Russian government has launched a diverse and devious set of activities that at first glance may appear chaotic. Russian military scholars and doctrine elegantly categorize these activities as related components of a single strategic playbook—information warfare. This concept breaks down the binary boundaries of war and peace, and views war as a continuous sliding scale of conflict, vacillating between the two extremes of peace and war but never quite reaching either. The Russian government has applied information warfare activities across NATO members to achieve various objectives. What are these objectives? What are the factors that most likely influence Russia's decision to launch a certain type of cyber operations against political infrastructure and how are they integrated with the Kremlin's other information warfare activities? To what extent are these cyber operations and information warfare campaigns effective in achieving Moscow's purported goals? This research addresses these questions and uses the findings to recommend improvements in the design of U.S. policy to counter Russian adversarial behavior in cyberspace by understanding under what conditions, against what election components, and for what purposes within broader information warfare campaigns Russia uses particular types of cyber operations against political infrastructure.

The book employs case study methods to identify patterns and areas of divergence across different cases that can inform the understanding of Russia's offensive cyber playbook. The case study–based method qualitative comparative analysis (QCA) was used to identify factors that correlate with the initiation of Russian cyber operations across seven cases of Russia-attributed cyber attacks against political infrastructure in different NATO states and invited members. These factors include economic, political, social, and military activities, as well as country characteristics such as the NATO membership status and geopolitical legacy of the targeted country.

The book also maps the role of Moscow's cyber operations in Russia's broader information warfare operations against political infrastructure by building a heat map, or a Hack Map, of the main political infrastructure that Russian cyber threat actors most frequently targeted across the different case studies. The research further used the case study method process-tracing to build a framework in which it visualized the range of Russian state-supported activities and showed the integration and potential interaction of these activities within each information warfare campaign.

By identifying factors associated with the launch of Russian cyber operations and by visualizing the main activities in each Russian information warfare operation, this research found patterns in Russia's offensive cyber operations that could facilitate the development of a theory about the factors that influence Russia's decision to employ different types of cyber operations against election targets, and how the state uses these operations in broader information warfare campaigns. The insights gained into how Russia employs this tool could enable the United States and other governments to detect, defend against, mitigate, and counter these campaigns more effectively. It would also allow broader public and private sector actors to anticipate likely scenarios where Russia could employ these tools and proactively address them.

ACKNOWLEDGMENTS

enjoyed writing this book because it not only provided me with the opportunity to spend a few years engrossed in reading the research of scholars and practitioners I deeply admire, but also gave me the wonderful excuse to travel to various countries in search of the clues that Russia's state-sponsored actors have left behind. During my research trips, I had my fair share of fun. While traveling across Eastern Europe, my hotel room was broken into and I was chased by a screaming Russian soldier who wanted to confiscate my camera. On another trip, I met Russian military veterans and may or may not have ridden a Soviet motorcycle. In between my adventures, I drew knowledge from local archives and significantly benefited from conversations with a number of experts who graciously provided feedback and recommendations, which vastly improved the quality of this publication.

The research is based on a dissertation that I wrote as a part of my PhD program at the Pardee RAND Graduate School. My dissertation committee members provided critical supervision. Christopher Paul, who agreed to take the helm and serve as the chair of this dissertation committee, guided my writing with enviable methodological elegance and wealth of knowledge. The arguments in this research are shaped by what I learned from Chris and I will be applying this knowledge throughout my career. Igor Mikolic-Torreira, who was a member of my dissertation committee, inspired and encouraged me from the beginning of this research and shepherded it from its inception to its completion. No logical inconsistency escaped his sharp eye while his limitless grace ensured that every criticism was gently delivered, yet never ignored. I am deeply grateful for the energy, expertise, and insights he offered. Quentin Hodgson, who also agreed to serve on my dissertation committee, believed in my potential and provided me with the platform to practice leadership and grow while conducting this research and during my time at the RAND Corporation. He is a mentor, a friend, and a partner in crime I am so grateful to have. Michael Daniel agreed to serve as the external reader for this research. He lent his monumental knowledge and experience, which significantly improved the arguments on these pages. His humility and patience with my questions throughout the process of writing this work were awe-inspiring.

My gratitude goes to the formidable Caolionn O'Connell, who gracefully shared her time and led my independent study at the RAND Corporation in preparation for writing this work. She not only pushed my research limits but also was the best St. Valentine's work date I have ever had.

Numerous other experts whom I met in the corridors of the RAND Corporation, at various conferences, or on field research trips contributed their ideas, shared invaluable leads on sources, or made introductions to critical contacts that enriched this analysis. My sincere thanks goes to Bruce McClintock, Katarzyna Pisarska, Zbigniew Pisarski, Rand Waltzman, Edward Geist, Damien Murphy, John Speed Meyers, Dominik Swiecicki, Björn Palmertz, Mikael Tofvesson, Piret Pernik, Merle Maigre, Liisa Past, Ellen Nakashima, Stephen Flanagan, Kenneth Geers, David Venable, Jair Aguirre, Jaclyn A. Kerr, Martti J. Kari, Keir Giles, Merike Kaeo, Bojan Stojkovski, Max Smeets, Bernt Tore Bratane, Christopher Chivvis, Marc Macaluso, Chris Karadjov, Mark Cozad, Romena Butanska, Eugene Han, Rouslan Karimov, Krystyna Marcinek, and Ljubomir Filipovic.

I would also like to express my deepest respect and gratitude to the following Russian scholars and practitioners: Vladimir Orlov, Evgeny Buzhinsky, Vadim Kozyulin, Yury Baluyevsky, Sergey Ryabkov, and Alexander Chekov for making time for my questions and helping me understand the nuances of Russia's position on various sensitive and controversial topics, even if our positions on these topics diverge. Sergey Chvarkov, deputy chief of Russia's Military Academy of the General Staff, allowed me to attend Russia's General Staff seminars on modern warfare. I was often the only non-Russian, non-military individual there, and yet I always felt welcome and was treated with respect. These events allowed me to gain unique insights into Russia's military thinking and into the debates of Russia's military elite.

The following experts deserve a special mention for making time to review major parts of this research and for sharing their remarkable expertise: Maria Raussau, Sale Lilly, Tihomir Bezlov, and my favorite coauthor on anything Russian, Joe Cheravitch.

I am deeply indebted to my wonderful acquisitions editor Padraic (Pat) Carlin, who saw potential in my scholarship and made the book you are now reading possible. Thank you, Pat, for your patience, guidance, and invaluable expertise. I would also like to thank the copy editor on my book manuscript, Carl Zebrowski, who genuinely impressed me with his attention to detail and commitment to improving every page of this narrative.

This research was generously funded by the Smith Richardson Foundation and the National Security Research Division at the RAND Corporation. The research was also sponsored through the Pardee RAND Graduate School awards: the Charles Wolf Jr. Dissertation Award, the Rothenberg Dissertation Award, and the Ford Foundation Award.

ABBREVIATIONS

AfD	Alternative for Germany (Alternative für Deutschland)
AI	artificial intelligence
AIVD	General Intelligence and Security Service of the Netherlands
ANSSI	French Network and Information Security Agency (L'Agence nationale de la sécurité des systèmes d'information)
APT	advanced persistent threat
BfV	Federal Office for the Protection of the Constitution (Bundesamt für Verfassungsschutz)
BMD	ballistic missile defense
BSI	Federal Office for Information Security (Bundesamt für Sicherheit in der Informationstechnik)
BSP	Bulgarian Socialist Party (Bulgarska Sotsialisticheska Partiya)
CCD COE	Cooperative Cyber Defence Centre of Excellence
CDU	Christian Democratic Union (Christlich-Demokratische Union)
CEC	Bulgarian Central Election Commission (Tsentralna izbiratelna komisiya)
CERT	computer emergency readiness team
CHAOS	cyber, hype, and associated operations
CIA	Central Intelligence Agency
CIA triad	confidentiality, integrity, and availability triad
CSS	cell site simulators
CSU	Christian Social Union (Christlich-Soziale Union)
CyCon	Conference on Cyber Conflict
DCCC	Democratic Congressional Campaign Committee
DDC	Defending Digital Campaigns
DDoS	distributed denial-of-service (attack)
DF	Democratic Front (Demokratska partija socijalista Crne Gore)
DHS	Department of Homeland Security

DIA	Defense Intelligence Agency
DNC	Democratic National Committee
DNS	Domain Name System
DoD	Department of Defense
DoJ	Department of Justice
DoS	denial-of-service (attack)
DPS	Democratic Party of Socialists (Demokratska partija socijalista Crne Gore)
EAC	Election Assistance Commission
EU	European Union
FAPSI	Federal Agency of Government Communications and Information
FBI	Federal Bureau of Investigation
FN	National Front (Front National)
FSB	Russian Federal Security Service (Federal'naya Sluzhba Bezopasnosti)
FSO	Federal Protective Service
GERB	Citizens for European Development of Bulgaria (Grazhdani za evropeiysko razvitie na Bulgariya)
GRAO	General Directorate for Civil Registration and Administrative Services (Grazhdanska registratsiya i administrativno obsluzhvane)
GRU	Russian Main Intelligence Directorate of the General Staff (Glavnoye Razvedyvatel'noye Upravleniye, Glavnoye Upravleniye)
IC	intelligence community
IoC	indicator of compromise
IRA	Internet Research Agency
ISP	internet service provider
IT	information technology
NATO	North Atlantic Treaty Organization
NGO	non-governmental organization
NSA	National Security Agency
OC	Open Campaign
ODNI	Office of the Director of National Intelligence
OSCE	Organization for Security and Co-operation in Europe
PST	Police Security Service (Politiets sikkerhetstjeneste)
QCA	qualitative comparative analysis
RCT	randomized controlled trial
SQL	structured query language
SVR	Russian Foreign Intelligence Service (Sluzhba Vneshney Razvedki)
TsRRSS	Center for Electronic Communications Surveillance
TTPs	tactics, techniques, and procedures
UN	United Nations
WADA	World Anti-Doping Agency

Introduction

I t was a regular working day in September of 2015. Yared Tamene, the technical support contractor at the headquarters of the U.S. Democratic National Committee (DNC), was sitting at his desk when he got an unusual phone call. The man on the line claimed to be Special Agent Adrian Hawkins of the Federal Bureau of Investigation (FBI). Special Agent Hawkins called to convey the troubling news that a Russian government agency had compromised the DNC's computer systems. Having doubts that Special Agent Hawkins was actually whom he claimed to be, Yared did not look too hard for the intruders and went on with his day.[1] Little did he know that the FBI agent was trying to prevent the most brazen state-sponsored cyber breach and subsequent documentation leak in U.S. election history. The IT specialist was completely oblivious to the fact that while he was calmly typing away at his desk, the same Russian agency that had plotted a coup d'état and assassinations against heads of state and weapons dealers in Eastern Europe, was currently roaming freely in the DNC networks. The Russian agency was harvesting data about Hillary Clinton's presidential campaign and was about to weaponize it in an unprecedented war against U.S. democracy that was going to rock the very foundations of U.S. governance.

Months before the 2016 U.S. presidential elections, Russian state-sponsored hackers breached the DNC and gained access to thousands of sensitive documents and emails related to the Hillary Clinton campaign, which the hackers subsequently disseminated through Western and Kremlin-sponsored personas and media.[2] In parallel to these activities, Russia-linked entities exploited Western social media platforms, notably Facebook, Twitter, and Instagram, to advertise the hacked material, promote anti-Clinton messages, and polarize the U.S. constituency through distributing socially divisive content.[3] These Russian state-supported activities pertain to a strategy that the Kremlin refers to as information warfare—a confrontation between states conducted for the purposes of achieving political goals.[4]

1

The cyber and information warfare operations against the 2016 U.S. elections are not an isolated event. Intelligence agencies and leaders of NATO member states have attributed a series of cyber operations targeting the political IT infrastructure of NATO countries and other post-Soviet states to the Russian government.[5] Such cyber operations include distributed denial-of-service (DDoS) attacks against Estonia in 2007 in the context of an incident caused by Estonia's decision to relocate a statue of a Soviet soldier, spear-phishing attacks against the presidential campaign of French candidate Emmanuel Macron in May 2017, and cyber operations against Bulgaria's Central Election Commission during Bulgaria's 2015 elections.[6]

These cases demonstrate that cyber operations attributed to the Russian government and conducted against political IT infrastructure have become increasingly prevalent in recent years. These cyber operations are components of broader Russian campaigns in which the Russian government employs a combination of military and nonmilitary measures, including cyber operations, disinformation, assassinations, and coup d'états to achieve its political objectives. These campaigns reflect the consensus reached among Russia's military and political leadership that the modern nature of interstate conflict is characterized by the conduct of adversarial activities through both military and nonmilitary means with a focus on eroding the social cohesion and the information environment of the adversary prior to and during conventional military activities.[7] The time of Russia's cyber operations and related adversarial activities against NATO member states roughly coincides with the establishment of general consensus among Russia's military leadership that Russia's definition of the conduct of warfare now includes nonmilitary and military measures. Russia's cyber activities against NATO states intensified after 2014, when that consensus was established and when Moscow's policies toward NATO and its member states became generally more aggressive and assertive.[8]

Through cyber operations against NATO member states, Russia demonstrated intent and capability to disrupt internet traffic and government communications, as well as to conduct cyber espionage. Although Russia-attributed cyber operations vary on multiple metrics, such as types and duration of the cyber operations and targets, existing research shows that the actors behind these malicious operations are often the same and their tactics, techniques, and procedures (TTPs) follow similar patterns.[9] Therefore, to identify the common triggers associated with the initiation of different types of cyber operations and understand the role of these cyber operations in Russia's information warfare in order to design effective policies to counter them, this research holistically examined all known cases of Russia-attributed cyber operations against political infrastructure in NATO members and countries invited to join NATO during military operations and in peacetime over the past fifteen years.

Various members of the U.S. political and military leadership have asserted that cyber operations against election targets and their role in broader Russian campaigns threaten to undermine the integrity of the Western democratic system of governance and compromise free elections.[10] Hacks against the United States and other states reveal a critical vulnerability of that infrastructure that can be exploited by adversaries to collect sensitive or classified data. Cyber operations in combination with disinformation spread via Russia-sponsored and Western social media have the potential to influence constituencies, disseminate false narratives for the benefit of an external actor, and encourage distrust in the legitimacy of democratic elections and institutions.

The Questions This Book Answers

Recognizing the gravity of this challenge, private companies, government agencies, and academic institutions have published and continue to release numerous studies on Russian cyber operations; the main perpetrators, targets, and other affected parties involved; the potential objectives of each operation; and its effectiveness. Despite the amount of analysis and high-quality investigative work already conducted on these critical issues, Western understanding regarding the conditions under which and how Russia employs its cyber capabilities offensively to serve foreign policy objectives is still evolving. Improving this understanding requires an examination of the evolution of the types of Russian cyber operations, such as confidentiality, integrity, or availability compromises described in chapter 2, as well as an analysis of how Russian agencies employ these operations in combination with other information warfare activities. Such a holistic analysis, which this research offers, can make a valuable contribution to the systematic and cumulative development of knowledge and theory about the past and likely future of Russian offensive cyber operations that can aid in formulating effective policies that Western states, and specifically the United States, can adopt to counter future Russian cyber activity.[11]

Russian state-sponsored cyber operations have become a persistent challenge for NATO and are likely to continue.[12] Effective policy to detect, prevent, and mitigate the consequences of such intrusions requires a foundation of systematic and methodologically rigorous research and analysis. To assist U.S. and other NATO policy makers in crafting a more effective policy against Russian cyber operations, this book analyzes under what conditions, in what contexts, and in what combinations with other nonmilitary and military measures Russia has employed certain types of cyber operations. In particular, this book explores what conditions have been associated with the employment of various types of Russian state-sponsored cyber operations against political IT infrastructure of NATO countries and invited members.[13] Related questions include what developments or changes in Russian policy or actions (if any) are associated with the use of different types of Russia-attributed cyber operations and what events or characteristics of the targeted country (for example, a particular diplomatic, military, or political incident regarding Russia) are associated with the use of different types of cyber operations? The book also examines the main actors involved (targets, defenders, attackers, etc.) and what political IT infrastructure in the targeted country the Russia government has targeted in each case. Furthermore, the research explores the other activities supported by the Russian government during the period of the cyber operations that may pertain to Russia's information warfare playbook.

The aim of the research is to map the anatomy of Russian cyber operations against political IT infrastructure and their role within Russia's information warfare operations.

The research evaluates the effectiveness of Russia's activities in achieving the objectives of the Russian government, and discusses what factors contributed to Russia's success or failure in each case. Based on these findings, the book recommends policy improvements that the United States and other NATO members could consider in defending their democracies against Russia's information warfare campaigns.

Main Criteria for Case Selection

To constrain the case studies to a manageable number while still allowing for sufficient analytical breadth and depth to answer the research questions, this research applied the following case selection criteria:

1. Target scoping: The research treats cyber operations against political IT infrastructure within a particular country as the unit of analysis/selection. This criterion is chosen because it allows for the analysis to focus on cyber operations specifically related to democratic processes and, in some cases, broader Russian campaigns against western elections, which are of particular concern to U.S. policy makers in the period of this analysis. Sven Herpig at the German Stiftung Neue Verantwortung defines political IT infrastructure as "the IT-systems, networks, and cloud services accounts of politicians, political parties, legislatures and any other institution engaged in the conduct of elections. These stakeholders and IT-infrastructures are at the core of any political system."[14]

    This research also includes cyber operations against agencies that belong to the information sphere and explains this framework in detail in chapter 2.

    The analysis focuses on cases of cyber operations against political IT infrastructure engaged in the conduct of elections on the territory of the state and excludes cases in which cyber operations have been launched exclusively against ministries of foreign affairs. This scoping criterion is applied because these institutions, although involved in managing extraterritorial voters though embassies, fall outside of the core agencies that organize and conduct elections on the state's territory. In cases where Russian state-sponsored cyber threat groups have launched cyber operations against foreign ministries in addition to operations against other political IT infrastructure, the analysis examines the operations against the ministries as well. This restriction also enables the researcher to focus on a manageable number of case studies.

2. Attribution: There are no universally accepted guidelines for attributing incidents in cyberspace. The standards of evidence for attribution vary widely among governments and private-sector companies, and so do the types of attribution. Andrew Grotto, for example, categorizes attribution into two types: analytic and strategic. The first category describes "what an analyst knows (or thinks he or she knows) about the identity of a malicious cyber actor."[15] Strategic attribution pertains to "what the analyst does with the analytic attribution, which includes keeping the judgment private, disclosing it to selected third parties, or making it public."[16] Other experts use the terms "technical attribution" and "political attribution" to delineate roughly the same

two categories of attribution.[17] The U.S. intelligence community (IC), for example, has clear guidelines on how to reach technical attribution for cyber incidents that the IC tracks. Once the technical attribution is achieved, the U.S. government makes a carefully weighted decision on whether to disclose the conclusion of the technical attribution process and how much of the evidence that contributed to the technical attribution to disclose publicly. The decision of the U.S. government is based on technical and geopolitical factors, and therefore, is more accurately categorized as a political or strategic, rather than technical or analytic, attribution.[18]

This research examines only cyber operations that have been publicly attributed to a group affiliated with the Russian government. This attribution criterion is considered satisfied if government intelligence services, another government agency, or cybersecurity companies that have worked on the particular cyber attack or intrusion make public attributions, or based on the terminology discussed in the previous paragraph, issue a strategic or political attribution, accepted as compelling by a broad cross section of cyber experts. The attribution must assert that Russian agencies such as the Federal Security Service (Federal'naya Sluzhba Bezopasnosti, or FSB) or the Main Intelligence Directorate (Glavnoye Razvedyvatel'noye Upravleniye, Glavnoye Upravleniye, or GRU), or criminal groups affiliated with the Russian government, were involved in the respective cyber operations. As a joint Central Intelligence Agency (CIA), National Security Agency (NSA), and Federal Bureau of Investigation (FBI) report assessing Russia's activities and intentions during the 2016 U.S. presidential elections states, "Every kind of cyber operation—malicious or not—leaves a trail."[19]

3. Evidence criteria: A significant methodological challenge with classifying Russia's methods of interference is the inability to possess complete information on most, if not all, of Russia's cyber operations and related information warfare activities. This criteria is closely related to the issue of attribution—to complete a meaningful case study, cyber operations need not only to be attributed to Russian state-supported cyber threat groups, but also to be sufficiently well documented. Therefore, the research examines only known and documented cases of cyber intrusions attributed to the Russian state. For the purposes of this research, a case is analyzed if there is more than anecdotal evidence and enough open-source information of an operation to allow the researcher to answer the research questions posed in this book.

Another major data collection limitation is the inability to possess perfect information about cyber attacks on political infrastructure not only because of the reluctance of governments and the private sector to release information about some cases but also because of the improvements in technology that facilitate defending information networks against cyber attacks. Because of the existence of automated systems that can divert and filter overloading web requests that are elements of DDoS attacks, there may be cases that have not been reported because these defenses have prevented the negative impacts of the DDoS attacks in their early stages.[20]

4. Geopolitical scoping: Only NATO member states and nations en route to obtain NATO membership are included in this analysis. Countries en route to joining the

alliance are examined in this research if they have been invited to start accession talks and have signed the accession protocol.[21] NATO agencies and NATO infrastructure are not studied in this research because they are not parts of national political infrastructures. This criterion is applied because of research considerations: there is data available in English, Russian, German, Bulgarian, Serbian, and French about Russian cyber operations against NATO states and invited members. Additionally, the author's familiarity with NATO and future members that Russia has targeted in the past provides an opportunity for productive field research and increases the likelihood that the researcher would collect unique evidence to enrich this analysis.

5. Temporal scoping: The cases of Russia-attributed cyber operations considered in this research occurred between January 2007 and January 2020. The author chose year 2007 as a temporal starting point because it marks the first large-scale and publicly known cyber operation against a state that was attributed to the Russian government—Russia's DDoS attacks against Estonia. There may have been other cases of Russian state-sponsored cyber operations against nation-states before 2007, but these are either not publicly known or fail to satisfy one of the other criteria that this research used to select the examined case studies. The ending temporal boundary is the start of 2020 because of the need to limit data collection and complete this work, and due to the paucity of data and usual delay of attribution announcements and evidence regarding recent cases.

These criteria allow the selection of a purposeful sample of diverse cases that would enable the researcher to trace the evolution and patterns of Russia's state-sponsored cyber operations.

Identifying the Cases This Book Analyzes

In compiling the list of candidate cases, in addition to academic databases such as JSTOR and EBSCO, and media and private sector websites, the research consulted the Timeline of Key Nation-State Cyber Operations created by the Center for Long-Term Cybersecurity, University of California–Berkley; *NATO Review*'s History of Cyber Attacks—A Timeline; the database of Significant Cyber Incidents compiled by the Center for Strategic and International Studies; and the Cyber Operations Tracker maintained by the Council on Foreign Relations.[22] Although the research included cases that have occurred between January 2007 and January 2020, these databases were consulted on a regular basis until March 2021 because of the potential for a public release of new information about cases included in this research.

Based on the above-mentioned criteria, the population of possible cases is Russia-attributed cyber operations on the political IT infrastructure of NATO member states and invited members since 2007 that are sufficiently well documented to research. Cases, such as Russian state-sponsored cyber operations against the 2018 U.S. midterm elections and the cyber operations against German parliament members in 2018, lacked data on the timing and targets of cyber operations and related Russian state-sponsored activities.[23]

This selection of case studies is a subset of all cases in which Russia has employed cyber operations and, therefore, the examined cases do not represent the entire universe of potential uses of cyber operations by the Russian state. Other subsets of the larger set of Russian cyber operations include cyber operations against critical infrastructure, including electrical grids, for example in the case of Ukraine in 2015 and 2016, and cases where Russian actors have used cyber operations against international organizations, for example, the cyber operation against NATO's headquarters in Brussels in 2013, the cyber operation on the Organization for Security and Co-operation in Europe (OSCE) in 2015, and the cyber operation against the World Anti-Doping Agency (WADA). This research also excludes cyber operations on economic or private IT infrastructure. Such cases that are out of the scope of this analysis include the cyber operation against the Warsaw stock exchange in 2014 and against France's TV5 Monde in 2015. Cases in which the Russian government has been *suspected* of attempting to meddle in elections but is not confirmed to have conducted cyber operations alongside the use of other information tools during these elections include, for example, the UK referendum on Brexit in 2016 and the Catalonian independence referendum in 2017; because of uncertain attribution such cases are also not examined here. These examples of cases of probable Russian cyber aggression or of Russian attacks against targets other than political IT infrastructure are included alongside all of the cases that do satisfy all inclusion criteria in table I.1. The excluded cases are still mentioned in the book as examples of other Russian operations but have not been subjected to detailed case study analysis. This research studies all identified cases that satisfy the abovementioned five criteria. Therefore, these cases constitute the full census of the population defined by these five constraints.

Seven cases in table I.1 meet the criteria of this research. These cases are:

1. 2007: DDoS attacks and other cyber operations against the Estonian official government websites as a part of broader cyber operations against Estonian IT infrastructure of media organizations, banking services, and other IT infrastructure;
2. 2015: Cyber intrusion into Germany's lower house of parliament, the Bundestag, which German authorities associated with Germany's 2017 parliamentary elections;
3. 2015: DDoS attack on the Bulgarian Central Election Commission and other political IT infrastructure during national elections and a referendum;
4. 2016: Cyber intrusions into the U.S. DNC and related targets, such as voter databases and software systems across the United States;
5. 2016: Attempted cyber intrusion into Norway's Labor Party as a part of a broader cyber operation whose other targets included Norway's army and intelligence services;
6. 2016: DDoS attacks against the websites of the government of Montenegro, NGOs, and media; and
7. 2016–2017: Cyber intrusions into the election campaign of French presidential candidate Emmanuel Macron.

TABLE I.1 A Selection Illustrating the Universe of Case Studies[24]

Targeted Country	Year	Attributed	NATO/Member en route	Political IT Infrastructure	Sufficient Documentation
Estonia	2007	Yes	Yes	Yes	Yes
Georgia	2008	Yes	No	Yes	Yes
Lithuania	2008	No	Yes	Yes	No
Kyrgyzstan	2009	No	No	No	No
Finland	2013	No	Yes	No	No
NATO	2014	No	No	No	No
United States	2014	Yes	Yes	No	No
Poland	2014	Yes	Yes	No	No
Ukraine	2014	Yes	No	Yes	Yes
The Netherlands	2015	Yes	Yes	No	No
France	2015	Yes	Yes	No	Yes
Bulgaria	2015	Yes	Yes	Yes	Yes
Ukraine	2015	Yes	No	No	Yes
Germany	2015	Yes	Yes	Yes	Yes
United States	2015–2016	Yes	Yes	Yes	Yes
OSCE	2016	Yes	No	No	No
Ukraine	2016	Yes	No	No	Yes
WADA	2016	Yes	Yes	No	Yes
Turkey	2016	Yes	Yes	Yes	No
Norway	2016	Yes	Yes	Yes	Yes
Montenegro	2016	Yes	Yes	Yes	Yes
France	2016–2017	Yes	Yes	Yes	Yes
The Netherlands	2017	Yes	Yes	Yes	No
Czech Republic	2017	Yes	Yes	No	No
Petya, NotPetya	2017	Yes	No	No	Yes
Pyeong Chang Olympic Games	2018	Yes	No	No	Yes
Germany	2017	Yes	Yes	No	No
United Kingdom	2018	Yes	Yes	No	No
United States	2018	Yes	Yes	Yes	No
Ukraine	2019	Yes	No	Yes	Yes
Finland	2019	No	No	Yes	No
Czech Republic	2019	No	Yes	No	No
United Kingdom	2019	Yes	Yes	Yes	No
Georgia	2019	Yes	No	Yes	No
Ukraine	2020	Yes	No	No	No

In most of the cases, more than one cyber operation has been attributed to Russian cyber state actors. These cyber operations were examined within the context of a single case study due to their temporal proximity and the likelihood that they were a part of the same Russian information warfare campaign.

The years indicated in this timeline reflect the time of the discovery of the known cyber operations(s) and do not delineate the period of the overall Russian information warfare campaign. These years served as a starting point but the start and end date of each Russian cyber and information warfare campaign were refined as the research progressed to include all known Russian state-supported activities that were a part of each information warfare campaign.

Methodology and Data Collection

To gain a better understanding of Russia's behavior in cyberspace and the role of cyber operations in Russia's information warfare operations, this analysis consulted a variety of secondary and primary data sources and employed a mixed-methods approach. Among the main data sources this research used were archival materials, journal and news media articles, books, and primary-source data collected through interviews. The main two approaches this book used to conduct comparisons of the different cases are qualitative comparative analysis (QCA) and process tracing, which form an appropriate combinatorial strategy for comparative-historical analysis of similarities and differences across a medium number of case studies. This section elaborates on these methods below under the subsection "Methods." In case studies where there is enough publicly available data, Lockheed Martin's Cyber Kill Chain model was used as a complementary mapping technique that facilitated a deeper understanding of the stages of Russian cyber operations.

DATA COLLECTION

To describe the evolution of Russia's institutions and main stakeholders involved in the decision-making and deploying of cyber capabilities, as well as to collect preliminary data on Russian cyber operations, the research conducted an initial systematic literature review using databases such as JSTOR, EastView, EBSCO, and Google Scholar. The research also consulted secondary literature from prominent researchers and research conducted by the Congressional Committee of Foreign Relations and the RAND Corporation.[25] To understand and analyze the role of cyber operations in Russia's information warfare, the research consulted Russian official documents such as Russia's Cybersecurity Strategy, National Security Strategy, and Military Doctrine, as well as Russian-language publications in prominent Russian military journals such as *Military Thought* (Voyennaya Mysl').

To enrich the analysis of each case study, the author talked with experts and individuals involved in or affected by Russian cyber operations. To select the discussants, the researcher created a list based on a review of the secondary literature and attendance of cybersecurity conferences such as the annual U.S.-based hacker conference DefCon and the annual Conference on Cyber Conflict, known as CyCon, organized by NATO's Center for Cyber Excellence in Estonia. The list contained the names of journalists who cover each case of Russian cyber operations, companies that publish technical information on these attacks, and individuals affected by each cyber operation or those who have been involved in managing it. The researcher further identified and attempted to talk with detained hackers who have been suspected or accused of playing a role in Russian-attributed cyber operations. Initially, the researcher created a diversity sample based on the collected data and then used a snowballing strategy to ask the individuals with whom she talked to recommend others for her to approach. The primary questions the researcher raised during the discussions aimed to collect additional information on the stages of each cyber operation and the role of the involved individuals. The researcher further solicited expert feedback on what other policies targeted countries could adopt to better respond to and mitigate the effects of Russia's cyber operations.

METHODS

The research commenced with a comprehensive literature review and a historical overview of the evolution and current status of Russia's cyber doctrine and forces, and their role in Russian foreign policy. To identify the main factors associated with the initiation of different Russian cyber operations and to draw comparisons between cyber operations against political infrastructure within and across cases, the book used qualitative comparative analysis.[26] This qualitative narrative was used to identify factors that were tested comparatively across all case studies. The method is appropriate because it allows for the variable-oriented documentation of similarities and differences across cases. QCA identifies factors associated with a phenomenon from supported hypotheses across case studies and allows for parsimony while still enabling the comparison of complex concepts. This method provides a holistic historical comparison by identifying binary factors (present or absent) in each case. The algebraic basis for this synthesis approach is Boolean algebra, which assigns 1 (if present) and 0 (if absent) to identified factors listed in so-called truth tables. The basic logic of Boolean algebra is that if any of the additive factors is present in the particular case, then the outcome is true (it occurs).[27] The number of rows in a truth table is equivalent to the number of combinations of values of the identified factors across the examined case studies. If there are more possible combinations of these factors than are observed across the examined case studies, the rows of the truth table are reduced to match the number of combinations of factors observed by the researcher. The application of a truth table offers a structured approach to complex problems and enables the identification of a minimum set of factors required for the occurrence of a certain outcome, called "prime implicants."[28]

The result of this comparative process is the reduction of factors to a minimum number of mandatory conditions that are sufficient or necessary to explain the observed phenomena under study, which in this case are different factors that are associated with the initiation of Russian cyber operations. The case studies literature differentiates between necessary and sufficient factors. As sociologist Charles Ragin explains, factors are deemed necessary if they "must be present for a certain outcome to occur," while a factor is sufficient if "by itself it can produce a certain outcome."[29] The combination of these factors provides the following categorization: a factor is considered both sufficient and necessary if that factor is the only one that is associated with an outcome without being included in a combination of factors. A factor is sufficient but not necessary if it produces an outcome but is not the only factor that can do so. A factor is necessary but not sufficient if it is present in all combinations with other factors in cases with a particular outcome.[30] A factor is neither sufficient nor necessary if it appears only in some cases of the combinations that are associated with a certain outcome.[31] For example, in the process of this research, the researcher attempted to identify a group of factors that, in combination, seem to be associated with the occurrence of a particular type of cyber attack. Let's label these factors X1, X2, and X3, and the type of attack Y. If this research reveals that the combination of X1 and X2 causes Y in one case study and the combination of X1 and X3 correlates with Y in another, then the researcher may conclude that if X1 is accompanied by X2 or X3 but not both at the same time, these two combinations result in Y. In this case X1 is a necessary but not sufficient factor for Y, while X2 and X3 are sufficient factors.[32] Sufficient factors must appear only in cases with one particular outcome and must be absent from comparable cases with a different outcome, while individual necessary factors may appear in cases with different outcomes but may not appear in the combination of necessary factors that must be present for an alternative outcome to occur.[33]

In identifying the absence or presence of necessary and sufficient factors in each case, the researcher also attempted to determine factors that may thwart the occurrence of a particular outcome when they are present or absent alongside the identified necessary and sufficient factors.[34]

The method was used to identify economic, political/diplomatic, social, media-related, and military factors that could be associated with the initiation of a particular cyber operation. The list of QCA factors was compiled based on a systematic literature review of academic articles, think tank reports, congressional testimonies, news sources, and expert opinion. The list of factors was tested with each case study. The final list produced as a result of the comprehensive cross-case QCA established the conditions associated with the initiation of Russian cyber intrusions. The identification of such factors can inform a theoretical framework that can be used to design effective policy responses to mitigate and counter Russian cyber intrusions.

The research compiled a detailed narrative for each case study based on already published literature and analyses of each case, and interviews with experts and individuals involved in or affected by Russia-attributed cyber operations. To compare and contrast the common and divergent stages, processes, and actors involved in each selected case of a Russian-attributed cyber operation and to demonstrate and document how each cyber operation is related to other information warfare tools, the book used narrative comparison. The particular method of narrative comparison this research employed to conduct within-case comparison is process tracing, defined as "systematic examination of diagnostic evidence selected and analyzed in light of research questions and hypotheses posed by the investigator."[35] Process tracing was used to establish a comparative framework for outlining the evolution of each cyber operation and its relation to broader Russian information warfare campaigns across case studies. The research applied an iterative process, characterized by a continuous dialogue between the emerging theory and evidence.

To identify the stages of each cyber operation and to assess the adequacy of cyber incidence response and defense, the analysis used Lockheed Martin's Cyber Kill Chain.[36] The Cyber Kill Chain model was applied to the data in cases with sufficient information because it is a classic framework used by cybersecurity experts to map stages of cyber operations, analyze the response of the defender, as well as compare the stages of each cyber operation and the responses across cases.

HYPOTHESES

The analysis commenced by outlining two hypotheses and proceeded to validate these hypotheses through the case studies. The hypotheses stem from an initial informal survey of the existing literature, primarily recently published works regarding Russia's information warfare tactics.[37] Considering the absence of strong theory to guide this inquiry, the research tested the following hypotheses:

> A systemic evaluation of the outlined case studies will reveal several distinct necessary and sufficient factors that are consistently present upon and therefore associated with the initiation of particular types of a Russia-attributed cyber operation. For example, the presence of a political candidate with an anti-Russian agenda or a candidate that the Russian government clearly prefers close to elections in the target state may be associated with cyber intrusions aimed at data collection and leaking. The presence of a disputed issue between Russia and the targeted state, such as an energy dispute or a historically relevant dispute, would be associated with cyberattacks, particularly DDoS attacks aimed at disputing the proper functioning of infrastructure. Former communist states are more likely to be targets of DDoS attacks, while Western governments without a communist legacy are more likely to be targets of cyber incidents aimed at collecting and leaking information.
>
> A cross-case analysis of Russia's cyber operations reveals a pattern of Russian cyber behavior and its integration with other Russian information warfare activities that can inform a discussion of Russia's information warfare playbook.

The policy implications from this analysis rest on the assumption that Russia will continue to develop, refine, and use its cyber capabilities to achieve a variety of foreign policy objectives unless and until Western states design an effective deterrence strategy that raises the strategic stakes to such an extent that the Russian government considers the costs of an operation too high and is therefore deterred from further employing such tactics. As FBI Director James Comey stated in a congressional testimony in March 2017, we can expect that the Russian government will continue. The Kremlin may not use identical tactics to those used in previous operations, but the record suggests that the Russian government tends to reuse those tactics that have proven successful.[38]

DEFINITIONS

Russian military and political leaders view the term *cybersecurity* as a Western notion and typically opt to use the Russian semantic equivalent "information security" (*informatsion-naya bezopastnost*). As the target audience for this research is Western academics and decision makers, the book uses the Western term "cyber operations" and other related terms defined in this section and chapter 1 to refer to Russia's activities in cyberspace.

This book uses the definitions of *cyber attack* and *cyber intrusion* outlined in the 2017 report by the U.S. Department of Defense Task Force on Cyber Deterrence. Cyber attack is defined as "any deliberate action that affects the desired availability and/or integrity of data or information systems integral to operational outcomes of a given organization." Such cyber attacks "may have temporary or permanent effects; they may be destructive of equipment or only disruptive of services; and they may be conducted remotely or by close access (including by insiders)."[39] The book also examines cases of cyber intrusions, which are breaches into information systems that do not affect data availability and/or integrity.[40] Such intrusions can be conducted for the purposes of data exfiltration and espionage, affecting data confidentiality.

Cyber operations, *cyber activities*, and *cyber campaigns* are used as composite terms that include both cyber attacks and cyber intrusions.

This research applies the Russian doctrinal understanding that cyber operations are a component of the broader concept of *information warfare*, which consists of both cyber operations and psychological operations (see the next chapter for a more detailed discussion). Information warfare is a strategy that the Russian government deploys during peacetime and war to advance Moscow's national interests.[41]

The research uses the definition of *information warfare* as outlined by Russia's Defense Ministry and publications by Russian senior military leaders and scholars. Based on these sources, information warfare is a major component of interstate relations and interstate confrontation, conducted both before the use of military force and during wartime through states' social and political movements and organizations, as well as through their armed forces. Each party seeks to inflict damage on and influence the information environment of the opposing party and protect its own in the interests of achieving set goals. Information warfare is a type of confrontation "in which information becomes its resource, means and purpose."[42] The term information warfare is discussed in more depth in the next chapter.

When examining Russia's cyber operations in each case study, this research describes the information warfare activities or operations that are attributed to the Russian government in each case. The range and categories of these activities is initially compiled on the basis of Russian doctrine, publications of senior Russian military, civilian researchers, and Western experts who have described Russia's activities in each case. Russia's information warfare activities include, but are not limited to, what the United States, NATO, and NATO nations call psychological operations, intelligence and counterintelligence activities, disinformation, electronic warfare, and destruction of computer capabilities.[43]

A Russian *information warfare operation* or *information warfare campaign* is defined as the composition of various types of information warfare and military activities used to achieve a broad set of objectives within the same case study.

BACKGROUND AND EXISTING DEBATES

The major debates in the cybersecurity literature that focus on Russian cyber operations and behavior in cyberspace fall under two categories. The first category is political science narratives that describe and analyze Russia's military science publications and cybersecurity doctrine. These narratives attempt to explain how cybersecurity is linked to Russian foreign policy. This literature contains little technical detail on the tactics and evolution of Russia's cyber capabilities and actors. The second body of literature focuses on mapping the stages of Russian cyber operations and describes the tactics, techniques, and procedures (TTPs) of the attackers. This literature contains a lot of technical jargon and does not put these tactics in the context of general political science literature on Russian security strategy.

Some literature focuses on explaining the role of cyber operations in Russia's strategic culture, and specifically, in Russia's information warfare as a part of Russia's evolving doctrine of modern conflict.[44] These analyses use slightly different definitions and provide a broad overview of the range of Russia's activities, including cyber operations and their relation to other Russian information warfare activities. They do not provide much detail on Russia's cyber capabilities or tactics or assess systematically the factors associated with the initiation of various cyber operations. Yet, some of these publications list a set of factors that could be associated with Russia's decision to support the launch of a cyber operation.

Moreover, in the political science literature, some research either examines Russian information warfare activities in various case studies, only mentioning disinformation operations, or primarily focuses on examining disinformation operations.[45] These studies fill in valuable under-researched areas in the Western understanding of Russian information warfare activities. Yet, they do not typically combine analysis of Russian state-sponsored media as one of the overt channels of Russian influence, with an examination of cyber operations. This research combines the two and maps strategic-messaging media campaigns on the timeline of events, searching for the patterns between cyber and psychology. This research further discusses other Russian state-supported activities such as protests, assassinations, and coup d'état, which alongside cyber and strategic-messaging operations, form a single information warfare campaign.

Another group of publications analyzes the technical footprint of Russian hackers and their methods. Excellent reports by cybersecurity companies and computer emergency readiness teams (CERTs) have made substantial contributions to our understanding of Russia's use of cyber operations. Such reports have been published by cybersecurity firms such as FireEye, CrowdStrike, and Palo Alto Networks, journalists, and U.S. and other government CERTs.[46] This literature explores the TTP of various adversaries and builds their cyber playbooks to facilitate researchers and network defenders who can use this information to improve their defenses against identified indicators of compromise (IOCs) used to profile and detect cyber adversaries.

Some of these publications also address the question of attribution. Although experts acknowledge that states and private companies are improving their ability to attribute cyber operations, researchers still raise concerns regarding the continued lack of a standardized, universally accepted methodology applicable to investigations to assess evidence. There is debate around what evidence is sufficient to attribute a cyber operation to actors and what elements of the investigative process of attribution governments should publish versus what elements they should maintain as classified.[47] The criterion of sufficiency is also driven by the purpose of the attribution and may be a higher threshold in cases where sanctions, instead of diplomatic warning, are considered as a response. Public attribution also varies from private attribution. The U.S. government often attributes attacks internally without disclosing attribution to the public.[48] Attribution also has a political dimension and, therefore, could be categorized as analytic and strategic, which is explained further in the section "Main Criteria for Case Selection" above.[49]

There is still a need to bridge the gap between these categories of research and understand the role of Russia-attributed cyber operations in Russia's evolving security policy and information warfare activities. Therefore, this research focuses on this issue.

BOOK OUTLINE

In chapter 1, the book describes Russia's modern conception of information warfare and the role of cyber operations in this understanding, as outlined in Russia's foreign policy documents, the writings of Russian and Western military science elite, and the speeches of the senior Russian leadership. The chapter proceeds by describing the known characteristics of Russia's agencies and cyber groups that employ cyber capabilities in fulfillment of Russia's cyber doctrine, their evolution, and their role in Russia's foreign policy.

The next chapter (chapter 2) uses the knowledge of Russia's conceptual understanding of information warfare to build several frameworks applied in the subsequent chapters to compare and contrast the different case studies. The first framework applies QCA methods to identify factors associated with the initiation of different types of Russian cyber operations. The second framework is a modification of a heat map, called a Hack Map, used to identify the political IT infrastructure components that Russian cyber groups target most and least frequently. The third framework visualizes Russia's state-sponsored cyber and psychological activities, and shows their chronological application and integration with the entire range of Russia's information warfare activities. The framework has been developed as a part of this research and is called CHAOS (Cyber, Hype, and Associated OperationS). Chapter 2 provides a detailed explanation of the various components of CHAOS.

Chapters 3 through 9 present a detailed investigation of Russia's information warfare in the seven case studies selected for this analysis. Chapter 10 synthesizes the divergent and convergent characteristics of each case revealed through the application of the frameworks presented in chapter 2 and draws general conclusions about Russia's cyber behavior, the factors that are associated with the initiation of Russian cyber operations, their role within Russia's general information warfare toolbox, and their effectiveness.

In chapter 11, the research offers policy recommendations that the U.S. government and other NATO governments can adopt to counter and mitigate the consequences of Russia's cyber operations and broader information warfare campaigns.

The final chapter summarizes some of the main findings of this cross-case comparative analysis and offers final thoughts on how to counter Russia's onslaught on democracies in the cyber wild west.

1

The Role of Cyber Operations and Forces in Russia's Understanding of Warfare

A Foundation for Subsequent Frameworks

To provide context for the role of Russia's cyber operations in Russian foreign policy, this chapter commences by examining Russia's current strategic outlook and Russia's perception of modern warfare as described in Russian official documents and in the writings of Russia's political and military leaders. The analysis then situates cyber operations in Russia's discussions of modern warfare and the contemporary means of waging and prevailing in a conflict. Analyzing cyber operations within the context of Russia's evolving perceptions of warfare informs Western decision makers' understanding of the rationale for Russia's interference. This approach offers a logical foundation for an analytical framework that outlines the main categories of activities that the Russian government is likely to employ to achieve political objectives in peacetime and during war. Since Russia's cyber operations are shaped by Moscow's objectives as well as its available capabilities, this chapter concludes by outlining the evolution and the current status of Russia's government agencies and related groups that are believed to employ cyber capabilities on behalf of the Russian government.[1]

Russia's Strategic Outlook

Russia's senior military and political officials argue that the current geopolitical environment is characterized by increasing tensions and growing likelihood of conflict, due primarily to the shifting balance of powers and erosion of the Western system of global governance. According to Moscow, in this volatile environment, aggressive states led by the United States have harnessed the potential of advanced technologies to craft a modern method of warfare that differs from the traditional twentieth-century model. Russian military and political leaders, forced to defend their territory, population, and allies against the threat of contemporary coercion and conquest, have embarked upon redefining their conceptualization of modern warfare. According to this modified view, information warfare (*informatsionnoye protivoborstvo*) and one of its tools, cyber attacks (*kiberataki*), are central to waging and winning contemporary conflicts. Drawing primarily upon examples of U.S.

interventions in the past three decades, the Russian military science literature emphasizes that information warfare is a principal component of modern warfare that serves as the cohesive agent and the blood of modern conflict, such that gaining information superiority (*informatsionnoye prevoskhodstvo*) over the adversary is critical for prevailing in war. In the context of warfare, information warfare operations are employed throughout periods of peace and during the deployment of military force. These operations are used to meet multiple objectives ranging from disabling critical infrastructure to eroding social cohesion within the territory of the adversary.

VOLATILE GLOBAL ENVIRONMENT AND GROWING LIKELIHOOD OF CONFLICT

Russia's intellectual elite and official documents paint a common picture of Russia's perceptions of the international order. They describe the international environment in a state of transition, in which Russia and its role as a global power is threatened by aggressive forces, primarily Western countries that strive to maintain the eroding Western-based system of governance. Russia's foreign policy concepts, national strategies, and military doctrines provide more detail on Russia's worldview. These documents espouse the narrative that the twentieth-century system of governance, largely built upon Western principles to benefit the United States and its allies, is unfavorable to Russia and its allies and is undergoing fundamental changes. Russia's four foreign policy concepts, published in 2000, 2008, 2013, and 2016, display a turn away from the optimism of the early post–Cold War period.[2] The 2000 foreign policy concept identifies U.S. unilateralism and the U.S.-centric approach to global governance as major sources of global instability that can increase tensions and aggravate interstate contradictions.[3] The 2008 and 2013 foreign policy concepts reiterate these arguments and stipulate that the West is experiencing relative decline while new centers of power, to include Russia, are emerging. The concepts criticize Western efforts to maintain its global "monopoly" and contain Russia again. The documents argue that the refusal of Western powers to relinquish their leadership leads to destabilization in the international environment, tensions, and even an arms race.[4] In this volatile environment, the risk of Russia being forced to engage in a conflict has increased.[5] Mirroring the bleak world conditions described in the foreign policy concepts, Russia's 2009 and 2015 national security strategies criticize the flawed regional and global architecture and contend that chances to maintain stability are decreasing.[6] The military doctrine of 2010 and its updated successor released in 2014, consistently echo Russia's antagonistic view of the global order, the United States, and NATO.[7]

Russia's senior political and military elites agree with the views presented in Russia's official documents. In his seminal 2007 speech at the Munich Security Conference, President Vladimir Putin asserted that the unconstrained use of military force is "plunging the world into an abyss of permanent conflicts" and, referring to the United States, warned that a unipolar world exemplified by one center of decision-making, authority, and force has pernicious effects on the whole system. Putin asserted that in this hostile environment, preserving peace by political means "becomes impossible."[8] Russia's longtime foreign minister Sergey Lavrov has consistently repeated the same vision. Lavrov stated in 2007 that the unipolar world acts as a mechanism for expansion of conflict worldwide.[9] In November 2017, Lavrov asserted that the efforts of a group of states spearheaded by the United States to adapt Cold War institutions to modern realities and establish a unipolar world order have failed. According to Lavrov, new security challenges are emerging and resistance to allowing emerging centers of power to exercise independent foreign policy will lead to chaos and instability, amid a growing number of conflicts.[10]

THE UNITED STATES AND NATO AS MAIN AGGRESSORS AND THREATS TO RUSSIA

Russia's strategic documents and leadership assign the primary blame for the increasing likelihood of conflict in the international environment to Western countries, and especially to the United States and NATO. Classic early examples used to illustrate this claim are the Gulf War in 1991, NATO's bombing of Yugoslavia in the 1990s, the war in Afghanistan in 2001, and the wars in Iraq in 2003 and in Libya in 2011, all of which Russia describes as illegitimate U.S.-led interventions aimed at regime change.[11] The list of these global conflicts is accompanied by the concept of prompt global strike and precision weapons, and by NATO's deployment of ballistic missile defense (BMD) since 2010, which Russia perceives as a threat to its strategic nuclear forces that undermines strategic deterrence.[12]

The aggressive policies of the United States and NATO are often mentioned in Russia's strategic doctrine. The 2009 national security strategy asserts that the failure of the existing global architecture, especially the transatlantic security structure, defined by NATO, threatens the provision of international security. The strategy also identifies the policy of leading countries aimed at achieving military superiority, primarily in strategic nuclear forces (likely a reference to the United States), as a threat to Russia's national security, while the deployment in Europe of elements of the U.S. global missile defense system significantly limits the opportunities for maintaining global and regional stability.[13] The 2015 security strategy even more explicitly states that the buildup of NATO's military potential, its further expansion, the deployment of its military infrastructure closer to Russia's borders, and its global activities "pursued in violation of the norms of international law" pose a threat to Russia's national security.[14] The 2010 Military Doctrine similarly includes NATO as a military danger to Russia and refers to the same policies of the Alliance, namely its potential eastward enlargement and deployment of military infrastructure close to Russia's borders as endangering Russian security.[15] The 2014 military doctrine similarly lists the alliance and its power projection, military infrastructure, and expansion as the first main external military danger to Russia. The doctrine lists the "creation and deployment of strategic missile defense systems" and the implementation of the prompt global strike concept and the deployment of precision weapons—strategies led by the United States—as the fourth main danger to Russia and global stability.[16]

Russian political and military officials also reference the policies of the United States and NATO as principal sources of instability and threat to Russian security. Reflecting this position, Russia's top political leadership has repeatedly stated that NATO's eastward expansion and buildup of military infrastructure closer to Russia's borders threatens strategic stability in the region. Moscow's political figures have also asserted that NATO's BMD system in Europe would aim to negate Russia's nuclear deterrence and exemplifies America's aggressively expansionist anti-Russian policies.[17] Lavrov, a supporter of these positions, stated in December 2020 that the United States and its NATO allies are pursuing the most aggressive form of containment policy toward Russia, inciting confrontation.[18] The chief of Russia's General Staff, General Valery Gerasimov, also reinforced these views and wrote in a 2017 article that NATO's military activity on its eastern flank weakens European security and presents a provocation to Russia. Gerasimov argued that primarily as a result of the deterioration of NATO-Russian relations, Europe transformed into a zone of heightened tensions. The potential for confrontation has increased on the background of a growing number of military forces and expanding military infrastructure in the Baltic countries, Poland, Romania, and Bulgaria, while the military dialogue at the NATO-Russia Council is discontinued. Alongside the deployment of missile defense, Gerasimov listed European military support for Kiev's regime as a main destabilizing factor, which provokes the extension of the conflict.[19] Over the past few years, General Gerasimov remained consistent in his views. In December 2020, he stated that NATO's military exercises near Russia's borders are anti-Russian and that the number of provocations toward Russia was increasing.[20]

Russia's scientific elite also supports the position of the military and political leadership. Viktor Vahrushev, associate professor at the Military Academy of the General Staff, asserted in 2017 that "the discrepancy between the U.S. struggle to preserve its global domination" and movement toward a "multipolar world" is a main source of contemporary conflicts. Vahrushev further stipulated that countries such as the former Yugoslavia, Afghanistan, Iraq, and Syria are "punished for their disobedience."[21] A former Ministry of Defense senior official and retired Russian general reiterated this view and stated that Russia is already at war with the United States—diplomatically, economically, and financially.[22]

The accepted views of a world in a state of conflict-prone transition where Russia is constantly threatened by an aggressive group of Western states led by the United States and a military alliance expanding eastward, which is increasing its military potential on Russia's doorstep, justifies a sustained focus on protecting Russia's territory and its allies. Such a threatening environment also necessitates a scientific understanding of the types of warfare Russia may be facing. Therefore, Russian military science largely attributes its vision of modern warfare and the changing character of war to be a product of studies of U.S. and NATO operations, rather than Russian activities, while the Russian leadership claims that its redefinition of warfare and military modernization and reforms are prompted by Western aggression, rather than by Russia's own expansionist policies and ambitions to increase its clout in the zone of Russian-privileged interests and beyond.

Russia's View of Modern Warfare: Increased Application of Nonmilitary Measures

Referencing conflicts waged by Western states, Russia's military scientists assert that modern warfare differs from twentieth-century conflicts. The fundamental difference lies in the conceptual shift of what constitutes the baseline of warfare. From Russia's perspective, the baseline of warfare, which originally centered on the use of armed force, has expanded and currently consists of an increased use of nonmilitary measures in combination with armed violence.[23] Russian and Western scholars have used a variety of terms to describe Moscow's view of warfare, such as the "Gerasimov doctrine," "hybrid warfare," "political warfare," "gray zone tactics," "influence operations," and "hostile measures."[24] These delineations contain certain differences but they all focus on depicting the established consensus that modern warfare is characterized by the increased integration of nonmilitary measures that can be employed to achieve strategic goals before, in conjunction with, or as a substitute for military measures.[25]

The view on the use of nonmilitary means as techniques to influence the minds of the adversary is not novel. Russian military scholars have deliberated over the benefits of such concepts even before the communist revolution and throughout the communist period, in parallel with the evolution of the application of these concepts. During Napoleon's war against Russia, Russia's military distributed leaflets with divisive messages aimed to lower the morale of the enemy.[26] Leading scholars, such as Russia's prerevolutionary strategic thinker Evgeny Messner, wrote about the blurring of lines between war and peace and the effects of employing information against the society of the adversary to achieve psychological effects.[27] During the Cold War, the training of the Soviet Red Army included lessons in generating sentiments among society that can be harnessed to "organize people's uprisings and partisan detachments in the enemy's rear."[28]

Despite the fact that the intellectual foundations of modern warfare had been shaped for decades, technological breakthroughs today have enabled the more pervasive application of these principles in modern warfare and discussions on their application have now become officially a part of Russia's military establishment.[29] In this context, the use of cyber operations has been enabled by the rapid development of information technologies and the widespread use of information in civilian populations as well as among military personnel. These technologies have changed the methods, nature, and techniques of military operations. Their wide adoption and proliferation have also created new information threats and challenges, as well as vulnerabilities that an adversary can exploit to prevail in conflict. The use of information methods enables the erosion, to the greatest extent possible, of the adversary's resistance capacity not only of its military forces but also of the whole population. In the current network-centric environment of command and control of military operations, achieving victory is dependent on achieving information superiority over the networks of the adversary and taking control over the information domain.[30] Information superiority is "the ability to collect, process, and distribute a continuous flow of information about the situation, while preventing the enemy from doing the same."[31] As Gerasimov asserts, no matter how powerful an adversary is and how perfect his weapons are, vulnerability in the adversary can always be identified.[32] According to the Russian military literature, these nonmilitary means that include cyber operations may be even more effective than traditional military measures in resolving interstate conflicts.[33] General Gerasimov even quantified the proportion of military to nonmilitary measures asserting that in current wars the ratio of military to nonmilitary means is 1 to 4. Although to date, no open-source publication or expert has been able to adequately explain the origins of this specific ratio, it nevertheless illustrates the large magnitude that nonmilitary measures occupy in conflict. Russian official documents as well as military leaders elaborate that such nonmilitary measures include media-related, economic, political, and diplomatic measures that are implemented using special operations forces, the protest potential of the population, and other indirect and asymmetric methods.[34]

Russia's Cyber Strategy: Cyber Operations as a Part of Information Warfare in Peacetime and during War

Russia's contemporary view of warfare serves as the strategic basis for understanding Russia's use of cyber operations because according to Russia's leadership, cyber operations are a major component of the nature of modern war, and are a part of the concept of information warfare.[35] Russia views information warfare as an activity occurring in the "information space"—which is roughly equivalent to the U.S. "cyberspace"—and defines information space in broad terms that reflect Moscow's doctrinal recognition of the technical and cognitive component of the domain.[36] According to Russia's 2011 Concept on the Activities of the Armed Forces of the Russian Federation in the Information Space, the "information space" is an "area of activity associated with the formation, creation, transformation, transmission, use, storage of information, which has an impact on individual and public consciousness, and on information infrastructure and information itself."[37]

Consistent with the definition of the information space, according to Moscow, information warfare also has two main components—a technical one and a psychological or cognitive one. Russia's 2011 Concept on the Activities of the Armed Forces of the Russian Federation in the Information Space defines information warfare as

> the confrontation between two or more states in the information space with the purpose of inflicting damage to information systems, processes and resources, critical and other structures, undermining the political, economic and social systems, [conducting] a massive psychological manipulation of the population to destabilize the state and society, as well as coercing the state to take decisions for the benefit of the opposing force.[38]

This definition clearly highlights the technical and cognitive elements of information warfare, placing cyber operations in this context.[39] Information warfare consists of components that are employed to manipulate the perception and decision-making processes of the opponent by exerting psychological pressure and components that are employed to affect the digital and technological infrastructure of the adversary.[40] Another critical aspect of information warfare that this definition highlights is the fact that this type of confrontation is conducted against both the leadership of the adversary and its general population.[41]

Some Russian scholars assert that the concept of information warfare provides a high-level strategic view of this relatively recent component of warfare. The essence of information warfare at the operational level, where information warfare is planned and conducted, is expressed through information operations.[42] Information operations are actions, synchronized in time, space, and objective, that aim to attain and maintain information superiority in support of the country's military strategy by influencing the information systems and information of the enemy. In this process, the country should also ensure that it enhances and protects its own information systems, infrastructure, and information.[43] For the purposes of this research, the term "information operations" is not used to identify the operational-level activities related to the Russian government to avoid adding another concept to this analysis and to avoid conflation with the already confusing usage of the term in U.S. military doctrine. The terms this research uses are "information warfare operations" or "information warfare activities."

The threats in cyberspace listed in Russian doctrine also reflect the broad interpretation of information warfare and its two elements—the technical one and the cognitive one (see table 1.1). When listing these threats, Russian doctrine stipulates that these are threats that foreign adversaries likely pose to Russian national security. This is a classic framing device of Russian military scholarship used to depict Moscow's own offensive methods. Hence, the threats in table 1.1 can serve as a basis to understand Russia's evolving offensive toolbox.[44]

Ensuring information superiority has transformed into the "alpha and omega" of modern Russian warfare. In modern conditions "information has become a kind of weapon" that "does not just add to the firepower, strike, and maneuver, but it transforms and unites them."[45] As the head of the Main Operational Directorate of the General Staff of the Russian Armed Forces, Colonel-General A. V. Kartopolov remarked in April 2015, "If in the past war was 80 percent combat operations, and propaganda was 20 percent, then in wars today 90 percent of activities consist of information warfare."[46]

Russian scholars seem to agree that the essence of information warfare is to exploit information and information systems for the purpose of influencing broader political processes in the economic, political, information, and social sphere. According to Russia's military elite, the aim of information warfare is "disorganizing or disorienting the political leadership and military command of the enemy, suppressing his will and leading his commanding units to make erroneous decisions."[47] Hence, information warfare is "at the forefront, [where] there is a battle for the minds and mass consciousness of the population."[48] Chekinov and Bogdanov similarly argue that information warfare, and specifically mass propaganda, is employed to incite discontent, demoralize, distract, and crush the spirit of the population and the military of the adversary in order to erode their will to fight.[49] Sayfetdinov proposes a similar purpose, stating that information warfare is "various ways of using information to mislead the enemy, undermine the will to resist, organize panic in his ranks, and generate betrayal." According to the author, the general goal of these activities is, therefore, "the purposeful use of information to achieve political, economic, military, and other goals."[50]

Makarenko similarly asserts that the main objects of influence during information operations include a wide range of targets: governing bodies of the state and the military

TABLE 1.1 Selected List of Threats as Outlined in Russian Cybersecurity Documents

Document	Threats	
	Psychological	Technical
Information Security Doctrine, 2000	• irrational, excessive restriction of access to socially necessary information; unlawful use of special means of influence • ousting Russian news agencies, the media from the domestic information market and increasing the dependence of the spiritual, economic, and political spheres of public life in Russia on foreign information structures • a decrease in the spiritual, moral, and creative potential of the Russian population	• development and distribution of programs that interfere with the normal functioning of information and information and telecommunication systems, including information protection systems • compromise of keys and means of cryptographic information protection • destruction, damage, or theft of machines and other storage media
Convention on Ensuring International Information Security, 2011	• factors creating a danger to the individual, society, state, and their interests in the information space • actions in the information space aimed to undermine the political, economic, and social systems of another state, destabilizing society • using the information infrastructure to disseminate information that incites ethnic, racial, and interconfessional enmity, racist, and xenophobic written materials	• targeted destructive impact in the information space on the critical structures of another state • countering access to the latest information and communication technologies, creating conditions for technological dependence in the field of informatization to the detriment of other states • information expansion, acquisition of control over the national information resources of another state
Basic Principles for State Policy in the Field of International Information Security until 2020, 2013	• carrying out hostile acts and acts of aggression aimed at discrediting sovereignty, violating the territorial integrity of states, and posing a threat to international peace, security, and strategic stability • interfering in the internal affairs of sovereign states, disturbing public order, inciting interethnic hostility	• destroying elements of critical information infrastructure • crimes, including those related to unlawful access to computer information, with the creation, use, and distribution of malicious computer programs
Information Security Doctrine, 2016	• increasing use by the special services of individual states of information and psychological influence aimed at destabilizing the domestic political and social situation in various regions of the world and leading to the undermining of sovereignty and territorial integrity • increase in materials in foreign media containing a biased assessment of the government policy of the Russian Federation	• an increase in the scale and coordination of computer attacks on objects of critical information infrastructure, increased intelligence activities of foreign states against the Russian Federation, as well as an increase in threats to the use of information technologies in order to damage territorial sovereignty, integrity, political and social stability of the Russian Federation

Source: Adapted from Lilly and Cheravitch, "The Past, Present, and Future of Russia's Cyber Strategy and Forces," 136.

services; key information systems of civil infrastructure such as telecommunications, the media, and industrial sectors; key informational military systems (communication systems, combat control, logistic support, reconnaissance, and weapons control); society as a whole (civilian population and military personnel); and electronic mass media.[51]

INFORMATION WARFARE CHANNELS AND TACTICS/ACTIVITIES

Information warfare constitutes a range of activities that are conducted by orders of the top leadership of a state.[52] These activities include impact on information technologies, hardware, and software; intelligence and counterintelligence; electronic warfare; and psychological operations.[53]

Information warfare is applied through strategic media messaging disseminated through all media channels that reach the population of the targeted country. The aggressive party uses information technologies to engage public institutions in the targeted country, such as mass media, religious organizations, NGOs, cultural institutions, and public movements receiving foreign financing.[54] To further help the demoralization of the population and ensure chaos, the adversary targets the disillusioned population and infiltrates these groups with provocateurs.[55]

Disinformation, or deliberate falsification of events, can also be considered among the principal information warfare components.[56] Information warfare aimed to misinform and mislead the adversary's political and military leaders may include a massive and carefully coordinated campaign through private and state-controlled media, diplomatic channels, top military agencies, and government departments. These actors may leak false information or orders. High-ranking political and military officers may be a part of the campaign and may be instructed to make public statements to ensure the success of the disinformation effort.[57]

In this context, cyber operations are an integral part of information warfare and their contribution in modern warfare is growing. Russian military leaders emphasize that in contemporary warfare, "Opposition in cyberspace is beginning to play an increasingly important role—right up to the conduct of combat cyber operations and cyber attacks."[58] Cyber operations can be used to execute targeted attacks on the communication systems of the managing entities at all levels.[59] Such operations can also be used to collect, destroy, modify, or deny access to confidential or damaging information that the adversary can exploit to further undermine the cohesion of the population and armed forces of the targeted state.[60]

Russia's military elite proposes various interpretations regarding how other nonmilitary measures relate to the above-mentioned core information warfare components. Some interpret nonmilitary state activities such as political and diplomatic activities as a part of information warfare. Molchanov, for instance, argues that diplomatic, political, and economic activities, as well as economic and political support for opposition movements and groups, are also components of information psychological influence.[61] Others consider such activities as separate nonmilitary measures that can be related to information warfare through the dissemination of information. Yarkov and Bolotov, for example, argue that nonmilitary measures include political, economic, financial, diplomatic, information, and other measures. The authors list information measures as types of the nonmilitary measures.[62] According to these military scholars, information warfare strengthens the effectiveness of other nonmilitary measures.[63] General Gerasimov also argues that other nonmilitary measures, such as economic blockades, economic sanctions, and the disruption of diplomatic relations with the targeted state, should be considered distinct from information warfare measures (see fig. 1.1).

Gerasimov's figure reveals another key component of information warfare, namely the fact that it can be employed during peacetime and during war.[64] In peacetime, cyber operations can be used in parallel or in combination with other nonmilitary measures

FIGURE 1.1 The Role of Nonmilitary Methods in Resolving Interstate Conflicts

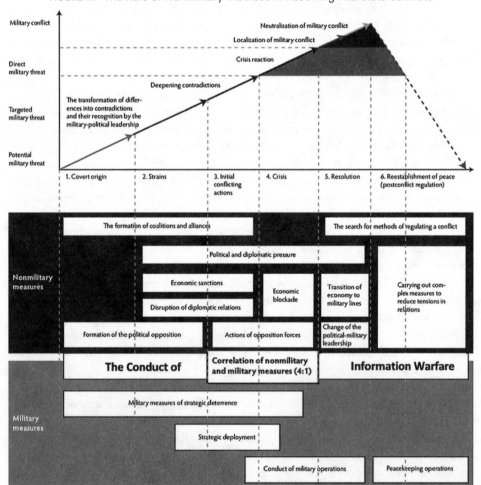

Source: Gerasimov 2013. Translation adapted from Charles Bartles. As of July 8, 2020: https://www.researchgate.net/figure/Graphic-from-Gerasimov-article-in-Voyenno-Promyshlennyy-Kurier-26-February-2013_fig2_329933852.

such as economic sanctions or diplomatic or political pressure.[65] During war, cyber operations are used to capture and maintain information superiority alongside military force and aim to amplify its effectiveness.[66] This range of military, political, economic, and other nonmilitary measures, blended with effective information warfare activities, will lead to victory.[67]

Regarding the exact domains through which these operations are conducted, Russia's military scientist S. R. Tsyrendorzhiev provides a helpful categorization. He contends that Russia's military policy can be conducted by government or nongovernmental actors across the following domains: foreign policy, military, sociocultural, and economic.[68] For the purposes of this book, economic sanctions, political and diplomatic pressure, protests, and other nonmilitary activities, separate from the core information warfare activities outlined above, are considered related nonmilitary activities or measures. For each case study, the book elucidates and visualizes the range of these activities and how they relate to the core information warfare activities.

Russia's Cyber Strategy in Practice: Forces and Capabilities

When analyzing each case study, this book refers to several state-sponsored cyber threat actors that have launched cyber operations against political IT infrastructure and related targets of NATO member states and partners on behalf of the Russian government. This section provides a brief introduction to these actors and their institutional positions, and elaborates on their operations and modus operandi in each case study. Russia's units that conduct cyber operations against political IT infrastructure are mainly associated with three divisions—the Foreign Intelligence Service (Sluzhba Vneshney Razvedki, or SVR), focused on foreign intelligence; the FSB, focused on domestic intelligence but also conducting foreign intelligence; and the GRU, focused on military intelligence. The most well-known and highly capable Russian APTs (advanced persistent threats) are APT 29 (Cozy Bear or Cozy Duke), APT 28 (Fancy Bear or Sofacy), and Sandworm.[69] APT 29 is believed to be a part of the SVR or the FSB.[70] The APT 28 group and Sandworm are likely subordinate units of the GRU.[71] Russia's three services are known to compete with one another, and this competition seems to be reflected in their cyber operations. Research by the companies Check Point Software Technologies and Intezer shows that Russian cyber threat actors affiliated with different services do not tend to share code, while teams in the same services share technical capacity.[72] In addition to Russia's main APTs, Russia's cyber operations benefit from the involvement of civilian hackers, including criminal groups who facilitate obfuscating attribution, and notionally private companies affiliated with government actors, such as the Internet Research Agency.[73]

THE FSB, SVR, AND THEIR MAIN AFFILIATED APTS

The FSB, the main successor to the KGB, was the chief intelligence agency conducting cyber operations beyond Russia's borders for most of the early post-Soviet period.[74] The FSB reports directly to Putin's office and the FSB's chief sits on Russia's security council (of which Putin is a member).[75] The agency can also report directly to the president himself due to long-standing informal connections built between the FSB's chief and Putin.[76] The FSB's functions include political intelligence, active measures, and counterintelligence.[77] In the 1990s and early 2000s, the FSB conducted its operations with the support of independent hackers, which conveniently facilitated the obfuscation of state attribution and served to alleviate the shortage of skilled hackers needed for some of FSB's operations.[78] The FSB improved its offensive cyber capabilities especially since its acquisition of Russia's equivalent of the NSA, the Federal Agency of Government Communications and Information (FAPSI), in 2003 and through its cooperation in developing offensive cyber capabilities with the Kvant Scientific Research Institute.[79] FSB's Center for Electronic Communications Surveillance (TsRRSS), also known as Unit 71330 or the 16th Center, is likely the FSB's main offensive cyber capability that conducts cyber espionage and collects signals intelligence abroad.[80]

The SVR is Russia's foreign intelligence service responsible for conducting intelligence activities, espionage, and electronic surveillance outside Russia's borders.[81] The service also emerged from a part of the KGB. Among the three services, the SVR is believed to be the one with the lowest status but has been recently expanding its structures, which may suggest it is also expanding its capacity to conduct cyber operations.[82] The SVR is known to employ sophisticated techniques and is likely responsible for the massive Solar Winds hack into government and commercial networks, discovered in 2020 and likely started in October 2019, which may emerge as the most significant breach of U.S. government and corporate networks in U.S. history.[83]

APT 29

APT 29 (Cozy Bear or Cozy Duke) is the primary cyber threat actor that researchers initially linked to the FSB. The exact agency APT 29 belongs to is still not definitively established, but accounts now tend to link APT 29 with the SVR.[84] The group is known since 2008 and is organized, well resourced, and dedicated. It primarily conducts espionage operations against governments and affiliated organizations such as media, think tanks, and NGOs in Europe, North America, Asia, Africa, and the Middle East. APT 29 tends to launch large-scale spear-phishing operations against thousands of individuals and uses "smash and grab" tactics, characterized by rapid and overt breach and data collection and exfiltration. APT 29 hackers use malware such as MiniDuke, CloudDuke, and HammerDruke.[85]

THE GRU AND ITS MAIN AFFILIATED APTS

The GRU is the main agency for foreign intelligence of the Russian military. The GRU's main objectives are providing the chief government organs and the military with all-source intelligence about Russia's adversaries, facilitating the successful implementation of Russia's defense and security policy, and assisting with maintaining Russia's military-technical security.[86] The GRU's chief formally reports to the chief of Russia's general staff and the defense minister.[87]

The GRU became a major player in Russia's reorganization of its cyber capabilities, which led to the GRU becoming the main Russian agency responsible for launching large-scale offensive cyber operations. The investment in the GRU's offensive cyber tools occurred alongside Russia's Defense Ministry program launched in 2013 to enhance military research and development and create military science units.[88]

In addition to a history of conducting offensive cyber operations, the GRU brought an institutional legacy of conducting psychological operations, dating back to the GRU operations as a part of the Soviet Red Army's special propaganda (*spetsprop*) units. The GRU operatives, therefore, had been trained in both the psychological and technical aspects of information warfare and realized the value of combining these two elements in their operations. In the GRU's mindset, the psychological operations are as important as cyber operations and both are at times conducted in parallel and in coordination with each other. The GRU units that used to conduct propaganda and decryption during the Soviet Union now conduct information warfare operations.[89] The GRU's main psychological operations unit is Unit 54777, which is under the 72nd Special Service Center.[90] The GRU's main cyber operations units are Unit 26165 and Unit 74455.[91] Unit 26165 was established during the Cold War as a military signals intelligence unit that operated with cryptography. The GRU's unit 74455, known as the Main Center for Special Technologies, has a shorter history but has already attracted international attention with its involvement in significant cyber operations, such as the 2016 intrusion into the DNC.[92] The GRU's daring and aggressive organizational culture reflects a wartime mindset and is evident in the service's operations, especially in cyberspace, where the GRU has adopted "the anything-goes approach."[93]

APT 28

APT 28 (Fancy Bear or Sofacy) has been operating at least since 2004 and is considered to be affiliated with Russia's GRU Units 26165 and 74455.[94] This APT has targeted governments, defense and financial industries, research institutions, and universities across the United States, Western Europe, Latin America, and Asia.[95] APT 28 uses credential harvesting through spoofed websites and phishing in the initial stages of its cyber operations. It uses the implant X-Agent, as well as X-Tunnel, DownRange, Foozer, and WinIDS. The group also tends to use domains that mirror the domains of their target organizations.[96]

Sandworm

Sandworm is another cyber unit associated with the GRU and is known to have operated at least since 2009.[97] Although this cyber-threat actor is best known for launching the most costly cyber attack to date, NotPetya, and for targeting critical energy infrastructure such as the two attacks against Ukraine's electric grid, Sandworm was also involved in disrupting political IT infrastructure and media operations in Ukraine.[98] It uses a variety of tools to conduct its operations, including BlackEnergy, PassKillDisk, and Gcat.[99]

Nongovernment Cyber Actors
In conducting some of their offensive cyber operations, Russia's security services have hired or coerced civilian hackers for decades.[100] The services are also known to provide immunity from prosecution if the hackers agree to work for the government when called and refrain from targeting .ru domains.[101] As the subsequent chapters demonstrate, the Russian government has used civilian hackers, such as enthusiastic university students who supposedly acted on their own volition compelled by a patriotic duty to defend the government's objectives during the cyber attacks against Estonia in 2007.

Conclusion

This chapter set the foundations for the subsequent frameworks and the analysis of case studies by describing Russia's threat perceptions and vision of contemporary warfare exemplified through the concept of information warfare. Russia's information warfare adopts a nonbinary view of war, based on which war and peace are no longer two distinct dimensions of interstate relations. Through the strategic prism of information warfare, confrontation is a constant state that exists on a sliding scale of conflict, vacillating between the two extremes of peace and war but never quite reaching either. Cyber operations are a part of Russia's information warfare toolbox and Russia's APTs leverage Moscow's cyber power in the continuum between peace and war, propelled and constrained by their guiding doctrine. The next chapter synthesizes the main elements of Moscow's information warfare concept and offers several frameworks for standardizing and visualizing the different activities of Russia's strategy. These frameworks systematize the practice of Russian military theory and serve as the foundations for identifying the patterns and contradictions in the different cases of Russian information warfare campaigns that this research investigates.

2

Frameworks for Predicting and Analyzing Cyber Operations in the Context of Information Warfare

A s the previous chapter demonstrated, Russia's information warfare strategy, rooted in Russia's threat perceptions and doctrine, has multiple layers and components. Its various aspects may make it hard to see the forest for the trees. This chapter offers several methods for untangling this complexity. Based on the main threats and concepts outlined in Russia's scholarship and doctrine on strategy, as well as on the author's examination of various Russian cyber and psychological operations, this chapter proposes several frameworks that can facilitate and standardize the depiction and analysis of Russian information warfare campaigns and their various elements. The aspects and stages of each framework can facilitate ordering the activities attributed to the Russian government in logical categories that allow standardizing the data collection on Russian information warfare operations and identifying divergent and convergent patterns in Russia's information warfare playbook across cases. This can enable the identification of common stages and tactics across operations, and can serve as the basis for more-targeted policy solutions that address each group of activities.

The chapter commences by introducing a framework that can identify factors associated with the launch of various types of Russian cyber operations against political infrastructure. The framework uses the case study methodology qualitative comparative analysis (QCA), described in the introduction, and calls for the collection of specific political, economic, social, and military indicators that may be associated with Russia's choice of which type of cyber operation to launch against another state. This analysis also examines other factors, such as the geographic and geopolitical affiliation of the targeted state, as well as Russian media coverage about that state or events related to that state.

This chapter also introduces a heat map—or in this case, a Hack Map—that can be used to identify the main political IT infrastructure elements that Russian-affiliated cyber threat actors target in different countries in a way that is also unique to this research. The data collection from each country is used to identify the most commonly targeted political IT infrastructure elements and draw conclusions on whether these elements have been targeted with the potential aim to exert actual physical or technical effects, or rather to exert psychological effects—the two main objectives of information warfare as explained in chapter 1.

Finally, the chapter proposes a framework developed as part of this research for visualizing various elements of Russia's information warfare campaigns. The framework visualizes the core components of Russia's information warfare, namely cyber operations and strategic messaging, including disinformation. This framework specifically identifies increases in the volume of strategic messaging through Kremlin-sponsored media and can serve to identify any potential correlation between spikes in media coverage and particular types of cyber operations. In addition, the framework shows a selection of political, economic, and social events related to the Russian government during the specific information warfare campaign to illustrate the wide range of information warfare activities. This framework depicts Russian cyber operations, hype in Russian-sponsored media, and associated operations and is, therefore, called CHAOS (cyber, hype, and associated operations).

A Framework for Identifying Factors Associated with the Initiation of Russian Cyber Operations

Informed by Russia's literature on strategic threats and measures employed in contemporary conflicts analyzed in the previous chapter, this section describes the way this research identified the set of factors used in the QCA analysis to identify the potential triggers for Russia's decision to employ different types of cyber operations.

THE DEPENDENT VARIABLE: TYPES OF CYBER OPERATIONS

Before outlining the main factors of the QCA framework, it is important to categorize the different types of Russian cyber operations that serve as the principal dependent variable on the basis of which case studies are grouped. This research uses the CIA (confidentiality, integrity, and availability) triad—a security model that groups cyber operations based on whether they compromise the confidentiality, integrity, or availability of data. The model is a well-known classification tool in the cybersecurity field and provides an appropriate embarkation point for this analysis.[1] In the CIA triad:

- Confidentiality compromises occur when a cyber operation results in unauthorized access to and/or use of data or systems. In case of beached data confidentiality, a cyber actor may use the data in different ways, which may include publicly releasing the data or parts of it, such as in the case of the 2017 breach into the political campaign of then French presidential candidate Emanuel Macron, or selling the data.
- Integrity is compromised when cyber threat actors gain unauthorized access to data and change the data or the system on which the data is stored. Data can be modified or deleted. In some cases, fabricated information can be added to and mixed in with authentic data and then released.

- Availability attacks result in denying or disrupting access to data or systems to users who otherwise are authorized to access the data. Such attacks do not affect the integrity or confidentiality of the data. They include DDoS attacks against websites that render them temporarily inoperable, as, for example, in the case of the DDoS attacks against Estonia's critical infrastructure and government websites in 2007.

In cases where Russian state-sponsored cyber threats executed cyber operations that compromised more than one element of the CIA triad, the analysis identified the primary CIA element that was compromised through the cyber operations in each case. The research mentioned other types of compromises that were known in each case but treated them as secondary to the analysis and did not list them in the dependent variable category of the QCA analysis.

In the final analysis, only two of the three types of cyber operations tend to dominate across the seven examined cases. These are availability and confidentiality compromises. Therefore, the QCA method identifies patterns that can discriminate only between the occurrence of these two observed types of cyber operations.

QCA FACTORS

When analyzing Russia's information warfare operations, a number of political scientists have argued that various factors could have affected Russia's decision to launch an information warfare campaign, including launching different types of cyber operations against various states. Some scholars for example, identify geographical proximity of the targeted state to Russia as a factor, others speculate that the presence of a pro-Russian candidate in upcoming elections is the reason for initiating different types of measures, yet others list the presence of a cultural or historical dispute, as in the case of Estonia, as a key reason.[2] Based on a review of these factors and the author's analysis of Russia's characterization of modern warfare and main threats, this research evaluates the presence or absence of the factors listed in table 2.1 to categorize the various nonmilitary and military activities that may have prompted the Russian government to employ a certain type of cyber operations in the context of each case study.

In case studies analyzing Russia's information warfare operations, the research identified the presence (marked as 1) or absence (marked as 0) of the following types of activities that may be associated with Russia's decision to initiate a certain type of cyber operations against a targeted state and may fall under the general description of bilateral relations prior to the initiation of cyber operations:

- Political or diplomatic activities: Activities by government representatives—for example, visits of Russian official delegations and diplomats, and speeches of Russian senior leaders related to the particular case under examination
- Social activities: Activities likely supported by a government but conducted by nongovernment actors, such as activists engaged in social protests supported by the Russian government and events organized by religious institutions

- Economic activities: Activities conducted by commercial entities or government-owned entities involved in commerce and focused on distributing, consuming or producing services or resources, for example, Russian-initiated cancellation of goods and services toward the targeted country. Economic activities include financial support for political parties or candidates.
- Military activities: Activities conducted by agencies and branches of the Russian military, such as deployment of forces. These activities also include actions by Russian military intelligence officers, such as the attempt to organize a coup d'état in Montenegro and the attempts to poison an arms dealer in Bulgaria. Twice.

As a major goal of Russia's information warfare is to psychologically affect the population and decision makers of a particular adversary through strategic messaging via state media channels, the analysis includes an examination of the media coverage of each case in Russian state-sponsored media outlets at the time of each information warfare campaign. Such media coverage can be considered as being influenced by Russia's political leadership because of sufficient evidence that shows Russian state control over Russia's domestic and international media sometimes directly through Russia's presidential administration.[3] As Christopher Paul and Miriam Matthews explain, Russia's propaganda model consists of disinformation and a "high number of channels and messages."[4] Therefore, a large quantity of messages, not only quality of content, is a part of Russia's "firehose of falsehood."[5] In accordance with this argument, this research focuses on examining relationships between the volume or quantity of media coverage as one aspect of Russian information warfare. In particular, the analysis examines the amount of media coverage, calculated as the number of articles, in Kremlin-sponsored media available in each targeted country that pertains to the elections in question (if the cyber operations were initiated around elections) or the country in general in cases where the government of the country has issued a policy that Moscow perceived as threatening and that prompted it to initiate cyber operations (such as the relocation of a Soviet statue, as in the case of Estonia). A spike in media coverage is identified as present (and marked as 1) if there is an observed increase in the number of articles in Kremlin-sponsored media prior to the cyber operations. A spike is considered present if there are more than three times the number of articles published in the examined Russian state-sponsored media in the period of the spike in comparison to the number of articles in the period immediately prior to the period of the spike.

If the cyber operations occurred during a period of elections in the targeted state, the analysis evaluates whether there are any pro-Russian or anti-Russian candidates and whether political parties or candidates have ties to the Russian government.

Historical legacies and current geopolitical affiliations affect Russia's foreign policy behavior. This is exemplified by Russia's policies toward the countries closest to its borders, which Moscow has publicly declared as its region of privileged interests. Russian military and political elites, as well as Russian policy, have demonstrated Moscow's effort to assert its control over its near abroad by political or even military means.[6] Such geopolitical differences may also affect Moscow's cyber calculus. Therefore, the book further identifies whether the country targeted by Russian information warfare was a part of the Soviet Union or the Eastern Bloc, and whether it is a member of NATO or is en route to NATO membership during the period of the examined Russian information warfare operations.[7]

The subsequent chapters explore each case study and identify the presence or absence of each of the factors in table 2.1. The table uses the example of Estonia to demonstrate how the QCA framework is applied to each case. For more information on Russia's information warfare campaign against Estonia, see chapter 3. Each chapter uses the technique of process tracing to methodologically examine the role of cyber operations within Russia's information warfare toolbox and related military and nonmilitary activities. This process can facilitate the identification of additional factors that can inform the QCA framework and can provide complementary insight into Russia's statecraft. For example, if the QCA method reveals that spikes in Russian-sponsored media coverage occur consistently before availability attacks, the United States and other NATO member states may consider this development as a warning indicator for Russian state-sponsored availability attacks and, hence, can monitor such media in anticipation of such spikes.

A Political Hack Map of Russian Targets

In addition to identifying factors associated with the launch of different cyber operations, the research used two frameworks to analyze Russia's exact targets within political IT infrastructure; in turn, this analysis revealed the most targeted elements. The research analyzes the type of cyber operations and the type of targeted political IT infrastructure. The analysis divides this infrastructure into three main groups, described in figure 2.1 below and analyzes the predominant potential effect of compromising each infrastructure. The research uses the depiction of the components of political IT infrastructure to identify the targets of Russian-sponsored cyber operations in each case study and provides an aggregation of the number of targeted components across cases. Hence, the framework is based on the concept of a heat map and the author chose to call it a Hack Map.

TABLE 2.1 Factors That Could Be Associated with the Initiation of Different Russian State-Sponsored Cyber Operations

Target	Type of cyber op (CIA)	Disputes in relations				Spike in media coverage before cyber ops	If cyber ops during elections		NATO member en route	NATO member	Frm. Eastern Bloc state	Frm. USSR state
		Polit	Soc	Econ	Mil		Anti-Ru candidate	Pro-Ru candidate				
Estonia (2007)	A	1	1	0	0	1	0	0	0	1	1	1

FIGURE 2.1 The Basis for Russia's Political Hack Map: Electoral Infrastructure, Facilitating Infrastructure, and Information Sphere

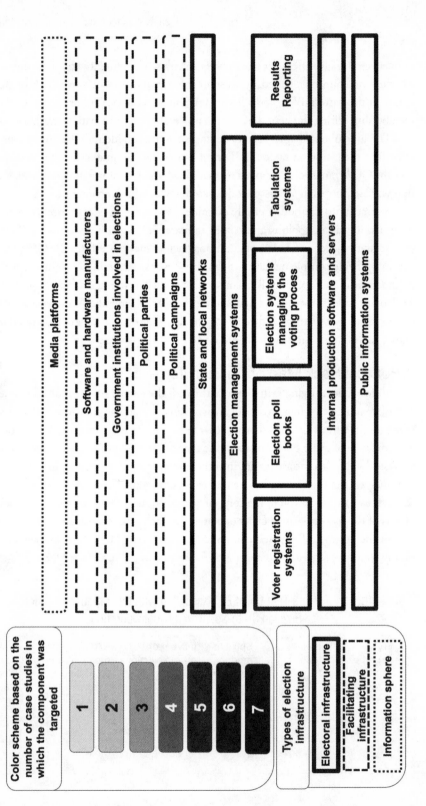

Figure 2.1. shows that the Hack Map consists of three categories of political IT infrastructure. The first category is electoral infrastructure. It consists of key technical components of the election IT system that, if destroyed or incapacitated, could "have a debilitating impact on security" and on the election process.[8] For this category, the book uses the list of technological components of the election systems designated by the U.S. Department of Homeland Security (DHS) as critical infrastructure. DHS designated the U.S. election systems as critical infrastructure in January 2017 as a consequence of the Russia-supported cyber operations during the 2016 U.S. presidential elections.[9] Although this DHS framework is created specifically for the United States, it represents a standard political IT infrastructure model applicable across countries.

These key technical components of the electoral IT infrastructure are

- state and local networks—includes emails and official networks that can connect with components of the election system;
- voter registration systems—used to gather personal information of voters;
- election systems that manage the voting process;
- election management systems—manage voting system databases, format ballots, and keep audit records;
- tabulation systems—record, aggregate, and present votes;
- results reporting—includes only systems used to deliver unofficial reporting on election night and does not include media platforms that further disseminate these results;
- public information systems—provide the public with information about the electoral process and results;
- election poll books—electronic systems used by staff at voting centers and polling locations to determine voter eligibility; and
- internal production software and servers—servers and software platforms that facilitate the political infrastructure environment.[10]

The second category is facilitating infrastructure. It refers to the IT systems, networks, and cloud services accounts of organizations, platforms, and individuals that facilitate the main political IT infrastructure but are still involved in the conduct of elections. These entities serve a supportive function and although they do not fall within the category of core electoral components, they are equally important to the conduct of elections. They include political campaigns, political candidates, and political parties involved in elections. This category also includes software and hardware manufacturers that support the election process. A potential breach into their networks or products may constitute a supply-chain risk.[11]

The third category is the general information sphere. It includes online and social media that may disseminate information about the election process or outcome and, therefore, may also be involved in the election process. In cases of cyber operations against media organizations, such cases are considered only if there is compelling evidence that the operations were related to the election process. Although more than one agency or system that pertains to each infrastructure component may be targeted in some cases, that component would be counted as targeted with a value of one without giving a specific number of the targeted entities within it. For example, if Russian APTs targeted two political parties in one case study, the Hack Map would reflect that the facilitating infrastructure of political parties was targeted but would not reflect that that number is equal to two in that particular case. In other words, for any one case, the value depends on whether the component was targeted at any level/intensity (1), or not (0). If the component was targeted, no matter how many times, the value for that component is 1. If the component was not targeted, the value is 0. The count in the color scale represents the number of case studies in which this component was targeted. In the summary chapter of this research, this diagram serves as a template for a heat map that represents in various shades the frequency of Russian cyber operations against each political IT infrastructure component across all examined case studies, also called a Hack Map. The final map would aggregate all cases with cyber operations against political parties and provide a sum of these cases, but not the number of cyber operations against all political parties across all cases. For example, if in one case Russian state-sponsored APTs targeted three political parties and in another case APTs targeted two political parties, each case would be given a value of 1 for the facilitating infrastructure of political parties. In the research summarizing the number of political IT components targeted across all cases, the total score would be 2: 1 for the first case study (which targeted three parties) and 1 for the second case study (which targeted two parties).

CYBER EFFECTS

As the intention of this work is to demonstrate the application of Russian information warfare doctrine through the eyes and mindset of Russia's leadership and not according to Western concepts, this research opted for a high-level categorization of cyber operations based on their effects that can be gleaned through Russia's doctrine and military literature.[12] As table 1.1 illustrated, the Russian leadership categorizes threats to the information space as threats primarily designed to exert effects on systems or processes and threats that are designed with the primary goal of exerting psychological influence over a group of people or an individual.

Some Russian military scholars follow a similar dual categorization specifically focused on cyber operations. According to N. A. Molchanov, offensive operations on computer networks can be allocated to either of two categories. The first is computer operations aimed to disorganize the networks, reduce their efficiency, render them impossible to use, or completely destroy them. The second category is cyber operations conducted to gain unauthorized access to information, extracting and using it for strategic purposes. Such purposes may include "distortion and substitution of content for disinformation," psychological operations, and counterintelligence operations.[13] S. Marinin similarly outlines four purposes of cyber weapons. These are, first, temporary disconnection of critical nodes of the communication infrastructure; second, "blocking of computer operations and functions"; third, "disruption and failure of automated control and communication systems"; and finally, "distortion and falsification of information and the spread of misinformation.[14] Similar to Molchanov's categorization, the first three purposes that Marinin lists can be categorized as using cyber operations to affect the functions of information systems and networks, while the last can be categorized as using cyber operations to exert psychological effects. Therefore, when examining each case study, this analysis identifies whether the state-supported cyber operations were designed to have primarily technical effects on election processes or psychological effects on a group of the population.

Cyber operations, such as phishing campaigns aimed at data exfiltration, against this category of targets usually have an objective of exerting psychological effects through exfiltration and exploitation of data. Even in cases where cyber actors defaced a website or launched a DDoS operation against it, technically rendering the website inoperable for a certain period, these operations mainly exert psychological effects because they cause only temporary damage, which may result in the temporary inability to publish election-relevant information on one platform. These operations, however, tend not to jeopardize the election process itself. In the case of cyber operations against Estonia in 2007, Russia-supported cyber actors compromised political IT infrastructure without intending to affect the election process but for the purposes of coercing the Estonian government to keep a statue of a Soviet soldier in the center of Estonia's capital. Although the intent in this case was not to disrupt the election process, the types of cyber operations and the targets can still indicate whether the attacks were intended to exert primarily psychological or technical effects.

Furthermore, these two categories are not mutually exclusive. Although the identification of the targeted infrastructure or entity can provide valuable clues as to whether an operation aims to exert technical or psychological effects, a clear differentiation between cyber operations aimed to exert purely technical or purely psychological effects rarely occurs in practice, and the same cyber operations may often exert both types of effects. For example, a DDoS attack against an election commission may be primarily aimed at disrupting the election process, but media coverage of the attack may still exert psychological impact on the population and decision makers by affecting voters' trust in the election outcome. The research, therefore, aims to identify the primary type of effect based on the technical knowledge of each cyber operation and its immediate impact.

This research treats cyber operations aimed at disrupting a core component of the election process as exerting or attempting to exert primarily technical effects. Website defacements and phishing campaigns resulting in data exfiltration and leaks are treated as operations aimed primarily to exert psychological effects. In case studies where multiple cyber operations have been attributed to the Russian government and where these operations have a combination of effects, they were categorized as operations aimed at exerting both technical and psychological effects.

Russia's CHAOS

This book further aims to illustrate the interaction between the two main elements of information warfare—the technical and psychological—by introducing a new framework designed to capture the process of integration between cyber operations and Kremlin-controlled strategic information flows, which may include disinformation. To that end, the research employs a framework designed to show how the two core information warfare elements are positioned and possibly interact with other associated activities that together constitute an entire information warfare operation. This framework was constructed following the logic of process tracing. It visualizes the multitude of cyber operations, psychological operations (exemplified in a narrower representation of state-sponsored media coverage), and other associated operations that all form a broad information warfare campaign against a targeted state. This framework reveals the correlations between the cyber attacks and events happening in the larger information space. It does this by plotting the timing of Cyber operations, the Hype in volume of media coverage (measured in number of articles), and Associated OperationS—CHAOS—that constitute a general template for Russia's information warfare campaigns.[15] As Russia's information warfare is aimed to sow distrust and division in a targeted state by amplifying extreme positions and provoking strong reactions that reduce the chances of reaching a consensus—in a way by attempting to cause chaos—the acronym CHAOS seems an appropriate simplification of Russia's complex campaigns. In particular, CHAOS contains the following categories:

- Cyber: this category contains a chronological list of the main known cyber operations during a single Russian information warfare campaign.
- Hype: this category includes a day-by-day count of media articles about the general issue that the literature has identified as the reason for Russia's information warfare campaign against a particular country. These issues could be a general election as in the case of the 2016 U.S. elections or the 2017 French presidential elections, or the relocation of an important Soviet symbol as in the case of Estonia in 2007. The analysis examines the volume of articles in Russian-sponsored media, which is accessible to the population of the targeted state. This coverage illustrates Russia's overt strategic messaging campaign aimed to influence the population of the targeted country. Ideally this section would have included an analysis of Russia's overt strategic messaging efforts as well. These would include analysis of social media content spread through trolls and bots associated with the Russian government. Such data, however, was unavailable for most examined cases and, therefore, was not added. Additional insight into the nature of Russian-sponsored media coverage could be derived from machine-learning tools for text analysis that could highlight the linguistic features, main themes, and rhetorical techniques of Russia's media content. However, the search engines used to collect some of the media coverage for the examined cases did not allow for automatic data download and allowed only partial or manual download of

the articles published by Russian state-sponsored media in each case. Due to these data collection difficulties, the author was unable to perform additional content analysis, which might have revealed patterns in Russian media coverage across cases that could have contributed to enriching our understanding of how the Kremlin weaponizes information.[16] Adding analysis on the volume of coverage from non-Russian media sources would enable a comparison of the volume of articles from the Russian-sponsored media with a more neutral outlet to identify whether Russia's spike in reporting is unique. However, this is not essential to this analysis—the aim of this media analysis is to identify the Kremlin's position and changes in that position to a topic through the volume of information about that topic, and whether the trends in reporting are unique or similar to the trends or volume of reporting in other outlets would be a useful addition, but not an essential one, to this research.

- Associated OperationS: this category includes political/diplomatic, social, economic, and military activities supported by the Russian government during the period of the information warfare campaign. These activities were described in the previous section. Associated operations also include a list of notable events and mitigation policies introduced by the targeted state to deter, contain, or reduce the negative consequences of Russia's state-sponsored activities.

The research uses the analysis of media coverage to search for patterns in the coverage that may be associated with the initiation of different types of cyber operations. The conclusion of the analysis on the relation between media coverage and cyber operations is subsequently added to the QCA framework.

Figure 2.2 provides an example of the framework in the case of the Russia-attributed DDoS attacks against Estonia in 2007, which is explained in detail in chapter 3. The x-axis represents the timeframe during which the activities associated with a single information warfare campaign took place. The y-axis displays the associated operations (government activities and rhetoric, economic activities, social activities, mitigation policies and events), media coverage as number of articles per day, and cyber operations. The figure displays four waves of DDoS attacks against Estonian institutions in this period. The figure also shows several spikes in Russian state-sponsored media coverage in this period. These spikes, or hype in media, occurred precisely prior to each DDoS wave. This observation suggests a potential correlation between hype in media coverage and this particular type of cyber operations in Russia's information warfare campaign against Estonia in 2007. When analyzing the other case studies in this book, the research explores whether this observation is confirmed in other cases of Russian state-sponsored DDoS attacks.

Conclusion

On the basis of the analysis of Russia's vision of information warfare in the previous chapter, this chapter proposed general frameworks for capturing and standardizing the justification and political infrastructure targets of Russia's state-sponsored cyber operations,

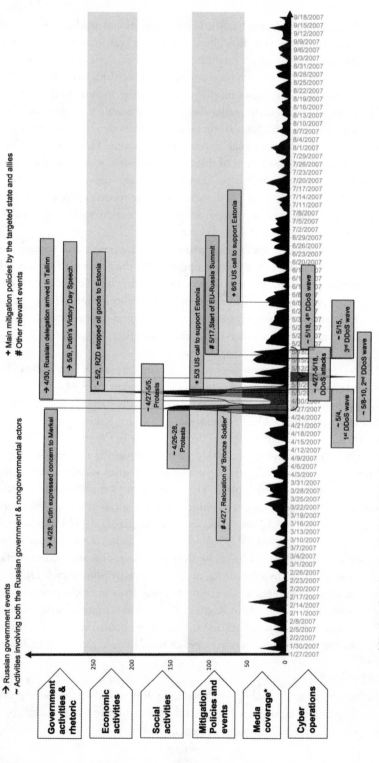

FIGURE 2.2 Russia's CHAOS in Estonia in 2007: A Selection of Cyber Operations, Media Coverage (Hype in Media), and Associated Operations

→ Russian government events

~ Activities involving both the Russian government & nongovernmental actors

+ Main mitigation policies by the targeted state and allies

Other relevant events

* Number of articles about Estonia published in top Russian media and internet agencies

Government activities & rhetoric

Economic activities

Social activities

Mitigation Policies and events

Media coverage*

Cyber operations

→ 4/28, Putin expressed concern to Merkel

→ 4/30, Russian delegation arrived in Tallinn

→ 5/9, Putin's Victory Day Speech

~ 5/2, RZD stopped oil goods to Estonia

~ 4/27-5/5, Protests

~ 4/26-28, Protests

4/27, Relocation of 'Bronze Soldier'

+ 5/3 US call to support Estonia

5/17, Start of EU-Russia Summit

+ 6/5 US call to support Estonia

+ 5/18, 4th DDoS wave

~ 5/15, 3rd DDoS wave

~ 4/27-5/18, DDoS attacks

~ 5/8-10, 2nd DDoS wave

~ 5/4, 1st DDoS wave

and the associated activities that constitute Russia's modern version of warfare. The first framework, shaped on the basis of qualitative comparative analysis, aimed to identify factors associated with different types of Russian state-sponsored cyber operations. The introduction of the visual depiction of the frequency of Russian cyber operations against various political IT infrastructure components, described as a Hack Map, can be a helpful visualizing tool that facilitates our understanding of the main targets of the Russian cyber groups.

The framework for capturing the entire range of activities that constitute a single Russian information warfare campaign, known as CHAOS, is a visualization technique that can serve several purposes. First, CHAOS captures in one figure the complexity and seeming chaos of a single Russian information warfare campaign. Such a distillation can be helpful not only for synthesizing large amounts of information in one image, but also for facilitating cross-case comparisons by standardizing the data collection for each case. This process can reveal common and divergent characteristics in each case. It can also help analysts, responsible for data collection, to identify all areas of potential Russian activity that they should examine.

The frameworks can be used to identify the most common patterns in Russia's cyber and information operations, such as types of cyber operations and associated factors (derived from the QCA framework), main political IT infrastructure targets (derived from the Hack Map), and key stages and general patterns in the interaction between the range of activities that constitute Russia's information warfare playbook (derived from CHAOS). Such analysis can help researchers and policy makers to see the entire forest of Russian information warfare activities. This strategic visibility can serve as a valuable step toward the identification of policies that can mitigate the effects of Russia's contemporary way of warfare and build resilience in democratic systems and populations against Russian interference.

The following chapters demonstrate the analytical prowess of these frameworks by applying them to seven known instances of Russia-attributed cyber operations against political infrastructure of NATO countries and invited members. The next chapters identify the common and divergent patterns in the factors that likely influenced Russia's decision to launch cyber operations, the most common political infrastructure targets that Russian state-sponsored cyber threat groups targeted in each case, and the integration of cyber operations within Moscow's general information warfare playbook in each case. Let's dive in.

3

Web War I

How a Bronze Soldier Triggered
a New Era in Cyber Warfare

The Russian-attributed DDoS attacks against Estonian government websites, IT infrastructure of Estonian media organizations, banking services, and other organizations in 2007, constituted the first publicly discussed instance in which cyber operations were used as a tool of statecraft in such overt and large-scale manner. During the course of 2007, the Russian government supported a series of information warfare activities against the government of Estonia that demonstrated the broad range of channels and actors that the Russian government can employ during information warfare campaigns.

This chapter commences by outlining the main reasons in Estonian-Russian relations likely associated with the Russian decision to launch cyber attacks against Estonia. The chapter then examines the main information warfare activities, including cyber attacks, likely associated with Russia's information warfare campaign and addresses the question of attribution. The Hack Map illustrates the political infrastructure components that the DDoS attacks targeted. An examination of the Kremlin-controlled media coverage assessed the volume of Russia's strategic messaging during the campaign. Finally, the research applies the CHAOS and QCA frameworks designed in chapter 2 to identify patterns in the integration of cyber attacks and other information warfare activities and potential factors associated with the initiation of Russia's cyber attacks.

Factors in Estonia-Russia Relations Potentially Associated with the Launch of Cyber Operations

It has been well established in the literature on this case that the immediate reason for the series of cyber attacks against Estonian infrastructure was the decision of the Estonian government to relocate a statue of a Soviet Red Army soldier from the center of the capital, Tallinn, to a peripheral location of the city. The Bronze Soldier statue, built in 1947, was a traditional location for the annual celebration of the Soviet liberation of Estonia from Nazi Germany.[1] Estonia is a former member of the Soviet Union and Soviet-Estonian relations occupies a major part of Estonian history.[2] As a result of an incident where Estonian nationalists used the venue of the monument to protest and express tribute to the Soviet regime in Estonia, the Estonian Reform Party Prime Minister Andrius Ansip spearheaded a political process to relocate the Bronze Soldier and rebury the soldiers' remains under it. The relocation of the monument triggered protests by pro-Russian groups, which escalated into three days of riots. As a result of the protests, 1 person died, 153 were injured, and more than 1,000 were detained.[3]

This episode represented one of the most contentious moments in Estonian-Russian relations.[4] A Russian delegation consisting of members of Russia's parliament (Duma) was dispatched to Estonia to ameliorate the situation.[5] The presence of the delegation, however, seemed to have escalated, rather than diffused the building tension. The delegation fueled the growing negative sentiments by spreading the false allegations that the Estonian government had damaged the statue while relocating it. As a result, Estonian foreign minister Urmas Paet canceled a scheduled meeting with the delegation.[6]

Before the removal of the Bronze Soldier in April, the Estonian government had already been concerned with the occurrence of ethnic clashes around the location of the statue. On January 10, 2007, the government passed the Protection of War Graves Act. The law allowed the Estonian government to authorize the reburial of persons who died in Estonian territory during war. This act laid the legal foundation for the relocation of the statue. A week later, on January 17, the Duma reacted to the law by officially releasing a statement expressing its criticism about this act, claiming it glorified Nazism.[7]

Russia's Information Warfare Activities

Activities associated with the Russian government in this period included social protests in Tallinn and Moscow, anti-Estonian policy proposals and political and religious rhetoric, and criticism against Estonia's government. In addition, the Kremlin was accused of launching cyber attacks, economic measures against Estonia referred to as "hidden sanctions," and a media campaign that included a proliferation of fake news and negative rhetoric continuing throughout 2007.

SOCIAL ACTIVITIES

Protests in Tallinn

The Russian government was accused of instigating the Tallinn-based protests and riots that took place as a result of the relocation of the Bronze Soldier. The evidence for these allegations consists of a series of meetings between Russian government representatives, pro-Russian groups, and protesters in advance of the riots.[8] Participation in the riots by representatives of Russia's youth movement Nashi, which is known to be created and supported by the Kremlin, further strengthened the argument.[9]

The protests started on April 26, 2007, when Estonian authorities commenced preparations to relocate the statue of the Bronze Soldier. The riots continued as the statue was removed on April 27, and subsided on April 28, after two nights of looting and rioting.[10]

Protests in Front of the Estonian Embassy in Moscow

Several pro-Kremlin youth groups that were created and/or funded by the Russian government participated in a week-long protest in front of the Estonian Embassy in Moscow.

These movements were Nashi (Ours), Molodaya Gvardiya Edinoy Rossii (Young Guard of United Russia), Rossiya molodoy (Young Russia), and Mestniye (Locals).[11] The protesters took down the Estonian flag and obstructed the movement of Estonian citizens and embassy personnel to and from the embassy.[12] Mirroring the Estonian government policy toward the Bronze Solider, the protest organizers further claimed they would support the dismantling of the building of the Estonian Embassy in Moscow.[13]

Besides the fact that the movements participating in the protests were linked to the Kremlin, other factors also suggested the protests were organized and likely supported by the Russian government. Regular meals were delivered for free to the protesters; participants were driven in mass from faraway locations, while tents, water appliances, and sound equipment were bought to support the protests. Such capabilities are atypical for spontaneous picketers and suggest premeditation.[14] The fact that the Russian police did not intervene when the protesters prevented Estonian representatives from entering the embassy suggests a level of government complicity with the activities of the protesters.[15]

The European Union and several countries expressed their support for Estonia and called on Moscow to end the protests around the Estonian Embassy.[16] The U.S. Senate and House of Representatives passed similar resolutions supporting Estonia on May 3 and June 5, respectively.[17]

POLITICAL ACTIVITIES: ANTI-ESTONIAN POLICY PROPOSALS AND DIPLOMATIC AND RELIGIOUS RHETORICAL SUPPORT

Through negative rhetoric and policy recommendations, Russian politicians and religious leaders engaged in an international and domestic public campaign to condemn Estonian actions. For example, in a note to Estonia's diplomatic corps, the Russian Foreign Ministry expressed "strong disagreement" with the decision of Estonia's government to relocate the Bronze Soldier.[18] In the note, Russia's foreign ministry warned that Estonian authorities should "refrain from actions that will have the most serious consequences for relations between Russia and Estonia."[19] On April 28, Putin himself expressed concern about the situation during a meeting with German chancellor Angela Merkel.[20] Putin further mentioned the Estonian events in his May 9 Victory Day speech.[21] Russian religious leaders also sided with the Russian government's position. Russian Patriarch Alexius II called the decision of the Estonian government to relocate the Bronze Soldier indecent and immoral.[22]

ECONOMIC ACTIVITIES AGAINST ESTONIA

The involvement of Russian companies in this case demonstrates their close links to the Russian government and the ability of political events to influence the economic direction of Russian businesses. Although the Russian government did not introduce any official sanctions against Estonian businesses, private Russian firms took their cues from senior political and religious leadership rhetoric to reduce their business with Estonia.[23]

On May 2, 2007, the Russian rail company RZD ceased delivering coal, oil, and petroleum to Estonia for several weeks. The company did not mention the controversy around the monument as a justification for its decision but claimed that urgent repairs were the reason for stopping oil deliveries.[24] The timing of this temporary delivery freeze coincided with Russia's political anti-Estonian position and can be viewed as a part of Russia's overall campaign to condemn and punish the Estonian government for its decision.[25] Following a similar line, some Russian companies stopped buying Estonian products.[26]

The transit trade to Estonia through Russia was also delayed by Russian authorities and pro-Kremlin activists. For example, authorities in St. Petersburg limited truck traffic delivering petroleum and coal products through Estonia's eastern border with Russia.[27] Pro-Kremlin Nashi activists further blocked trucks on the Estonian-Russian border near Ivangorod.[28] Russian transit trade through Estonia's railways declined by 29 percent in May 2007 in comparison to the previous month and contributed to a 1.5-percent decrease in growth of Estonia's gross domestic product in 2007.[29]

Besides trade with and transit to Estonia being hindered, Russian investment in Estonia was also temporarily impacted.[30] Two years after the events, Minister Lavrov commented that Russians were united behind the Russian government position and justified the economic response because "most of our compatriots understood and supported these actions."[31]

RUSSIA-AFFILIATED DDOS ATTACKS AND WEBSITE DEFACEMENTS

During the incident, Estonia was subjected to a series of cyber attacks against Estonian political parties, government ministries, media, and banks.[32] The entire cyber attack campaign lasted for twenty-two days, between April 27 and May 18, 2007. The majority of the attacks can be described as denial of service (DoS) or distributed denial of service (DDoS) attacks. The focus, method, and volume of the attacks changed over the twenty-two days.[33] These attacks can be grouped into four periods, outlined in table 3.1.[34]

TABLE 3.1 Main Waves of DDoS Attacks against Estonia in 2007

4 May	In the days before the first wave of DDoS attacks, pro-Kremlin groups organized DDoS attacks to Estonia's ISP and governmental websites. Attack scripts were posted on the web so that computer-savvy Russian sympathizers could participate in DDoS attacks. The attackers used global botnets and proxy servers in different countries, and probably faked their IP addresses to obfuscate attribution.
8–10 May	Estonia's websites were attacked with various tools such as SQL injections during Russia's Victory Day celebrations around May 9. Script kiddies may have been encouraged by President Putin's Victory Day speech. The most massive DDoS attack with botnets occurred on May 9. The massive May 9 attack, Russia's Victory Day, was the longest and lasted about 10 hours. The May 9 attack was preceded by encouragement on many websites, where the organizers called for an attack on that date. The attack started a little after 11 p.m. Tallinn time on May 8, suggesting the attackers may have been based in Russia, Moscow time, where it was the start of May 9.
15 May	During this wave of DDoS attacks, the hackers attacked Estonian government websites and banks.
18 May	The attacks on this day were primarily targeting government websites and coincided with the EU-Russia Summit, which took place on May 17 and 18, 2007.

Sources: Juurvee and Mattiisen, *The Bronze Soldier Crisis of 2007*, 29–30; Jose Nazario, "Politically Motivated Denial of Service Attacks," *Arbor Networks*, 2010, https://www.senki.org/wp-content/uploads/2017/10/12_NAZARIO-Politically-Motivated-DDoS.pdf (accessed March 9, 2021); Rain Ottis, *Analysis of the 2007 Cyber Attacks against Estonia from the Information Warfare Perspective* (Tallinn, Estonia: NATO Cooperative Cyber Defence Centre of Excellence, 2018), https://ccdcoe.org/uploads/2018/10/Ottis2008_AnalysisOf2007FromTheInformationWarfare Perspective.pdf (accessed March 25, 2021); President of Russia, "Events Russia-European Union Summit May, 17–18, 2007," May 18, 2007, http://en.kremlin.ru/events/president/trips/48843 (accessed March 9, 2021).

FIGURE 3.1 Russia's Political Hack Map against Estonian Targets

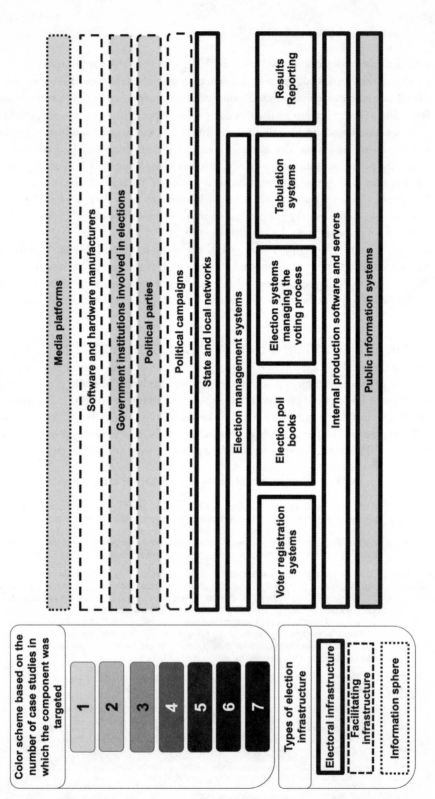

Methods used during the DDoS attacks included malformed web queries, ping flood, and email spam. A few attempts were made to hack into systems, using SQL injection, for example. Some of these attacks against noncritical systems succeeded.[35] Some sites were defaced and redirected users to images of Soviet soldiers and Martin Luther King quotations. On April 29, hackers defaced the ruling Reform Party's website and left a message that Estonia's prime minister and his government were asking forgiveness of Russians and promising to return the Soviet statue to its original site.[36] Therefore, the attacks can be categorized as availability and integrity attacks, with the majority being availability attacks.

The majority of the attacks focused on noncritical services such as public websites and email. Some concentrated on more critical targets, such as online banking.[37] Critical infrastructure, such as systems in the energy and transportation sector, was not targeted.[38]

Figure 3.1 indicates the elements of the political infrastructure that the DDoS attacks affected. The cyber operations targeted components of all three categories of political infrastructure. The legend on the upper left side of figure 3.1 shows that each targeted election component is counted only once. The legend on the lower left side of the figure indicates the three types of political IT infrastructure and suggests that electoral infrastructure has a heavy outline; facilitating infrastructure has a dashed outline; and information sphere has a dotted outline. Using this framework, figure 3.1 shows that in this case, Russian cyber groups targeted one component of Estonia's electoral infrastructure, two components of Estonia's facilitating infrastructure, and media platforms, which are a part of Estonia's information sphere.

In this case, attacks against the political infrastructure primarily focused on facilitating infrastructure and included DDoS attacks and website defacements. Therefore, these attacks likely aimed to have a dual psychological and technical effect on the targeted country.

ATTRIBUTION OF INFORMATION WARFARE OPERATIONS

Although Estonian officials publicly blamed Russia for the cyber attacks, there is only circumstantial evidence linking some of the discussed activities, including the cyber operations in Estonia, directly to the Russian government. Estonian IT experts and officials carried out investigations and concluded that some evidence assigned attribution to Russian state institutions. NATO and EU experts, however, found no evidence to prove Russian state-sponsored involvement. Despite the lack of definitive evidence, the scope and timing of the attacks, and the refusal of the Russian government to assist the Estonian authorities in prosecuting suspects involved in the attacks in Russian territory, suggests the Kremlin may have been at least complicit in the execution of these attacks, if not involved in orchestrating them.[39] In addition, although the Russian government denied involvement in the attacks, in 2009, a Russian parliament deputy publicly claimed that his assistant conducted the cyber attacks, but he refused to reveal the identity of that person. In the same period, members of the pro-Kremlin movement Nashi claimed they were responsible for the cyber operations.[40]

Furthermore, the actions of the Russian leadership, including President Putin's Victory Day speech against Estonia, which coincided with an increase in cyber operations against Tallinn and anti-Estonian rhetoric propagated by the Russian media, may have contributed to subsequent events and could be considered as enabling factors or conditions. Given the paucity of evidence to prove such a claim with certainty, it is prudent to refrain from claiming premeditation, or even backing, by the Russian leadership for all ensuing events in this case study. There are, however, a multitude of actors and events backed up by the Kremlin that seem to have contributed to different aspects of the information warfare campaign outlined in this chapter.[41]

PRO-KREMLIN MEDIA COVERAGE

The Kremlin state-sponsored media coverage of the events continued throughout the development of the controversy. The coverage was in line with Russia's official anti-Estonian position condemning the Estonian government policy toward the Bronze Soldier and the handling of the events surrounding it. This coverage contained the same general elements within Estonia and Russia, and was amplified by the cyber attacks and rhetoric of Russian political leaders.

The most-watched Russian-language media channels in Estonia include First Baltic Channel (PBK), which rebroadcasts material from the Russian state-owned Channel 1, NTV, Russian Television Channel (Rossia/RTR), and Russian Television (RTV). These media channels either broadcast content from Russian channels or produce and air content specifically for the Estonian public. The channels have ties to the Russian government and typically portray news in line with Russia's official government position.[42] During the time of the incident, Russia's media covered the story with a negative spin on Estonia's decisions. The media also falsely reported that the Estonian government had cut the Bronze Soldier statue before relocating it, hence introducing an element of disinformation in its reporting.[43] The media also emphasized police brutality during the protests and covered a member of Night Watch—an organization created by Russian-speaking activists to guard the Bronze Soldier—threatening Estonia with civil war.[44] Russian media in Russia also covered the events, including the cyber attacks. Some of the most-watched Russian national channels such as Channel One and Russia One, which are mostly government controlled, and NTV, which is owned by the state-controlled Gazprom, covered the issue.[45] Russian TV news also aired a fabricated image of the Bronze Soldier that depicted the full-body statue of the soldier without a torso and with only his boots remaining in place as an illustration of the rumor that the statue was cut into pieces, which was disinformation.[46]

To examine the integration of media coverage by Russian state-sponsored media and the other elements of Russian information warfare, especially cyber attacks during this period, this research conducted an analysis of Russian media channels known to reflect Russia's position. The research analyzed media content that was available to Estonian audiences at the time of the period under examination and that the Estonian public, particularly Russian speakers, may have watched.[47] To compare media coverage on Estonia with

FIGURE 3.2 Russian State-Sponsored Media Coverage Related to Estonia's Bronze Soldier

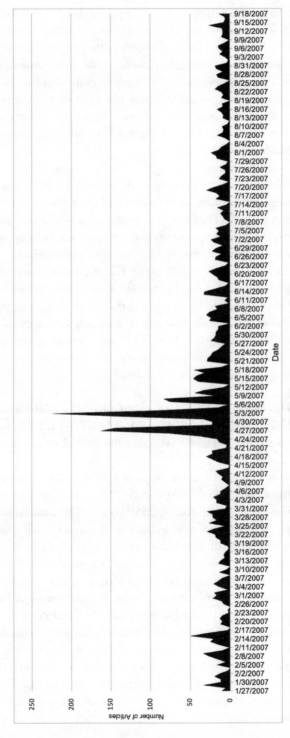

Source: Data compiled through the database Integrum. Examined media included Russian state-sponsored information agencies TASS and Ria Novosti (which as of 2013 was renamed to Rossiya Segodnya) and newspapers: *Kommersant, Komsomolskaya Pravda,* and *Izvestiya*

previous media coverage, the analysis covered the period three months before the Bronze Soldier controversy and three months after the last known DDoS attack (January 27 to September 18, 2007).[48] Figure 3.2 shows the result of the analysis. Several major increases in media coverage are observed during the campaign. An examination of the articles also suggests that their content was consistent with the content in other Russian media, namely the articles expressed criticism toward Estonia's treatment of the statue of the Bronze Soldier. The next section juxtaposes the analysis in figure 3.2 with the other information warfare components discussed in this chapter to identify any potential connections among the different Russian-linked activities.

In addition to disinformation and negative media coverage about Estonia disseminated through Russian media, activists wrote commentaries on media websites to further condemn the Estonian government for the removal of the Bronze Soldier. In this period, social media platforms such as Facebook and Twitter were still nascent technologies and their use as channels for organizing activists and spreading and amplifying strategic messages was not yet as prevalent as it is today. Therefore, commentaries on media websites, particularly Delfi.ee and the dating portal Rate.ee, served as the venues for freely expressing and sharing personal views. To prevent the use of their platforms for spreading tension, some websites, including Delfi, blocked the option for online commentaries on April 27. Ideally, this research would have analyzed the data from these platforms to provide a more comprehensive analysis of Russia's strategic messaging campaign during this case, however, according to a recent report by the Estonian-based International Center for Defense and Security, this data is not available.[49]

Russia's Interference in Estonia: Associated Factors and Mapping the Information Warfare Campaign Using CHAOS

Figure 3.3 visualizes the main activities related to the 2007 Russian information warfare campaign against Estonia.

Figure 3.3 shows a marked increase in pro-Kremlin media coverage about Estonia just before the start of the series of DDoS attacks. Moreover, there is a marked spike in media coverage prior to each of the four main waves of DDoS attacks. This finding suggests that there may be a potential relation between the start of each attack and Russia's strategic messaging. As much of the media coverage focused on criticizing Estonia for its policy toward the Bronze Soldier, it is reasonable to assume that the media coverage may have encouraged nongovernment hackers to join the DDoS attacks, making media coverage a part of Russia's cyber recruitment efforts. In the summary of factors presented in table 3.2 that could be associated with the initiation of DDoS attacks in this case, it is reasonable to indicate that there was an increase in negative media coverage with a value of 1. Another notable potential association is that between increased Russian media coverage and the two main periods of protests in Tallinn and Moscow. The two highest increases in media coverage occurred as the protests were taking place. Hence, the media coverage may have also encouraged protesters to maintain their activities or other individuals to join these activities.

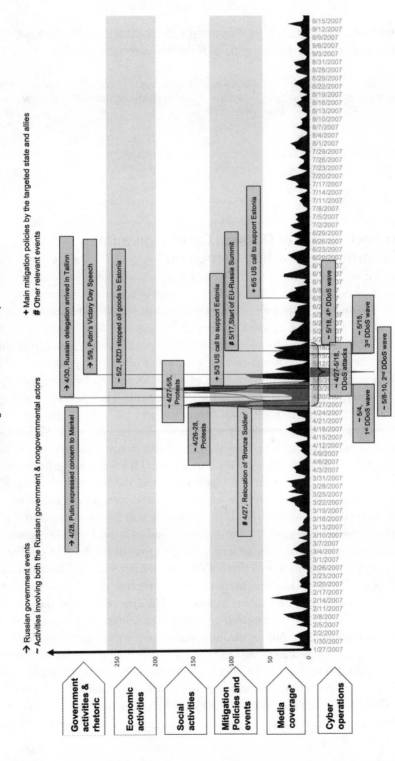

FIGURE 3.3 Russia's CHAOS in Estonia in 2007: A Selection of Cyber Operations, Media Coverage, and Associated Operations

→ Russian government events

~ Activities involving both the Russian government & nongovernmental actors

+ Main mitigation policies by the targeted state and allies

Other relevant events

* Number of articles about Estonia published in top Russian media and internet agencies

Government activities & rhetoric

Economic activities

Social activities

Mitigation Policies and events

Media coverage*

Cyber operations

→ 4/28, Putin expressed concern to Merkel

→ 4/30, Russian delegation arrived in Tallinn

5/9, Putin's Victory Day Speech

~ 5/2, RZD stopped oil goods to Estonia

~4/27-5/5, Protests

~ 4/26-28, Protests

4/27, Relocation of 'Bronze Soldier'

+ 5/3 US call to support Estonia

5/17, Start of EU-Russia Summit

+ 6/5 US call to support Estonia

~ 5/18, 4th DDoS wave

~ 5/15, 3rd DDoS wave

~4/27-5/18, DDoS attacks

~ 5/8-10, 2nd DDoS wave

~ 5/4, 1st DDoS wave

TABLE 3.2 Factors That Could Be Associated with the Initiation of the Particular Type of Cyber Operations Observed during the 2007 Russian Information Warfare against Estonia

Target	Type of cyber op (CIA)	Disputes in relations				Spike in media coverage	If cyber ops during elections		NATO member en route	NATO member	Frm. Eastern Bloc state	Frm. USSR state
		Polit	Soc	Econ	Mil		Anti-Ru candidate	Pro-Ru candidate				
Estonia (2007)	A	1	1	0	0	1	0	0	0	1	1	1

The Effectiveness of Russia's Cyber Operations and Information Warfare Campaign

Compelled by Estonia's decision to relocate a historical symbol of gratitude to the Soviet Union, the Russian government used a broad range of activities, channels, and actors to wage an information warfare campaign against Estonia in 2007. The range of the known Russian-backed activities includes protests in Estonia and Russia, economic pressure against Estonian business, hostile government rhetoric, strategic messaging campaigns through Russian state-sponsored media, and a series of cyber operations. In this case, attacks against the political infrastructure primarily focused on facilitating components and include DDoS attacks as well as website defacements. Therefore, these attacks likely aimed to have a dual psychological and technical effect.

When examining the sequence of activities visualized using the CHAOS framework, a notable pattern that emerges from the data is that the pro-Kremlin media coverage consistently increased before each of the four waves of DDoS attacks, indicating potential association between the volume of media coverage and the launch of these attacks. The increase in media coverage may have served as a call to arms for hackers, sympathizing with Russia's position, to join in the DDoS attacks against Estonian targets.

How effective were Russia's cyber operations and additional activities during this information warfare campaign in achieving the objectives of the Russian government? If examined in isolation from the other information warfare activities, the immediate objective of the DDoS attacks was likely to cause disruption of communication and the functionality of websites and servers in Estonia. The attacks achieved these effects, but only temporarily, because the Estonian government took immediate measures to mitigate the effects of these attacks. Among the immediate measures that Estonia took as the attacks were still occurring were identifying and blocking of bots from root Domain Name System (DNS) servers. Estonia's president allowed the continuation of attacks on his website so that attackers do not refocus on more critical infrastructure. Additionally, Estonia's Computer Emergency Readiness Team (CERT) contacted internet service providers (ISPs) worldwide and persuaded them to blacklist attacking computers. Estonia further blocked all .ru addresses.[50]

When examined as components of Russia's broader strategy against Estonia in reaction to Estonia's decision to relocate the Bronze Soldier, the effectiveness of the cyber operations in this context seems to diminish. The Russian leadership clearly expressed criticism toward the relocation of the soldier, and it is conceivable to assume that one of the objectives of the cyber operations was to coerce the Estonian government into agreeing to keep the Bronze Soldier at his original location. However, Estonia still relocated the soldier. Moreover, the cyber operations prompted a number of countries and international organizations to increase their cooperation with Estonia and to assist the country in mitigating the immediate effects of the cyber operations. Several NATO member states, including Germany, Italy, Latvia, Lithuania, Slovakia, and Spain, funded Estonia's CERT. NATO also provided assistance. One of the key long-term policy changes as a result of the DDoS attacks is the fact that NATO established a cyber center of excellence in the territory of Estonia to demonstrate NATO's support to its Baltic member. The Center, called the NATO Cooperative Cyber Defence Centre of Excellence (CCD COE) was established in Tallinn and hosts annual NATO-wide cyber exercises as well as an international cybersecurity conference known as the Conference on Cyber Conflict (CyCon) , which the author had the pleasure to attend and speak at several times.[51]

Although the two nights of protests in Estonia were unprecedented at that time and have not been repeated ever since, they did not exert any long-term negative effects on Estonia's civil society. The sanctions against Estonian businesses appear to have had only a short-term impact.[52] These activities also did not appear to have achieved a reversal in the Estonian government's decision to relocate the Bronze soldier.

The cyber resources and support that Estonia received and the permanent location of NATO's CCD COE in Estonian territory indicate that in this particular case, Russia's use of cyber operations did not seem to have achieved Russia's desired results and likely led to unintended and undesirable consequences for Russia. That said, the case was recorded in cyber history as the first instance of a large-scale and overt cyber operation launched against a nation-state and placed Russia's cyber aggression among the tools of Russian foreign policy and statecraft. In this respect, the case was successful in elevating the status of Russia's cyber capabilities and in signaling to the West that relations with Russia were growing increasingly hostile, especially in cyberspace.[53]

4

Blowing Up Its Own
Trojan Horse in Europe
DDoS Attacks against Bulgaria's Political Infrastructure, Assassinations, and Explosions[1]

During Bulgaria's local elections, which took place on October 25, 2015, the Bulgarian state infrastructure responsible for communicating election information to the Bulgarian population sustained the most powerful series of DDoS attacks in the territory of the entire Balkan Peninsula until that day.[2] Bulgarian counterintelligence attributed the attacks to Russian state-sponsored hackers.[3] Considering Bulgaria's century-old cultural, economic, and political ties to Russia, Moscow's decision to launch cyber operations against a partner nation appears perplexing. Russia's deployment of its first-class cyber forces seems even more counterintuitive in this case because the particular election during which Russia's cyber operations occurred was not a national one. It was an election for regional representatives and thus was much less consequential than national elections.[4]

To shed light on the possible reasons behind the decision of the Russian government to launch cyber operations against Bulgarian political infrastructure on election day, this chapter examines the environment of bilateral relations in which Russia's cyber operations occurred and outlines the range of known information warfare activities that the Russian government supported at that time. After briefly describing the long legacy of relations between Bulgaria and Russia, this chapter highlights the main issues of contention that emerged between the two countries prior to the Bulgarian local elections. Political and economic tensions that occurred between Moscow and the Bulgarian government in Sofia in the years prior to the elections provided a reasonable list of justifications that could explain Russia's choice to employ cyber tools against its former communist partner. The close ties between Russia and several Bulgarian opposition parties may have served as supplementary incentives for Moscow to intervene in the election process in support of Bulgaria's pro-Kremlin parties. A major irritant in Russian-Bulgarian relations that may have prompted Moscow to use its cyber forces revolved around Bulgaria's arms and ammunition export business, which increased significantly during that period. An attempted poisoning of one of Bulgaria's main arms dealers by Russia's GRU officers, which the chapter discusses, indicates the gravity of the types of actions that the Russian government was willing to undertake to address this issue. The chapter further examines Russia's sponsored cyber operations against Bulgaria's political infrastructure and maps the targeted components on the Hack Map outlined in chapter 2. The analysis then discusses Russia's influence over the Bulgarian media and Moscow's strategic messaging during the election period as another dimension of Russia's information warfare campaign against Bulgaria at that time. The chapter concludes by visualizing the range of activities attributed to Russian state-sponsored actors with the CHAOS framework, highlighting a few key lessons learned from this case and evaluating the effectiveness of Russia's operations.

Factors in Bulgaria-Russia Relations and the Bulgarian Election Environment Potentially Associated with the Launch of Cyber Operations

Once called Russia's Trojan horse in the European Union, Bulgaria has deep historical and cultural connections with Russia.[5] Numerous episodes in Bulgarian history link Moscow to Sofia and ensure Russia's influence over Bulgaria. The 1870s war between the Russian and the Ottoman Empires was a part of Russia's strategy to expand its influence in Europe. Most Bulgarians today, however, remember that war as the time when Russia liberated Bulgaria from the Ottoman Empire. Some Bulgarians still feel deeply indebted to Russian General Mikhail Skobelev, who, as Bulgarian history and literature attest, valiantly crossed the Danube River on his white horse and liberated large Bulgarian territories from Turkish occupation in 1878.[6] During the Cold War, Bulgaria was colloquially known as the sixteenth Soviet republic and maintained strong ties with the Soviet Communist Party. Russia's influence over the Balkan country is evident not only in the Russian names of monuments, streets, and churches across Bulgaria, but also in the durable individual relationships that Bulgarian and Russian elites continue to sustain. These close ties are reinforced by mutual experiences. Many of Bulgaria's politicians, businessmen, military officers, and intellectuals received their education from Soviet, and later Russian, top-tier educational institutions. Russian language can be heard in many Bulgarian cities on the Black Sea coast where Russian citizens have purchased homes. In addition to historical and cultural ties, Bulgaria is dependent on Russia for energy imports—Moscow supplies the vast majority of Bulgaria's nuclear fuel, oil, and gas.[7] Despite its strong connections to Moscow, Bulgaria opted in the post–Cold War era to formally discard its Russo-centric heritage of Pan-Slavism and join the West by becoming a member of NATO and the European Union. The long-standing legacy of relations with Moscow, however, continues to influence Sofia's geopolitical direction, which vacillates between Brussels and Washington on one hand, and Moscow on the other.

Given the close ties between Russia and Bulgaria, the launch of cyber operations on election day appears perplexing at first. However, an examination of the political and economic landscape prior to the elections reveals the existence of several major lines of disagreement between Sofia and Moscow that may have prompted Russia to use its cyber capabilities on election day against the political infrastructure of its Balkan brethren. The cyber attacks occurred in a period of economic and political tensions between the leading party and the opposition regarding the strategic direction of the country and its relations with Russia.

The coalition government in power, dominated by the political party Citizens for European Development of Bulgaria (Grazhdani za evropeiysko razvitie na Bulgariya, or GERB) adopted a Euro-Atlantic political direction and an anti-Russian stance on a number of issues relevant to the Russian government. The GERB-led coalition supported the EU sanctions against Russia in response to Moscow's invasion of Ukraine.[8] Moreover, in 2014, Bulgaria updated its security doctrine to reflect Russia's actions in Ukraine and expressed a changing perspective on Russia. The document ascertained that Russia posed a threat to Bulgaria and expressed concern over Bulgaria's energy dependence on Russia, connections between Russian and Bulgarian business and political elites, and Russian influence in the Bulgarian media. Bulgarian pro-Russian parties vociferously criticized the document and insisted it would poison relations with Moscow. Russia unequivocally expressed its opposition to the updated strategy. Russian Vice Premier Dmitriy Rogozin commented that the document represented a betrayal of Russia. Under pressure, the Bulgarian government toned down the anti-Russian language in the report and published an updated version in which Russia was not listed as a direct threat to Bulgaria. Nevertheless, the new version preserved some of its anti-Russian connotations. It contained a reference to Russia's strategic application of economic pressure and its annexation of Crimea, which the report condemned as illegal.[9]

Economic discord with Russia also existed prior to the 2015 Bulgarian elections. Diversifying energy supply to Europe away from Ukraine was a priority for Russia. Since the conflict in Ukraine, Moscow aimed to reduce its dependence on Ukraine as a transit country for Russian natural gas and looked to build alternative transit channels through other countries, including Bulgaria.[10] Bulgaria and Russia have been discussing the creation of the South Stream pipeline that would transfer Russian natural gas from Russia through Bulgaria, Serbia, Hungary, and Slovenia to Austria. The construction of the pipeline had the potential of elevating Bulgaria's status as a strategically important partner of Russia and the West through its enhanced role as a gas transit nation. In 2014, however, the European Commission declared that the gas pipeline project violated EU competition laws because Russia's company Gasprom controlled the majority of the pipeline's capacity. The EU legal framework required the capacity to be accessible to other gas suppliers. Russia rejected the new policy and, in December 2014, Putin announced the cancellation of South Stream. The Russian president publicly criticized the Bulgarian government for not adhering to the initial South Stream agreement and acting against its national interest.[11] Russia commenced negotiations with Turkey for the construction of an alternative pipeline, which would circumvent Bulgaria and deprive it of transit fees.[12]

The Bulgarian government further irked Moscow when in early September 2015 it refused to grant Moscow permission to fly over Bulgaria. The Russian government officially asked its Bulgarian counterpart for permission to use its airspace to transport cargo to Syria in military transport planes. The Bulgarian government declined Russia's request and explained that the reasons for the refusal were doubts about the purposes of the flights and the type of cargo that the Russian military planes would carry.[13] Bulgarian Defense Minister Nikolay Nenchev explained that the Ministry of Defense received information that the Russian military planes that were about to fly over Bulgaria did not carry humanitarian aid but weapons.[14] Russia condemned Bulgaria's decision as a U.S. plot.[15]

Analysts speculate that another economic tension that existed between Russia and Bulgaria at that time pertained to the increase of Bulgaria's production and exports of weapons and ammunition.[16] The value of Bulgaria's arms exports increased approximately five times in 2015, relative to the previous year.[17] Some of Bulgaria's weapons export destinations were markets that were traditionally dominated by Russian suppliers. Bulgaria also increased weapons exports to Ukraine when the country was actively fighting the Russian military.[18] The existing tension in arms exports may have represented another incentive that prompted the Russian government to disrupt Bulgaria's electoral process on Election Day. Two attempts to poison a Bulgarian arms dealer, his son, and his executive director, which were attributed to Russian GRU officers, act as corroborating evidence to this hypothesis. The next section of Russia's information warfare activities elaborates on these poisoning attempts and other potential related activities, including explosions in Bulgarian weapons facilities.

RUSSIAN CONNECTIONS TO PARTIES RUNNING IN THE OCTOBER ELECTIONS

Despite the long history of fruitful and constructive Bulgarian-Russian relations, the changes in Bulgaria's security doctrine, the refusal to open Bulgarian airspace to Moscow, the dissolution of the South Stream project, and the sharp increase in arms exports, which occurred under GERB's leadership, suggest that the political direction of Bulgaria's leading party, whose representatives were competing in the October 2015 elections, was not aligned with Russia's foreign policy interests.

The main party in opposition during the October 2015 elections—the Bulgarian Socialist Party (Bulgarska Sotsialisticheska Partiya, or BSP)—had a long and extensive record of relations with Russia. The party is the direct successor of the Bulgarian Communist Party, which governed the country during the Cold War.[19] Many of BSP's leaders were educated in Russia's universities and have various business connections to Moscow.[20] The BSP adopted several positions aligned with Russian foreign policy objectives. For example, the BSP had consistently called for the cessation of sanctions against Russia and rebalancing of Bulgarian relations with Russia. The BSP also supported South Stream and criticized the government's failure to keep the project.[21]

In the months prior to the October 2015 elections, the divergent views of the president and current government on one hand and the BSP and its supporters on the other became evident during a series of nationwide protests organized with the involvement of the BSP. The demands of the protesters included rejection of the proposal to establish a NATO command center in Sofia and an appeal that Bulgaria not implement NATO and EU policies that will transform the country into a "frontline state" against Russia. One of these protests took place on February 10, 2015, in front of the Bulgarian presidential palace. Bulgaria's former vice president, General Angel Marin, also participated in the protests, supporting the protesters and their cause.[22] The BSP does not reveal details about the exact origins of its financing.[23] Although there is no publicly available evidence to suggest that the protests were facilitated by the Russian government, BSP's positions were closely aligned with the interests of the Kremlin.

In addition to BSP, another more-recently-founded Bulgarian party called Attack (Ataka) was gaining popularity among marginalized groups and advocated for policies favorable to Moscow's interests. Attack was established in 2005 by then TV presenter Volen Siderov and since has transformed itself into the party of extreme nationalistic views. The party vociferously opposes Bulgaria's NATO membership and advocates for no military bases of foreign countries on Bulgarian territory.[24] Similar to the BSP, Attack does not disclose the complete list of its financial supporters.[25] However, some experts and Western government representatives indicate that Attack maintains close ties with the Russian Embassy in Sofia, and that the embassy's members likely influence Attack's anti-American and anti-U.S. positions. These experts further attest that Moscow may be also shaping the manner in which Attack's views are reflected in Bulgarian media outlets influenced by Russia (see section "Pro-Kremlin Media Coverage" below).[26] Other analysts are bolder in their assessments and directly allege that Russia provides financial support for Attack. A former member of the party, Valeri Simeonov, directly accused Siderov of receiving funding from a Russian Orthodox foundation.[27] Attack does not conceal its interactions with Russian government representatives and publicizes photographs and information about these meetings in the party's newspaper, which carries the name of the party. The party and Russian diplomats openly discuss their mutual position against the deployment of U.S. and NATO bases on Bulgarian territory.[28] Attack's leaders have also visited Russia and met with senior Russian government representatives. For example, Attack's leader, Siderov, met with the chairman of Russia's parliament duma Sergey Naryshkin in 2012 and during his visit relayed a flattering message to President Putin.[29]

It was in this environment of contentious issues of consequence for Bulgarian-Russian relations and existing ties between the Russian government and opposition parties advancing agendas aligned with Russia's geopolitical interests, that Bulgaria was about to hold local elections.

Russia's Information Warfare Activities

On October 25, 2015, Bulgaria held nationwide elections for local government representatives, specifically mayors and municipal council members. Alongside casting their ballots for local representatives, the Bulgarian voters were asked to vote on a referendum to assess public opinion on introducing electronic voting. The elections, although consequential for local administrations, were not expected to represent a pivotal moment in Bulgarian election history. They were not as consequential for foreign policy as parliamentary or presidential elections, which are national-level elections and determine the general political direction of the country. Yet on election day the Russian government deployed its first-class cyber forces. This section examines the publicly available information about the Russian-attributed cyber operations and other activities related to the Russian government that may have been a part of a unified information warfare campaign. On a quest to identify any patterns in the volume of media coverage that may be associated with the launch of the cyber operations, the section further analyzes Russian state-sponsored media coverage in Bulgaria.

ATTEMPTED POISONING OF AN ARMS DEALER AND HIS SON

In 2015, Russian military intelligence officers attempted to poison the same Bulgarian national at least twice. The Bulgarian in question was Emilian Gebrev, one of the most prominent Bulgarian arms producers and dealers at that period. Although he was temporarily hospitalized, Gebrev survived both poisoning attempts. The first one likely took place on April 27 and the second one occurred between May 24 and 30. After the first poisoning attempt, Gebrev's son and the executive director of Gebrev's weapons company, Emko, were also hospitalized with the same symptoms as Gebrev. In the years following the poisoning attempts, Bulgarian investigators did not find any evidence that pointed at potential perpetrators and did not discover any links to Russia. Three years later, however, an international investigation into the poisonings uncovered the involvement of a Russian GRU unit that was also implicated in the attempt to assassinate former Russian spy Sergei Skripal in the United Kingdom.[30]

Intelligence officials hypothesize that Russia's GRU officers targeted Gebrev due to his small-arms and ammunition business, which likely irritated Moscow. As the previous section explained, Bulgaria emerged as a major arms and ammunition exporter to markets that were traditionally dominated by Russian-made Kalashnikovs.[31] The Bulgarian arms dealer sold weapons to these markets. Moreover, Gebrev had active business connections with weapons factories in Ukraine, whose soldiers were fighting Russian nationals and service members, including those from the GRU in the east, in a historic war that was as much about territory as it was about Ukraine's geopolitical direction. In addition to creating potential friction with Moscow because of his buyers, Gebrev might have attracted Moscow's wrath through other deals. He tried to acquire a weapons factory called Dunarit, which the Russian oligarch Konstantin Malofeev, who is close to the Kremlin, was also competing to purchase. Some experts examined the competition over that property as another justification for Russia's decision to assassinate Gebrev.[32]

SUSPECTED RUSSIAN SABOTAGE IN EXPLOSIONS AT WEAPONS FACILITIES

Over the past decade, there have been dozens of explosions in Bulgarian weapons manufacturing or storage facilities. The official versions of the reasons for these incidents have typically been technical malfunction or lack of adherence to technical working protocols. Some of these explosions, especially since the end of 2014, have been particularly devastating. For example, an explosion in October 2014 in the Bulgarian military factory Midzhur resulted in the death of fifteen people.[33] Although the initial investigations into the series of explosions investigated possible sabotage but concluded that they were not deliberate, the British investigation into the poisoning of former Russian agent Skripal and his daughter spurred new discoveries into the assassination attempts on Gebrev, which also led the Bulgarian authorities to reopen some of the cases of explosions and investigate them for potential Russian involvement. As a result of more scrutinous inquiries, investigators in the United Kingdom informed Bulgarian authorities that they discovered that a Russian citizen linked to the Russian government visited Bulgaria two weeks before the first attempted poisoning of Gebrev. The visit of that individual coincided with two explosions at weapons facilities that were property of the largest Bulgarian military-industrial company, which is owned by the Bulgarian government. The first explosion took place on March 21, 2015, in an ammunition depot that belonged to the weapons manufacturer VMZ-Sopot. The particular facility was located near the village of Iganovo. The second explosion occurred on April 14, 2015, near the same village but in an ammunition production facility owned by the same weapons manufacturer.[34] At that time VMZ-Sopot became the largest Bulgarian exporter of ammunitions to Syria, which irritated Moscow. Gebrev was also involved in selling VMZ-Sopot's products.[35] During the initial investigation into the causes of the explosions, Bulgarian authorities asserted that the version of sabotage was also investigated as a possible reason for the explosions, but no concrete evidence to link this theory to the Russian government was found at that time.[36] In February 2019, former Bulgarian defense minister and former ambassador to NATO Boyko Noev stated that there may be a connection between the visit of that Russian citizen and the two explosions. Noev explained that the Russian citizen may have caused the explosions in an attempt to sabotage Bulgarian weapons production and added that "there are many circumstances and facts that suggest that representatives or people connected in some way to Russia are involved in activities in Bulgaria that are directed against the Bulgarian arms industry."[37]

In June 2015, another explosion occurred at a testing range of VMZ-Sopot. The explosion resulted in the death of one individual who was an American citizen and a DoD contractor. The investigation into the case at the time concluded that this was a training accident caused by faulty ammunition.[38] No publicly known subsequent investigations have uncovered other reasons for the explosion, but the timing and the death of an American citizen appear suspicious, to say the least.

RUSSIA'S CYBER ATTACKS AGAINST BULGARIA

As Bulgarian citizens headed to the polls to vote in the October local elections, Russian cyber threat actors launched a series of DDoS operations against political infrastructure. The cyber attacks targeted the official websites of Bulgaria's Central Election Commission, the General Directorate for Civil Registration and Administrative Services (Grazhdanska registratsiya i administrativno obsluzhvane, or GRAO), the Bulgarian Interior Ministry, and the Ministry of Foreign Affairs. The cyber operations were DDoS attacks, which were likely conducted to disrupt access to data and could, therefore, be categorized as availability attacks.[39] As a result of the attacks, all four websites were temporarily shut down or inaccessible to the public.[40]

All four targeted organizations were directly or indirectly involved in the electoral process. The websites of each organization either contained information for the general

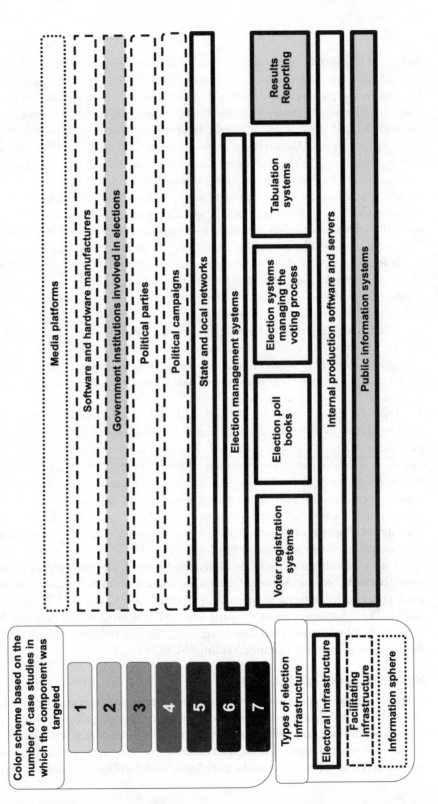

FIGURE 4.1 Russia's Political Hack Map during the 2015 Bulgarian Elections

population regarding how to vote or were going to be used to post voting results.[41] GRAO (Grazhdanska registratsiya i administrativno obsluzhvane, or General Directorate for Civil Registration and Administrative Services) is a part of the specialized administration of the Ministry of Regional Development and Public Affairs. GRAO has two departments—Methodology and Control, and Electronic Information Processing. In addition to its two main departments, GRAO has twenty-eight territorial units in the administrative centers of Bulgaria's districts.[42] The electronic information processing website was the target of the October 2015 cyber operation.[43] Bulgarian citizens use GRAO's webpage to identify their specific voting district and the location where they should vote. The website of the Bulgarian Central Election Commission (Tsentralna izbiratelna komisiya, or CEC) experienced the DDoS attacks. CEC's targeted website is the platform that CEC uses to publicize voting results. The Ministry of Foreign Affairs website contained information on voting locations outside Bulgaria, which was useful information for Bulgarian diasporas interested in casting their votes. The website of Bulgaria's Ministry of the Interior provided useful guidelines for Bulgarian citizens whose identification documents had been stolen or lost and who wanted to exercise their right to vote.[44]

Based on this information, figure 4.1 shows what elements of the political infrastructure the DDoS attacks targeted according to the categorization of political components outlined in chapter 2. The map reveals that the majority of targets pertained to electoral infrastructure and affected the availability of data. These types of attacks could exert both psychological and technical effects.

The DDoS attacks were quickly contained—GRAO's information services department subscribed to the service CloudFlare and the Ministry of the Interior followed that example as the DDoS attacks continued. The ministry's website continued to receive requests (1.8 billion over a few hours), but because the ministry already subscribed to the service, on the day following the elections the service diverted the traffic or cut traffic requests from abroad, and the ministry's website continued to function. GRAO's website sustained only a temporary shutdown because CloudFlare blocked traffic to the website from abroad. The chief of Bulgaria's CERT at that time, Vasil Gruncharov, said the attacks were neutralized within an adequate timeframe.[45]

A few weeks after the attacks, on November 10, 2015, during a meeting of the Bulgarian National Security Advisory Council, representatives of Bulgarian counterintelligence presented information to support the argument that GRU's APT 28 executed the attacks. The information about the particular APT was given to the Bulgarian intelligence services by "a partner intelligence agency."[46] Various Bulgarian officials, including the Bulgarian president at that time, confirmed GRU's role.[47]

PRO-KREMLIN MEDIA COVERAGE

In addition to cyber operations, the Russian government may have used media channels accessible to the Bulgarian public to spread strategic messaging aligned with Moscow's political objectives. Russia's influence in Bulgarian media is substantial and occurs through various channels and agents.[48] In September 2014, then Bulgarian president Rosen Plevneliev stated that "90% of the media in Bulgaria work for Russian masters."[49] Although

Plevneliev's assessment of the magnitude of Russia's media reach may be exaggerated, a brief analysis of the multiple forms of Russia's influence in the Bulgarian media space would make the former president's statement plausible.

The Russian government supports media outlets that publish in Bulgarian, such as Russian Diary (Ruski Dnevnik), hosted by the Russian media outlet Russia Beyond the Headlines (RBTH), funded by the Russian government.[50] Russian channels are broadcast on Bulgarian cable networks and Russia maintains positive relations with publishers of major Bulgarian newspapers, such as the newspaper *Duma* (*Word*), which is the official newspaper of the BSP.[51] A study conducted by the Sofia-based Center for the Study of Democracy concluded that *Duma*, alongside newspapers *Zemia* and *Attack* (the official newspaper of the party Attack) have "direct ties to Russia" either through influence on the content the newspapers publish or through ownership of them.[52] In 2011, then Russian president Dmitriy Medvedev decorated *Duma*'s editor for his "contribution to the upkeep of Russian monuments in Bulgaria."[53] Pro-Russian journalists, media anchors, and reporters further ensure that Russia's position in Bulgarian news is heard.[54] Russian influence is also exerted through a Russia-backed community of social media content creators such as internet trolls and bloggers.[55] Another channel through which the Russian government exerts influence over Bulgarian news is through an increased number of websites and blogs that observe a pro-Kremlin line, such as Alterinformation.wordpress.com, Afera.bg, and Fakti.bg. Information from these blogs and websites is further reproduced on social media.[56]

There are no Bulgarian-language editions of the Russian outlets *Sputnik News* and *RT*, which are Russian state-sponsored media outlets that are known to reflect the Kremlin's position abroad.[57] Therefore, to analyze whether Russia's state-sponsored media in Bulgaria adopted a position in favor of one political party over another and engaged in a strategic messaging campaign around the time of the cyber operations and during the October 2015 election cycle, this section examined the coverage of the two main contending parties, GERB and BSP, in the Russian-sponsored website Russian Diary published in Bulgarian.[58] The analyzed coverage starts three months before the first known poisoning attempt against Gebrev and ends three months after the DDoS attacks on election day (January 27, 2015, to January 25, 2016).[59] Figure 4.2 represents the results of the daily coverage and illustrates the minimal number of coverage that the two parties received in Russia's Russian Diary—eleven articles over the entire period. This number could hardly serve as the basis for drawing any meaningful conclusions about potential alteration in the volume of media coverage.

To verify the lack of patterns in Russian-influenced media coverage about the two main parties during the period of the DDoS attacks, the analysis also examined the coverage in one of the Bulgarian newspapers whose coverage is known to be influenced by Russia, namely the newspaper *Trud* (*Labor*).[60] The author chose to examine the coverage in this newspaper because it was available online and because the newspaper is known to be influenced by the Russian government.[61] Figure 4.3 displays the number of articles per day in the period from January 27, 2015, to January 25, 2016, that mention GERB and BSP.

Due to the fact that Labor is not under the direct ownership of the Russian government like *RT* or *Sputnik News*, it is difficult to distinguish between the extent to which

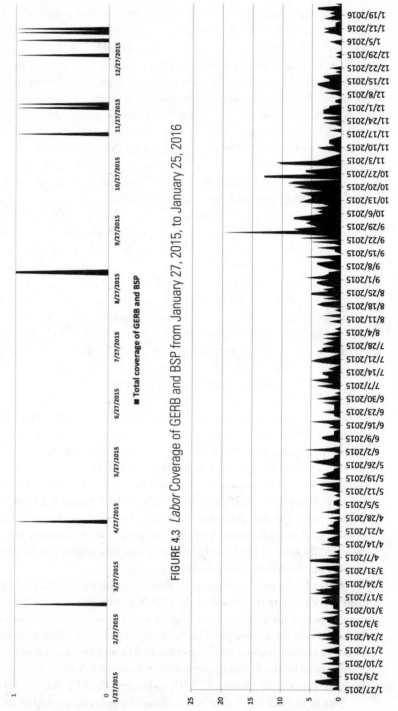

FIGURE 4.2 Russian Diary Coverage of GERB and BSP from January 27, 2015, to January 25, 2016

FIGURE 4.3 *Labor* Coverage of GERB and BSP from January 27, 2015, to January 25, 2016

Moscow is responsible for the volume and content of coverage during the Bulgarian elections and the extent to which Bulgarian editors exercised autonomy over the analyzed coverage. Assuming that the coverage is at least partially influenced by *Labor*'s ties with Russia, even if not completely dictated by it, the analysis examined the amount and type of news about the two parties as a proxy for Russia's strategic messaging in this period. Unlike in the coverage of Russian Diary shown in figure 4.2, the coverage about the two parties in *Labor* shown in figure 4.3 revealed a spike in the volume of reporting about the two parties on election day and an increased coverage in the month before the election.

To identify whether any themes that were particularly negative about the relatively anti-Russian political party GERB existed in the media coverage, or whether any themes that would undermine the election results, and thus the legitimacy of the elections in the eyes of the constituency, were prevalent in the media coverage during the period under investigation, the analysis examined the contents of the article in the months prior to and after the elections. In the weeks prior to the elections, *Labor* published relatively balanced coverage about the candidates from the two main competing parties.[62] Despite occasional articles critical of GERB's policies, most articles referring to GERB portrayed the party in a positive light and there was no consistently negative reporting of GERB's candidates.[63] The postelection coverage contained articles about potential violations of the election process, such as intimidation of candidates and forgery of ballots. The articles covered violations raised both by GERB and BSP candidates. Allegations about voting violations raised by GERB representatives occasionally pointed at GERB as the perpetrator or the party responsible for allowing these violations to occur.[64] Despite the violations reportedly conducted by GERB, the *Labor* coverage still reflected that the BSP leadership accepted the election results and did not blame them on a forged election process but on other issues, systemic to the country, such as the type of democracy in Bulgaria.[65] Based on this information, *Labor*'s reporting of the two main parties during the election period does not seem to contain any consistently strong negative bias toward GERB or its candidates. Therefore, if *Labor*'s coverage is regarded as a proxy for Russia's strategic messaging at that time, it does not appear that the Russian government is particularly in favor of or against any of the two main contending parties.

There are several hypotheses to explain this lack of negative media coverage. First, Russia may be using other channels to convey specific positions. Such channels include other Bulgarian media outlets, blogs, and social media platforms. Some analysts argue that due to Russia's well-established influence in Bulgarian newspapers and TV channels, the already existing Bulgarian media channels may constitute an even more effective conduit of Russian strategic messaging. The effectiveness of reflecting Russia's position through domestic media in Bulgaria may also be the reason why Russia did not regard the need to establish Bulgarian versions of *RT* and *Sputnik News*.[66] If this is the case, other media should be examined in this section. However, the author did not have access to social media data from this period, and due to the inability to identify with any level of certainty what Russia's influence on the coverage in Bulgarian newspapers was at the time, the author did not examine the coverage about BSP and GERB in social media.

A second explanation may be that the Russian government may not have considered these particular Bulgarian elections as critical enough to launch a media campaign. Moscow may have considered them as an opportunity to test its cyber capabilities. There is evidence to suggest that in 2015, the GRU had been testing a tool for DDoS attacks from Bulgaria's territory. A *New York Times* article reported how an executive of Russia's military company Rostec who was close to the Russian military flew a Russian programmer to Sofia, where a Bulgarian company demonstrated to the programmer how a novel software tool could stage DDoS attacks. During the demonstration, the company briefly crashed the websites of the Ukrainian Ministry of Defense and Russian news website Slon.ru. The Russian programmer was asked how the software could be improved. The Russians planned to purchase the software from the Bulgarian firm.[67] The DDoS attacks on election day may have been another demonstration of this tool, or of another one.

Another objective of Russia's cyber operation might have been to send a signal to Bulgaria's leadership regarding its policies on sanctions against Russia, South Stream, and Bulgarian arms exports without having a broader agenda of disrupting the election process or influencing the election outcome.[68] These alternative explanations are not mutually exclusive and could have all factored in Moscow's decision to go on the cyber offensive against Bulgaria's political IT infrastructure.

To assess the Russian-influenced media coverage of Bulgarian arms exports during the period under investigation, the author examined all articles published in *Labor* between January 27, 2015, and January 25, 2016, that referenced "arms exports," "weapons," or "arms" in their titles. The author found only eight relevant articles, which was too small a sample size to draw any methodologically rigorous conclusions about trends in this narrative (see fig. 4.4). Despite the lack of consistent media coverage of Bulgaria's weapons trade potentially influenced by the Russian government, the Kremlin may have still had a strong interest in influencing Bulgaria's arms exports, but the activities that the Russian government may have supported to do so may not have included strategic messaging campaigns in Bulgarian media, or at least in Bulgaria's newspaper *Labor*. As the main decision makers in Bulgaria regarding weapons exports are the government and private companies, it is conceivable to assume that the Kremlin may have chosen a more targeted strategy to influence their decisions. This strategy could have included applying pressure to the government through the attempted poisoning of the Bulgarian arms dealer Gebrev, starting explosions in Bulgarian weapons facilities, or DDoS-ing political infrastructure on election day—activities described earlier in this chapter.

QCA and Visualization of Russia's Cyber Attacks and Other Activities

Bulgarian authorities and analysts have provided sufficient clarity into the role of Russian state-sponsored hackers during the DDoS attacks against key components of Bulgaria's political infrastructure. Adequate proof also links assassination attempts against Bulgarian arms dealers to Russian intelligence. The influence of the Russian political elite on Bulgarian media channels has also been well established, and data shows an increase in

FIGURE 4.4 *Labor* Coverage of Bulgarian Arms Exports from January 27, 2015, to January 25, 2016

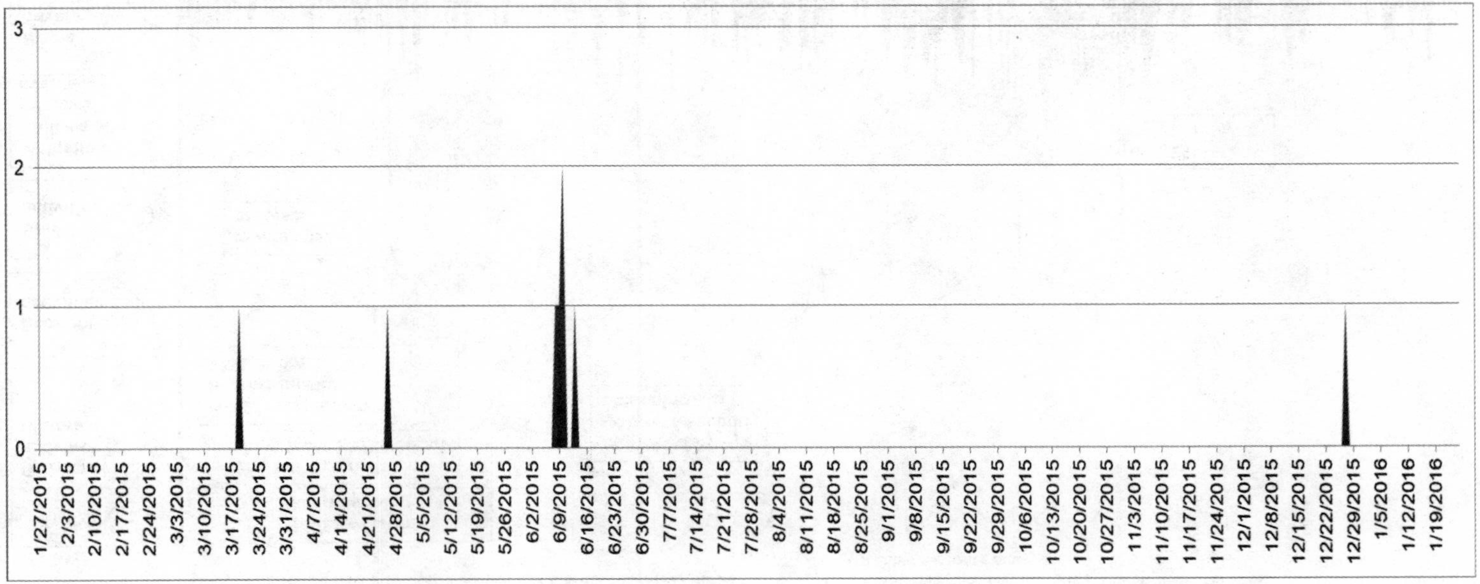

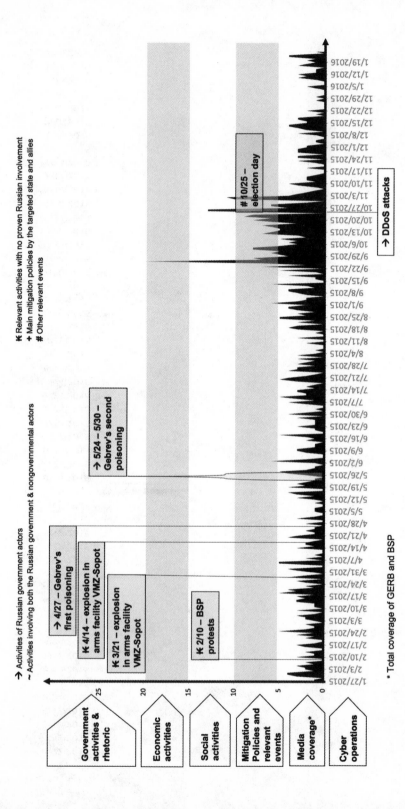

FIGURE 4.5 Russia's CHAOS in Bulgaria

TABLE 4.1 Factors That Could Be Associated with the Initiation of the Particular Type of Cyber Operations Observed during the 2015 Bulgarian Elections

Target	Type of cyber op (CIA)	Disputes in relations				Spike in media coverage before cyber ops	If cyber ops during elections		NATO member en route	NATO member	Frm. Eastern Bloc state	Frm. USSR state
		Polit	Soc	Econ	Mil		Anti-Ru candidate	Pro-Ru candidate				
Bulgaria (2015)	A	1	0	1	1	0	1	1	0	1	1	0

media coverage about the two main parties competing in the October 2015 elections in the month prior to the elections. However, the media coverage did not contain strong and consistent negative bias toward the pro-NATO party GERB or consistent strong narratives questioning the legitimacy of the election process. Considering the conclusions of the media analysis, the lack of information about other Russian-sponsored activities in Bulgaria at that time that could be considered part of a Russian state-sponsored information warfare campaign or any definitive information on Russia's intentions behind the cyber operations, it is unclear whether the Russian government conducted these activities with a common objective or whether they coincidentally occurred in temporal proximity to one another.

Figure 4.5 visualizes the known activities linked to Russian state-sponsored entities and Russian-influenced media coverage at that time, with the caveat that the attempted assassinations of Gebrev, the explosions in Bulgarian weapons facilities, Russia's cyber operations on election day, and the media coverage potentially influenced by Russia during the election period may not have been conducted with a unified purpose. That said, the fact that the attempted poisonings of Gebrev and the DDoS attacks were both probably conducted by the GRU further suggests that there could have been some level of coordination, or at least awareness of these activities within the GRU.

Table 4.1 applies the QCA framework to the information gathered in this chapter. This data is added to the conclusion of this research, which offers a cross-country analysis using the QCA framework.

The Effectiveness of Russia's Cyber Operations and Information Warfare Campaign

Despite Bulgaria's being a member of NATO and the European Union, its foreign policy is still a balancing act. Bulgaria's deeply ingrained cultural, historical, political, and economic bonds with Russia continue to influence the direction of Bulgarian politics, which is formally connected with Western organizations but continues its special relationship with Russia. In the months prior to the October 2015 elections, several political and economic issues in Russian-Bulgarian relations exacerbated tensions in the ties between the two states. In addition to its national security doctrine that designated Russia as a threat and condemned Russia's annexation of Crimea, Bulgaria's refusal to allow Russian flights over Bulgarian airspace, a failed project to approve South Stream's construction through Bulgaria on Russian terms, and an increase of Bulgarian weapons exports to Russian markets and adversaries irritated Moscow's leadership.

In this environment, increasingly unfavorable to Moscow, the Russian government may have chosen to authorize cyber operations against Bulgaria's political infrastructure on election day for several reasons. The Kremlin may have aimed to disrupt the election process. However, the websites of the attacked institutions did not experience major disruptions on election day, so if Russia's objective was to disrupt the election process, Russia's cyber operations did not appear to have been effective in achieving that objective.

Furthermore, if the Russian government had interest in influencing the process or outcome of the Bulgarian elections, Russia's positions toward the contending election candidates could have become obvious through the Kremlin-influenced media coverage in Bulgaria at that time. The analysis of this case revealed that there was no extensive coverage of the election and no increase in reporting on election day or afterward in media in Bulgaria. However, an analysis of the media coverage of a Bulgarian newspaper with known Russian influence revealed some patterns. There was an increase in reporting about the two parties on election day and in the month prior to election day, which is a typical media response, considering that elections are an important topic in the country. However, there was no consistently negative coverage of the leading party GERB prior to or after the elections, which suggests that the Russian government may not have aimed to influence the election outcome.

In addition, there was no known evidence of Russian state sponsorship of protests or other notable events that could be associated with a general strategy of the Russian government aimed at influencing the elections. Nevertheless, protests organized by the main opposition party, the BSP, were advocating for policies in line with Russian interests, and although there is no evidence of the direct financial or other support of the Russian government for these protests, further research into BSP's financial contributions, which the party does not disclose, may reveal a financial link to the Kremlin.

Russia's justification behind the cyber attacks may not have been directly related to the process or outcome of the elections. Russia could have aimed to test its capabilities and Bulgaria may have seemed an appropriate cyber range. Considering that the targeted websites experienced disruptions, this objective could have been successfully achieved. The lack of specific anti-GERB media coverage, and of other Russian state-sponsored activities suggesting Moscow's interest in influencing the elections, would support this conclusion.

Furthermore, Russia may have used the cyber operations as a manner through which to express disapproval of the policies of the leading party GERB. Other activities attributed to Russian government actors at that time include the two poisoning attempts of the Bulgarian arms dealer and potentially staging explosions at weapons facilities. These activities would further support the hypothesis that the Russian government was irked by

Bulgaria's policies around that time. The fact that the Russian cyber operations and the attempted assassinations were both conducted by GRU units provides another potential link between the different activities, suggesting that they could have been conducted with a common purpose.

If Russia used the cyber attacks on election day to send a message of disapproval to Bulgaria, the message did not seem to have resulted in any marked change in the main foreign policy priorities of the country. The Bulgarian government continued to support sanctions against Russia in relation to its annexation of Crimea, continued to keep Russian jets away from Bulgarian airspace, and did not reverse its policy on South Stream.[69] Bulgaria's weapons exports also remained high in the following year.[70] Hence, Russia's cyber operations appear to have been equally ineffective in accomplishing a meaningful change in the issues of Bulgarian foreign policy important to Moscow.

5

The 2016 and 2020 U.S. Presidential Elections, or Why the Devil Wears Gucci, Not Prada[1]

In the summer of 2015 and in April 2016, Russian hacker groups associated with Russian intelligence services instigated a series of cyber operations, gaining access to the emails of numerous election and party officials and breaching the networks of the Democratic National Committee (DNC) and the Democratic Congressional Campaign Committee (DCCC). In the subsequent months leading to the November 2016 U.S. presidential elections, a massive amount of sensitive campaign data and personal emails obtained as a result of these intrusions were released to the public, strategically timed to coincide with major political events. On October 7, 2016, the U.S. Office of the Director of National Intelligence (ODNI) and the Department of Homeland Security (DHS) officially accused the Russian government of conducting these cyber breaches and attempting to interfere in the 2016 U.S. presidential elections.[2]

Various government investigations and analyses have since confirmed that Russia's information warfare campaign during the 2016 elections was multifaceted and unprecedented in its scope and sophistication.[3] Russian government-supported activities that facilitated this operation were initiated at least as early as 2014. Several key documents released by the U.S. intelligence community (U.S. IC), the U.S. Justice Department, the U.S. Senate Intelligence Committee, and independent social media experts show that Russia's campaign consisted of a multilayered information warfare operation that included intelligence gathering, exploitation of U.S. social media platforms and U.S.-based computer infrastructure, financial fraud, and impersonation of U.S. citizens. The campaign also included multiple cyber operations against all U.S. states and other political organizations such as the DCCC, dissemination of propaganda and disinformation, and sponsorship of political rallies in support of various political candidates and divisive social issues.[4] The aim of Russia's information warfare campaign around the 2016 elections was to disseminate disinformation, deepen societal divisions, "undermine public faith in the U.S. democratic process, denigrate Secretary Clinton, and harm her electability and potential presidency."[5]

Although the Russian government used a similar playbook that included cyber operations across other NATO members after 2016, the Kremlin is not known to have directed any consistent cyber operations against political targets related to the 2020 U.S. elections. The Russian government was accused of attempting to interfere in the 2020 elections but the known methods it used did not include cyber operations. A report released by the U.S. intelligence community alleged with high confidence that the Russian government attempted to undermine the 2020 U.S. presidential campaign of then presidential candidate Joseph Biden by influencing public perceptions through media and prominent individuals. For example, the Kremlin used pro-Russian foreign assets, such as a Ukrainian legislator and member of Ukraine's parliament, to leak private information relating Biden to corruption in Ukraine.[6] Evidence suggests that the Russian government used strategic messaging against the 2020 U.S. elections but it did not deploy its cyber forces in this particular case. Because the presence of a publicly attributed Russian state-sponsored cyber operation is a main requirement for the examination of a case of Russian interference in this book, this chapter does not examine in detail Russia's activities related to the 2020 U.S. elections.

This chapter focuses on the 2016 U.S. elections and identifies the context and factors associated with the Russian 2016 information warfare campaign. It begins by describing the general state of U.S.-Russian relations at the time of Russia's activities and the relevant characteristics of the U.S. electoral campaign. This section is followed by an analysis of the range of Russian information warfare activities around the time of the election and a subsequent description of the threat actors, targets, and types of Russia's cyber operations. The Hack Map visualizes the components of the U.S. political IT infrastructure that the Russian APTs targeted. The chapter proceeds by analyzing Russian state-sponsored media coverage around the time of the cyber operations. The QCA framework described in the previous chapter then identifies the presence or absence of factors that may be associated with the start of Russia's cyber operations. Using the process-tracing method and the CHAOS framework, this chapter further examines how Russia's cyber operations fed into the range of activities Moscow applied in this information warfare operation to achieve a synergetic interference. Finally, the chapter presents conclusions on the role and effectiveness of Russia's cyber operations in the general toolbox of information warfare operations.

A Note on Standards of Evidence

The conduct of the 2016 U.S. elections and the potential involvement of foreign states such as Russia and Ukraine, received unprecedented attention by all branches of the U.S. government, the U.S. IC, and the media. Allegations and speculations even questioned the veracity of the assessments that Russian state-sponsored threat actors breached the DNC servers.[7] Due to the contentious nature of this case, a note on the standards of evidence this chapter considered is in order. In analyzing this case, this book considered only information that has been backed up by actual evidence and endorsed by professional organizations whose job it is to assess the evidence on the particular issue. For example, this book accepts the argument that two Russian APTs breached the servers of the DNC because well-regarded cybersecurity companies, the U.S. intelligence community, and intelligence communities of other states, endorsed this position.[8] Similarly, this book does not venture into evaluating the argument of possible Ukrainian interference in the elections because of testimonies by well-regarded foreign policy professionals who have debunked these claims as false.[9] The analysis does not take into account allegations about potential collusion between former U.S. president Donald Trump and the Russian government because of the highly politicized nature of these discussions and because, despite detailed government investigations into the matter, none have yet revealed any concrete evidence to substantiate the claims of collusion between the political campaign of then presidential candidate Trump and the Russian government during the 2016 U.S. election campaign.[10]

Factors in U.S.-Russia Relations and the U.S. Election Environment Potentially Associated with the Launch of Cyber Operations

An examination of the literature reveals the presence of various U.S.-Russian political, diplomatic, and economic disputes, as well as certain characteristics of the 2016 U.S. election in particular, that may have prompted the Russian government to authorize cyber operations against the United States. In 2014 when the Russian government initiated information warfare activities against the United States, U.S.-Russian relations had significantly deteriorated. Russia's illegal annexation of Crimea in April 2014 and the subsequent prolonged and bloody conflict in Eastern Ukraine compelled the United States and other Western nations to adopt a series of measures to demonstrate their opposition to Russia. These measures aimed to influence Russia's behavior, and deter Moscow from expanding its aggressive foreign policy in Ukraine and beyond.[11] Some of the policies that the West and the United States adopted included: expelling Russia from the Group of 8 (G-8) summit, discontinuing any practical cooperation within the framework of the NATO-Russia Council, and imposing a series of targeted sanctions against Russian economic sectors and especially Russian individuals related to Russia's war in Ukraine.[12] The United States had also been vocally criticizing Russia's activities in Syria.[13] Russia's support for Syrian president Bashir Al-Assad served to drive another wedge between Washington and Moscow.[14] President Putin himself has publicly blamed the United States for the disclosure of the Panama Papers and the Olympic doping scandal, demonstrating his disapproval of U.S. policies against Russia.[15]

In addition to deteriorating bilateral relations and specific events that may have influenced Russia's decision to interfere in the 2016 U.S. elections, there are specific characteristics of the 2016 U.S. election candidates that could have factored in the Russian leaders' decision to launch cyber operations against the DNC and other political entities during the elections. A number of experts refer to Hillary Clinton's record toward Russia in her political career as one of the potential reasons for Moscow's election interference. FBI Director

James Comey testified that Putin detested Secretary Clinton and preferred Trump as U.S. president.[16] Already in her position as a U.S. senator, Clinton supported the U.S. invasion of Iraq, and as secretary of state she supported NATO's campaign against the Muammar Qaddafi regime in Libya, which Putin and the Russian government opposed.[17] Clinton's outspoken criticism against the legitimacy of the 2011 Russian parliamentary elections, which Putin's party won, further widened the divide between the two political leaders.[18] Putin has openly blamed Hillary Clinton for the subsequent large-scale Russian protests against his government in 2011 and 2012.[19] The Russian leadership also expressed concern with regard to her public positions on human rights violations in Russia; Russia's annexation of Crimea, which Clinton opposed; and increased sanctions against Russia.[20] Moscow envisioned that if Clinton became president, it would be nearly impossible to remove sanctions against Russia, which was a question of personal importance to Putin.[21] Moscow was also apprehensive about Clinton's cabinet and the potential increased influence of Senator John McCain and Victoria Nuland, among others.[22]

Accounts further suggest that candidate Donald Trump would have been a more agreeable choice for Russia and that Putin "developed a clear preference for President-elect Trump."[23] As a 2019 Senate Intelligence Committee report outlines in detail, Trump developed business and personal relationships with various Russian oligarchs close to the Russian president prior to running for office and also pursued business with Russia during the election campaign.[24] After Trump chose to hold the Miss Universe competition in Russia, he even received a personal gift from Putin in November 2013.[25] Furthermore, Trump's policy positions on matters of interest to Russia during the election campaign made him a preferable candidate for the Russian leadership. For example, Trump indicated he would consider lifting sanctions against Russia and recognizing the Crimean Peninsula as a part of Russia. Trump also did not outspokenly criticize Russian human rights violations and personally praised Putin.[26]

Russia's Information Warfare Activities

It was in this environment of deteriorating relations with the United States, and of political candidates with articulated positions and records of interaction with Russia, that Moscow launched an information warfare operation against the 2016 U.S. presidential election. This operation was personally ordered by President Putin[27] and constituted a combination of centrally mandated information warfare activities.[28] The Russian government sent operatives to the United States to lay the groundwork for the information warfare campaign. The Kremlin used its state-sponsored social media channels to plant and disseminate disinformation in Russian, but also in U.S. social media, purchased and disseminated advertisements on U.S. social media websites, launched a series of cyber operations, and used social media accounts managed by Russian paid internet bloggers (trolls) and automated internet accounts (bots) to spread targeted information. This information was designed to increase tensions, erode the social cohesion of the American public, and harm the electability of various presidential candidates, most notably Secretary Clinton.

POLITICAL ACTIVITIES

The Internet Research Agency

Russia's campaign was partially coordinated by a Russian organization based in St. Petersburg with the generic name Internet Research Agency (Agenstvo Internet Issledovaniy, or IRA), which is known to have existed at least since 2013.[29] Since at least June 2014, the IRA has been obscuring its operations by working through other Russian entities and has received government funding through another Russian organization called Concord Management and Consulting LLC.[30] The IRA's activities against the United States were only a part of a broader interference operation. Other elements of the project involved targeting Russian audiences and the population of other foreign countries.[31]

The IRA was structured as a corporate entity rather than a government operations agent. It was directed by a management board and was divided into departments, including a data analysis department, a search-engine department, and a graphics department. Since at least April 2014, the IRA also had a department known as the "translator project." The staff of that department targeted the U.S. population and was delegated with conducting operations with the objective to "spread distrust towards the candidates and the political system in general" and fuel "political intensity through supporting radical groups, users dissatisfied with [the] social and economic situation and oppositional social movements."[32] The IRA did this through social media, using platforms such as Facebook, Twitter, YouTube, and Instagram to target the U.S. population.[33]

Trips to the United States

Russia's campaign to interfere in the U.S. elections commenced at least as early as 2014, when two Russian citizens, Alexandra Krylova and Anna Bogacheva, traveled to the United States to gather information for Russia's subsequent operations against the U.S. political system, leading to the 2016 U.S. presidential elections.[34] From approximately June 4 to 26, 2014, Krylova and Bogacheva visited California, New Mexico, Nevada, New York, Colorado, Illinois, Michigan, Louisiana, Texas, and New York and produced an intelligence trip report. The trip of these two individuals was followed by the visit of another Russian operative to Atlanta, Georgia, from November 26 to 30, 2014.[35] While in the United States, the individuals purchased space on U.S.-based computer servers to conceal the fact that the social media operation was directed by Russia. The Russian operatives established a virtual network and created hundreds of email and social media accounts. By setting up the accounts from U.S. servers, the individuals made them appear established by persons who resided in the United States. The Russian operatives also used fake or stolen U.S. identification documents, identities, and fraudulent bank accounts to make their media presence appear authentic.[36]

SOCIAL ACTIVITIES

Exploitation of U.S. Social Media Platforms

Russia's use of social media platforms to spread disinformation, socially divisive content, and leaked materials was broad and strategic. The primary agents in this operation were the IRA employees who exploited the infrastructure set up during trips to the United

States to create fake personas and obfuscate the origins of their media content.[37] In particular, the IRA used Instagram, Facebook, Twitter, Reddit, Pinterest, YouTube, LinkedIn, 4chan, Tumblr, and others to disseminate its messages, purchase campaign advertisements, and promote campaign rallies.[38] To reach a broader audience and amplify the impact of posted content, Russian actors used thousands of bots and trolls.[39]

Around February 2016, the IRA staff received instructions on the types of content it should circulate regarding the U.S. presidential campaigns. These instructions included explicit tasking to disparage the presidential campaign of then candidate Clinton and support the campaign of then candidate Trump.[40] IRA staff was also tasked with creating "political intensity through supporting radical groups, users dissatisfied with [the] social and economic situation and oppositional social movements."[41]

Analyses that examined in detail the content of IRA social media accounts, targeted audiences, and account names over the course of the U.S. presidential campaigns indicate that although the IRA staff exploited the topic of U.S. elections, the majority of the IRA content consisted of divisive social issues. These issues included discrimination, race, gun rights, and immigration. The objective of these messages was likely to "pit Americans against one another and against their government."[42] This objective is consistent with Russia's information warfare strategy described in chapter 1. The group most targeted in the IRA campaign was African Americans and the most preferred topic of the campaign was race and related matters. An analysis of Russia's Facebook advertisements corroborates this conclusion. Over 60 percent of IRA's Facebook ads contained a reference to race while they were targeted at African Americans in urban areas.[43] The focus on African Americans is also evidenced in the IRA Facebook pages. For example, the IRA staff created group pages on Facebook and Instagram, where it posted content on topics such as the Black Lives Matter movement (a group called Blacktivist). The size of some of these groups reached thousands of online followers by 2016.[44] Similar focus on racial issues was seen across social media platforms. About 96 percent of IRA's content on YouTube was related to racial issues, while five of the IRA's top ten Instagram accounts were targeted at African Americans.[45] Voter suppression among potential democratic voters also seemed to be among the goals of the IRA content. [46] The IRA messages often conveyed disunity, hopelessness, and contempt.[47]

IRA staff used social media groups to rally Americans in opposition or in support of socially divisive issues and had a broad reach. When Russia-linked Facebook group, Being Patriotic, for example, posted a message calling Americans to oppose proposals to increase the settlement of refugees in the United States, the post was shared, liked, or viewed by over 750,000 Facebook users.[48] Facebook estimated that approximately 126 million Americans were exposed to content disseminated by Russia-linked pages and users from 2015 to 2017.[49]

IRA employees also created and controlled Twitter accounts that looked quite authentic and likely deceived many of their followers into believing the accounts were genuinely American. For example, the IRA controlled a Tennessee GOP Twitter account with handle @TEN_GOP, which claimed to be administered by a U.S. political party and attracted more than 100,000 online followers.[50] Some of the materials posted by IRA accounts on Twitter were retweeted or cited by Trump campaign members, including Eric Trump, Kellyanne Conway, and Donald J. Trump Jr., which amplified the IRA's messages.[51] Testimony by a Twitter executive in October 2017 revealed that from September 1, 2016, to November 15, 2016, Twitter identified 36,746 Russia-linked automated accounts or bots that produced election content. These accounts generated about 1.4 million election-related tweets, which received 288 million impressions.[52] In January 2018, Twitter increased that number, reporting that over 50,000 IRA-linked automated accounts tweeted content related to the U.S. elections.[53] Twitter also identified over 3,800 IRA-linked accounts that engaged 1.4 million Twitter users.[54]

On Instagram, the IRA's presence was even more prolific than on Facebook. Similar to what the IRA did on other social media platforms, it used Instagram to spread disinformation and socially inflammatory content. The IRA created 133 Instagram accounts and published over 116,000 posts, reaching 187 million total engagements.[55] As the research manager at the Stanford Internet Observatory, Renée DiResta testified, "Instagram dramatically outperformed Facebook in terms of reach and in terms of likes and in terms of engagement."[56]

As early as 2015, IRA staff also started purchasing advertisements on social media to promote IRA-administered social media groups and inflammatory social content.[57] Paid ads however, did not appear to be the key of the IRA operation, considering the small number of these advertisements and the fact that they were viewed by relatively few people.[58] From at least April to November 2016, IRA staff and affiliates purchased, produced, and distributed advertisements promoting the election of then candidate Donald Trump and criticizing candidate Clinton.[59] The majority of the ads however, did not directly mention any of the political candidates. Instead, in alignment with the rest of the content of the IRA information warfare operation, the ads focused on divisive issues, including immigration, gun rights, and police brutality. The ads did not reflect only one side of a debate but at times supported opposite positions and encouraged rally attendance. Based on this content, analysts conclude that one of the objectives of the ads was to exacerbate polarization.[60] In November 2017, Facebook officials testified that approximately 11.4 million people in the United States had been exposed to advertising content linked to Russian accounts between 2015 and 2017 (44 percent of the total views, known as impressions, from the ads were generated before the elections on November 8 and the rest, after that date). The advertisements were commissioned by the IRA, which paid about $100,000 for about 3,400 ads—a minor sum in comparison to the IRA's overall monthly budget of more than $1.25 million.[61] The Daily Beast provided an alternative estimate of the ad's reach, stating they may have been seen by between 23 and 70 million individuals.[62]

Support for Protests
IRA staff were also involved in organizing, instigating, and funding political rallies on U.S. territory since approximately June 2016, using false identities and doctored PayPal accounts, sponsoring advertisements, paying unwitting U.S. individuals to participate in

or to help to organize rallies, and contacting real U.S. persons to ask them to partake in or promote the rallies. The IRA conducted these activities from Russia using identities of fictitious U.S. activists and claiming to be based in the United States. To advertise rallies and attract the American population, IRA personnel reached out to U.S. activists and administrators of social media groups asking that they advertise the rallies. IRA staff also used its Facebook groups and Twitter accounts to promote these events. For example, around June and July 2016, IRA staff and affiliated individuals used the Twitter account @March_for_Trump, the Facebook group Being Patriotic (which had more than 216,000 followers), and other IRA-controlled accounts to organize two rallies in New York. The IRA used fictitious identities to contact real U.S. individuals and offer them money to solicit their support in organizing these rallies. The first rally, called "March for Trump," took place on June 25, 2016, and the second one, "Down with Hillary," took place on July 23, 2016.[63] Around late July 2016, the IRA and affiliated individuals used the same social media accounts and techniques to organize several rallies in Florida, referred to as the "Florida Goes Trump" rallies, which took place on August 20, 2016.[64] Following the rallies in Florida, the IRA staff organized similar rallies in support of presidential candidate Donald Trump in New York and Pennsylvania.[65]

The IRA-sponsored political rallies continued after the 2016 election when social tensions among the U.S. population were still significantly high, as a large number of the American public was disappointed with the result of the presidential election. In that period, IRA staff and affiliated individuals organized rallies in support of both sides of the political spectrum, allegedly attempting to widen the social divide through exacerbating social divisions. For example, after the November 2016 election, on the same day—November 12, 2016—the IRA staged two rallies in New York, one in support of President-elect Trump and one against him.[66] The November anti-Trump protest gathered between 5,000 and 10,000 protesters.[67] A Russian media report assessed that the IRA spent around $80,000 to subsidize approximately 100 Americans who organized 40 protests across the United States.[68]

RUSSIA'S CYBER OPERATIONS

Cyber operations targeting various components of the political infrastructure at the federal and state level were a significant part of Russia's information warfare campaign against the U.S. political process and the 2016 presidential election. Russia's APT 28 and APT 29 were both involved in cyber operations but various U.S. investigations singled out GRU's APT 28 as the group that conducted the most notable operations. APT 28's operations included the intrusion into the networks of the DCCC and the DNC. APT 28 also gained access to emails of Clinton campaign officials and employees, including Clinton's campaign chairman, John Podesta. APT 28 exfiltrated and subsequently strategically released large amounts of personal and campaign data from Clinton's campaign.[69]

Cybersecurity firm SecureWorks estimated that entities accused by the U.S. government of being affiliated with the Russian government attempted to breach into approximately 5,000 email accounts of politicians, DNC members, journalists, and Secretary

Clinton's campaign staff. The techniques the attackers used were not sophisticated novel methods or zero-day exploits. Instead, the attackers used the relatively well-known technique of phishing emails that require low technical knowledge and trick the target into clicking on a link, which leads to the installation of malware used to exfiltrate content from the victim's email account.[70] The hackers also exploited a vulnerability in Microsoft's Windows software to attack U.S. political institutions.[71]

Investigators found that Hillary Clinton's presidential campaign chairman John Podesta was one of thousands of individuals who were targeted by APT 28 from March to November 2016, as a part of its mass phishing operation. In March 2016, APT 28 managed to breach Podesta's email account and obtain personal correspondence and information that was subsequently leaked to the public.[72]

Russia's APTs launched their most notable, known, successful cyber intrusion against the DNC—a facilitating political organization in the election process based on the framework developed in chapter 2—in the summer of 2015 and in April 2016. In this intrusion, APT 28 (specifically unit 26165) and APT 29 installed malware on DNC servers that enabled them to continuously exfiltrate information and send it to command-and-control servers (see table 5.1).[73] APT 29 was the first to breach the DNC servers in the summer of 2015 after sending spear-phishing emails to over 1,000 individuals.[74] In or around April 2016, GRU's APT 28 managed to infiltrate the networks of the DNC's sister organization, the DCCC.[75] Once in the DCCC's systems, the hackers used a virtual private network (VPN) connection to establish a link with the main computer network of the DNC.[76] From April through June 2016, APT 28 exfiltrated "thousands of politically sensitive documents" from the DNC and the DCCC servers.[77] APT 28's alleged goal was to access research files compiled by the DNC on opposition candidate Trump.[78] The APT stole documents and emails from both the DCCC and the DNC servers.[79]

A Senate Intelligence Committee report released in 2019 indicated that Russian actors probably targeted political infrastructure in all 50 U.S. states. The operations targeted election-related websites, election service companies, election system software, and voter registration databases. Most of them consisted of scanning the networks and did not infiltrate any systems.[80] The GRU also targeted election officials, including secretaries of state and county governments, county websites, state boards of elections, and private companies that provided political infrastructure such as voter registration software.[81] Although most of the attacks failed to infiltrate the targeted voting systems, in June and July 2016, law enforcement and state election administrators reported that election systems databases in Arizona and Illinois were breached.[82] In Illinois, hackers breached a database of the Illinois Board of Elections and accessed up to 200,000 voter records through the voter registration database. The data, which was exfiltrated, contained voters' identifying information such as names, addresses, and birthdays. Some records also included drivers' license numbers and the last four digits of a voter's Social Security number.[83] Despite the scope of Russia's 2016 cyber operations, investigations have determined that there was no evidence of manipulation of voter registry files, votes, voter tallies, or voting machines.[84]

TABLE 5.1 Cyber Attacks against the DCCC and DNC on
Lockheed Martin's Cyber Kill Chain

Cyber Kill Chain Stage	DCCC Hack	DNC Hack
	APT 28 (GRU)	APT 28 (GRU)
Reconnaissance	• Spear phishing and spoofing campaign • Scanned the DCCC network to identify technical specifications, network vulnerabilities, and connected devices	• Scanned the DNC network to identify technical specifications and network vulnerabilities
Weaponization	• Prepared versions of its X-Agent malware to install on the DCCC networks	• Prepared versions of its X-Agent malware to install on the DNC networks
Delivery	• Stole DCCC employee credentials through a spear-phishing campaign	• Activated X-Agent's keylog and screenshot functions to steal credentials of a DCCC employee who was authorized to access the DNC network
Exploitation	• Used the stolen credentials of a DCCC employee • Gained access to the DCCC computer network	• Gained access to approximately thirty-three DNC computers
Installation	• Installed versions of their X-Agent malware on at least ten DCCC computers. • X-Agent allowed APT 28 to monitor employees' computer activity, steal passwords, and maintain access to the DCCC network	• Installed X-Agent malware on the DNC network to explore the DNC network and steal documents
Command and Control (C2)	• X-Agent implanted on the DCCC network transmitted information to a GRU-controlled server located in Arizona, referred to as AMS panel • APT 28 logged into the AMS panel to use X-Agent's screenshot and keylog functions during monitoring and surveillance activities	• Monitored the X-Agent malware from the AMS panel, using screenshot and keylog malware, among others
Actions on objectives	• APT 28 searched for and identified computers on the DCCC network that contained information related to the 2016 U.S. presidential elections • APT 28 used X-Tunnel (another GRU malware) to move the stolen documents outside of the DCCC networks through encrypted channels	• APT 28 captured data from the victim computers • The AMS panel collected thousands of keylog and screenshot results from the DNC computers

Source: United States of America v. Viktor Borisovich Netyksho, Boris Alekseyevich Antonov, Dmitriy Sergeyevich Badin, Ivan Sergeyevich Yerakov, Eleksey Aleksandrovich Morgachev, Nikolay Yuryevich Kozachek, Pavel Vyacheslavovich Yershov, Artem Andreyevich Malyshev, Aleksandr Vladimirovich Osadchuk, Aleksey Aleksandrovich Potemkin, and Anatoliy Sergeyevich Kovalev, Indictment, 18 U.S.C. sections 2, 371, 1030, 1028A, 1956 (U.S. District Court for the District of Columbia, July 13, 2018), at 6–13, https://www.justice.gov/file/1080281/download (accessed March 28, 2021); Select Comm. on Intelligence, *Russian Active Measures Campaigns and Interference in the 2016 U.S. Election*, Volume 5: *Counterintelligence Threats and Vulnerabilities*, S. Rep. No. 116-XX, at 171–182 (August 18, 2020).

FIGURE 5.1 Russia's Hack Map during the 2016 U.S. Elections

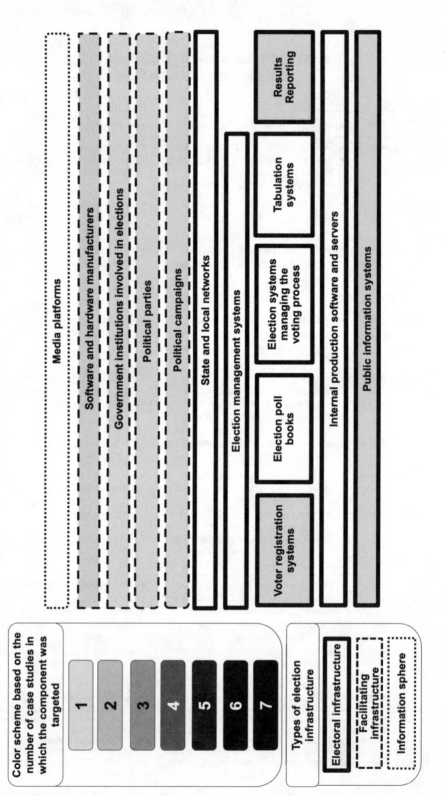

Russia also breached three suppliers of political infrastructure that provide "back-end systems" for verification of voters' eligibility to cast their ballots.[85] An investigation revealed that malware was placed on the company VR Systems, which supplies voter registration systems and electronic poll books, but the investigation again did not find evidence that any election processes or relevant data were manipulated.[86] Figure 5.1 indicates the elements of the political IT infrastructure that Russian APTs targeted during the 2016 U.S. presidential election. The majority of the targeted elements are parts of the facilitating infrastructure and can be categorized as confidentiality compromises.

Based on this information, Russia's cyber operations during the 2016 U.S. elections can be categorized as mainly aimed to exert psychological effects rather than technical ones.

ATTRIBUTION OF THE CONDUCTED CYBER ATTACKS

Various private security companies, U.S. federal agencies, and foreign governments asserted that the cyber operations during the 2016 U.S. presidential election were directed by Russia's senior leaders, particularly by Russian President Putin himself.[87] The publicly released series of attribution reports and statements linking the cyber attacks to the Russian government commenced in May 2016, when the private security company Crowd-Strike was first to discover the DNC breach and publish the announcement on June 14, 2016. CrowdStrike had knowledge of the DNC breach because the DNC had hired the company to analyze and respond to the suspected intrusion.[88] Other cybersecurity firms, to include Fidelis and FireEye, confirmed that the DNC hack was a part of a series of cyber operations executed by Russia's agencies the GRU and the FSB and their APTs 28 and 29, respectively.[89] In mid-June, a lone hacker under the name Guccifer 2.0 claimed responsibility for the DNC hack and also claimed to have infiltrated Hillary Clinton's email. Guccifer 2.0's claims, however, were debunked, and U.S. government agencies as well as cybersecurity firms confirmed that Guccifer 2.0 is a smokescreen for the Russian GRU. Similarly, the website DCleaks.com, used to release some of the exfiltrated data, was also attributed to the Russian government, particularly the GRU.[90]

Several key U.S. federal government documents confirm these attribution findings. In September and October, representatives of the Senate and House Intelligence Committees attributed the DNC hacks to Russia's government. On October 7, 2016, Secretary of Homeland Security Jeh Johnson and the Director of National Intelligence James Clapper released a joint statement accusing Russia of attempting to interfere in the 2016 U.S. elections and being behind the attacks against state voter registration websites.[91] In January 2017, the Office of the Director of National Intelligence (ODNI) released a report in which the organization assessed with "high confidence" that the Russian government and its agencies conducted the operation, designed "to undermine public faith in the US democratic process, denigrate Secretary [of State] Clinton, and harm her electability and potential presidency."[92] A subsequent report by the Senate Intelligence Committee critically examined and agreed with the conclusions of the ODNI assessment.[93] Intelligence agencies of other governments, including the Netherlands and the United Kingdom, also confirmed the link between GRU operatives and the DNC leaks.[94]

INTEGRATION OF CYBER OPERATIONS INTO STRATEGIC MESSAGING

After the successful hacks, the GRU—mainly unit 74455 in cooperation with unit 26165—used the GRU-managed site DC Leaks, the fake persona Guccifer 2.0, and WikiLeaks to systematically release documents exfiltrated during the cyber operations, indicating strategic intent. The major document releases coincided with events critical to elections that disrupted the Democratic campaign or assisted the Trump campaign in addressing some major developments that were expected to create a negative impact on the campaign.[95]

The first set of documents leaked from those stolen as part of the DNC hack was made public on June 15, 2016, by an online persona that went by the name of Guccifer 2.0, who claimed to have singlehandedly infiltrated the networks of DNC headquarters. Guccifer 2.0 released a confidential document about Trump's professional record and personal characteristics, as well as half a dozen additional private documents to the Democratic Party regarding Democratic campaign donors and the Clinton campaign political strategies.[96] Guccifer 2.0 also published other DNC documents upon requests from bloggers and publications.[97] Although the documents that Guccifer 2.0 released stirred the media and created momentary setbacks for the Clinton campaign, the media coverage of these initial documents was minor in comparison to the negative coverage and revelations that came to light as a result of the subsequent massive document releases via WikiLeaks. Investigations by the U.S. Select Committee on Intelligence have proven the communication and coordination between WikiLeaks and the GRU in this process.[98]

On July 22, 2016, WikiLeaks released another major set of documents—19,252 emails and 8,034 attachments stolen from key members of the DNC that were accessed through the breach of the DNC servers.[99] This release was only three days before the Democratic Party National Convention, which took place July 25 to July 28, 2016.

On October 7, 2016, WikiLeaks released a second major tranche of documents. The release occurred just hours after DHS and ODNI issued a statement accusing the Russian government of interference in the election through cyber operations. The release also coincided with the *Washington Post* announcement of the *Access Hollywood* videotape in which Trump described his unflattering female courting tactics. The released documents stolen from Podesta's email were extensively covered by media, fueling the allegations that Clinton was a corrupt candidate.[100] Throughout October and early November, WikiLeaks released in phases thirty-four sets of emails stolen from Podesta's personal email account during the last month of the heated presidential race. The total number of emails released from Podesta's personal account amounted to approximately 60,000.[101]

Alongside WikiLeaks, the website DC Leaks published correspondence of other individuals who were targeted in the same cyber attacks, including Clinton campaign staffer William Rinehart and former secretary of state Colin Powell. The U.S. intelligence community and experts believe that DC Leaks was specifically established to serve as a platform from which the cyber groups would leak the documents stolen from the DNC servers.[102]

After being released on WikiLeaks and DC Leaks, the appropriated private and sensitive information was picked up and disseminated through numerous Russian and Western media channels, as well as by high-profile political figures. The leaked information provided material for frequent news reports, undermined the message of the democratic campaign, and created tensions among its staff members in the critical last months before the presidential election. The released email correspondence revealed disagreements inside the Clinton campaign, including discord over donations. The leaks also revealed private correspondence among staff members who had a low opinion of Clinton.[103]

Russia's state-sponsored media channels, *Sputnik News* and *RT*, frequently published articles covering the information released by WikiLeaks and DC Leaks between June 2016 and November 2016. These media widely covered the DNC report on Trump, the allegations that the Clinton campaign had access to debate questions in advance of presidential debates, and that Clinton's campaign had exerted pressure on Bernie Sanders, leading him to step down from the race for the democratic nomination.[104]

Dozens of reputable Western newspapers, television stations, and radio stations, as well as bloggers around the United States, published reports quoting the materials and pursued reporting on the basis of the information that had come to light through documents procured through hacking. Such media included the *New York Times*, the *Wall Street Journal*, and the *Washington Post*. Through covering developments about the stolen and leaked information, these media provided additional outlets for Russia's operation and amplified its outreach, increasing the effects of the cyber intrusions. Guccifer 2.0 and DC Leaks also provided documents directly to reporters upon request.[105]

The Trump campaign also took advantage of the opportunity to besmirch the reputation of its Democratic opponent. Members of the Trump campaign sought information about WikiLeaks releases in advance and prepared strategies to share and promote the released information.[106] Trump himself encouraged the release of documents by WikiLeaks and publicly encouraged the organization to continue to release private communication.[107] Trump further cited many of the stolen emails on the campaign trail.[108] One account indicated that in the month prior to the election, Trump mentioned WikiLeaks over 160 times.[109]

Russian hackers also obtained confidential documents by the DNC's sister organization, the DCCC. The released documents also suggested strategic intent. They pertained to Democratic candidates running in some of the most competitive races for House seats in the country. These emails appeared in congressional races in nearly a dozen states. The emails tainted the image of some of the Democratic candidates and may have contributed to them losing their races. For example, Democratic candidate Annette Taddeo lost her primary race in Southern Florida after secret campaign documents obtained through the DCCC were leaked.[110]

PRO-KREMLIN MEDIA COVERAGE

As chapter 1 explained, Russia's information warfare operations include a deliberate dissemination of strategic messaging, including disinformation and propaganda through various media. In addition to disseminating content through social media, the Russian government used state-sponsored pro-Kremlin channels, namely *RT* and *Sputnik News*, to spread similar strategic narratives as the ones on social media—fictitious and provocative content aimed to sow divisions within the U.S. population, denigrate Hillary Clinton, and support Trump's campaign.[111] These media are known to represent the views of Russia's presidential administration and their content is monitored and directed by the Kremlin.[112] *Sputnik News*, which is owned by the Russian government, aims to reach foreign audiences and is available in the United States.[113] During the presidential campaign, *Sputnik*'s coverage of Hillary Clinton was consistently negative while its coverage about Donald Trump was "increasingly favorable."[114]

Data about IRA's social media presence on various platforms is based on voluntary self-reporting by social media companies and may be incomplete due to the clandestine nature of Russian bloggers and bots. An analysis of Russian state-sponsored media coverage can present a more holistic picture of trends and topics that the Kremlin considered relevant to emphasize during the elections because of the overt nature of these platforms.[115] Such analysis can be used to identify periods of high and low coverage of specific topics of the U.S. elections. The data can then be juxtaposed against the initiation of Russian state-sponsored cyber operations in an attempt to discover potential association. In the case of the 2016 U.S. elections, this book examines the media coverage produced by *Sputnik News*.[116]

To conduct the analysis, the research examined all *Sputnik* coverage that contained the name of any of the two main presidential candidates in the text or title (see figure 5.2). The analysis did not include articles on socially divisive issues that do not mention the two presidential contenders, because although such articles may be linked to Russia's aim to influence voters' preferences, it is harder to ascertain that that coverage is directly related to Russia's attempts to influence the 2016 elections in Russian-sponsored media, as opposed to attempts to sow chaos among the U.S. population in general, agnostic regarding the election process. As the research investigates patterns between cyber operations and other elements of Russian information warfare, the start date is January 1, 2016, or three months before the first spear-phishing campaign by the APT 28 against DNC, DCCC, and Clinton campaign employees. The end date is February 8, 2017, or three months after the elections.[117] The aim of this analysis is to determine whether there were any spikes (or hype) in Russia-sponsored media reporting around the time of the main cyber operations and periods of data exfiltration from the DNC, the DCCC, and Podesta's emails, which, as the sections above explained, all commenced in March 2016. The analysis also examined the presence or absence of increased media coverage around the periods of the major data releases on July 22 and October 7, as well as on election day.

The results of this analysis, displayed in figure 5.3, show that there were no significant spikes in reporting related to either of the two major candidates during or immediately after the major data releases. The data nevertheless indicates a gradual increase in reporting during the months of October and the beginning of November before election day, November 8. The significant rise in reporting around November 8 suggests increased interest in the U.S. elections. In October and early November, coverage referring to the leaked documents through WikiLeaks constituted a major part of the total coverage about the two presidential candidates. This illustrates the integration of cyber operations

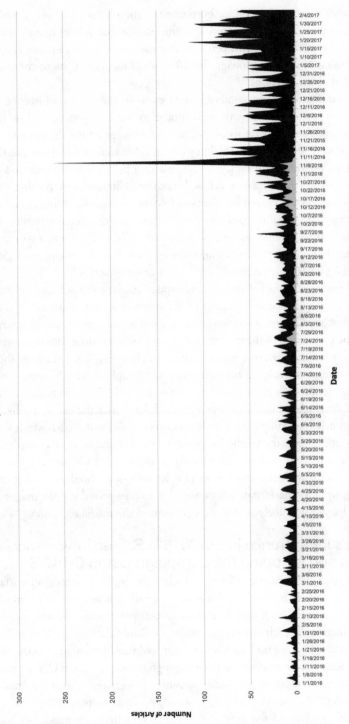

FIGURE 5.2 *Sputnik* Coverage of Hillary Clinton and Donald Trump from January 1, 2016, to February 8, 2017

■ Part of total coverage including WikiLeaks   ■ Total coverage of Donald Trump and Hillary Clinton

into Russia's strategic messaging. Furthermore, the media coverage of topics related to President-elect Trump and Clinton after the election was relatively more than the coverage about the candidates in the period before the election. This finding is consistent with the conclusion of analyses showing that IRA's social media campaigns continued and even increased after the elections.[118]

An examination of the content of articles about the two candidates before and after the elections reveals recurrent themes, similar to the ones proliferated by Russian state-sponsored trolls and bots on social media. The coverage before the elections was negative toward Clinton. It focused on the information exfiltrated as a result of the Russian hacks on Clinton's political campaign, Clinton's use of a private email server, and other alleged transgressions.[119] An article even accused candidate Clinton of supporting extremism.[120]

Themes after the November elections in *Sputnik News* were similar and were focused on covering U.S. social discord and polarization over the election results. The coverage also continued to include stories that portrayed Hillary Clinton as a corrupt and unreliable leader. The coverage included anti-Trump protests and movements, U.S. voter fraud, and ongoing investigations into Clinton's private email server.[121]

The findings about the volume and type of media coverage, especially after election day are in line with Russia's strategy of information warfare outlined in chapter 1. The chapter described information warfare as a continuous process aimed at sowing discord among the population of the targeted state by exploiting various socially contentious issues, rather than focusing on one topic, such as an election. These findings show common patterns in terms of volume among Russia's overt and covert information warfare channels. Considering how surprising the result of the 2016 U.S. elections was for many, the increased coverage about the presidential candidates after the election is likely consistent with other news reporting from non-Russian-state-sponsored media, which would weaken, although not negate, the predictive power of the volume of media coverage as a part of Russian information warfare. Nevertheless, while the trend in reporting volume may be consistent with news reporting from non-Kremlin-sponsored media outlets, the many references to DNC hack materials during the election period suggest that an information warfare element was likely at least a component of the media reporting.

Russia's Interference in the 2016 U.S. Elections: Associated Factors and Mapping the Campaign Using CHAOS

As this chapter demonstrated, Russia launched a complex information warfare operation against the 2016 U.S. elections. Due to the significant amount of detail of each information warfare activity, it may be easier to detect patterns across campaigns and identify critical junctures if each main component of Russia's campaign is visually depictured. Figure 5.3 displays chronologically the main political/diplomatic, social, and economic events of Russia's information warfare campaign against the 2016 U.S. elections discussed in this chapter. The figure also indicates some of the major mitigation policies that U.S. agencies adopted in reaction to Russia's activities. To assess potential patterns of increased media coverage around the time of the launch of state-sponsored cyber operations, the

FIGURE 5.3 Russia's CHAOS during the 2016 U.S. Elections: A Selection of
Cyber Operations, Media Coverage, and Associated Operations

→ Activities of Russian government actors   + Main mitigation policies by the targeted state and allies
~ Activities involving both the Russian government & nongovernmental actors   # Other relevant events

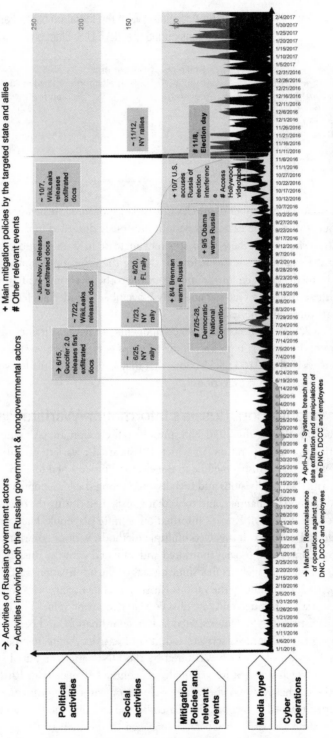

* Articles about Hillary Clinton and Donald Trump published in Russian media are represented by the dark shaded area above the x-axis.
Articles pertaining to the DNC leaks as a part of the overall media coverage are represented by the smaller light gray shaded area along the x-axis.

TABLE 5.2 Factors That Could Be Associated with the Initiation of the Particular Type of Cyber Operations during the 2016 U.S. Elections

Target	Type of cyber op (CIA)	Disputes in relations				Spike in media coverage	If cyber ops during elections		NATO member en route	NATO member	Frm. Eastern Bloc state	Frm. USSR state
		Polit	Soc	Econ	Mil		Anti-Ru candidate	Pro-Ru candidate				
U.S. (2016)	C, I	1	1	1	0	0	1	1	0	1	0	0

figure illustrates the number of articles in Russian sponsored media, *Sputnik News*, in the United States during the examined period, previously discussed in this chapter (fig. 5.2). The analysis shows that there is no apparent increase in state-sponsored media coverage based on the examined sources before or during the cyber operations, but there was an increase in media coverage in the month prior to the elections. As figure 5.2 illustrates, many of these articles in October and early November included a reference to the released documents through WikiLeaks.

Table 5.2, which reflects the main components of the QCA framework given in chapter 2, summarizes the main policies in the relations between the two states and the specific characteristics of the 2016 U.S. elections that may have affected the Russian government's decision to interfere in the elections.

Observations about Russia's Information Warfare Playbook

Russia's actions during the 2016 U.S. presidential election are an example of a Russian information warfare operation, in which Russia used a variety of state-sponsored and existing media platforms to meddle in the electoral process of a foreign state, attempting to exacerbate societal divisions and fuel discord among the U.S. population. An examination of the activities, channels, and tools that Russia used during the operation reveals several important aspects of Russia's information warfare playbook. First, the operation was large-scale and complex. It involved multiple methods, various government departments, private companies, and proxies sponsored and affiliated with the Russian government.

Second, evidence suggests that some aspects of the information warfare operation were likely uncoordinated among the various Russian intelligence agencies and involved a large volume of trials with uncertain rate of success and strategic value. The cyber attacks conducted against the DNC demonstrated lack of coordination, and perhaps even competition, among Russia's security services and their offensive cyber teams. The private security company CrowdStrike, which was hired by the DNC after the initial series of Russian attacks, and which detected Russia's malware, conducted analyses of Russia's cyber tactics and concluded that Russia's cyber actors were acting without coordinating their activities. CrowdStrike reached this conclusion based on the fact that the Russian groups compromised the same systems and separately engaged in the theft of the same credentials.[122]

These findings are consistent with a report by the European Council on Foreign Relations, which documents the competitive relationship between Russia's main intelligence services, which rarely share intelligence and deconflict their operations, despite the fact that they have overlapping responsibilities.[123] The cyber operations against all U.S. states also show that Russia's APT cast a wide net, which suggests that Russia did not have a grand strategy for how to influence the election process but that the strategy evolved over the course of the election season. This indicates that there was an operational approach to embrace the uncertainty of American elections.

Third, Russia's unprecedented brazen behavior, especially with regard to its cyber operations and the leaked information about the Clinton campaign, also suggests a high level of risk and potential to accept a high level of failure. Research now takes for granted the fact that Trump won the election, but during the course of the election campaigns, this outcome was uncertain. The Russians themselves were not convinced that Trump would win. This became clear by the fact that pro-Russian bloggers had prepared a media campaign, Democracy RIP, to launch and question the legitimacy of the election, if Clinton had won.[124]

Fourth, the analysis illustrates how Russian state-sponsored hacks are integrated with Russian media campaigns and strategic messaging during an information warfare campaign. The research suggests a level of coordination between the APTs, which exfiltrated data from the Clinton campaign, IRA staff, and media platforms such as WikiLeaks and pro-Kremlin newspapers that proliferated and amplified the contents of the leaked information. This coordination or synchronization does not appear to be only in content but also in volume, demonstrated by the increased coverage of leaked materials before the elections and the continuation of negative coverage after the elections in pro-Kremlin media and by IRA staff on social media.

Fifth, the types of cyber operations (mainly affecting the confidentiality and integrity of data) that Russia's APTs launched during this information warfare operation suggest a preference to affect psychological rather than technical processes.

Finally, Russia's readiness to continue its social media efforts denigrating U.S. democracy and the continuation of negative social media and pro-Kremlin media coverage on Clinton after the elections indicate that Russian efforts against the elections were only a part of Russia's broader information warfare campaign aimed not at influencing the election outcome but at eroding democratic governance.

The Effectiveness of Russia's Cyber Operations and Information Warfare Campaign

It is difficult, if not impossible, to estimate the effect that Russia's release of illegally obtained information had on the outcome of the 2016 presidential election, but it is clear that the DNC hacks constituted a critical event for Washington. For the first time in U.S. history, a state adversary used advanced cyber capabilities to meddle so extensively and publicly in the U.S. political process.[125]

No study to date has conclusively assessed the extent to which Russia's interference influenced the election outcome, but even without such an assessment, Russia's various activities caused a series of disruptions to the presidential campaign of Clinton and damaged her image. The media coverage of the leaked documents suggested that the DNC was partial toward Clinton and preferred her candidacy over that of Bernie Sanders, and raised questions of whether he was unfairly treated. In the immediate fallout of the crisis, DNC chairman Debbie Wasserman Schultz submitted her resignation. The release of the first major batch of documents complicated the DNC's management of the Democratic Party National Convention and marred Clinton's presidential nomination at the convention. [126]

The effectiveness and scope of Moscow's information warfare activities may have been influenced by a series of policies adopted by the U.S. government at that time. The U.S. government took measures to address Russia's interference while Russia's information warfare activities were still ongoing, and senior U.S. officials believed that these efforts prevented the Russian government from conducting more brazen activities. [127] In the months prior to election day, the administration of President Barrack Obama attempted to prevent further Russian interference through direct discussions with Russia's leadership. At least five warnings to Moscow were conveyed through various channels. Secretary John Kerry, CIA director John Brennan (on August 4, 2016), and Ambassador Susan Rice (on October 7, 2016) conveyed warnings to their Russian counterparts. [128] President Obama himself met with Putin on September 5 at the Group of 20 (G20) summit and warned him against further election interference attempts. [129] The U.S. government also formally accused Russia of election interference, on October 7, 2016. [130] On October 31, for the first time, the administration used the "cyber hotline," specifically designed to communicate directly with Russia's presidential administration in cases of cyber incidents, to warn Moscow against interfering on election day. [131]

Senior U.S. administration officials involved in addressing the Russian threat at the time determined that these unofficial efforts yielded the desired results. A justification for this assessment may be the fact that Moscow halted some of its covert activities after these exchanges and that there was no major cyber operation on election day. However, analysis after the elections revealed that Russia did not discontinue all its information warfare activities. For example, IRA staff continued its campaign on social media, and Russian hackers continued to try to infiltrate political infrastructure at the state and local levels. [132]

The U.S. government could have addressed Russia's interference during the 2016 elections more assertively. However, a number of reasons prevented the government from adopting a stronger stance. According to Michael Daniel, who at that time served as special assistant to President Obama and cybersecurity coordinator on the National Security Council (NSC) staff, the government was expecting espionage operations against the political campaigns, which had happened before, but not the types of hack-and-leak operations that the Russian government conducted. Such weaponization of exfiltrated data was a new threat and the government did not have a blueprint for how to respond proportionately to it. In addition, a strong firewall existed between the White House, other senior policy officials, and the political campaigns. That administrative compartmentalization entailed that addressing breaches into political campaigns or parties fell outside the purview of senior leaders at the While House and the NSC. Such matters were the responsibility of the FBI. The ability of the U.S. senior leadership to respond to

Russia's DNC and other hacks was also complicated by the fact that the parts of the political IT systems that the White House and the NSC could address are managed by state and local election administrative officials. Therefore, a response to Russia's hacks required coordination between the U.S. senior leadership and state and local governments, which had to be built on connections and trust among all these groups, which had not been well established at that time.[133]

Daniel further asserted that the U.S. government did not react immediately to Russia's strategic messaging campaigns via social media because the government was not aware of the scope and scale of Russia's activities at the time of these operations. Most of this information emerged in 2017 after the elections and after Obama left office. Hence, during the 2016 elections, the Obama administration focused on containing Russia's cyber operations against state and local election infrastructure where the U.S. administration could see the threat, and less on addressing Russia's strategic messaging campaign, which the U.S. administration was not aware of at that time.[134]

The Obama administration was also reluctant to mount a more aggressive response against Russia's election interference because it feared it could be viewed as biased and perceived as using the federal government apparatus to support Hillary Clinton. Furthermore, the administration was concerned that if it discussed Russia's electoral interference more publicly, it would facilitate Russia's efforts to cast doubt on the legitimacy of the electoral process.[135]

After the elections, the government introduced more specific policies aimed to punish Russia and prevent a similar Russian information warfare campaign against the U.S. elections in the future. These policies included a series of sanctions, expelling Russian diplomats, and closing down U.S.-based Russian diplomatic facilities.[136] In addition, DHS made significant improvements in enhancing coordination between state and local election officials, and the federal government. It designated political infrastructure as a critical sector, improved cyber vulnerability assessments, and offered other types of assistance that enhanced election IT networks' defenses.[137]

Besides government efforts, social media platforms, notably Facebook, Twitter, and YouTube, adopted a series of measures to identify and prevent malicious and inauthentic use of their platforms by Russian and other state actors. These companies have also coordinated with the government by providing data of Russian IRA staff, estimating the reach of the IRA and continuing to delete and suspend accounts on their platforms that the companies identify as being linked to the Russian government.[138] Although there is a lot of room for improvement with regard to the transparency of algorithms used to identify malicious users and their reach, sharing information about these users across platforms and publishing ads funded by non-U.S. government agencies, the policies introduced since the 2016 election are a push in the right direction and demonstrate the foundations of a wide-ranging and multidimensional approach to the threat posed by Russian information warfare, which itself is characterized as broad and multifaceted. The fact that no similar Russian activities are known to have targeted the 2020 U.S. presidential elections suggests that the efforts by U.S. government agencies and the commercial and nonprofit sectors may have contributed to deterring Russian interference.

6
Phishing in Norway's Nets in 2016
Where Sputnik Crashed and Burned[1]

In the fall of 2016, Russia launched a cyber operation against Norway, one of NATO's founding countries. The operation targeted a large number of government organizations including the Norwegian Ministry of Foreign Affairs, the Ministry of Defense, and Norway's Labor Party.[2] The cyber operations occurred in a period of political, economic, and military tensions between Russia and Norway. These bilateral issues may have contributed to Russia's decision to launch cyber operations against the Nordic nation. This chapter examines the discord that existed in Russian-Norwegian relations before the launch of cyber operations and outlines other activities associated with the Russian government at the time. The Hack Map and the CHAOS framework aid in the process. The chapter concludes with assessing the potential reasons behind the cyber operations and their effectiveness.

Factors Potentially Associated with the Launch of Cyber Operations

The Nordic region is strategically important to Moscow. Norway shares a land border with Russia and plays an active role in the Arctic region, which is an area of growing economic and security interest to Russia.[3] As a member of the alliance, Norway's border to the east represents NATO's direct border with Russia, which also makes Norway a country of military importance to the Kremlin.[4]

Since 2014, Norway's relations with Russia, which were traditionally positive, experienced friction specifically related to economic, political, and military issues.[5] Although not a member of the European Union, Norway sided with the official EU position on Russia's operations in Ukraine and criticized Moscow for illegally invading its neighbor.[6] Norway further imposed the same sanctions against Russia as the EU in response to Russia's annexation of Crimea in March 2014.[7] Norway's political direction irked the Russian leadership and various Russian representatives lamented Norway's decision to impose sanctions.[8] In response to the sanctions against Russia, Moscow banned food imports from

Norway on August 7, 2016. Norwegian fishermen were impacted by Russian sanctions because until that time, Russia was the largest market for Norway's seafood industry, which is not reliant on government subsidies and is export-dependent.[9]

In addition to political and economic disagreements, decisions of the two countries in the military sphere resulted in increased tensions. In October 2016, a Russian naval fleet sailed near Norway on route to Syria, where the fleet was going to enhance Russia's combat mission.[10] The naval flotilla, deployed at a time when NATO accused Russia of provocative military maneuvers, passed very close to the Norwegian city Trondheim and consisted of an unusually large number of military vessels, including Russia's only aircraft carrier, *Admiral Kuznetsov*, and seven other ships.[11]

A few days after Russia's naval flotilla sailed by Norway, the Nordic nation announced it would allow the stationing of 330 U.S. Marines on its territory in 2017. The marines will be stationed at Norway's Vaernes military base, located east of Trondheim, for a trial period as a part of the policy to boost interoperability and training among NATO members. This announcement represented a shift from Norway's characteristic approach of prohibiting foreign military forces on its territory, and was met with disapproval from Russia.[12]

Russia's Information Warfare Activities

The Norwegian intelligence services assert that Russia conducts information warfare activities in Norway through think tanks, private companies, the secret services, research communities, and the media. Russia's activities in Norway include attempts to amplify disagreements between the northern parts of Norway, bordering Russia, and Oslo on issues relevant to Moscow. Such issues include environmental policy and sanctions against Russia. As in previous cases this research analyzed, Russia uses traditional and social media in Norway to conduct its strategic messaging campaigns.[13] Despite reports that indicate that Russia has attempted to influence debates in Norway, as of January 2021 there have not been any known prominent examples of Russian disinformation or strategic messaging campaigns in Norway.[14] As of February 2021, there was also no publicly available information to suggest that any political party or a member of a political party in Norway have received financial or other types of support from an agency or a representative associated with the Russian government. Furthermore, there are no accounts of Russian state-supported public protests or other public activities in Norway that may exert disruptive political effects.

CYBER OPERATIONS

On February 3, 2017, the Norwegian Police Security Service (PST) accused Russia's APT 29 of attempting to infiltrate the parliamentary group of Norway's Labor Party and other institutions in the fall of 2016. The breach was likely unsuccessful.[15] The Labor Party is the largest Norwegian political party and has traditionally been a supporter of defense policy and security cooperation through Norway's NATO membership.[16] The party

FIGURE 6.1 Russia's Hack Map during the Cyber Operations against Norway in the Fall of 2016

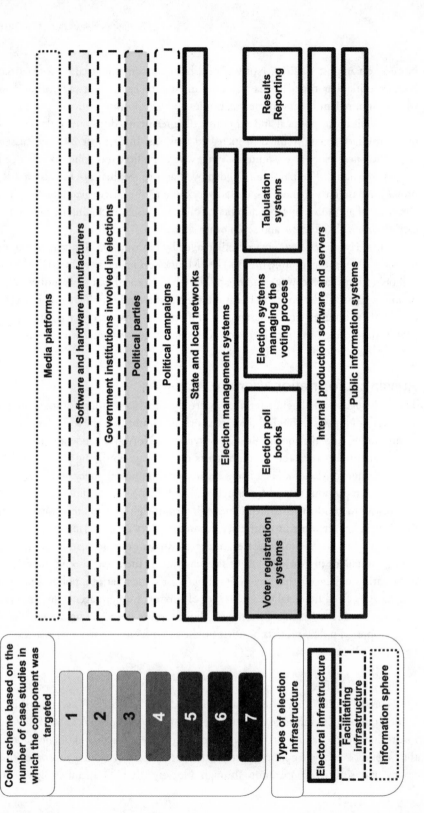

was previously led by Jens Stoltenberg, who assumed the position of secretary general of NATO in 2014.[17] As a political entity that participates in Norwegian elections, the Labor Party constitutes a component of the facilitating infrastructure of Norway's political system that a Russian state-sponsored cyber threat group targeted (see fig. 6.1).

The PST did not provide more specificity on the time of the operations or the exact networks that the cyber threat actors attempted to compromise. The other targets during the same cyber operation included the Norwegian Ministry of Foreign Affairs, Ministry of Defense, security services, the radiation protection agency, and a school. APT 29 sent emails to nine email accounts of members of these organizations.[18] The emails were a part of a spear-phishing attempt. According to PST, there was no indication that APT 29 gained access to classified information.[19] Based on the publicly available information about the type of cyber operations, they can be categorized as attempted compromises of data confidentiality that were likely conducted to exert psychological effects.

The Norwegian authorities did not provide any specific reasons for the objective of the Russian state-sponsored cyber operations.[20] Although the cyber operations against Norway were compared to the hack against the DNC that was a part of an effort to influence the 2016 U.S. elections, the PST did not link the attacks to Norway's next elections scheduled for September 11, 2017.[21] The annual report on the Norwegian Intelligence Services likewise did not provide reasons for these specific intrusions and explained that the 2016 cyber operations took place in a period of "more aggressive and targeted" Russian cyber operations against Norway, especially for the purposes of intelligence gathering from government and military targets. In the years prior to the 2016 attempted intrusions, Russian cyber threat actors had continuously attempted to gain access to Norwegian government networks.[22] Therefore, the cyber operations against the Labor Party could be viewed as components of an increased Russian intelligence activity against Norway. Norwegian intelligence indicated that Russian intelligence services may have been looking for information that could enable the Kremlin to influence the Norwegian authorities' position on sanctions against Russia or to circumvent or undermine these sanctions. Another objective for the potential intelligence gathering operation could have been to find sensitive information related to the production and supply of energy from Norway, which is a major energy supplier to European countries and a competitor to Russia. Russia might have been seeking information that would cast doubt on the reliability of the energy supply from Norway in an attempt to take over some of Norway's markets. Another intelligence gathering objective could be the status of ongoing Norwegian space research in the Arctic.[23] Thus, the cyber operations in the fall of 2016 could be considered another episode of Russian intelligence gathering, which may be, but does not necessarily have to be, related to the Norwegian parliamentary elections in 2017.

RUSSIAN STATE-SPONSORED MEDIA COVERAGE

Russia's influence in the Norwegian media space seems more limited than in other countries, such as Bulgaria and Montenegro. The story of Russia's *Sputnik News* services in Norway suggests that Moscow's classic pro-Kremlin channels for disseminating Russia's strategic messaging did not seem to be effective in Norway. Russia established a Norwegian language service of *Sputnik News*, called *Sputnik Norge*, in April 2015. The news service focused on delivering anti-NATO and anti-EU news coverage tailored to local audiences.[24] The outlet lacked command of the Norwegian language and, judging by the meager number of Twitter and Facebook followers of the *Sputnik Norge* accounts, the negative coverage about European values and conspiracy theories did not seem to gain popularity among the Norwegian audience. Analysis asserts that partially for these reasons, Russia closed down Sputnik's Norwegian version in March 2016—less than an year since the outlet was established. After the shutdown of *Sputnik Norge*, *Sputnik International* news service in English would occasionally produce coverage about Norway, which is typically focused on critically reporting on a weakness or a problem in the region.[25]

To assess the volume of coverage about Norway in Russian state-sponsored media in the region, which was accessible to Norwegian citizens during the period of attempted Russian state-supported cyber operations, the analysis examined all articles published in *Sputnik International* in English three months prior to the indicated period of cyber operations and three months afterward. As Norway's security services did not provide specific dates on which the attempted intrusions took place but reported only that they took place in the fall of 2016, the analysis examined media coverage from June 22, 2016 (three months before September 22, 2016, which marks the beginning of fall), to March 21, 2017 (three months after December 21, 2016, which marks the end of the fall season).[26] This period falls outside of the period in which *Sputnik Norge* existed, which suggests that any Russian state-sponsored coverage targeted at Norwegian audiences that could have been relayed through *Sputnik Norge* was likely redirected through *Sputnik International* and was captured by this analysis.

Figure 6.2 shows no visible increase in the volume of media coverage about Norway during any particular days in the period under investigation. The lack of any media spikes in Russian state-sponsored media during confidentiality compromises is consistent with the previously analyzed cases of Germany and the United States.

As traditional media outlets did not seem effective in Norway, analysis indicates that in recent years the Russian government started to rely increasingly on spreading its message through less regulated social media platforms.[27] The 2020 annual report of Norway's intelligence services noted that false accounts (trolls) and automated accounts (bots) are a part of Russia's information warfare activities.[28] The narratives spread on social media and may target individuals, such as journalists who have written critical reports of Russia, with the aim to discredit or intimidate them.[29] Russian strategic narratives also target broader groups in an attempt to erode their trust in elections, politicians, government agencies, and the media.[30] In the past few years, Russia has exploited media platforms, including Twitter and Facebook, to counterbalance Norwegian media coverage critical of Russian policies particularly on issues related to the environment and the Arctic.[31] Based on Russia's seeming reliance on social media in Norway, future research into Russia's attempts to influence the Norwegian public and its decision makers should include analysis of Russian state-linked accounts on the main social media platforms available in Norway.

FIGURE 6.2 Russian *Sputnik International* Coverage of Norway

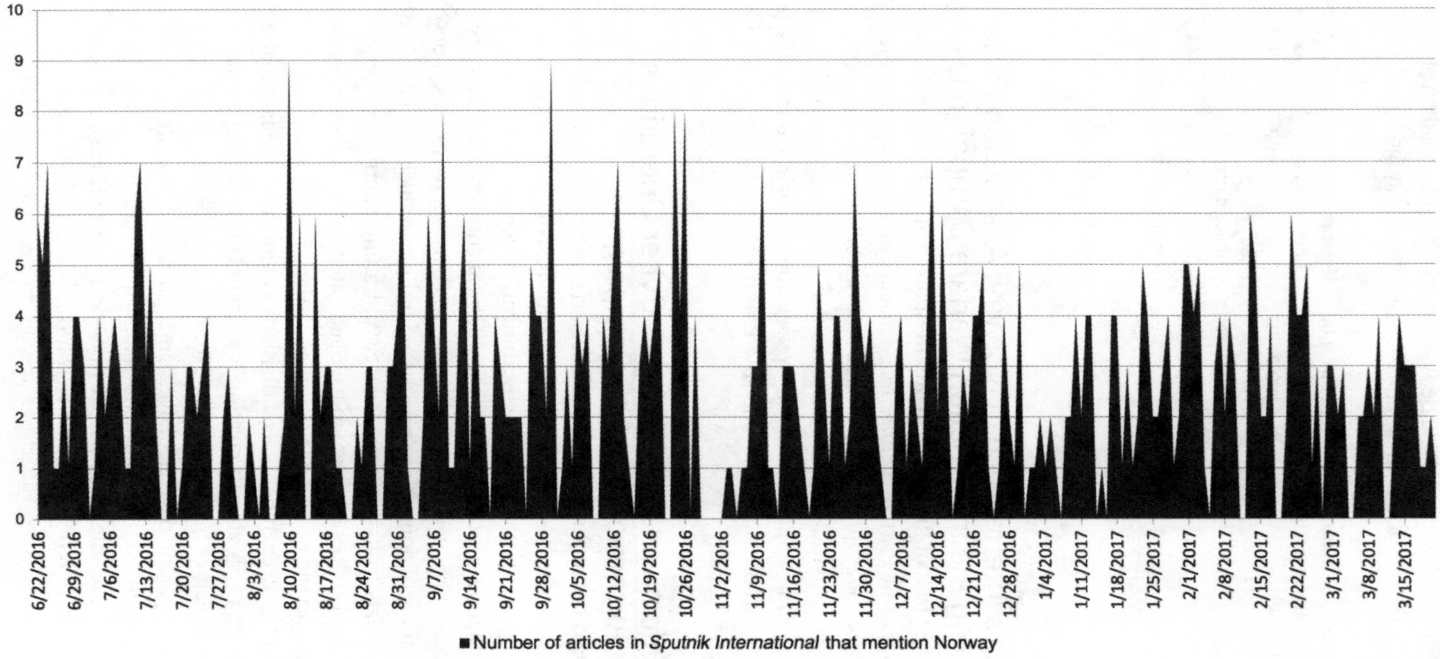

■ Number of articles in *Sputnik International* that mention Norway

TABLE 6.1 Factors That Could Be Associated with the Initiation of the Particular Type of Cyber Operations against Norway in the Fall of 2016

Target	Type of cyber op (CIA)	Disputes in relations				Spike in media coverage before cyber ops	If cyber ops during elections— no link between attacks and elections made		NATO member en route	NATO member	Frm. Eastern Bloc state	Frm. USSR state
		Polit	Soc	Econ	Mil		Anti-Ru candidate	Pro-Ru candidate				
Norway 2016	C	1	0	1	1	0	0	0	0	1	0	0

Russia's Interference in Norway: Associated Factors and Mapping the Information Warfare Campaign Using CHAOS

Due to the lack of known Russian state-sponsored activities in Norway beyond the cyber operations and Russia's *Sputnik International* coverage, applying the CHAOS framework to this case looks quite impoverished (see fig. 6.3). The main conclusion from juxtaposing Russia's activities against Norway in that period is that there is no apparent increase or decrease in the volume of media coverage about Norway during the period of the cyber operations. Table 6.1 shows the absent and present factors of the QCA framework in the case of Norway.

The Effectiveness of Russia's Cyber Operations and Information Warfare Campaign

Compared to the Russian information warfare activities in all other countries examined in this analysis, there is a relative lack of known activity in Norway. In addition, the activities instigated by the Russian government, which could be categorized as being related to information warfare, such as the 2016 sanctions against Norway's food industry, do not seem to have generated significant negative long-term effects on Norway's economy. Despite the sanctions, Norway's seafood industry, which was heavily affected by the sanctions, appears to have rebounded well and found alternative markets.[32] Russia's strategic messaging also does not seem to have generated a mass following or contributed to stimulating any activities, such as protests and other types of social disturbance in Norway, that could lead to deepening societal divisions or violence. The fact that *Sputnik Norge* closed in less than a year after its creation is a testament to the impotence of Russia's traditional media channels of influence in the Nordic nation.

The apparent paucity of Russian information warfare activities and the failure of the few existing ones to influence Norwegian audiences could be attributed to several factors. It is possible that such activities exist, but they have not been documented in the open-source literature. Another reason that some analysts support is that Norway, which has been subjected to Russian aggression for decades, has built resistance against Russian

FIGURE 6.3 Russia's CHAOS in Norway: A Selection of Cyber Operations, Media Hype, and Associated Operations

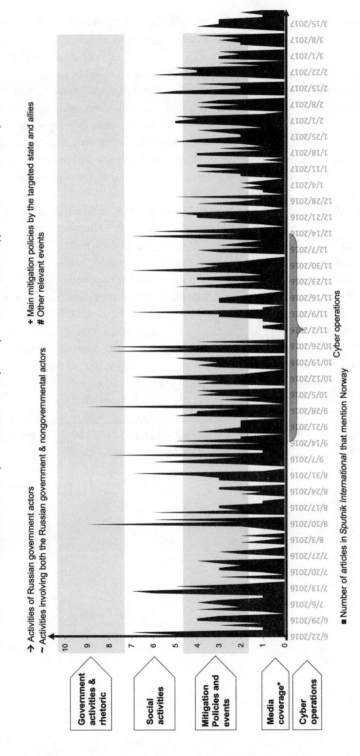

information warfare activities. The vulnerabilities that Russia has exploited to expand its influence in other countries, such as deeply ingrained historical connections to Russian political, economic, and cultural groups in the case of Bulgaria or large groups of constituencies who support the opposite sides of polarizing issues in the case of the United States, seem to be largely absent in Norway. Norway's population reports one of the lowest favorability ratings toward Russia among all European countries. Norway also has some of the lowest levels of corruption in the world, while Norway's educational system fosters critical thinking. Such dynamics may help to prevent the dissemination of any pro-Russian narratives through traditional or social media and to inoculate Norway's citizens against rashly believing in information originating from disreputable or dubious sources.[33]

Perhaps precisely because Norway's population is relatively resilient to Russia's traditional range of information warfare activities, such as inciting protests as in the case of Estonia in 2007. Russia attempted to exert its influence through cyber operations and targeted strategic messaging campaigns, which, as Norway's intelligence services argue, are likely to become more sophisticated.[34] In this case, cyber operations did not appear to have been a tool used to complement and amplify the effects of other Russian state-supported information warfare activities, such as in the cases of the U.S. DNC hack during the 2016 U.S. elections.

The case of Norway is a success story and merits further study. Future research could explore more thoroughly and rigorously the reasons why *Sputnik Norge* did not manage to attract a large following in Norway. Such analysis could be valuable to Western decision makers because it could improve their understanding of the types of factors that could effectively counterbalance Russian strategic messaging. Additional research into Russia's use of social media in Norway could also enrich decision makers' ability to identify methods to detect, contain, and mitigate Russia's activities on social media.

7

How the Tiny Balkan Nation
of Montenegro Withstood
a Russian-Sponsored Coup

On October 16, 2016, the people of Montenegro headed to the polls to cast their votes in a historic parliamentary election. The outcome of the election was of monumental significance that transcended the borders of this tiny Balkan country with a population of just over 620,000. The election results were a critical part of a process that would signal the country's preference whether to integrate with the West or maintain its allegiances to Russia and the East. Prior to the election, a large portion of the Montenegrin constituency had indicated its penchant for strengthening relations with Western institutions, particularly NATO and the European Union.[1] As chapter 1 indicated, the Russian government would consider such a shift destabilizing and detrimental to its interests. The geopolitical stakes were too high for Moscow to remain an idle spectator in this unfolding strategic realignment.

In the months leading to Montenegro's elections, Russia employed a wide range of information warfare measures in an attempt to keep Montenegro outside NATO's and EU's orbits. On election day, Montenegro's government, a pro-Western political party, an NGO, and media websites sustained a series of cyber operations.[2] These operations continued in the months following the elections and were attributed to Russia. They constituted an aspect of a multidimensional Russian state-sponsored information warfare campaign that included Russian financial support for pro-Russian political parties, NGOs and social movements, an unsuccessful coup d'état, political rhetoric, strategic messaging, and instigation of protests.

This chapter begins by outlining the most likely reasons that influenced Russia's decision to launch a series of cyber operations against Montenegro in 2016 and 2017 and elaborates on the additional aspects of Russia's state-sponsored interference during this period. The chapter analyzes Russia's cyber operations and visualizes them using the Hack Map of electoral and facilitating political infrastructure. The chapter concludes by applying the CHAOS framework to the known Russian activities and highlights the main lessons learned from this case regarding Russia's information warfare campaign and its effectiveness.

Factors Potentially Associated with the Launch of Cyber Operations

Russia's cyber operations against Montenegro occurred in a period of political tensions between the two countries. Previously a part of former Yugoslavia, Montenegro has long-standing relations with Russia dating back to Russia's Tsar Peter the Great.[3] In the post–Cold War period, Montenegro was drifting away from its traditional geopolitical configuration that presupposed cultivating close ties with Russia and was actively pursuing NATO membership—a strategic decision that, as chapter 1 demonstrated, the Russian government considered threatening to its interests.[4]

Russia's relations with Montenegro were also strained because of Montenegro's rejection of Russia's request to use Montenegro's Adriatic port for refueling and maintenance of Russian warships. Russia first made the request to the government of Montenegro to allow Russian warships to temporarily dock at Montenegrin ports in September 2013. During that time, Russia was searching for access to European ports where Moscow could be allowed to replenish its vessels on their way to Syria, which was fighting a civil war. Russia likely remembered Montenegro's rejection in 2016, when a Russian carrier and its battle group could not gain approval to use any European ports to refuel on route to Syria.[5] Montenegro's refusal to grant Russia access to its port facilities may have contributed to Russia's realization that Russia needed to change Montenegro's current pro-Western government to secure not only its naval interests but also its broader geopolitical grasp over the small but strategically placed Balkan nation.[6]

In addition to factors in the bilateral relations of the two countries that may have influenced Russia's decision to interfere in Montenegro's electoral process, the main contending parties had clearly established pro- or anti-Russian agendas. The 2016 elections were critical to Montenegro's political direction and to Russia's interests because the main parties competing in the elections had clear positions in favor of or in opposition to Montenegro's accession to NATO. Joining the alliance automatically implied sacrificing closer ties with Russia.[7] Arguably, the main objective of the October 2016 elections was to demonstrate that the majority of the Montenegrin population supported NATO membership.[8]

Furthermore, in the years prior to the election, the Russian government demonstrated a clear preference for Montenegro's anti-NATO parties and actively supported them and other organizations that advocated for a pro-Russian agenda. For example, the anti-NATO party that gathered the most opposition votes during the October elections, the Democratic Front (DF), promised to reverse Montenegro's pro-Western direction and withdraw Montenegro's support for sanctions against Russia.[9] Montenegro joined the EU and imposed sanctions against Russia in March 2014 under the country's pro-NATO leadership, which was running against the DF in the October 2016 elections.[10]

Russia's Information Warfare Activities

In the months leading to Montenegro's parliamentary elections, the Russian government supported a variety of activities in the political, social, and media spheres ranging from strategic messaging campaigns to a coup against one of Montenegro's leading political figures. The deteriorating political relations likely affected bilateral economic trade, especially in the agricultural and tourism sectors.[11] This section outlines the main known channels and agents of influence linked to Moscow in this period. Analysts contend that the general reason for the intensification of Russia's information warfare campaign was to destabilize Montenegro and derail its prospects of becoming a member of NATO.[12] The evidence in this section confirms this hypothesis and so does the fact that most of Russia's known operations took place after December 2, 2015, when NATO officially invited Montenegro to begin accession discussions.[13]

POLITICAL ACTIVITIES

Political Rhetoric

Russia's government agencies reacted swiftly to Montenegro's official announcement of its decision to join the alliance and maintained a consistently negative position on the matter. On the day of NATO's announcement, Kremlin spokesperson Dmitry Peskov stated that NATO's eastward expansion would "lead to retaliatory measures from Russia."[14] The Russian Foreign Ministry simultaneously released a statement in which it declared correspondingly that

> we perceive the decision of foreign ministers, participants in the December 1–2 North Atlantic Council meeting in Brussels, to launch NATO accession talks with Montenegro as an openly confrontationist move which is fraught with additional destabilizing consequences for the system of Euro-Atlantic security. . . . This new round of the alliance's expansion directly affects the interests of the Russian Federation and forces us to respond accordingly.[15]

Additional statements by Russian political representatives reinforced the official hostile government rhetoric. Foreign Ministry spokesperson Maria Zakharova, for example, used Twitter to echo the ominous pledge for a veiled retaliation by announcing on July 14, 2016, that "the current Montenegro authorities will bear full responsibility for the consequences of their anti-Russian stance."[16]

Support for Pro-Russian Political Parties

Russia supported pro-Russian political parties and anti-NATO civil movements. The Russian government is believed to have financially supported the pro-Russian DF. Due to the fact that the DF does not reveal the sources of its financing, it is difficult to estimate the exact amount of Russia's contributions, but various analysts hypothesize that they are substantial, and even amount to millions of dollars.[17] The party was originally a marginal force in Montenegro's political landscape but evolved into the chief opposition party.[18] Similar to the political party Attack in Bulgaria, the DF does not hide, and it even promotes, its connections with Russian authorities.[19] DF leaders frequently travel to Moscow and meet with representatives of Russian government agencies or foreign relations institutes. During these meetings, DF delegations have interacted with various high-ranking current and former Russian officials. Among these officials were Russian vice president Dmitry Rogozin and Russian general Leonid Reshetnikov. General Reshetnikov is a retired SVR officer whom a former Bulgarian president referred to as "the right hand of Mr. Putin on the Balkans."[20] Sergey Zheleznyak, a former deputy speaker of Russia's parliament and member of Putin's political party reportedly advised DF representatives to oppose NATO accession for Montenegro and propagate the alternative narrative that Montenegro should establish itself as a neutral country and become the "Balkans Switzerland."[21] This information suggests that the Russian government had a favored political party competing in the October elections that may have served as another incentive for Moscow to attempt to influence the election outcome.

Support for NGOs and the Orthodox Church

Russia reportedly aided anti-NATO NGOs in Montenegro such as the Montenegrin Movement for Neutrality and No to War, No to NATO.[22] The Balkan Federation of Russian Speaking Organizations (BaFRO) is another organization with strong ties to Russia's political leadership and to pro-Russian movements, such as the biker organization Night Wolves, that are known for their radical views and for promoting closer ties with Russia. The Night Wolves endorse ideas about Russian claims to territories outside of Russia based on history, ethnicity, and religion. BaFRO was established in Montenegro and allegedly partners with Russian NGOs such as the Russian state-sponsored Russkiy Mir Foundation.[23]

Russia also uses its influence in the Orthodox Church to enhance support for Russian society and opposition to NATO. The predominant religion in Montenegro is Orthodox Christianity, and as such, the Orthodox Church plays an important role in shaping Montenegrins' values and viewpoints. The Russian government, which is connected to the Russian Orthodox Church, is known to use the church to promote values that are in apparent contradiction to the Western world and its institutions. Orthodox priests partake in anti-Western strategic messaging and their actions are covered by Russian state-sponsored media.[24] For example, before NATO's meeting in December 2015, when it was clear that NATO would invite Montenegro to join the alliance, the DF and the Serbian Orthodox Church, openly supported by Russia, backed a series of protests in Montenegro. The protest organizers intended to incite a wave of nationwide demonstrations leading to a "people's awakening" aimed to overthrow the current Montenegrin government, prevent Montenegro's NATO accession, and return to Russia.[25] The protests were not only in response to external factors; DF reportedly called for the protests in reaction to changes in Montenegro's legislature that would favor the ruling Democratic Party of Socialists (DPS).[26] The protests were initially peaceful but escalated and turned violent on October 24, 2015, when the police intervened to prevent about 5,000 people from storming the parliament.[27]

An Attempted Coup d'état

One of the most brazen activities that the Russian government undertook during this information warfare campaign was an attempted coup d'état against Montenegro's pro-Western government. Russia was implicated in a failed attempt to cause instability, incite violence, and harm Montenegro's prospects of joining NATO by instigating a coup d'état plot and detaining, or even assassinating, Montenegro's main pro-NATO champion, Prime Minister Milo Djukanovic. The prime minister was the leader of the DPS, which was competing in the October elections.[28] On September 26, 2016, Russian former GRU military intelligence officers Vladimir Popov and Eduard Shishmakov met with Serbian nationalist Aleksander Sindjelic in Moscow. The two former GRU operatives shared a plan to overthrow Montenegro's pro-NATO leadership if it won the October 16 elections, and they offered Sindjelic the opportunity to participate, which he agreed to do. Popov and Shishmakov provided financial support for the purchase of weapons and ammunition. The plan dictated that in case of electoral victory by Djukanovic's party, members of the pro-Russian DF would facilitate the organization of a protest in front of Montenegro's parliament. The protest would happen on election day and would include a group of armed individuals who would open fire on the protesters, storm the parliament building, capture or assassinate Prime Minister Milo Djukanovic, announce that the elections were invalid, and declare the pro-Russian DF the winner.[29] After the meeting, the Serbian nationalist hired the Montenegrin Mirko Velimirovic and paid him to purchase ammunition and rifles in support of the coup d'état.[30] The plot failed because a few hours before the protests, Velimirovic turned himself in to the police and reported the plan to the authorities. The Russian former intelligence officers implicated in attempting to execute the assassination were caught by the Serbian authorities and deported to Russia.[31] In May 2019, a Montenegrin court sentenced the two Russian military intelligence officers in absentia to over ten years in jail because of their involvement in organizing the coup d'état.[32] In February 2021, however, the Court of Appeals of Montenegro overruled the verdicts.[33]

ECONOMIC ACTIVITIES

The increasing tensions over Montenegro's geopolitical direction affected the country's economic relations with Russia, especially Montenegro's agricultural, wine, and tourism industries.

Soon after Montenegro announced it would impose sanctions against Russia alongside the EU as a result of Russia's annexation of Crimea, Russia responded with an agricultural embargo on Montenegrin imports in August 2014.[34] In April 2017, Russia also banned wine imports from Montenegro, which Montenegro's prime minister condemned as a politically motivated decision that Russia made because of Montenegro's NATO membership. Until that time, Russia was the fifth-largest importer of Montenegrin wine.[35]

The bilateral political tensions also affected Montenegro's tourism industry. Russian citizens constituted the largest percentage of tourists to Montenegro, and their numbers increased from 2006 to 2016. In 2016, revenue spent by Russian tourists in Montenegro amounted to approximately 5 percent of Montenegro's GDP. After the October 2016 elections, Russian government representatives openly discouraged Russian citizens from traveling to Montenegro. In March 2017, for example, Russian foreign minister Lavrov warned that Montenegro was jeopardizing its economic ties with Moscow by becoming a NATO member. Lavrov's statement was followed by a negative campaign in Russian state media depicting Montenegro as filthy and dangerous for Russian tourists. These developments may have impacted the number of Russian tourists to Montenegro, which declined in subsequent years.[36]

CYBER OPERATIONS

Another element of Russia's interference is a series of cyber operations against a wide range of Montenegrin entities, including some that are parts of Montenegro's political IT infrastructure.[37] In the days prior to the elections and on election day, DDoS attacks temporarily disrupted the services of several major Montenegrin online media known for their pro-Western bias, including the popular media Café Del Montenegro and radio Antena M. The cyber operations also targeted the portal of Montenegro's government and the mobile carrier T-Kom. During the same wave of DDoS attacks, hackers targeted Montenegro's ruling party, the DPS. The Montenegrin authorities concluded that these were the "strongest ever" attacks against Montenegro's information systems until that time.[38] Figure 7.1 identifies the types of political infrastructure targets of these DDoS attacks. The cyber operations disrupted network traffic and the functions of a range of websites. Therefore, the cyber operations can be categorized as availability attacks, aimed to cause technical effects. Disrupting the operations of media outlets would also result in severing communications networks, which would also exert psychological effects.

The Montenegrin government embarked upon a detailed investigation of the cyber attacks but as of February 2021 has not publicly attributed the election day DDoS attacks against the DPS to Russian state-sponsored cyber threat actors.[39] Private companies, such as Booz Allen Hamilton, indicated that the DDoS attacks against the DPS were also conducted by Russian actors.[40]

Montenegro's government agencies and various cybersecurity companies reported that cyber operations against government and private sector institutions in Montenegro continued after election day and drastically increased in the year after the October 2016 elections. The publicly available evidence indicates that these operations were launched against the information systems of entities that did not constitute components of Montenegro's political infrastructure at that time.[41] The Hack Map of electoral, facilitating, and information sphere components of political IT infrastructure in chapter 2 identifies the components targeted during this period in figure 7.1.[42] Therefore, this chapter focuses on the DDoS attacks that occurred during the October 2016 elections and targeted political infrastructure.

RUSSIAN STATE-SPONSORED MEDIA COVERAGE

Russia launched various state-sponsored traditional and social media outlets that most likely were intended to serve as conduits of Russian influence on Montenegro's population. In order to avoid Montenegro's media laws, which the Montenegrin government can use to revoke the license of Montenegro-based Russian media, Russia has also set up

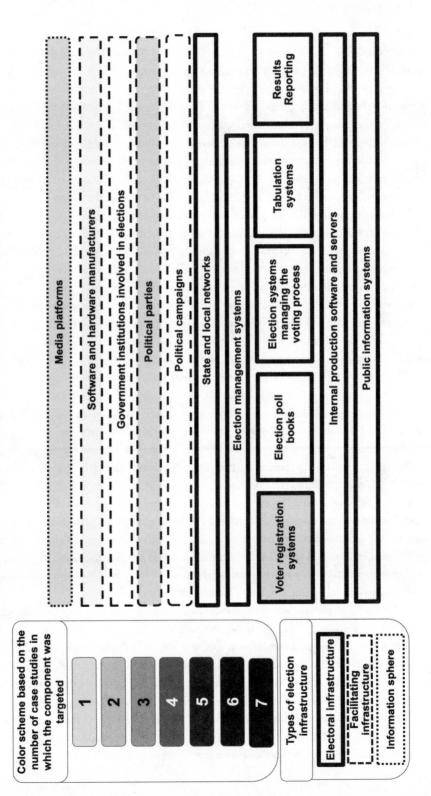

FIGURE 7.1 Russia's Political Hack Map during the 2016 Cyber Operations against Montenegro

media channels in Montenegro's neighboring country Serbia. These media, which numbered about 100 outlets in 2017, broadcast their content in Serbian—one of the main languages spoken in Montenegro. These media include *New Russia* (*Novaya Russia*), *South Front*, and the Serbian-language version of *Sputnik News* called *Sputnik Srbija*. The latter is one of the most well-established channels for conveying the Kremlin's viewpoint. Through these media, the Russian government launched a strategic messaging campaign against Montenegro's incumbent pro-Western government.[43] According to Ambassador of Montenegro Vesko Garčević, Russia's campaign was especially intense in the months before Montenegro received an official invitation from NATO to join the alliance on December 2, 2015. The campaign also intensified in the weeks prior to and during the parliamentary elections on October 16, 2016. Russia's state-sponsored media depiction of Montenegro at that time was primarily negative, describing the country as politically unstable and corrupt, and propagating the argument that NATO's decision to invite Montenegro into the alliance aimed to challenge Russia. The same media and pro-Russian social networks and web portals supported pro-Russian and anti-Western political movements and described Russia as a guardian of Orthodox values and Orthodox peoples—Orthodoxy is the dominant religion in Montenegro.[44] During the election period, the pro-Russian media also circulated narratives about voting irregularities.[45]

To examine whether Russia's state-sponsored media increased its coverage prior to the cyber operations, the analysis looked at the volume of coverage about the two main parties—the pro-NATO DPS and the pro-Russian DF—in *Sputnik Serbija*. Due to the fact that Russia's information warfare activities against Montenegro were likely related to Montenegro's invitation to join NATO, which was officially announced in 2015, the media analysis covers the period of the entire Russian information warfare campaign between Montenegro's official invitation to join NATO until the period of Montenegro's accession. To compare media coverage before and after the period of the campaign, this analysis examines the coverage three months before and after the period in question. Specifically, the analysis starts on September 2, 2015, which is three months before Montenegro's official invitation to join NATO (the alliance issued a formal invitation to Montenegro on December 2, 2015), and ends on September 5, 2017, which is three months after Montenegro officially joined NATO (June 5, 2017).

The results of the analysis show a spike in coverage on election day, but not before it (see fig. 7.2). Consistent with the trend observed after the 2016 U.S. elections, the figure also shows an increase in the volume of media coverage in the two months after the elections, which was more than the coverage in the two months prior to the elections. The articles that mentioned DPS and its leadership in the preelection period address themes such as casting doubts on the legitimacy of the October election by reporting that the DPS committed election fraud by pressuring voters and paying for votes.[46] Another theme was that the DPS leadership was incompetent, corrupt, and unfit to govern Montenegro, while DF was a better alternative that "can provide freedom and security."[47]

FIGURE 7.2 Russian *Sputnik Srbija* Media Coverage of DPS and DF

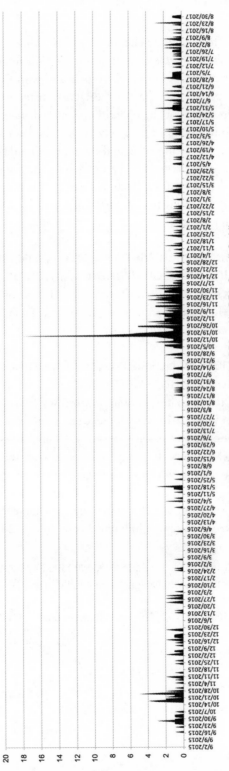

■ Number of articles per day that mention DPS and/or DF in *Sputnik Serbija*

In the months following the elections, *Sputnik Srbija* continued to spread similar divisive narratives about the illegitimacy of the election results and the DF being the better alternative to a corrupt DPS leadership, in line with Russia's foreign policy goals. One narrative was that despite the fact the DPS won the elections, a large portion of Montenegro's voters voted for the opposition, which demonstrated there was a sizable Montenegrin group that opposed joining NATO.[48] Another narrative that *Sputnik Srbija* proliferated was that the attempted coup d'état on election day was organized to prevent the DF from winning the elections.[49] The attempted coup d'état plot proved the elections were not conducted under normal circumstances and their results should, therefore, be considered invalid.[50] According to that version of events, the DF was a more viable candidate than the corrupt DPS.[51]

Russia's Interference in Montenegro: Associated Factors and Mapping the Information Warfare Campaign Using CHAOS

Figure 7.3 visualizes some of the activities that received direct or indirect support by groups associated with the Russian government in this period. Table 7.1 summarizes the factors of the QCA framework present in this case.

The Effectiveness of Russia's Cyber Operations and Information Warfare Campaign

Analysts agree that the main justification for Moscow's information warfare campaign in Montenegro in 2015 and 2016 was Montenegro's decision to join the NATO alliance, which Russia doctrinally and publicly opposed. Despite Russia's extensive information warfare campaign, Montenegro's pro-NATO forces won the October 2016 elections. Prime Minister Djukanovic, who was the target of the unsuccessful Russia-backed coup plot, emerged victorious with 41 percent of the votes. Djukanovic publicly interpreted this outcome as a vote for NATO membership for Montenegro.[52] The Balkan nation officially became NATO's twenty-ninth member on June 5, 2017.[53] Russia's unsuccessful

TABLE 7.1 Factors That Could Be Associated with the Initiation of the Particular Type of Cyber Operations against Montenegro in 2016 and 2017

Target	Type of cyber op (CIA)	Disputes in relations				Spike in media coverage before cyber ops	If cyber ops during elections		NATO member en route	NATO member	Frm. Eastern Bloc state	Frm. USSR state
		Polit	Soc	Econ	Mil		Anti-Ru candidate	Pro-Ru candidate				
Montenegro (2016–2017)	A	1	1	1	1	0	1	1	1	0	1	0

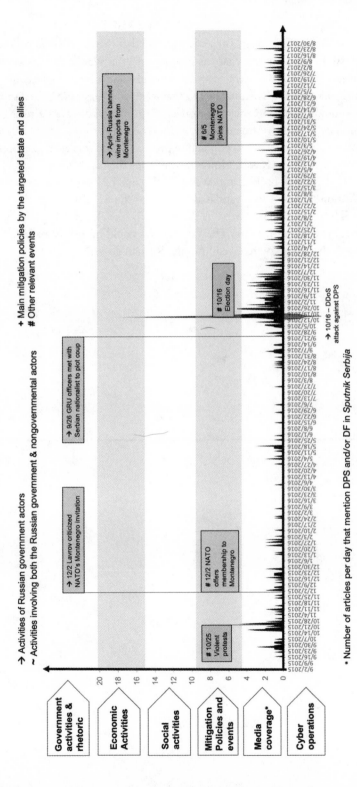

FIGURE 7.3 Russia's CHAOS in Montenegro in 2015–17: A Selection of Cyber Operations, Media Hype, and Associated Operations

→ Activities of Russian government actors
~ Activities involving both the Russian government & nongovernmental actors
+ Main mitigation policies by the targeted state and allies
# Other relevant events

→ 12/2 Lavrov criticized NATO's Montenegro invitation

→ 9/26 GRU officers met with Serbian nationalist to plot coup

→ April- Russia banned wine imports from Montenegro

6/5 Montenegro joins NATO

10/16 Election day

12/2 NATO offers membership to Montenegro

10/25 Violent protests

→ 10/16 – DDoS attack against DPS

* Number of articles per day that mention DPS and/or DF in *Sputnik Serbija*

Government activities & rhetoric

Economic Activities

Social activities

Mitigation Policies and events

Media coverage*

Cyber operations

attempts to derail Montenegro's accession proved that this tiny Balkan nation could withstand Russia's onslaught and chart its own path to the West.[54] Russia's sanctions against Montenegro also did not seem to exert a long-lasting negative effect on the country's economy. Although the deteriorating bilateral relations adversely impacted some of Montenegro's economic sectors, Russian investment in this period did not decrease below 10 percent of foreign direct investment and even increased in the period from 2013 to 2017.[55]

Montenegro's pro-Western population persevered and managed to geopolitically shift the country away from Russia. However, similar to the case of the German elections (see chapter 9), the Russia-backed, anti-Western DF gained 21 percent of the votes during the 2016 elections. These votes translated into 18 of the 81 seats in the Montenegrin parliament. The party did not emerge as the winner in the elections but still earned a role in Montenegro's decision-making. The DF's success could be at least partially attributed to the support that the party received from the Russian government.[56]

8

Trying to Trump En Marche! Russia's Interference in the 2017 French Presidential Elections[1]

The 2017 French presidential elections serve as another example of an information warfare campaign against political IT infrastructure of a NATO member state. The campaign started at least as early as October 2016, with a series of attempts to infiltrate the presidential campaign of then French presidential candidate Emmanuel Macron, who became the main target of information warfare activities in the context of the 2017 French presidential elections. In addition to cyber operations, the information warfare activities against Macron included a sustained disinformation operation, consisting of fabricated documents and a proliferation of offensive rumors on social media and Russian state-sponsored media. Trolls and bots on social media, as well as Russian state-sponsored media, leaked information obtained through a successful hack of Macron's political campaign. The leaked information became a part of the strategic messaging operation against Macron and his campaign.

With the benefit of hindsight about Russia's activities around the 2016 U.S. presidential elections, the French government and nongovernment organizations prepared for the possibility of Russian interference before the 2017 elections. Government agencies offered cybersecurity training to political parties while the French media enhanced its fact-checking capabilities to better detect potential disinformation. The Macron campaign independently increased its resilience against cyber intrusions by, for example, creating false data to confuse any unwelcome network intruders. Researchers and practitioners largely view the French multidimensional approach to a potential Russian information warfare campaign as a success.[2] Unlike during the 2016 U.S. election cycle, when the chairwoman of the Democratic National Committee resigned because Russian state-sponsored cyber groups hacked and leaked information from the DNC servers, no similar resignations followed the successful hack and leak of data from Macron's campaign. Furthermore, although there is no methodologically sound analysis that proves whether Russia's interference in the 2016 U.S. elections contributed to or resulted in the election of Donald Trump, experts refer to the fact that Emmanuel Macron won victory in both French presidential rounds, on April 23 and May 7, as another demonstration of the failure of Russia's operation against France.

This chapter begins by describing the factors that may have affected Russia's decision to interfere in the French election process, specifically the status of relations between Paris and Moscow, highlighting some of the main points of contention in the bilateral relationship. This section also examines the financial connection between the French candidates and the Russian government, and their disposition toward topics relevant to Russia. The chapter proceeds by outlining the main information warfare activities associated with Russian state-sponsored actors during the French elections and addressing the question of attribution. The Hack Map illustrates the main political components that Russia's APTs targeted in this case. After describing the various information warfare activities, the chapter applies the CHAOS framework to visualize the relation between the hack-and-leak operation, the main election rounds, and the trends in strategic messaging through Russia's state-sponsored media channels. In conclusion, the chapter discusses the effectiveness of Russia's activities and some of the main lessons learned from this case.

Factors Potentially Associated with the Launch of Cyber Operations

Despite a strong historical and cultural relationship with Russia, the French government had found itself on the opposite side of Russia on several major political, social, and economic issues in the years preceding the 2017 French presidential election. The French leadership criticized Russia's policies in Ukraine. In 2014, then French president Francois Hollande joined the majority of the international community in publicly condemning Russia's annexation of the Ukrainian Peninsula of Crimea. Hollande did not recognize the status of Crimea as Russian territory.[3] The French president maintained this policy in his following years in office as well, even though he advocated that NATO members should consider Russia a partner, rather than a threat.[4]

In the early stages of the Ukraine crisis in 2014, under the spotlight of the international community, former president Hollande stopped the execution of a high-profile agreement between France and Moscow. The agreement stipulated that France build and deliver two *Mistral*-class warships that the Kremlin had commissioned.[5] The ships, for which Russia had paid approximately $1 billion in advance, were helicopter carriers, and President Hollande refused to execute the delivery of the ships after Russia's annexation of Crimea. Despite Russia's strong opposition to Hollande's decision, France sold the ships to Egypt.[6] France further supported the imposition of EU sanctions against Russia in response to Moscow's invasion of Ukraine.[7] President Holland continued to express support for the extension of the sanctions against Moscow after 2014 due to the lack of progress on implementing the Russian-Ukrainian ceasefire agreement.[8] In response to the EU sanctions against Russia, Moscow imposed its own sanctions against EU countries, including France. The sanctions affected raw materials, agricultural goods, and other products.[9] A demonstration of the tense relationship between Hollande and Putin was

Hollande's refusal to attend the official opening of a Russian cultural center near the Eiffel Tower in October 2016. In response, Putin canceled a planned visit to Paris.[10]

RUSSIA'S PREFERENCE FOR AND LINKS TO FRENCH POLITICAL PARTIES

The main presidential candidates competing for the French presidency in 2016 and 2017 had either established relations with the Russian political leadership or articulated clear positions on Russia. Already in 2014, the Russian government demonstrated its support for the far-right presidential candidate Marine Le Pen and her ultranationalist National Front party (FN), which was a main contender in the 2017 French presidential race. An investigation conducted by the French investigative platform *Mediapart* revealed that Le Pen's party borrowed 11 million euros from Kremlin-linked Russian financial institutions and oligarchs in 2014 and planned to borrow an additional 3 million euros in 2016 for the purposes of "financing the electoral campaign."[11] FN borrowed the money from Russia after the party was rejected by French banking institutions on the basis of its links to anti-Semitism and white supremacy.[12] The money was directly transferred to accounts managed by Marine Le Pen or her father, Jean-Marie Le Pen, the former leader of FN.[13] Additionally, the close ties between Russia and Marine Le Pen are visible through Le Pen's positions on Russia—a country that she considered an example to emulate.[14] Le Pen had publicly supported Russia's position on a number of important issues. Le Pen endorsed Russia's policy in Syria and Ukraine and called for collaboration with Russia against terrorism and a willingness to "energize an alliance between the U.S., France and Russia in the fight against Islamists."[15]

Marine Le Pen's main competitor in the 2017 French presidential race emerged to be Emmanuel Macron. Contrary to Le Pen, Macron publicly rejected an alignment with the Kremlin. He defended the continuation of sanctions against Russia for its annexation of Crimea as long as the Minsk II agreements on Ukraine that aimed to establish a ceasefire in Eastern Ukraine were not enforced. Macron's position on Syria was also inconsistent with Russia's view. Macron insisted that to reach a peaceful solution with the Syrian parties, all sides should participate in the negotiation, but President Assad should not be a part of that negotiation without standing trial for his crimes.[16]

Russia's Information Warfare Activities

It was in this environment of existing political, social, and economic disagreements, as well as the presence of two French presidential candidates with opposing positions on Russia, that the Russian government made the decision to employ information warfare activities in an attempt to interfere in the French presidential election. The main activities that cybersecurity companies and experts attributed to the Kremlin included the two core elements of information warfare: a targeted strategic messaging campaign aimed at psychological manipulation conducted via social platforms and Russian state-sponsored media, and a range of cyber operations against the Macron political campaign, which resulted in the leaking of information obtained as a result of these cyber operations. Trolls and bots on social media proliferated messages about the leaked information, which became a part of the disinformation operation against President Macron.

In addition to cyber operations and disinformation campaigns, the Russian government may have attempted to influence the French elections through the NGOs and religious organizations linked to the Kremlin. Russia has sponsored a number of French-based organizations that cultivate social and religious ties with France and advocate Russia's position. For example, Vladimir Yakunin, a former Putin confidante who was minister and chief of Russia's state-owned Russian Railways, was the copresident of the Paris-based Association Dialogue Franco-Russe. The association promotes the cultivation of stronger Franco-Russian ties and amelioration of relations.[17] Another similar organization is the Institute for Democracy and Cooperation, which is chaired by a former Duma deputy Natalya Narochnitskaya. The institute advocated a pro-Kremlin position in its activities without being directly linked to the Russian government.[18]

The presence of Russia's Orthodox Church in France is another channel for influence and promotion of Russia's policies. French media reported French government concerns over the possibility that Moscow may use a recently erected Russian church at the heart of Paris for surveillance. The church and Russia's general religious presence in France are seen as an attempt to influence Russia's 200,000 Orthodox diaspora in France.[19]

Although as of February 2021 no publicly available information suggests that NGOs linked to the Russian government or Russia's Orthodox Church conducted any activities to influence the 2017 French election, they are mentioned here to highlight the possibility for further research into the role of these organizations into Russia's information warfare campaigns.

RUSSIA'S CYBER OPERATIONS

Russian-affiliated cyber groups launched a range of cyber operations against the political campaign of presidential candidate Macron, political parties, and local government entities.[20] These cyber operations included attacks against the confidentiality, integrity, and availability of data. At least from October 2016 to mid-March 2017, cyber actors used spear phishing and spoofing.[21] There were 2,000 to 3,000 attempts to hack the Macron presidential campaign. The attackers sent emails to Macron campaign officials with links to websites baiting them to reveal their email passwords. The targets were primarily mid-level campaign management staff.[22] Other targets included emails of local French governments, high-profile individuals, and other French politicians.[23] These cyber operations resulted in at least five successful compromises—five of Macron's colleagues had their personal and professional emails hacked.[24] In addition to spear phishing, cyber actors launched DDoS attacks that temporarily shut down the website of the Macron campaign.[25] The subsequently released documents were edited, affecting the integrity of data and, hence, constituted an integrity attack.[26] These cyber operations seem to have been conducted for the purposes of both psychological and technical effects.

Based on this information, figure 8.1 shows the components of the political IT infrastructure that Russian agencies targeted during this period. Russia's APTs targeted primarily facilitating infrastructure.

FIGURE 8.1 Russia's Political Hack Map during the 2017 Cyber Operations against France

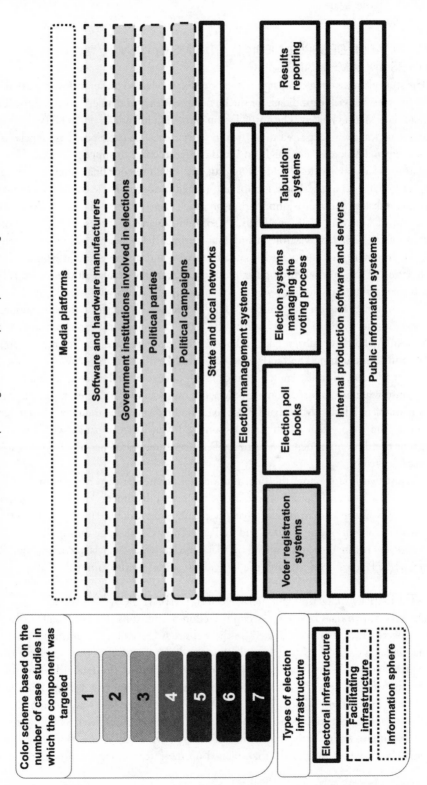

EXPLOITATION OF SOCIAL MEDIA PLATFORMS BY FRENCH USERS AND AMERICAN TROLLS

The strategic messaging campaign against candidate Macron began in January 2016 when he emerged as a viable candidate for the French presidency and an opponent of pro-Russian candidate Marine Le Pen. The anti-Macron campaign included French Le Pen supporters and Americans who appeared to be Trump supporters. The latter posed as French citizens, and targeted Macron's campaign on social media in order to support Le Pen. They used platforms such as Twitter, Reddit, Discord, and 4chan to coordinate their campaign and spread their messages.[27] These groups also posted messages in the comments sections on media websites. Journalist John Harkinson called these groups "Marine Le Pen's 'Foreign Legion' of American Alt-Right Trolls."[28] Common themes that these groups used in their attempts to denigrate Macron included allegations that Macron was an aristocrat who hated common men, supported Islamic terrorism, and his government would be a continuation of the previous unpopular president.[29] A major strategy of these groups before the second round of elections was to convince French voters who were likely to vote for Macron not to vote on election day.[30] This theme was consistent with voter suppression efforts spread by Russian trolls during the 2016 U.S. elections, explained in chapter 5. Moreover, about two dozen fake Facebook accounts may have been created to monitor Macron's campaign staff and individuals close to Macron on Facebook.[31]

In addition to trolls, French politicians supportive of Le Pen contributed to spreading unsubstantiated information about Macron on social media. For example, the member of parliament Marion Marechal-Le Pen, Marine Le Pen's niece, used her Twitter account to circulate a story that Saudi Arabia sponsored Macron's campaign, which was a false rumor based on no evidence. Marine Le Pen herself retweeted her niece's post before her niece deleted it.[32]

Just two hours before the final presidential debate between Macron and Le Pen, a user with a Latvian IP address posted two fabricated documents on the platform 4chan claiming Macron had an offshore bank account. American extremist groups and others spread the allegations on Twitter, and Le Pen even raised the issue during the presidential debate and before the rumor spread on social media, which led Macron campaign staff to believe Le Pen was working with the individuals spreading the rumors.[33]

INTEGRATION OF CYBER OPERATIONS INTO STRATEGIC MESSAGING

On May 5, two days before the second election round, thousands of emails stolen from the Macron campaign were posted on the website Archive.org. The documents included manipulated data.[34] Links to these data were posted on Pastebin and a website emleaks (which may stand for En Marche Leaks) that mirrors the site established in the U.S. case named DC Leaks. Within an hour the links were shared on 4chan. Then links to the data appeared on Twitter. The first to share a link to the files was William Craddick, who previously contributed to spreading the U.S. conspiracy known as Pizzagate.[35] The American pro-Trump activist Jack Posobiec also shared a link to the data using the hashtag #MacronLeaks. WikiLeaks then picked up the threat, citing the link to the data on

Pastebin and amplified it. French Le Pen supporters, including the vice president of NF, paid attention to WikiLeaks' tweets and spread the message about the files further.[36] An army of bots and trolls promoted the leaked information on Twitter with the hashtag #MacronLeaks. The hashtag appeared in almost 500,000 tweets in 24 hours.[37] The Macron leaks did not attract significant attention—the number of Twitter accounts involved in the spread of the information was only 23,036, a small fraction of Twitter's more than 300 million user accounts in that period.[38] Moreover, the conversation about the leaks quickly shifted from anti-Macron messages to tweets focused on countermessaging, mocking the information about the leaks or emphasizing a relationship between the leaks and Russia in order to demonstrate foreign interference. As Ben Nimmo concluded, this Twitter campaign did not appear to influence the French political dynamics.[39]

On July 31, 2017, WikiLeaks released a searchable archive that contained over 21,075 emails, dating between March 2009 and April 24, 2017, from Macron's campaign that WikiLeaks claimed it verified. The platform published an additional 50,773 emails whose authenticity WikiLeaks had not confirmed. Overall, the leak consisted of 71,848 emails, 26,506 attachments, and details of 4,493 senders.[40] Pro-Kremlin media publicized information about the WikiLeaks database, but the coverage was minimal in comparison to *Sputnik News*'s coverage of the U.S. DNC leaks.[41]

ATTRIBUTION OF THE HACK-AND-LEAK OPERATION AND THE STRATEGIC MESSAGING CAMPAIGN

As of 2021, the French government had not publicly attributed the cyber operations against the Macron campaign to any particular cyber group or state. However, several cybersecurity companies and renowned cybersecurity experts attributed the operations to the cyber threat actor APT 28, associated with Russia's GRU.[42] These companies include the Japanese cybersecurity firm Trend Micro, which identified similarities in the malware and IP addresses used during the attacks against the Macron campaign and the intrusions against the DNC. Although Trend Micro stated it could not verify with absolute certainty that the perpetrators of the cyber operations was APT 28, the company's representative assessed that in addition to the similarities in techniques between the Macron hack perpetrators and the DNC hack perpetrators, the group behind the Macron hack "certainly appears to pursue Russian interests."[43] Additionally, the cybersecurity company Threat-Connect reported that the Macron hackers used the same email platform and servers that were previously associated with APT 28.[44]

The leaked documents offered another set of clues pointing to Russia. The cybersecurity firm Proofpoint identified that some of the documents were edited on computers that had operating systems in Russian. Some of the Excel spreadsheets that were among the leaks contained information on the last person who had edited the documents, and the name of that person was listed as Georgiy Petrovich Roshka. A person with that name registered for a 2016 conference as a representative of Unit 26165, which is GRU's cryptography unit. These indicators suggest that Russia's GRU was at least partially involved in the cyber operations.[45] As the vice president for intelligence of the cybersecurity firm

Flashpoint asserted, all these indicators suggest that we can assess with "moderate confidence" that APT 28 was the perpetrator of the cyber operations.[46]

Regarding attribution of the strategic messaging operation against the Macron campaign, the role of the Russian government can be clearly identified through negative narratives about Macron and the proliferation of fabricated information via the Russian state-sponsored media *Sputnik France* and *RT*. Attribution to the Russian government or Russian actors, however, has not been established with regard to the trolls, bots, and other accounts on social media that systematically criticized the Macron campaign. The majority of these accounts originated in North America, especially the United States, or France, and several of the key anti-Macron social media users who amplified information about the Macron leaks were American citizens known for their far-right extremist views. Experts have hypothesized that the Russian government may have coordinated or assisted these groups in supporting the campaign of Le Pen and opposing that of Macron, which is a reasonable assumption given the overlapping interests of these groups and the Russian government (to support nationalist political parties, which in both the United States and France appear to be pro-Russian). These actors may also have worked in parallel toward the same objective without necessarily working together.[47]

As of this writing, no investigations prove that Russian state-sponsored actors were present and involved in these social media campaigns, but a U.S. indictment released in October 2020 asserted that at least one social media account controlled by the GRU played a role in this campaign by contacting French individuals and offering to supply them with documents stolen from the Macron campaign. The indictment did not reveal whether the GRU account shared any of the stolen data the user claimed to possess.[48]

PRO-KREMLIN MEDIA COVERAGE

Media sponsored by the Russian government in France include *RT* and *Sputnik France*. As members of the Macron campaign asserted in the course of 2017, and as President Macron himself firmly stated while standing next to President Putin at a press conference after the French elections, Russia used Kremlin-sponsored media *RT* and *Sputnik* as "organs of influence" to spread propaganda during the French presidential campaign.[49] These Russian media outlets distributed negative rhetoric and disinformation through media articles critical of Macron.[50] A study of the coverage of *Sputnik France* conducted by Ben Nimmo in the early stages of the presidential election campaign showed an anti-Macron bias. The *Sputnik France* coverage included trying to link Macron to allegations of corruption and a high unemployment rate. At the same time, the *Sputnik France* coverage of Le Pen was mainly positive and amplified messages and positions of her party, NF.[51] For example, *Sputnik France* articles portrayed Macron as an agent of the United States who is supported by a gay lobby.[52] *Sputnik France* also covered an unsubstantiated rumor that he had an extramarital homosexual relationship.[53]

The Russian state-sponsored media in France also covered the documents leaked through the hacks into the Macron party. Figure 8.2 shows the amount of coverage about the leaks as a portion of the general coverage about Macron and Le Pen during this election

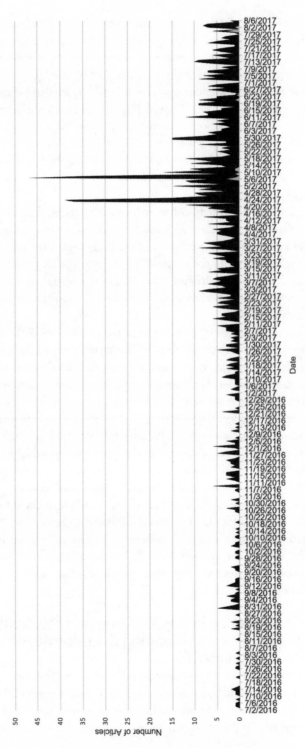

FIGURE 8.2 Russian State-Sponsored Media Coverage

cycle in *Sputnik France*. To draw comparisons between coverage before and after the main information warfare activities in this case, the period this research examined starts on July 1, 2016 (three months prior to the known commencement of spear-phishing operations against the Macron campaign), and ends on August 6, 2017 (three months after the second round of the French presidential elections). The figure shows that information about the amount of coverage of the two main presidential candidates increased in the period preceding the elections and significantly spiked on the days of each election round and the two days immediately following election day. The coverage was markedly negative toward Macron and positive toward Le Pen. In addition, the figure reveals that the coverage related to the Macron leaks did not constitute a major part of the coverage about the two candidates in that period.

The figure also shows that, consistent with the analytical conclusions in the case of Russia's interference in the 2016 U.S. elections, the volume of coverage about President Macron and Le Pen after the elections was markedly higher than the volume of coverage about the candidates before the elections. Such strategy is in accordance with one of the aims of Russia's information warfare—to use existing societal grievances or divisive issues to amplify societal divisions and distrust in democratic institutions not only around elections, but continuously.

The *Sputnik* coverage in French in the weeks after the 2017 elections contained articles suggesting violations on voting day, indicating a rigged voting process and invalid election results. One article, for example, claimed that hundreds of Marine Le Pen bulletins were stolen.[54] Another article covered complaints of violations on voting day, which included damaged ballots for Le Pen.[55] Other reporting emphasized a lower voter turnout during the second election round and the highest abstention rate since 1969 on election day of the second round and covered protests in France against Macron's victory.[56]

The content of *Sputnik France* after the elections continued to contain occasional unflattering remarks about Macron and his victory, such as commentaries that Macron was elected "without enthusiasm."[57] *Sputnik France* cited criticism toward the French election outcome by foreign political leaders—for example, it chose to highlight the comment by the former leader of the United Kingdom Independence Party, Nigel Farage, who tweeted that France chose "5 more years of failure."[58] Even in articles reporting that Macron received congratulations on his victory from various world leaders, *Sputnik France* mentioned information that suggested the election results did not represent the opinion of the entire French population.[59]

Russia's Interference in the 2017 French Presidential Elections: Associated Factors and Mapping the Information Warfare Campaign Using CHAOS

In the period before the 2017 French presidential elections, actors associated with the Russian government launched a strategic messaging campaign and likely initiated a series of cyber operations against the presidential campaign of Macron and in favor of Le Pen. Figure 8.3 applies the CHAOS framework to this case and juxtaposes the analysis of

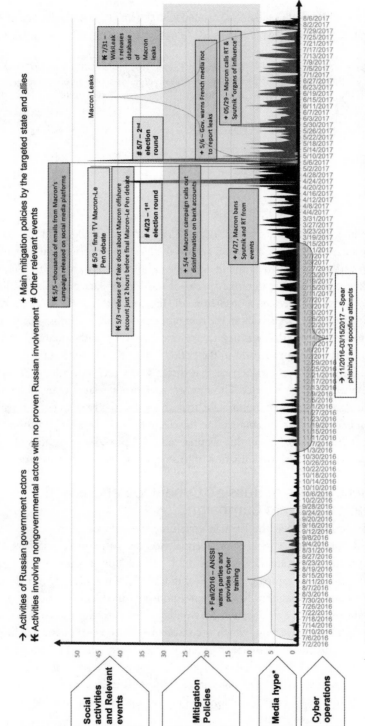

FIGURE 8.3 Russia's CHAOS in the 2017 French Elections

→ Activities of Russian government actors   + Main mitigation policies by the targeted state and allies
Ҡ Activities involving nongovernmental actors with no proven Russian involvement # Other relevant events

Social activities and Relevant events

Mitigation Policies

Media hype*

Cyber operations

Ҡ 5/5 –thousands of emails from Macron's campaign released on social media platforms

5/3 – final TV Macron-Le Pen debate

Ҡ 5/3 –release of 2 fake docs about Macron offshore account just 2 hours before final Macron–Le Pen debate

4/23 – 1st election round

5/7 – 2nd election round

Macron Leaks

Ҡ 7/31 – WikiLeaks releases database of Macron leaks

+ 5/6 – Gov. warns French media not to report leaks

+ 05/29 – Macron calls RT & Sputnik "organs of influence"

+ 5/4 – Macron campaign calls out disinformation on bank accounts

+ 4/27, Macron bans Sputnik and RT from events

+ Fall/2016 – ANSSI warns parties and provides cyber training

→ 11/2016–03/15/2017 – Spear phishing and spoofing attempts

* Articles about Emmanuel Macron and Marine Le Pen published in Russian media are displayed along the x-axis in darker gray. The subset of articles pertaining to the Macron Leaks are highlighted in lighter gray.

TABLE 8.1 Factors That Could Be Associated with the Initiation of the Particular Type of Cyber Operations Observed during the 2017 Russian Information Warfare against France

Target	Type of cyber op (CIA)	Disputes in relations				Spike in media coverage before cyber ops	If cyber ops during elections		NATO member en route	NATO member	Frm. Eastern Bloc state	Frm. USSR state
		Polit	Soc	Econ	Mil		Anti-Ru candidate	Pro-Ru candidate				
France (2017)	C, I, A	1	0	1	0	0	1	1	0	1	0	0

pro-Kremlin *Sputnik France* coverage during the election campaign and the main events related to the hack-and-leak operation against the Macron campaign, and the mitigation policies by various French government agencies and the Macron campaign itself that may have facilitated the relative minimal spread of the leaked data on social media and its minimal coverage on Kremlin-sponsored media in comparison to the spread of the leaked information from the DNC hack in the case of the 2016 U.S. elections. The figure shows that the media coverage that was negative toward Macron slightly increased after the two rounds of elections in comparison to the period before the elections, in accordance with Russian information warfare doctrine that dictates that such operations are continuous and not limited to election cycles. The coverage specifically related to instilling distrust in the French election outcome supports the hypothesis that the Russian government aims to erode trust in democratic governance and the elections are only one opportunity to do so.

Considering the analysis in this chapter, table 8.1 provides a synthesis of the potential factors associated with the initiation of this type of Russian cyber operations.

The Effectiveness of Russia's Cyber Operations and Information Warfare Campaign

The modus operandi that the Russian government employed in France resembled the one it used during the 2016 U.S. presidential election. In particular, hackers seemed to have attempted to replicate the success of the U.S. hack-and-leak operation. The hackers infiltrated the election campaign of then candidate Macron and unidentified individuals leaked the stolen information. Russian state-sponsored media in France also covered the election campaign with a distinct anti-Macron bias. The nature of this coverage continued in the weeks after the election, which is consistent with the goal of Russia's information warfare to sow distrust in democratic governance and leadership. In contrast to the case of the 2016 U.S. elections, the leaked information did not spread on social media and the preferred Kremlin candidate did not win. Therefore, Russia's information warfare campaign against the 2017 French elections did not seem as effective in achieving the objectives of the Russian government.

The reasons for the relative lack of success of Russia's information warfare campaign may be partially attributed to the immediate policies that key stakeholders in the French elections adopted before the elections. The French government and media took a number of steps before the elections to prepare for the possibility of a hack-and-leak campaign or disinformation spread by the Russian government. For example, in the fall of 2016, the French Network and Information Security Agency (L'Agence nationale de la sécurité des systèmes d'information, or ANSSI) warned all French political parties of the potential they could be targets of cyber attacks and offered cybersecurity training to party representatives.[60] Macron's campaign prepared in advance by using a technique known as "cyber-blurring." Campaign staff created fake email accounts and documents on the campaign's networks to divert hackers from the authentic information.[61] On April 27, 2017, Macron's campaign banned reporters who work for Russia-sponsored *Sputnik France* and *RT* from attending its events.[62]

French media increased its vigilance against disinformation and fake news by increasing its fact-checking methods. For example, *Le Monde* launched its Décodex project, which verified the reliability of information sources.[63] During the government investigation into the leaked data from Macron's political campaign, the French electoral commission further warned the media that republishing the leaked data could be considered a criminal offence.[64]

There is no direct evidence on the basis of which to attribute the disinformation campaign on social media to Russia, which means the Russian government may have learned from the U.S. case and started to work with proxies, or it may just not have seen the need to launch a campaign on social media. Yet, if we consider the spread of the Macron leaks and other anti-Macron messages on social media as a part of Kremlin's information warfare, the disinformation campaign on social media also did not succeed in spreading the anti-Macron information. This may also be partially attributed to specific structural characteristics of the French media space. There is a low penetration of social media in France in comparison to the United States. Other factors that may have limited the success of a social media disinformation campaign are the preference of the French population to receive information from mainstream media and the low popularity of alternative media sources in France.[65]

9

The Hack of the Bundestag and Aiding AfD[1]

As France was wrapping up its tumultuous presidential elections, Germany was preparing for its own. On September 24, 2017, the German voters were about to elect the main political parties that would constitute the nineteenth German parliament. Some experts argue that Russia's information warfare campaign to influence the 2017 German federal election commenced as early as 2015.[2] In 2015, the lower house of the German parliament, the Bundestag, sustained a cyber intrusion. During the intrusion, hackers exfiltrated over 16 gigabytes of information from the parliament's network.[3] The German intelligence service and cybersecurity companies attributed the hack to Russia. The German political leadership articulated its main policy response a few years later.[4] After years of relative silence, German chancellor Angela Merkel revived the issue with a bang in May 2020. The chancellor publicly ascribed attribution for the cyber operations to Russia's military intelligence agency, the GRU, and called for the first-ever EU sanctions against Russia in response to a cyber intrusion.[5]

This chapter examines Russia's 2015 hack of the Bundestag within the context of Russia's information warfare. Although Russia's intrusion into the Bundestag networks occurred prior to the cyber operations in Bulgaria, the United States, Norway, Montenegro, and France, this case is examined last because the German authorities linked Russia's 2015 cyber operation in Germany to Germany's 2017 elections. Much of Germany's response to Russia's cyber operations and other information warfare activities was informed by Germany's awareness of Russia's actions in the previous cases. This chapter starts by outlining the potential reasons that influenced the decision of the Russian government to launch a cyber operation against the German parliament and proceeds by examining the various aspects of Russia's information warfare campaign and the response of the German government in that period. In this section, the Hack Map facilitates the visualization of the political infrastructure targets during the 2015 cyber operations. The chapter continues by analyzing the interaction and integration of the different Russian-linked information warfare activities using the CHAOS framework and places the factors that could have led to Russia's decision to employ its cyber capabilities in the QCA table whose components are outlined in chapter 2. The chapter also examines Germany's policy response and the effectiveness of Russia's cyber operations and general information warfare campaign at that time.

Factors Potentially Associated with the Launch of Cyber Operations

The relations between Germany and Russia before Russia's cyber operations against the Bundestag were characterized by political and economic tensions. Despite the long history of amicable political and business relations between the two countries, especially in the energy sector, Germany supported the introduction and maintenance of EU sanctions against Russia in response to Russia's 2014 annexation of Crimea.[6] In response to the sanctions, Russia imposed its own sanctions against raw materials, agricultural products, and foodstuffs from EU member states, including Germany.[7] The investigation of Russian involvement in the downing of Malaysian flight MH-17 over Ukrainian territory and Russia's support for the conflict in Eastern Ukraine further added to the list of disagreements between the two states. These controversial issues led Chancellor Merkel to state that Germany's "strategic relationship" with Moscow had concluded.[8] Merkel's persistent support for EU sanctions against Russia and her criticism of Russian human rights violations and interference in foreign elections established her as a political opponent to the Putin regime.[9]

Russia's Information Warfare Activities

The Russian government's attempts to influence the 2017 German elections included developing ties with and supporting the pro-Russian German political party Alternative for Germany (Alternative für Deutschland, or AfD). Experts also linked a series of Russia-attributed cyber operations against German political entities in 2015 to Russia's efforts to interfere in the 2017 German elections.[10] In the months before the 2017 elections, Russia also employed strategic messaging, including disinformation, and spread narratives supportive of the AfD and critical of Chancellor Merkel and her party, the Christian Democratic Union (Christlich-Demokratische Union, or CDU). The nationwide protests that formed in relation to a fabricated story, known as the Lisa case, which Russia's foreign ministry reinforced, can be considered as another element of Russia's campaign to fuel existing discontent with the CDU's immigration policies.

Other possible channels and agents of influence through which the Kremlin could advance its interests in Germany included German politicians, businessmen, and journalists. For instance, former German chancellor Gerhard Schroeder accepted a position on the board of the Nord Stream pipeline project. Russian civil society organizations, such as the Dialogue of Civilizations Research Institute, founded in Berlin in 2016 and financed by Putin's confidante Vladimir Yakunin, are also suspected to be potential channels for Russian influence.[11] Due to the paucity of evidence to suggest substantive involvement of these potential conduits of Russian influence in Russia's campaign during the 2017 German elections, this chapter does not examine these connections in detail but mentions them here in the hope that other researchers may find studying the role of these organizations in conveying Moscow's influence during the 2017 elections sufficiently intriguing to render further exploration.

POLITICAL ACTIVITIES: RELATIONS WITH GERMAN POLITICAL PARTIES

The Russian government developed ties with Germany's far-right political party AfD, whose positions to improve German relations with Russia and remove the EU sanctions against Moscow align with Russian interests.[12] During the campaign leading to the September 2017 German elections, the AfD benefited from favorable publicity and comprehensive coverage of its election campaign in Russian-sponsored media relative to the minimal coverage the AfD received in German media. The AfD reporting in Russian media outlets may have increased the party's appeal among the ethnic Russian voters in Germany. The inclusion of Russian native speakers among the AfD political candidates likely further increased the popularity of the party among the ethnic Russian voters in Germany and in the Kremlin. Based on AfD estimates, ethnic Russians in Germany accounted for approximately one-third of the AfD support base.[13]

Another demonstration of political affiliations between AfD and Russia is evident through the personal meetings of AfD leaders with Russian political elites. In 2015, the AfD leader Alexander Gauland traveled to St. Petersburg and met with Russian billionaire Konstantin Malofeev, known for his support of Russian interests, and members of Putin's party, United Russia.[14] Malofeev may have also influenced Russia's information warfare operation in Bulgaria, through his interest in purchasing a weapons factory, which is discussed in the chapter on Bulgaria. In February 2017, the AfD leader, Frauke Petry, also visited Russia and met with Russia's former presidential deputy chief of staff, Vyacheslav Volodin.[15] In another demonstration of political affiliation between the AfD and Russia, the AfD youth division sought ties with the youth wing of the Russian political party United Russia.[16] German intelligence sources also assert that Russia provided financial support for AfD before the September 2017 elections through an intermediary by selling gold below market prices.[17]

Other German political parties have positions aligned with Russian foreign policy interests, but direct Russian financial or political support for them has not been definitively established. These parties include the extreme-left party, the Left (Die Linke), and the extreme anti-immigrant movement Pegida, which advocates its alliance with Russia and has flown Russian flags at its rallies. The fact that some of these parties' positions align with Moscow's policy agenda does not necessarily suggest that the parties receive Russian state support. The alignment of interests may be a consequence of an inadvertent convergence of perspectives because of Germany's cultural conservatism and negative attitudes toward globalization, further EU integration, and anti-Americanism that exists among some German groups. Hence, this partial convergence of agendas may indicate only political correlation and may not be a product of relations with Russian leaders and Russian influence.[18]

Based on the documented Russian links to Germany's AfD, it is reasonable to stipulate that the 2017 German elections included at least one pro-Russian party that developed a relationship with Russian political leaders.

RUSSIA'S CYBER ATTACKS AGAINST GERMANY

The cyber operations attributed to Russian state-sponsored APTs prior to the 2017 German elections were mostly confidentiality compromises. As of April 2021, none of the known cyber operations resulted in the release of hacked data, as opposed to the 2016 U.S. case, and, therefore, the attacks did not seem to compromise data integrity. The Russian APTs targeted primarily facilitating infrastructure of the political infrastructure and likely aimed to produce psychological effects rather than technical disruptions.

In April and May 2015, the Bundestag experienced a cyber intrusion that lasted several weeks. The German domestic intelligence agency attributed the operations to Russia's APT 28 and accused Russia of gathering political data that Moscow could choose to release before the 2017 German elections. The German domestic intelligence agency attributed a series of cyber operations against lawmakers, the CDU, and other institutions affiliated with the party to APT 28, but there was no evidence that any data was exfiltrated during these intrusions.[19] The hereby presented analysis, hence, focuses on the 2015 intrusion into the Bundestag as the most notable and damaging cyber operation that was conducted in the period before the 2017 German elections and was linked to Russia's attempt to influence the elections.[20]

German authorities estimate that the cyber operations began on April 30, when German parliamentarians received an email that was constructed to appear as if it were sent from an official UN account (the sender's address had the extension @un.org) when in reality the email was sent from APT 28. The email was titled "Ukraine conflict with Russia leaves economy in ruins" and referred recipients to a link to a UN bulletin. The link led to a fabricated UN page that installed a Trojan on the computer of the mail's recipient, which provided a backdoor into the Bundestag. The hackers also used XTunnel, the same malware that was employed in the DNC cyber operation in the United States, discussed in chapter 5. The intruders' timing was intentional. The next day, May 1, was a holiday and the Bundestag IT team had the day off. On that day, APT 28 infiltrated the Bundestag networks, uploaded additional malware, including Mimikatz, which is used to perform searches for administrator passwords, and created official access to the Bundestag networks that enabled it to appear as a regular user.[21]

In April and May 2015, APT 28 implanted malware in at least 25 places in the Bundestag's network that provided it with access to over 12,000 users and 5,600 computers. The APT stole over 16 gigabytes of data—mailboxes and hard drives from at least sixteen parliamentarians' offices, including the office of Chancellor Merkel and Vice President of the Bundestag Johannes Singhammer, a member of the Christian Social Union (Christlich-Soziale Union, or CSU) party, a sister party to the CDU. As a result of the attack, the Bundestag network was shut down for four days. News reports cited an unpublished analysis from 2016, which indicated that intrusions of this type were likely directly authorized by the office of President Putin.[22]

Germany's Federal Office for Information Security (Bundesamt für Sicherheit in der Informationstechnik, or BSI) emergency team finally removed the last known APT 28 malware from the Bundestag servers and shut down APT 28's access to the Bundestag on May 20, 2015. The cyber intruders siphoned data from the network until the last day. Although the emergency team could identify most of the data that was exfiltrated during the intrusion, the Bundestag system at that time was set to record network traffic for seven days, and it then would be deleted. Because of that system, it is not known what data was exfiltrated during the first seven days the intruders had access to the Bundestag's network.[23]

In the months preceding the 2017 German elections, German officials speculated that the GRU could release some of the data stolen through the Bundestag intrusion in an attempt to influence the outcome of the elections.[24] Germany's chief of domestic intelligence, for example, stated that the intrusion was a component of a Russian campaign in which Russia "is trying to generate information that can be used for disinformation or for influencing operations."[25] The publicly available evidence validates this hypothesis. Adhering to the pattern observed during the 2016 U.S. elections and the 2017 French elections, in January 13, 2017, unknown individuals registered two websites, btleaks.info and btleaks.org, whose designation pattern matched that of APT 28's previous websites used to publicize exfiltrated information from the DNC and the Macron campaign— DCleaks.com in reference to the documents leaked from the DNC intrusion and emleaks in reference to Macron's party En Marche. Judging by the name of the websites (*bt* in the name of the websites stands for Bundestag), they were likely to be used to post any information stolen from the 2015 Bundestag intrusion.[26]

This type of election interference seems to be potentially more effective and, thus, more likely than an attack on Germany's political infrastructure. Germany does not use electronic voting machines and uses paper ballots instead. Computers are used to aggregate the data but the system used for that is encrypted and not connected to the internet, which makes cyber operations against some components of the political IT infrastructure unlikely.[27]

Based on the available data, the types of cyber operations attributed to Russia were launched against the facilitating infrastructure components indicated in figure 9.1.

ATTRIBUTION OF THE CONDUCTED CYBER ATTACKS

BSI attributed the series of spear-phishing emails that targeted German political parties to APT 28 and Germany's domestic intelligence agency, the Federal Office for the Protection of the Constitution (Bundesamt für Verfassungsschutz, or BfV), also attributed the 2015 cyber intrusion into Germany's Bundestag to Russia's APT 28.[28] Applying APT 28's operational pattern observed during the DNC hack and the 2016 U.S. presidential elections to Germany, some German officials and experts inferred that Russia's APTs may be intended to use documents obtained through the 2015 Bundestag intrusion to influence

FIGURE 9.1 Russia's Political Hack Map Associated with the 2017 German Elections

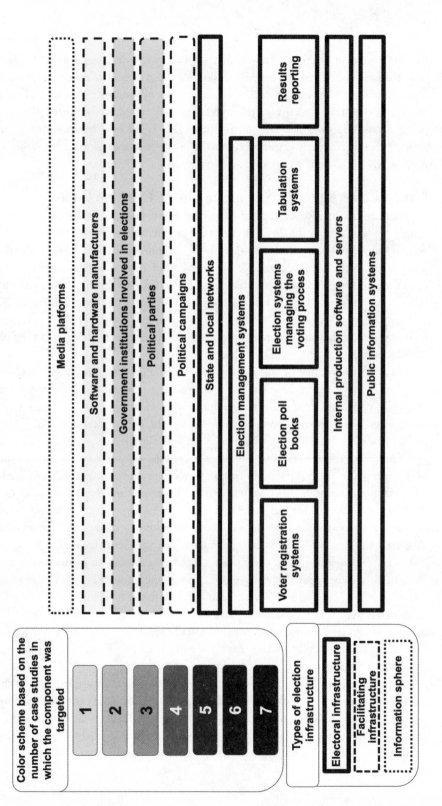

the 2017 German elections.[29] Some analysts, however, hypothesized that Russia's APT may not have conducted the cyber intrusion for the purposes of collecting compromising information. Similar to the case of Russia's cyber operations in Norway, discussed in chapter 6, the main objective of the Bundestag hack may have been to collect data on personal positions on topics relevant to Russia that could help Moscow during negotiations.[30] In this context the intrusion may be considered an espionage operation whose purpose was not directly to gather data relevant to the 2017 elections.

Media Coverage and Social Activities: The Lisa Case

Expectations that the Russian government may release documents obtained through the Bundestag hack during the 2017 elections did not materialize. As of March 2021, there was no known publication of such data. Even without leaked information, the Russian government likely employed a range of other known tools that pertain to the types of tactics used during information warfare campaigns. Prior to the 2017 elections, Russian state-sponsored media outlets focused their narratives on criticizing Chancellor Merkel and her party's policies while circulating positive coverage about AfD. Such narratives can be interpreted as the Russian government's attempt to influence the German population through strategic messaging, as described in chapter 1.[31]

To assess the volume of Russian-sponsored media coverage during Russia's information warfare campaign against Germany in this period, figure 9.2 displays the number of articles published by the German language version of *Sputnik News*, called *Sputnik Deutschland*, that mention the main party led by Chancellor Merkel, the CDU, as well as the main party known to have developed ties with the Russian government, the AfD.

The aim of the analysis is to examine the presence or absence of significant increase of coverage about the two parties during and after the cyber operations against the Bundestag that may have been associated with Russia's intentions to influence the 2017 German elections. The timeline for the analysis, therefore, is January 30, 2015, to December 24, 2017.[32] The period starts three months before the known date of the intrusion of the Bundestag in April 2015 and ends three months after the German elections in September 2017. The analysis shows that there was no significant increase in media coverage before or during the cyber operation. There is a spike in media coverage around election day (September 24, 2017), which is expected and similar to the media spikes in Russian state-sponsored media observed during the 2016 U.S. and 2017 French elections. Unlike Russia's media coverage after the U.S., Montenegrin, and French elections, there was no notable increase in Russian media coverage about the two parties in the months after the German elections.

An examination of the Russian state-sponsored media coverage in the month after the elections shows that *Sputnik Deutschland* lauded the "brilliant" entry of AfD into the parliament, while pointing the voter support lost by the CDU.[33] The Russian-sponsored media interpreted the election outcome as a symptom of a divided German society and as an indicator of diminishing support for Chancellor Merkel's refugee policy, which "was finally voted out."[34]

FIGURE 9.2 Russian State-Sponsored Media Coverage

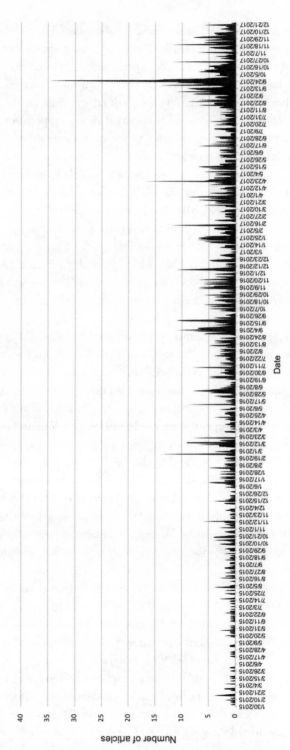

Number of articles

Date

■ Total coverage of CDU and AfD

The absence of increased volume of coverage about the CDU and the AfD in the months after the elections may be due to the fact that the main topics Russian state-sponsored media focused on were not necessarily articles about the two parties but divisive issues that both parties had clear and opposing positions on. For example, Germany's refugee and immigration policy was arguably the most critical issue on the political agenda for the federal elections. CDU and AfD supported diverging positions on the topic, with Chancellor Merkel's party advocating for a more open Germany while AfD advocated for restrictions on immigration access.[35] German society was divided over Germany's decision to accept a large number of immigrants from the Middle East. Immigration policy transformed into a wedge issue during the 2017 German federal elections and influenced the election outcome in favor of Chancellor Merkel's critics.[36]

The author attempted to examine the coverage of these topics by *Sputnik Deutschland* in the studied period—however, as of February 2, 2021, the official website of *Sputnik Deutschland* has been inaccessible, which precludes any data collection and analysis of the media coverage.[37] Based on information displayed on the website of *Sputnik News*, the German version of *Sputnik News* seems to have been replaced with the media SNA News.[38]

Russian-language bot accounts on Twitter amplified pro-AfD messages and concerns about election manipulation. The messages retweeted by the bots encouraged German citizens to monitor the election process due to possible election fraud, suggesting the potential for voter manipulation that could cast doubts on the legitimacy of the election outcome.[39] The accounts, however, were very few in comparison to accounts amplifying divisive political messages during the 2016 U.S. elections and did not seem to have a significant impact on the voting campaign, judging by the number of their followers and shares of their content on social media.[40] A BuzzFeed investigation shed light on the potential Russian involvement in a pro-AfD social media campaign by publicizing information from an interview with a Russian hacker who claimed that he was a member of a thirty-one-member group of hackers who amplified pro-AfD messages. Similar to the case of the 2017 French elections, however, it remains unclear whether the Twitter campaign was conducted under the guidance of an organization affiliated with the Russian government.[41]

A vivid example of the connection between the Russian government and disinformation campaigns was the 2016 Lisa case. The case refers to the story that developed around a thirteen-year-old ethnic Russian girl named Lisa, who claimed to have been kidnapped and violated by Muslim migrants after she temporarily disappeared in January 2016. The German police swiftly discovered that the story was fabricated and revealed the real story that Lisa escaped from her family to meet with her boyfriend. Regardless of the fact that the narrative about Lisa's assault by migrants was debunked, Russian-state Channel One (Perviy Kanal) broadcast the story. Russian foreign media, including *RT Deutsch*, *RT*, and *Sputnik News*, circulated the story further. The story spread over social media and protests in Germany were organized over Facebook. The protests involved members of the ethnic Russian minority in Germany and neo-Nazi groups. Russian media covered the demonstrations, which then brought them to the attention of German media.[42]

Russian government organizations also got involved in the story. Foreign Minister Sergey Lavrov contributed to the growing tensions surrounding the incident by himself commenting on the case.[43] The foreign minister criticized Germany's government for its management of the case and referred to the alleged victim as "our Lisa." The Russian Embassy in London amplified Lavrov's message and strengthened the legitimacy of the case by publicizing it on the embassy's Twitter account.[44] Lavrov's involvement and that of other senior Russian diplomats provided a layer of legitimacy to the story and elevated it to international attention.

The amplification of the false narrative through Russian media and Russia's senior leadership likely contributed to galvanizing the ethnic Russian population and the subsequent nationwide protests in Germany regarding the Lisa case against Angela Merkel's immigration policies. One of the protests took place in front of Merkel's chancellery in Berlin on January 23.[45] The Lisa case and Russia's involvement could have influenced the German constituency and raised the profile of AfD because immigration policy was a prominent issue in Germany at that time.[46]

Russia's Interference in Germany: Associated Factors and Mapping the Information Warfare Campaign Using CHAOS

This section applies the CHAOS framework to the case of Russia's information warfare against the German federal elections in September 2017 (see fig. 9.3). It visualizes chronologically the main cyber operation attributed to Russian state-sponsored actors, the key social activities, and the main known activities of the Russian government that may have influenced German voters' preferences, specifically in favor of AfD. Table 9.1 displays the present and absent elements of the QCA framework in Germany.

TABLE 9.1 Factors That Could Be Associated with the Initiation of the Particular Type of Cyber Operations Observed against the Bundestag in 2015

Target	Type of cyber op (CIA)	Disputes in relations				Spike in media coverage before cyber ops	If cyber ops during elections		NATO member en route	NATO member	Frm. Eastern Bloc state	Frm. USSR state
		Polit	Soc	Econ	Mil		Anti-Ru candidate	Pro-Ru candidate				
Germany (2015)	C	1	1	1	0	0	1	1	0	1	1 (half)	0

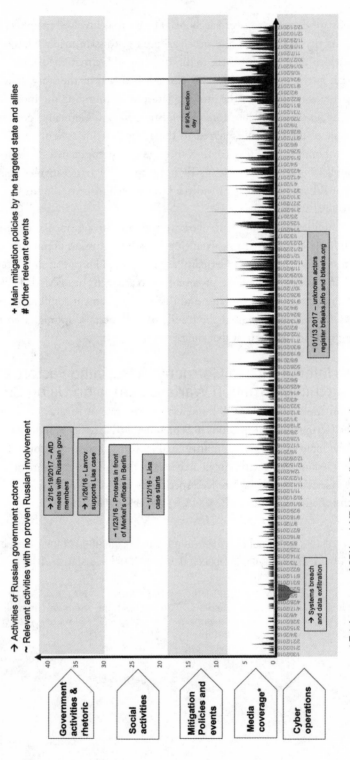

FIGURE 9.3 Russia's CHAOS in Germany in 2015–17

→ Activities of Russian government actors
~ Relevant activities with no proven Russian involvement

+ Main mitigation policies by the targeted state and allies
# Other relevant events

→ 2/18-19/2017 – AfD meets with Russian gov. members

→ 1/26/16 - Lavrov supports Lisa case

~ 1/23/16 - Protests in front of Merkel's offices in Berlin

~ 1/12/16 - Lisa case starts

9/24, Election day

~ 01/13 2017 – unknown actors register btleaks.info and btleaks.org

→ Systems breach and data exfiltration

* Total coverage of CDU and AfD in *Sputnik Deutschland*

Government activities & rhetoric

Social activities

Mitigation Policies and events

Media coverage*

Cyber operations

Germany's Policy Response

The German government introduced a number of policies to prevent further Russian cyber operations against German political entities similar to Russia's 2015 intrusions. Germany also took measures to prepare for other Russian government activities that may influence the 2017 German elections.

Immediate Response

Germany's policy responses to the 2015 cyber intrusion included immediate responses to mitigate the effects of the intrusion and the creation of a long-term strategy to improve resilience against cyber operations and strategic messaging campaigns. The German government established a policy to respond to Russia's actions by publicly exposing and holding the Russian government accountable through international recognition of its culpability for the attacks and appeal for sanctions.

Swifter interagency communication and exchange of data to expose the intrusion during the management of the case could have ensured faster response. As in the case of the DNC, when the FBI had evidence to indicate the potential intrusion, and interagency communication would have facilitated a prompter discovery of the cyber operations, in the case of Germany, a foreign cybersecurity company and BSI had information that could have ensured an earlier response or even prevention of the cyber intrusion.[47] On May 12, Germany's domestic intelligence agency informed the Bundestag and the BSI of the intrusion. The message was not received by the BSI emergency team until three days later, on May 15, because of bureaucratic delays, and a BSI team traveled from Bonn to Berlin to address the intrusion.[48] The time between discovering the intrusion and the BSI's response could have been curtailed through more efficient interagency communication.

Furthermore, the BSI maintained a list of approximately 160,000 servers identified as suspicious. The BSI was aware of the server that APT 28 used in this particular attack, and on April 13, two weeks in advance of the Bundestag's intrusion, the BSI blocked data emanating from that server. The action protected Germany's executive branch, but because the BSI is not responsible for protecting the Bundestag, it did not share information about the server with the IT defense team at the Bundestag. Had the BSI shared that information before April, it likely could have prevented or significantly minimized the effects of the intrusion.[49]

General Policies Enhancing Germany's Resilience to Russian Information Warfare

A variety of measures taken by the German government and nongovernmental actors since the 2015 Bundestag intrusion and specifically around the 2017 elections likely improved Germany's ability to withstand Russian operations and may have deterred more active Russian interference than was observed.

Since the 2015 cyber intrusion, Germany has adopted a series of broader policies to enhance its resilience to Russian cyber and disinformation interference. Some of these policies include establishing a cyber defense center, as well as creating the Cyber and Information Space Command as a branch of the armed forces.[50] In November 2016, Germany adopted a cybersecurity strategy overseen by the BSI. Under the guidelines of the strategy, rapid-reaction cyber forces have been created across various government institutions, including within the BSI. They are tasked to respond to cyber operations against government and critical infrastructure.[51]

Nongovernmental organizations in Germany are also contributing to improving the country's resilience against information warfare by releasing publications on Russia's various activities and raising awareness among the population. Germany's research institutes such as the Stiftung Neue Verantwortung, the Stiftung Wissenschaft und Politik, and the German Council on Foreign Relations conduct high-quality research on Russia's interference, which is a necessary step to understanding the threat such interference poses and to designing effective policies to counter it. Independent organizations such as Correctiv monitor the media space and report on disinformation.[52] In addition to measures enhancing cybersecurity, media outlets created fact-checking teams to address potential disinformation.[53]

Specific Policies Prior to the 2017 Elections and Beyond

In the months prior to the September 2017 elections, there was a broad consensus among German federal agencies and experts that Russia was likely to interfere in the elections to delegitimize the election results and the democratic process.[54] The German authorities expected Russian interference and, in addition to enhancing the resilience of their networks and preparing to debunk disinformation, they sent signals to Moscow that such interference would incur damaging consequences for the Russian government.

Before the elections, German officials publicly warned Russia against interfering and hinted that such Russian activities would face consequences. Germany's president, Frank Walter Steinmeier, for example, warned, "If Moscow interferes with the Bundestag elections . . . , that would be damaging for both sides." Chancellor Merkel also raised the issue of possible Russian interference directly with President Putin during a meeting in Sochi, as did other Chancellery representatives.[55] Such public warnings are deliberate and aim to act as deterrence to possible future Russian cyber and disinformation interference, and prepare the German public for possible responses in case they occur.[56]

Policies to enhance resilience included regular penetration tests of the computer networks of the federal election authority. The Bundestag and party campaigns further consulted with specialists on cyber hygiene to minimize the potential success of cyber intrusions.[57] In 2016, all German parties competing in the 2017 elections except for AfD agreed to refrain from using paid trolls or bots in their election campaigns.[58] In June 2017, Germany's parliament passed a law authorizing that social media companies can be fined up to 50 million euros if they failed to remove content that is obviously illegal within 24 hours of its publication or, for less-obviously illegal content, failed to assess and remove it within seven days.[59]

Soon after the German secret service discovered the creation of the two websites btleaks.org and btleaks.info in 2017, the German domestic intelligence agency was tasked with monitoring these websites hourly for any published information in expectation that the websites would be used to leak information stolen from the 2015 Bundestag intrusion. These efforts, in combination with an established "gentleman's agreement" among the competing parties not to exploit leaked information against each other, may have deterred the Kremlin from posting any of the exfiltrated information.[60]

Social media companies also prepared to counter Russian disinformation interference in the 2017 elections. For example, Facebook announced it increased monitoring of its platform for malicious accounts and removed thousands of fake accounts prior to the election to prevent the spread of disinformation.[61]

In 2020, enabled by an EU sanctions framework passed in 2019, Germany revived the issue of the 2015 hack again. In April 2020, Germany's federal public prosecutor identified Russian Dmitri Badin—suspected of being a military intelligence officer—as the individual responsible for the 2015 intrusion and issued a warrant for his arrest. On May 28, Germany announced it would call for EU sanctions against him in response to the 2015 hack. The United States had already indicted Badin in 2018 for the 2016 U.S. election interference.[62]

The Effectiveness of Russia's Cyber Operations and Information Warfare Campaign

Having the benefit of forewarning from Russia's operations in the United States and France, German officials anticipated Russian interference in the September 2017 federal elections and introduced policies to effectively counter it. Prior to the elections, actors linked to the Russian government were involved in a series of activities that negatively impacted Chancellor Merkel's party and reputation. In this case, a 2015 cyber intrusion of the Bundestag followed a similar pattern to the 2016 DNC intrusions and revealed Russia's malicious intent and readiness to interfere in the domestic affairs of NATO states. German officials and experts hypothesized that an objective of the intrusion may have been to influence the elections and anticipated a data release of documents that Russia's APT 28 exfiltrated during the intrusion of the Bundestag. The creation of websites linguistically similar to the ones created during the 2016 U.S. elections and the 2017 French elections, which Russian actors used in the 2016 U.S. case to upload the stolen data, corroborate this argument. There is a possibility that these websites were a false flag operation and may have been created by another cyber group not related to Russia. If, however, the websites were created by a Russian APT, this would suggest a similar modus operandi to previous Russian interference, pointing to a deliberate Russian state-sponsored operation. Germany's multilayered strategy to build resilience against further Russian cyber intrusions and disinformation campaigns may have contributed to Russia's decision to diverge from its previous pattern and not release documents stolen from the Bundestag (as it did in the case of the U.S. elections).

In addition to potentially considering the release of information obtained through the hack of the Bundestag, Russia attempted to affect the election process through its state-sponsored media in Germany. Russian media outlets expressed clear preference for AfD in their coverage during the election period, which may have increased the support for AfD, especially among the Russian immigrant population in Germany. One of the most visible examples of the effectiveness of Russian disinformation efforts at the time was exemplified in the Lisa case. It revealed the connection between Russian disinformation operations spread through Russian media outlets and the highest level of Russia's diplomatic echelons, exposing another thread in the complex coordination mechanisms of the Kremlin's interference campaigns.

Despite increased government and public awareness in Germany, the Russian government still supported several lines of activities that shaped its information warfare campaign against Chancellor Merkel's policies. As in the case of France, the Russian government developed relations with German political parties sympathetic to Moscow's foreign policy agenda. Such connections may have increased the appeal of these parties among the ethnic Russian population in Germany and may have exerted an effect on the voting results. Not only did the AfD gain seats in the parliament for the first time since World War II, but it also collected the third-largest share of votes.

10

Cross-Country Analysis and Effectiveness of Russia's Cyber Operations and Information Warfare Campaigns

aving presented a summary of each case in the previous chapters, this book now aggregates the data compiled through the QCA framework, the Hack Map, and CHAOS in each case and offers a cross-country comparison. The chapter identifies the factors that are most likely associated with Russian choices about which types of cyber operations to launch against targeted political infrastructure. The chapter then analyzes the data about the particular targeted political infrastructure components across each country and compiles a Hack Map showing the frequency and type of components that Russian state-sponsored cyber actors targeted the most across the seven case studies. The chapter proceeds by outlining commonalities and differences in Russia's information warfare playbook derived from the visualization of information warfare campaigns through the CHAOS framework and discusses the role and integration of cyber operations within Russia's information warfare campaigns. The chapter concludes by offering an analysis of the effectiveness of Russia's cyber operations and information warfare campaigns, based on Russia's most likely short-term and long-term objectives.

Cross-Country QCA Analysis and Main Conclusions

Table 10.1 represents an aggregate visualization of the QCA factors present and absent across all included case studies of Russian state-sponsored cyber interference. All cases of cyber operations attributed to APTs linked to the Russian government can be categorized as primarily either availability or confidentiality compromises. In the cases of the United States and France, Russian APTs were accused of launching a few instances of integrity or availability attacks, and as these attacks represented a relatively small part of the other type of cyber operations in each case, they are considered as secondary and not listed in the table. Table 10.1 groups the cases on the basis of the primary types of cyber operations attributed to Russian state-sponsored cyber threat actors in each country. Therefore, Estonia, Bulgaria, and Montenegro constitute the group that has been targeted primarily by availability attacks, and the United States, Norway, France, and Germany constitute the second group that has been mainly targeted by confidentiality compromises.

An examination of the factors potentially associated with the initiation of availability or confidentiality compromises reveal a few notable patterns. According to the data, political tensions with Russia are present across all countries examined in this analysis. This observation, however, cannot serve as definitive evidence that the presence of political tensions across all cases is a prerequisite for Russian cyber operations. To draw such a conclusion, the analysis would have to include an examination of cases where the Russian government did not launch cyber operations, and such cases are not included in this analysis. Table 10.1 also shows that social, economic, or military tensions are present across some of the cases and do not reveal any clear patterns across the different types of cyber operations. A spike in Kremlin-supported media coverage before the launch of cyber operations is present only in the case of Estonia, which, again, is not sufficient to demonstrate a potential correlation between increased media coverage and the start of a cyber operation. The presence or absence of political candidates with pro-Russian or anti-Russian agendas also does not appear to be a reliable indicator that could be associated with the initiation of a certain type of cyber operation. Whether the targeted state is a NATO member, a NATO member en route, or a former member of the Soviet Union also

TABLE 10.1 Factors That Could Be Associated with the Initiation of Different Russian State-Sponsored Cyber Operations

Target	Type of cyber op (CIA)	Disputes in relations				Spike in media coverage before cyber ops	If cyber ops during elections		NATO member en route	NATO member	Frm. Eastern Bloc state	Frm. USSR state
		Polit	Soc	Econ	Mil		Anti-Ru candidate	Pro-Ru candidate				
Estonia (2007)	A	1	1	0	0	1	0	0	0	1	1	1
Bulgaria (2015)	A	1	0	1	1	0	1	1	0	1	1	0
Montenegro (2016)	A	1	1	1	1	0	1	1	1	0	1	0
U.S. (2016)	C	1	0	1	0	0	1	1	0	1	0	0
Norway (2016)	C	1	0	1	1	0	0	0	0	1	0	0
France (2017)	C	1	0	1	0	0	1	1	0	1	0	0
Germany (2017)	C	1	1	1	0	0	1	1	0	1	0	0

does not appear to be a reliable indicator that is consistently present or absent across cases of either availability or confidentiality compromises.

The only variable that seems to be consistently present across cases of availability attacks and consistently absent across cases of confidentiality attacks is whether or not the targeted state was a member of the Eastern Bloc. The data suggests that Russian cyber threat actors tend to launch availability attacks primarily against former Eastern Bloc states, which in this analysis are Estonia, Bulgaria, and Montenegro. Confidentiality attacks are the preferred type of cyber operations against NATO members that are not former members of the Eastern Bloc, which in this analysis are the United States, Norway, France, and Germany. Availability attacks lead to disruption and, hence, appear more brazen and hostile, while confidentiality compromises are less disruptive to infrastructure and tend to be more subtle in comparison. This suggests that Russian state-sponsored APTs are likely to be more aggressive in cyberspace in countries that were members of the Eastern Bloc and more cautious in their operations against Western NATO members. The reason for this more unrestrained confrontation toward members of the former Eastern Bloc may be due to the perception of the Russian decision-making elite that Russia's near abroad is a zone of privileged interests for the Russian government where Moscow is historically and culturally entitled to exert more control.[1]

Cross-Country Hack Map Analysis and Main Conclusions

Figure 10.1 represents the Hack Map of all political infrastructure components targeted by Russian APTs across all examined cases. The analysis reveals that Russian APTs are more likely to target facilitating rather than electoral IT components in NATO member states or countries that have received official invitations to join the alliance. Russian APTs are known to have targeted electoral components of the political infrastructure only twice—in the case of the 2016 U.S. elections and in the case of Bulgaria's 2015 elections. In the case of the United States, the evidence suggests that Russian APTs did not attempt to disrupt voter registration systems, while in the case of Bulgaria, Russia's cyber operations were much bolder and resulted in temporarily disrupting the operations of a part of Bulgaria's election reporting infrastructure. This observation corroborates the conclusion from the QCA framework that stipulated that Russian state-sponsored activities tend to be more aggressive in countries that are former Eastern Bloc members.

Figure 10.1 further reveals that the most-targeted facilitating infrastructure across the examined cases is political parties. In all cases, the targeted political parties supported policies unfavorable to Russia's strategic interests. Therefore, anti-Russian parties appear to be the most likely targets. The analysis shows that the second-most-frequent targets of Russian APTs are government institutions involved in elections. The types of operations in most of these cases were confidentiality compromises, and they were likely conducted to gain access to information that Russian state-sponsored actors could subsequently leak or use for other purposes, likely aiming to exert psychological, rather than technical, effects over decision makers or the broader population.

FIGURE 10.1 Russia's Political Hack Map: Targeted Political Infrastructure across Cases

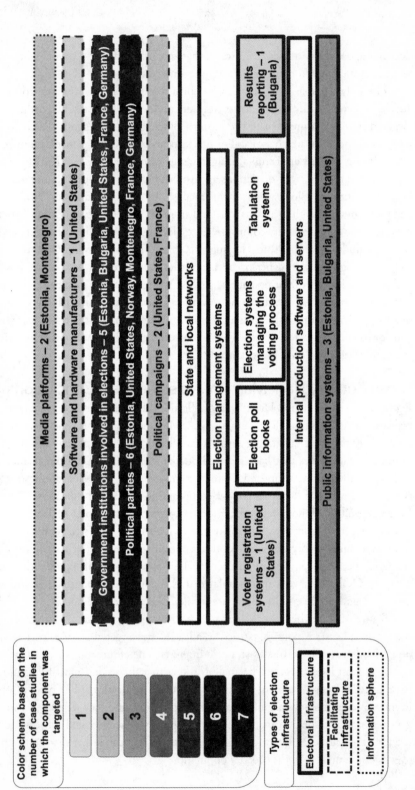

Cross-Country CHAOS Analysis and Main Conclusions

The application of the CHAOS framework across the seven cases reveals a number of insights about the range and integration of Russian information warfare activities. An overview of the seven CHAOS figures applied to each case reveals that the range of activities tends to be broader and more aggressive in countries that were former members of the Eastern Bloc, which is a conclusion in line with the observed bolder types of cyber operations in these cases. The QCA analysis showed Russian APTs typically launch large-scale DDoS attacks against government infrastructure in Estonia, Bulgaria, and Montenegro, while the same APTs conduct limited DDoS attacks and mainly phishing campaigns and other confidentiality compromises in the United States, Norway, France, and Germany. The two examples of the widest range of Russian information warfare activities are Estonia, where the Russian government supported economic, political, social, media, and cyber operations in 2007, and Montenegro, where the Russian government supported government, economic, media, and cyber operations, as well as a failed coup d'état plot against the pro-NATO government of Montenegro. The case of Bulgaria further complements our understanding of the range of hostile measures that the Russian government is willing to undertake to achieve its goals. A series of explosions in weapons facilities and two failed poisoning attempts paint a glaring picture of a Russian regime that displays little to no restraint in aggressive intelligence operations, at least in part to convey a message, even in countries that are members of NATO.

THE C IN CHAOS: CROSS-CASE ANALYSIS OF RUSSIA'S CYBER OPERATIONS

A cross-country analysis of Russia's cyber operations suggests that the Russian government primarily uses cyber operations against political infrastructure either to collect intelligence on political parties or candidates competing in elections using phishing campaigns as in the cases of the United States, France, and Germany, or to disrupt election processes on election day using primarily DDoS attacks as in the cases of Bulgaria and Montenegro.

When examining the role of these cyber operations as part of Russia's broader information warfare operations it becomes clear that the motivations behind these operations are quite diverse. *Russia does not use cyber operations against political infrastructure for the sole purposes of influencing the election process or outcome. Broader objectives include applying coercion on the government of the targeted state in an effort to change that government's policy on issues that may not be related to the elections.* The case of Russian DDoS attacks against Estonia and Bulgaria demonstrate this point. Another objective is breaching networks for the purposes of espionage and the collection of information on various political positions relevant to the Russian government as in the case of Norway.

THE H IN CHAOS: CROSS-CASE ANALYSIS OF RUSSIAN-SPONSORED MEDIA COVERAGE

A cross-country analysis of the Russian-sponsored media coverage of each information warfare campaign reveals several trends. The examined coverage typically played an important role in disseminating disinformation and strategic messaging campaigns. The media echoed the positions of the Russian government and supported the pro-Russian candidates in cases where the information warfare operations were conducted during election periods. In cases where countries held elections, media coverage tended to spike on election day as in the cases of the United States, France, Germany, Montenegro, and Bulgaria.

In the case of the 2016 U.S. elections, the 2016 Montenegro elections, and the 2017 French elections, there was also increased media coverage about the political candidates in the month after the elections in comparison to the month prior to the elections. Such coverage was typically divisive and inflammatory. It was negative toward the anti-Russian candidates and positive toward the pro-Russian ones. In some cases, the media coverage contained general allegations of voter fraud and attempted to amplify the perception of illegitimate elections, especially in the cases of France and Montenegro, where the anti-Russian candidates won. This finding is in line with Russia's information warfare doctrine described in chapter 1, which stipulates that Russia conducts information warfare continuously. Moscow's attempts to sow popular distrust in governance would not stop after the elections, which are only one event, but would continue after the elections when Russia may attempt to exploit socially divisive themes that could increase suspicion in democratic institutions and drive communities further apart.

The trend of increased media coverage in the months after an election in the targeted state are not confirmed in the cases of Germany and Bulgaria. In the case of Germany, there was no observed increase in media coverage after the elections, but the narrative remained negative toward Chancellor Merkel and positive toward Russia's preferred AfD. The lack of increased postelection media coverage in Germany may be due to the fact that in Germany a topic that emerged as a key wedge issue among the population was immigration. *Sputnik Deutschland* may have chosen to amplify coverage of that issue rather than coverage of Chancellor Merkel or AfD. Due to the fact that the German version of *Sputnik News* was taken down in the beginning of 2021, the author could not perform an analysis of the volume of coverage on immigration issues in that period to confirm or reject this theory. In the case of the Bulgarian elections in 2015, there was an increase in media coverage about the competing parties on election day but not afterward, and that coverage did not appear to be as negative toward the less-preferred Russian candidate as in the cases of the United States and Montenegro. This finding is in line with the hypothesis that Russia's cyber operations on election day may not have been conducted with the purpose to influence the election process but to send a signal to the Bulgarian government regarding its weapons export policy and other issues important to the Kremlin, which are unrelated to the elections.

Overall Effectiveness of Russia's Cyber Operations and Information Warfare Campaigns: Is Being the Top Villain Worth It?

Table 10.2 summarizes the effectiveness of Russia's cyber operations and broader information warfare campaigns in each examined country based on the main identified short-term and long-term goals of the Russian government described in the analysis of each case study. The table identifies the short-term and the long-term effectiveness of Russia's state-sponsored activities and ascribes success, failure, or "unclear" to each category based on the evidence collected in each case. The table identifies some activities as accomplishing short-term success but long-term failure if they temporarily achieved their objective. For example, DDoS attacks are assessed as a short-term success if these attacks caused a temporary disruption to people, processes, and technology as opposed to a short-term nuisance with no actual consequence. DDoS attacks are typically assessed as a long-term failure when they successfully disrupted communications and operations but their effects were mitigated by the targeted state relatively swiftly. The cyber adversary is likely well aware of these types of short- and long-term effects, but the analysis still includes both types to accentuate the typically short-term utility of DDoS attacks. In a few cases the table lists the effectiveness as unclear because of the lack of robust research to prove the precise effect of the activities. In these cases, the absence of analyses that can ascertain the level of influence that Russia's information warfare activities exerted equates to the unclear outcome. In each of these cases, given sufficient resources and time, researchers could theoretically conduct a number of studies to assess the extent to which Russia's interference may have affected the population and processes in each targeted state. These studies could include surveys, randomized controlled trials (RCTs), and psychological experiments. The results of these studies could be quite valuable to policy makers of NATO member states. For example, a randomized control trial can be used as the methodological foundation for a study assessing the potential impact of the documents leaked as a result of the DNC hack on voter preferences and behavior in the 2016 U.S. elections. The outcome of these analyses may provide clarity about the relative (lack of) impact of Russia's

TABLE 10.2 Effectiveness of Russia's Information Warfare Campaigns across Cases

Case	Activity	Objectives	Effectiveness
Estonia			
	Cyber operations	Disrupt communications and operations	Short-term success, long-term failure
	Information warfare campaign	Bronze Soldier remains in the center of Tallinn	Failure
	Information warfare campaign	Harm Estonia economically and politically	Short-term success, long-term failure
Bulgaria			
	Cyber operations	Disrupt communications and operations	Short-term success, long-term failure
	Information warfare campaign	Coerce the Bulgarian government into changing its policy on weapons exports and other issues	Failure

(continued)

TABLE 10.2 (*continued*)

Case	Activity	Objectives	Effectiveness
United States			
	Cyber operations	Exfiltrate information	Success
	Cyber operations as part of information warfare	Integrate exfiltrated information into strategic messaging	Success
	Information warfare campaign	Deepen societal divisions and distrust in institutions	Unclear
	Information warfare campaign	Influence the election outcome in favor of Donald Trump	Unclear
Norway			
	Cyber operations	Exfiltrate information	Failure
Montenegro			
	Cyber operations	Disrupt communications and operations	Short-term success, long-term failure
	Information warfare campaign	Prevent Montenegro from joining NATO	Failure
	Information warfare campaign	Harm Montenegro economically and politically, including through a coup d'état	Short-term success, long-term failure
	Information warfare campaign	Influence the election process in favor of the Democratic Front	Success
France			
	Cyber operations	Exfiltrate information	Success
	Cyber operations as part of information warfare	Integrate exfiltrated information into strategic messaging	Failure
	Information warfare campaign	Influence the election outcome in favor of Le Pen	Failure
	Information warfare campaign	Deepen societal divisions and distrust in institutions	Unclear
Germany			
	Cyber operations	Exfiltrate information	Success
	Cyber operations as part of information warfare	Integrate exfiltrated information into strategic messaging	Failure
	Information warfare campaign	Influence the election process in favor of AfD	Success
	Information warfare campaign	Deepen societal divisions and distrust in institutions	Unclear

various information warfare activities. Decision makers can use such results to prioritize which types of Russian activities that may occur in the future they should address, and what policies to deter and mitigate these potential activities appear commensurate with their potential impact.[2]

The summarized information reveals a mixed scorecard of success and failure. Russia's cyber operations across all cases appear successful in achieving Russia's most likely short-term objectives. The caveat of this conclusion is that the case studies and specific cyber operations examined in this analysis largely determine this outcome. In each case of confidentiality compromises, Russian APTs experienced numerous failures in attempting to breach political infrastructure networks and eventually achieved success. In addition, there are likely numerous cases of Russian cyber operations against other government political infrastructure that this study does not cover due to lack of publicized information on these cases. If this study takes into account all these failed attempts and unknown cases of cyber operations, the assessment on the effectiveness of Russia's cyber power may change.

Russia's overall information warfare campaigns, however, seem to have achieved only partial success. Yet, the possible successes, although some of them are methodologically difficult to ascertain, may be sufficient to justify the failures and prompt the Russian government to continue using and refining its information warfare toolbox. Furthermore, the lack of clear red lines set by NATO members and of significant costs to the Russian government in cases of failures of its information warfare operations likely affects the calculus of the Kremlin and emboldens it to continue its information warfare onslaught. Even in cases where the likelihood of success is low, the likelihood that the costs to Moscow will be low as well may also prompt it to proceed with using its interference playbook. The cyber operations are a part of the information warfare campaigns and, therefore, the analysis shows that in some cases they have not been successful in achieving Russia's desired objectives. Russia uses cyber operations in combination with strategic messaging campaigns but with mixed success. Such integration worked during 2016 U.S. elections but was unsuccessful in France and Germany. The Russian information warfare campaign may have also achieved partial success in Germany and Montenegro, where pro-Russian parties gained seats in their respective parliaments.

Regardless of whether Russia's information warfare operations achieved their short-term and long-term goals, the media hype about Russia's cyber operations and related activities by itself serves Russia and could be considered as another benefit to the Kremlin. The furor over GRU's interference in the 2016 U.S. elections, for example, went a long way in building Russia's reputation as a first-class cyber power, which is consistent with Moscow's effort to establish itself as a great power on the world stage.[3] The focus by the French and German leadership on the Russian government and its potential influence over the elections in these two states, as well as the attention by U.S. authorities to the 2018 U.S. midterm and 2020 presidential elections, further directed attention to Moscow's cyber capabilities and perpetuated these debates, while also channeling resources and research toward understanding the TTPs and strategies of the sophisticated cyber bears. Despite the fact that NATO member states and NATO bolstered their cybersecurity policies, and U.S. Cyber Command was led to pursue more offensive operations, Moscow could perceive these developments as partially positive because they give the Kremlin perceived cyber power.[4]

Main Takeaways of the Cross-Case Analysis and the Effectiveness of Russia's CHAOS

The identified cases include a temporal gap in Russia's use of cyber operations and information warfare against NATO members. The first case, which is Russia's DDoS attacks against Estonia, occurred in 2007, while the second case, Russia's cyber operations against Bulgaria, occurred eight years later, in 2015. The subsequent five examined cases occurred within months of each other. Although this research examines only a small number of cases, which methodologically limits the appropriateness of broad generalizations, the resumption of Russian offensive cyber operations in 2015 coincides with a general deterioration of NATO-Russian relations and an increasingly aggressive Russian foreign policy that roughly began with Russia's annexation of Crimea in 2014. In that period, the Russian government also increased its efforts to cultivate technological innovation, improve cyber capabilities, and expand direct recruiting programs, combining will with capacity.[5] In this context, Russia's cyber operations and information warfare campaigns against the West can serve as a barometer of the overall state of NATO-Russian relations over the past fifteen years.

Based on the aggregate analysis, we can draw the following conclusions about Russia's offensive behavior in cyberspace, which confirm the two hypotheses outlined in this book's introduction. The first conclusion confirms the first hypothesis, which stipulates that the case studies will reveal factors that are consistently present across cases of similar types of cyber operations and, hence, are associated with the initiation of these cyber operations. The QCA analysis revealed that the main factor that may be associated with Russia's choice to launch availability attacks or confidentiality compromises is whether or not the targeted state was a member of the Eastern Bloc. In other words, proximity to Russia matters. Russian APTs tend to use large-scale availability attacks against NATO members that were members of the Eastern Bloc and confidentiality compromises against other NATO members.

Second, the Russian government targets mainly facilitating components of the political infrastructure, specifically political parties. Considering the types of operations, the Kremlin appears to launch these operations mainly to exert psychological, rather than technical, effects on the population of the targeted state or its decision makers.

Third, Russia uses cyber operations usually in combination with other information warfare activities to achieve a common objective. This finding confirms the second hypothesis outlined in the introduction, which asserts that the cross-case analysis of Russia's cyber operations reveals a pattern of Moscow's behavior in cyberspace and its integration with other information warfare activities that may be used to improve U.S. policy against Russia's activities. The research revealed that other information warfare activities that Moscow uses include economic sanctions, political rhetoric, strategic messaging, and disinformation. In countries that are former members of the Eastern Bloc, Russia tends to use more aggressive information warfare measures than it does in other NATO nations, such as coup d'états and assassinations. The purposes of Russia's cyber operations are diverse and include manipulating elections, coercing a government into changing its economic or other policy, and collecting data for espionage purposes.

The cross-country analysis further shows that Russia did not achieve all its objectives through information warfare. Despite Russia's onslaught, Estonia relocated the Bronze Soldier, Macron became president in France, Chancellor Merkel won reelection, Norway did not have to mitigate the consequences of any leaked data, Montenegro joined NATO, and Bulgaria continued to export weapons, maintained the direction of its other policy decisions that irked Moscow, and had legitimate local elections. Yet, Russia's information warfare activities may have contributed to a few notable successes. Donald Trump was the U.S. president for four years, while AfD and the Democratic Front gained a pro-Russian vote in the German and Montenegrin parliaments. Another general success for the Russian government is its elevated strategic status as a sophisticated cyber power. For a country that values international status, assuming the position of the top villain in cyberspace carries its own benefit. Unless NATO member states raise the costs of Russia's information warfare activities and enhance their resilience against them, Russia's successes seem sufficient to justify a continuation of Russian information warfare campaigns. The next chapter examines each component of Russia's information warfare playbook and proposes recommendations that the United States and other governments may consider adopting to defend data and democracy from further Russian interference.

11

Policy Recommendations for Defending against Russia's Information Warfare Activities

overnments of NATO member states, including the United States, have made immense progress in introducing policies, creating agencies, and allocating resources to detect, counter, and mitigate the effects of various aspects of Russia's information warfare operations.[1] This chapter, while acknowledging the critical role of these steps in protecting political infrastructure and democratic communities from Russian interference, does not repeat them here and instead focuses on using the data collected from each case examined in this book to highlight the policies that appeared to have been effective in combating Russian interference that governments may consider adopting going forward. This chapter first outlines several recommendations for improving data collection and analysis, and then discusses policies to address the two main components of information warfare: cyber operations and psychological operations, focusing on strategic messaging. It proceeds by outlining policy proposals that address the remaining associated information warfare operations and concludes by offering recommendations for future research.

Improve Data Collection and Knowledge about the Different Information Warfare Activities That the Russian Government Supports

The conclusions of this research and, therefore, the policy recommendations that follow on the basis of these conclusions are only as good as the data available for each case. Collecting data on Russian information warfare activities is a challenging process, constrained by the clandestine nature of most of these operations and the reluctance of targeted entities to share data on particular cyber operations and other activities. To be able to analyze Russian cyber operations, states should publish more information on the cyber operations and the cyber threat actors that have targeted their infrastructure. This would facilitate defenders' ability to understand and identify Russia's cyber playbook, and the TTPs of APTs, which would consequently assist with improving networks' resilience by designing indicators of compromise (IoCs) and geopolitical indicators that defense teams at different organizations can monitor to detect Russian intrusions. This would enhance the knowledge of geopolitical factors and triggers that improve defenders' ability to predict a cyber operation before the point of breach.[2]

Limited availability of data on Russian state-supported accounts on social media platforms and databases of Russian state-sponsored media coverage also hindered the analysis of the case studies. As the research in this book demonstrated, the Russian government uses these platforms to organize protests and polarize constituencies of NATO states. Social media platforms do not widely and readily share such data with researchers, while very few databases collecting Russian state-sponsored media coverage in smaller countries such as Bulgaria, Estonia, and Montenegro exist. Monitoring and collecting data on Russian state-sponsored strategic messaging campaigns on social media platforms beyond Twitter and Facebook would also improve researchers' knowledge of Russian influence. Platforms such as 4chan, local social media apps, and forums specific to each country can provide additional insights into Russian state-sponsored operations. Investigations should also examine potential Kremlin influence on seemingly local groups such as Anonymous in Bulgaria, whose positions closely mirror those of the Russian government.[3]

Another limitation to the data collection efforts was the lack of transparency on financial sources of political parties. In the cases of Bulgaria and Montenegro, political parties suspected of receiving funding from the Russian government are not legally obligated to disclose the origins of their funding. Improving the legal requirements regarding transparency of party financing and connections with foreign governments in these particular countries would facilitate the ability of NATO governments to understand and analyze the full extent of Russian networks of influence on their territories, as well as be a small step toward curtailing such activity.[4]

In addition to ensuring transparency in parties' financing, governments of NATO member states may consider leveling the playing field for various parties and candidates during national, state, and local elections, by supporting online platforms that enable the interaction between political candidates and constituencies without requiring massive financial resources. Online community platforms such as Open Campaign (OC) connect political candidates with their potential voters and enable them to focus on local issues and causes. Through the provision of a low-cost platform for communication and interaction, platforms such as OC ensure that any targeted financing for a particular party or representative is offset by the ability of politicians to access voters directly. OC, which political candidates in the United State and India already use, enables political discourse while eliminating or significantly reducing the need for financial resources required to organize meetings with potential voters, produce campaign materials, and hire professional companies to conduct polls, petitions, and surveys.[5]

More data collection is necessary to shed light on connections between the Russian government and the Russian Orthodox Church, religious groups, and NGOs in NATO states, as well as organizations active in political lobbying, such as the National Rifle Association in the United States.[6]

Besides the need for a more holistic understanding of the various activities of Russian information warfare operations against various NATO members, there is a strong need for analysis to understand the relative effects of Russia's various activities. Such analysis, which was briefly discussed in the previous chapter, could include RCTs that identify the potential effects of various disinformation narratives or different types of cyber operations on the perceptions, opinions, and behaviors of specific constituencies. These studies can identify which types of disinformation narratives are most likely to exert what effects on what types of information consumers. This knowledge can consequently facilitate the introduction of tiered and informed policies that surgically target the elements of Russian information warfare that are likely to cause the most harm.

Address the C in CHAOS: How to Defend against Russia's Most Likely Cyber Operations against Political Infrastructure

The aggregate Hack Map in the previous chapter illustrated that Russian APTs have been more likely to target facilitating rather than electoral IT components of the political infrastructure.[7] The former are more challenging to protect than the latter because of the sheer number of facilitating infrastructure components and their large attack surface. In addition, the U.S. and other governments may not have authority over many of the diverse owners of that facilitating infrastructure and, therefore, may not be able to monitor, protect, and defend it. Hence, providing a holistic defense to all components is likely impossible. Focusing on the specific facilitating infrastructure components most likely to be targeted and the possible types of attacks Russian APTs are likely to use are necessary operational steps to narrowing down the types of threats to defend against. The seven analyzed cases revealed that the Russian government uses phishing campaigns and DDoS attacks, most often against political parties and campaigns. To enhance resilience against cyber operations targeting political parties and campaigns, governments may consider adopting the following recommendations:

- Introduce mandatory cybersecurity awareness and incident response training for all members of political parties and campaigns, their staff, and volunteers who participate in local, state, and national elections.

  As the cases of France and Germany illustrated, the governments of the two countries introduced such cybersecurity training in preparation for their national elections. This training may have increased the resilience against Russia's cyber operations during the respective elections. This training should also include incident-response exercises and guidelines that parties and campaigns can refer to in the event of a cyber incident. The analysis presented in this book further illustrated that the Russian government targets primarily political parties and campaigns that do not support Russia's agenda. Therefore, political entities that have clearly articulated positions on topics that are relevant to the Russian government and diverge from the Kremlin's preferred stance could be especially vulnerable to Russian state-sponsored cyber assaults and, hence, should particularly consider adopting this recommendation.

As the case of Russia's interference against the 2016 U.S. elections illustrated, Russian state-sponsored APTs are known to target parties and campaigns that compete for national- and state-level elections. This information suggests that cybersecurity training should be offered not only to party and campaign staff that run for national elections but also to their counterparts that run for local and state elections. Not all local- and state-level campaigns, however, are well resourced and possess the necessary funding to secure the top-level cybersecurity training and assistance that the campaigns require to defend themselves against sophisticated state-level cyber threats.

To ensure the provision of such training, the U.S. government may consider allocating funding for the expansion of such cybersecurity services. The U.S. Election Assistance Commission (EAC) could be a potential channel through which funding for such services is allocated—however, the EAC focuses exclusively on the conduct of elections and does not work directly with parties.[8] The U.S. government may consider expanding the EAC's mandate to cover the provision of cybersecurity assistance for political parties and campaigns. Such a shift in the EAC's mandate, however, would require additional resources and a potential administrative restructuring. A more viable alternative for the management and distribution of such funding that would not require refining the mandate of the EAC could be to use structures already existing outside of the U.S. government that focus on this issue. One of these organizations is the NGO Defending Digital Campaigns (DDC).[9] DDC offers access to cybersecurity products, training, educational materials, incident response guidance, and incidence response checklists to campaigns and political parties at low or no cost. DDC serves as an intermediary between cybersecurity companies that would like to offer their services and products to parties and campaigns on one hand and parties and political campaigns on the other.[10] During the 2020 U.S. elections, DDC provided outreach to more than 500 campaigns and introduced cybersecurity products for 183 campaigns and committees across 42 states.[11] The U.S. government may consider expanding the capabilities of DDC by funding its work.

- Conduct interagency coordination exercises outside of election cycles.

In the cases of the DNC in the United States and the Bundestag in Germany, the FBI and the BSI, respectively, possessed information that, if properly communicated to and used by Russia's targets in advance, would have accelerated the initiation of activities to contain the cyber intrusions or could have prevented them altogether. Since these cases, NATO member states have significantly improved interagency communication, malware sharing, and general information exchange between law enforcement, federal agencies, and political parties regarding malicious threat actors. Many agencies have designed incident response protocols and practice them in tabletop exercises and other simulations.[12] This research demonstrated that Russia's cyber operations that target political infrastructure can be conducted years prior to an election. Therefore, interagency exercises should be conducted not only during election cycles but constantly to ensure interagency response and coordination of activities that can detect, intercept, and mitigate the effects of Russia's cyber operations quickly and effectively at all times.

- Maintain continuous threat monitoring and assessment of Russian information warfare activities.

    Since Russia's interference in the 2016 U.S. elections, the U.S. IC has been paying increased attention to the potential external threats to political parties and election processes, which affects intelligence collection and targets in the run up to elections.[13] The findings of this research indicate that Russia's information warfare campaigns, and specifically strategic messaging campaigns, continue *after* the elections as well. Therefore, the U.S. IC should remain vigilant of threats to political parties and campaigns, as well as to the broader population, after election cycles. As the cases of Russia's interference in the United States, Montenegro, and France illustrated, Kremlin-supported strategic messaging can include falsified narratives about voter fraud and illegitimate election processes. The chapter on Russia's interference in Montenegro's elections further demonstrated that Moscow's information warfare operations can include attempts to stir insurrection and cause civil unrest on election day. Russia's information warfare is sustained and unceasing, and, therefore, so should be our defenses.

Address the H in CHAOS: How to Enhance Resilience against Disinformation and Strategic Messaging Campaigns

Think tanks, academic institutions, companies, government entities, and international organizations have published numerous valuable reports analyzing the content, spread, and effects of strategic messaging campaigns. These analyses often contain pertinent recommendations on the types of interventions that could be effective in detecting, containing, and mitigating the impacts of various Russian strategic messaging operations.[14] Based on the seven cases examined here, some of the interventions that seemed to have effectively improved countries' resilience to these specific Russian government activities include

- Government-mandated legal requirements for media outlets to remove any disinformation from their platforms or face substantial penalties. Such laws were introduced in France and Germany, and likely contributed to the limited spread of leaked information obtained through an intrusion into the networks of Macron's presidential campaign. However, such laws are likely unconstitutional in the U.S. environment and, therefore, alternative regulation such as enabling offended parties to sue publishers of false information and force them to take it down may be a more realistic alternative.
- Agreement between political parties that pledge not to exploit any information about their opponents that has been exfiltrated through a cyber operation. Such agreements were present among some political parties in the cases of Germany and France.
- Agreement between media outlets to exercise restraint and carefully consider the origins of information and the consequences of publicizing information released as a result of a foreign state-sponsored cyber operation related to election candidates. During the 2020 U.S. elections, some mainstream U.S. media, drawing on lessons learned

from the 2016 election, determined to exercise more caution in publishing stories based on information that may have been disseminated by foreign governments in an attempt to influence the election process. Some of the most reputable U.S. media outlets also issued guidance to their newsrooms regarding covering any information obtained through cyber incidents. The guidelines for the *Washington Post*, for example, stressed "deliberation and communication." Before reporting on the release of hacked or leaked information, the guidelines said, senior editors should assess the newsworthiness, authenticity, and provenance of the information. "Our emphasis should be on making a sound and well-considered decision—not on speed," said the guidelines, issued by the *Post*'s then executive editor, Marty Baron.[15] Such guidelines could be publicized and endorsed by all major media outlets to ensure the institutionalization and wide acceptance of best practices and standards that prevent journalists from becoming unwitting participants in Russia's information warfare campaigns, while still maintaining journalistic integrity and informing the public about critical issues. The fact that the story about the laptop of President Joe Biden's son, Hunter Biden, did not receive excessive coverage during the 2020 U.S. election cycle indicates an improvement and increased awareness of U.S. media outlets regarding potential information warfare operations.[16]

- Introducing curricula in all schools and universities to improve media literacy and foster healthy skepticism about media sources and information consumption. Such training should include basic information on state-sponsored malicious information warfare activities and their objectives. The failure of Russia's *Sputnik Norge* in Norway and the limited spread of leaks from the Macron campaign on social media platforms in France are evidence of societies with high media literacy that other countries can study and learn from.

As the analysis of the United States and France revealed, Russia's divisive strategic messaging campaign continues in the days and months after the elections. This pattern seems accurate especially in cases where the pro-Russian party or candidate did not win the particular election. Therefore, NATO governments should be prepared to address narratives that elicit strong emotional responses and may divide their constituencies over sensitive social issues or narratives that cast doubt on the legitimacy of the election process.

Address the AOS in CHAOS: How to Defend against Russia's Other Information Warfare Operations

The cases analyzed in this research demonstrated that Russia's information warfare activities are much broader than cyber operations and strategic messaging campaigns. Other activities include assassination attempts, as in the case of Bulgaria, and even a coup d'état plot, as in the case of Montenegro. Such brazen Russian interventions should be investigated extensively and should face significant consequences. In Montenegro, the implicated Russian GRU officers faced trial but their conviction was thrown out on appeal.[17] In Bulgaria, the two attempted poisonings of weapons dealer Emilian Gebrev did not result even in a trial. Further investigations into the potential link between Russian citizens and explosions in Bulgarian weapons facilities also did not appear to have taken place. The absence of an adequate response from the Bulgarian government demonstrates to Moscow that its aggressive and illegal actions could go unpunished and serves as an invitation for further similar state-sponsored activities. The Bulgarian government, as well as other NATO governments, should address such interventions with more scrutiny and commensurate responses.

Regarding enhancing resilience against Russian sanctions, diversifying the economies of industries that consider Russia a main export market would be a reasonable solution and a guarantee against future economic disruptions. The case of Norway's seafood industry represents an example of a market that managed successfully to pivot away from exports to Russia.

The analyzed cases also revealed Russian government support for local protests, either through direct financing or the organization of protesters, as in the cases of Estonia, the United States, and Montenegro, or through overt government criticism of the targeted country that may encourage such activities, as in the case of the Lisa affair in Germany. There is no universal antidote against protests. Moreover, in democracies, holding peaceful demonstrations is a legal right that citizens can choose to exercise to express their positions. However, Russian information warfare doctrine stipulates that Moscow does not have the same objectives for domestic protests that local citizens have. The Russian government supports public demonstrations in NATO member states because it aims to incite protests for the malicious purposes of deepening societal divisions, creating instability in the targeted state, and even inciting a forceful violent government change or coup d'état. The cases of Russia's information warfare campaigns against Estonia, the United States, Germany, and Montenegro examined in this book contain direct examples of such Russian state-sponsored activities. Therefore, NATO member states should detect, contain, and ideally eliminate any Russian government involvement in supporting such demonstrations. Collective efforts by law enforcement agencies and social media companies are already in progress across NATO member states to limit the influence of Russian state-sponsored actors who may be inciting such demonstrations. Inoculating the population to Russian strategic messaging through media literacy and awareness of Russian information warfare campaigns, mentioned in the previous section, is also a valuable policy for containing Russia's attempts to incite protests. Addressing divisive domestic issues and introducing policies to alleviate racial, ethnic, and economic disparities among local populations are related complex efforts that the Russian government targets and exploits. The attempts of NATO member states to address these issues would further strengthen these countries' ability to resist Russian strategic messaging campaigns.

Final Thoughts about Russia's Assault on Democracies in the Cyber Wild West

This book has two main goals. First, it aims to identify indicators associated with the initiation of different types of Russian cyber operations that could facilitate policies aimed to detect and mitigate the effects of Russian cyber operations. Second, the analysis creates frameworks for systematically visualizing the range of Russian cyber operations against political infrastructure and their interaction with other information warfare activities. These frameworks can help data collection and analysis of Russia's information warfare playbook and can inform a discussion about various types of policy interventions to counter Russia's malicious activities. To achieve these goals, the research describes the main elements of Russia's information warfare doctrine and demonstrates how the Russian government uses cyber operations and other information warfare activities against seven NATO member states to achieve various geopolitical goals. Informed by the analysis of the seven case studies examined in this research, each chapter offers a list of general conclusions derived from the analyses regarding the policies that seemed to have been most effective in preparing for, deterring, and mitigating the negative consequences of the different components of Russia's information warfare campaigns.

This research demonstrates that Russia's information warfare breaks down the binary boundaries of war and peace, and views conflict as a continuum, which hardly ever reaches the "zero" of peace or the "one" of a full-blown war, although in some cases, it gets close. Russia's information warfare playbook is multifaceted and conducted through multiple channels customized to each targeted NATO member. Russia tends to conduct availability attacks against former members of the Eastern Bloc and confidentiality compromises against other NATO member states. Moscow targets mostly facilitating infrastructure components of the political IT infrastructure and most frequently targets political parties supporting policies unfavorable to Moscow's interests. The cyber operations against these parties aim either to disrupt their political campaign or to gain access to information that Moscow could subsequently release publicly and integrate into broader strategic messaging campaigns. The Kremlin rarely conducts cyber operations in isolation as the sole information warfare activity. Cyber operations are often accompanied by broader strategic messaging campaigns conveyed through Russian state-sponsored media outlets and social media channels. Other information warfare activities, such as protests, economic sanctions, coup d'états, and assassinations, can also be components of Russia's information warfare campaign. The Russian government tends to resort to physical violence in former members of the Eastern Bloc and refrains from using such aggressive tactics in the territory of other NATO member states.

The effectiveness of Russia's cyber operations and information warfare activities varies, based on Russia's purported objective and the particular targeted country. Availability attacks cause temporary disruption to the operations of networks and the flow of communications, but countries tend to restore these functions fairly rapidly. Confidentiality compromises have been more successful in achieving disruptions and influencing domestic elections, specifically in the case of the 2016 U.S. elections, but Moscow has not been able to replicate the magnitude of that success in Germany and France, where it conducted similar cyber operations. It is difficult to provide a methodologically rigorous assessment on the extent to which Russia's information warfare operations have amplified societal divisions and distrust in institutions and democratic governance. However, evidence suggests that the spread of disinformation and divisive content in the hereby examined cases at times contributed to exacerbating these issues, at least temporarily, as in the cases of Estonia, the United States, and Germany, where the Russian government used disinformation and strategic messaging to support protests. In Germany and Montenegro, pro-Russian political parties that the Russian government supported gained seats in their respective parliaments. These political gains are significant. As Russia's information warfare is not episodic but a continuous process, these victories can act as lighter fluid for far-right movements and extreme anti-Western ideologies and can inspire the continuation of divisions and disagreements among the communities of NATO member states.

Best practices revealed across the seven cases indicate that a number of policies might have managed to limit the pernicious influence of Russia's information warfare activities. Such policies include introducing mandatory cybersecurity awareness training for political parties, improving interagency communication and malware sharing practices, gentlemen's agreements among parties and media outlets to refrain from publicizing leaked information, introducing media literacy, and addressing specific economic, racial, and ethnic inequalities that may persist in various NATO member states. Improving data collection and our understanding of links between various local organizations and the Russian government would greatly expand the ability to map the components of Russia's information warfare operations and to design policies to effectively address their negative effects.

Russia's information warfare campaigns do not happen in a strategic vacuum, and even if Russian state-supported actors are allowed to act with a certain level of autonomy when executing the different operations discussed in this research, the general direction of operations is approved from the corridors of the Kremlin—the top leadership of the country. Warnings from senior-level government officials, sanctions, indictments, and other similar policies can send clear signals to the Russian government that such operations will incur costs. A layered strategy that addresses all aspects of Russia's information warfare playbook, while also taking into consideration the most likely targets of Russia's democratic onslaught, seems to be the most appropriate approach.

NOTES

PREFACE
1. This sentence was inspired by California governor Arnold Schwarzenegger's message after the failed U.S. coup d'état on January 6, 2021. Although this book makes no claims that the riots that took place on that day were incited by the Russian government, the research presented in this study demonstrates the multiple parallels that exist between the events on January 6, 2021, and the strategic messaging campaigns, protests, and coup d'états that Russian state-sponsored actors have supported in NATO countries. Arnold Schwarzenegger, "Governor Schwarzenegger's Message Following This Week's Attack on the Capitol," *YouTube*, January 10, 2021, video, 0:46, https://youtu.be/x_P-0I6sAck, accessed February 17, 2021.

INTRODUCTION
1. Eric Lipton, David E. Sanger, and Scott Shanedec, "The Perfect Weapon: How Russian Cyberpower Invaded the U.S.," *New York Times*, December 13, 2016, https://www.nytimes.com/2016/12/13/us/politics/russia-hack-election-dnc.html (accessed March 21, 2021).
2. Select Comm. on Intelligence, Russian Active Measures Campaigns and Interference in the 2016 U.S. Election, Volume 5: Counterintelligence Threats and Vulnerabilities, S. Rep. No. 116-XX, at 178–258 (August 18, 2020), https://www.intelligence.senate.gov/sites/default/files/documents/report_volume5.pdf (accessed March 24, 2021).
3. Director of National Intelligence, Joint Statement from the Department of Homeland Security and Office of the Director of National Intelligence on Election Security (October 7, 2016), https://www.dhs.gov/news/2016/10/07/joint-statement -department-homeland-security-and-office-director-national (accessed March 26, 2021); Select Comm. on Intelligence, Russian Active Measures Campaigns and Interference in the 2016 U.S. Election, Volume 2: Russia's Use of Social Media with

Additional Views, S. Rep. No. 116-XX, at 4–11, https://www.intelligence.senate
.gov/sites/default/files/documents/Report_Volume2.pdf (accessed March 26, 2021).

4. The concept is defined further in this chapter's section "Definitions" and in chapter 1.

5. The term "political IT infrastructure" is defined in the section "Main Criteria for
Case Selection" in this chapter.

6. Bilyana Lilly, "Bringing Order through CHAOS: A Framework for Understanding Russian Cyber Operations and Disinformation during the 2020 U.S. Elections
and Beyond," *CyberWire,* November 2, 2020, https://www.thecyberwire.com/stories
/572863ea3b074fc3867caa362c6bef5a/bringing-order-through-chaos-a-frame
work-for-understanding-russian-cyber-operations-and-disinformation-during-the
-2020-us-elections-and-beyond (accessed March 24, 2021). See the respective chapters on these cases in this book.

7. See chapter 1; Ministry of Defense of the Russian Federation, Encyclopedia, s.v.
"informatsionnoe protivoborstvo" [information warfare], http://encyclopedia.mil
.ru/encyclopedia/dictionary/details.htm?id=5221@morfDictionary (accessed March
26, 2021); Valeriy Gerasimov, "Tsennost' nauki v predvidenii" [The value of science
is in foresight], *Voyenno Promyshlennyy Kuryer,* February 26, 2013, http://vpk-news
.ru/articles/14632 (accessed March 24, 2021); Igor' Panarin, *SMI, propaganda i informatsionnyye voyny. Teoriya informatsionnogo protivoborstva* [Mass media, propaganda,
and information wars. Information warfare theory] (Moscow: "Pokolenie," 2012),
http://propagandahistory.ru/books/Igor-Panarin_SMI—propaganda-i-informat
sionnye-voyny/28 (accessed March 24, 2021).

8. Bilyana Lilly and Joe Cheravitch, "The Past, Present, and Future of Russia's Cyber
Strategy and Forces," in *20/20 Vision: The Next Decade,* ed. T. Jančárková, L. Lind-
ström, M. Signoretti, I. Tolga, and G. Visky (Tallinn, Estonia: 12th International
Conference on Cyber Conflict, NATO Cooperative Cyber Defence Centre of Excel-
lence, 2020), 131, https://ccdcoe.org/uploads/2020/05/CyCon_2020_8_Lilly_
Cheravitch.pdf (accessed March 25, 2021); Center for Strategic and International
Studies, "Russian Foreign Policy: Research and Analysis Regarding All Aspects of
Russia's Foreign Policy," updated July 15, 2019, https://www.csis.org/programs/russia
-and-eurasia-program/archives/russian-foreign-policy (accessed March 26, 2021).

9. See, for example, Blake E. Strom, Andy Applebaum, Douglas P. Miller, Kathryn C.
Nickels, Adam G. Pennington, and Cody B. Thomas, "MITRE ATT&CK Design
and Philosophy," July 2018, https://www.mitre.org/sites/default/files/publications
/pr-18–0944–11-mitre-attack-design-and-philosophy.pdf (accessed March 24, 2021);
Eric M. Hutchins, Michael J. Cloppert, and Rohan M. Amin, "Intelligence-Driven
Computer Network Defense Informed by Analysis of Adversary Campaigns and
Intrusion Kill Chains," *Leading Issues in Information Confrontation & Security Research*
1, no. 1 (2011): 7–8, https://www.lockheedmartin.com/content/dam/lockheed
-martin/rms/documents/cyber/LM-White-Paper-Intel-Driven-Defense.pdf (accessed
March 24, 2021); FireEye iSight Intelligence, *APT28: A Window into Russia's Cyber*

Espionage Operations? special report, 2014, https://www.fireeye.com/content/dam /fireeye-www/global/en/current-threats/pdfs/rpt-apt28.pdf (accessed March 26, 2021).

10. Congressional Task Force on Election Security, Final Report (January 2018), https:// homeland.house.gov/imo/media/doc/TFESReport.pdf (accessed March 26, 2021); Abby Vesoulis, "States Are Trying to Stop Election Meddling. But the Real Risk is Public Confidence," *Time*, March 5, 2019, https://time.com/5543649/2020-elections -voter-security-states/ (accessed March 24, 2021).

11. The issue of limitations of capabilities will be examined with the caveat that what Russian and Russia-affiliated threat actors have done does not necessarily demonstrate the whole range and scope of their capabilities but serves as an illustration of them. In other words, if they have not exploited a certain vulnerability, this does not necessarily mean they do not have the capacity to do so.

12. Joe Cheravitch and Bilyana Lilly, "Russia's Cyber Limitations in Personnel Recruitment and Innovation, Their Potential Impact on Future Operations, and How NATO and Its Members Can Respond," in *Cyber Threats and NATO 2030: Horizon Scanning and Analysis*, ed. A. Ertan, K. Floyd, P. Pernik, and T. Stevens (Tallinn, Estonia: NATO Cooperative Cyber Defence Centre of Excellence, 2020), 48.

13. The term political IT infrastructure is defined in the section "Main Criteria for Case Selection" in this chapter.

14. Sven Herpig, *Cyber Operations: Defending Political IT-Infrastructures* (Germany: Stiftung Neue Verantwortung, June 2017), 3.

15. Andrew Grotto, "Deconstructing Cyber Attribution: A Proposed Framework and Lexicon," *IEEE Security & Privacy* 18, no. 1 (January/February 2020): 12.

16. Grotto, "Deconstructing Cyber Attribution," 12.

17. Quentin Hodgson (senior international and defense researcher of the RAND Corporation), in discussion with author, February 19, 2021; Michael Daniel (president and chief executive officer of the Cyber Threat Alliance, special assistant to President Barack Obama, and cybersecurity coordinator on the U.S. National Security Council staff from June 2012 to January 2017), in discussion with author, February 19, 2021.

18. Daniel, discussion, February 19, 2021.

19. Office of the Director of National Intelligence, *Background to "Assessing Russian Activities and Intentions in Recent US Elections": The Analytic Process and Cyber Incident Attribution*, January 6, 2017, at 2, https://dni.gov/files/documents/ICA _2017_01.pdf (accessed March 26, 2021).

20. Business.com, "The Best DDoS Protection Services of 2020: How to Choose a DDoS Protection Service," updated February 7, 2018, https://www.business.com /categories/best-ddos-protection-services/ (accessed March 26, 2021).

21. Montenegro is the only country examined in this research that was not a NATO member during the analyzed Russian state-sponsored information warfare campaign. NATO invited Montenegro to start accession talks in December 2015, and

NATO members signed the accession protocol on May 19, 2016. North Atlantic Treaty Organization, "Relations with Montenegro (Archived)," updated December 14, 2017, https://www.nato.int/cps/en/natohq/topics_49736.htm (accessed March 26, 2021).

22. Center for Long-Term Cybersecurity and Microsoft, *Digital Accountability: Designing Futures for Cyber Attack Attribution, Background Document* (Berkeley, California: July 17, 2018), 6; *NATO Review*, "Cyber—The Good, the Bad, and the Bug-Free: The History of Cyber Attacks—A Timeline," https://www.nato.int/docu/review/2013/cyber/timeline/en/index.htm (accessed March 26, 2021); the CSIS database records significant cyber incidents since 2006. It focuses on cyber attacks on government agencies, defense, and high-tech companies, or economic crimes with losses of more than $1 million: Center for Strategic and International Studies, "Significant Cyber Incidents," https://www.csis.org/programs/cybersecurity-and-governance/technology-policy-program/other-projects-cybersecurity (accessed April 2, 2021); Council on Foreign Relations, "Cyber Operations Tracker," https://www.cfr.org/interactive/cyber-operations/search?keys=russia (accessed March 26, 2021).

23. Center for Strategic and International Studies, "Significant Cyber Incidents."

24. Ivo Juurvee and Mariita Mattiisen, *The Bronze Soldier Crisis of 2007: Revisiting an Early Case of Hybrid Conflict* (Tallinn, Estonia: International Centre for Defence and Security, August 2020); Council on Foreign Relations, "Cyber Operations Tracker"; Tom Espiner, "Georgia Accuses Russia of Coordinated Cyberattack," *CNet*, August 11, 2008, https://www.cnet.com/news/georgia-accuses-russia-of-coordinated-cyberattack/ (accessed March 24, 2021); John Leyden, "Russian Spy Agencies Linked to Georgian Cyber-Attacks. Follow the Bear Prints," *Register*, March 23, 2009, https://www.theregister.co.uk/2009/03/23/georgia_russia_cyberwar_analysis/ (accessed March 24, 2021); John Markoff, "Before the Gunfire, Cyberattacks," *New York Times*, August 12, 2008, https://www.nytimes.com/2008/08/13/technology/13cyber.html (accessed March 24, 2021); Andrzej Kozlowski, "Comparative Analysis of Cyberattacks on Estonia, Georgia, and Kyrgyzstan," *European Scientific Journal February* 3 (2014): 240–41; "Russian Turla Behind Foreign Ministry Hacking," *Finland Times*, January 14, 2016, http://www.finlandtimes.fi/national/2016/01/14/24215/Russian-Turla-behind-foreign-ministry-hacking (accessed March 24, 2021); "Russian Group behind 2013 Foreign Ministry Hack," *Yle*, January 13, 2016, https://yle.fi/uutiset/osasto/news/russian_group_behind_2013_foreign_ministry_hack/8591548 (accessed March 24, 2021); Adrian Croft and Peter Apps, "NATO Websites Hit in Cyber Attack Linked to Crimea Tension," *Reuters*, March 15, 2014, https://www.reuters.com/article/us-ukraine-nato/nato-websites-hit-in-cyber-attack-linked-to-crimea-tension-idUSBREA2E0T320140316 (accessed March 24, 2021); Evan Perez and Shimon Prokupecz, "Sources: State Dept. Hack the 'Worst Ever,'" *CNN*, March 10, 2015, https://www.cnn.com/2015/03/10/politics/state-department-hack-worst-ever/ (accessed March 24, 2021); Ellen Nakashima, "New Details Emerge about 2014 Russian Hack of the State Department: It Was

'Hand to Hand Combat,'" *Washington Post*, April 3, 2017, https://www.washington post.com/world/national-security/new-details-emerge-about-2014-russian-hack-of -the-state-department-it-was-hand-to-hand-combat/2017/04/03/d89168e0–124c -11e7–833c-503e1f6394c9_story.html?utm_term=.9d6cc3a7c930 (accessed March 24, 2021); Carnegie Endowment for International Peace, "Appendix: A Review of Past Cyber Incidents Involving Financial Institutions," 13, http://carnegieendow ment.org/files/Carnegie_Cyber_Financial_Data_white_paper_appendix.pdf (accessed March 26, 2021); Glib Pakharenko, "Cyber Operations at Maidan: A First-Hand Account," in *Cyber War in Perspective: Russian Aggression against Ukraine*, ed. Kenneth Geers (Tallinn, Estonia: NATO Cooperative Cyber Defense Center of Excellence, 2015), 60; "Russian 'Spies' Accused of Trying to Hack MH17 Inquiry," *AFP*, October 23, 2015, https://tribune.com.pk/story/978152/russian-spies-accused-of -trying-to-hack-mh17-inquiry/ (accessed March 24, 2021); Matthew Schwartz, "French Officials Detail 'Fancy Bear' Hack of TV5Monde," *Bank Info Security*, June 12, 2017, https://www.bankinfosecurity.com/french-officials-detail-fancy-bear -hack-tv5monde-a-9983 (accessed March 24, 2021); "Russian Hackers Blamed for TV5 Cyber Attack," *Euronews*, June 10, 2015, https://www.youtube.com/watch ?v=KuDzqYUwygc (accessed March 24, 2021); Momchil Milev, "Khakerite, udarili bŭlgarskite izbori, veroyatno sa atakuvali i Klintŭn" [The hackers who hit the Bulgarian elections probably attacked Clinton as well], *Kapital*, July 27, 2016, https:// www.capital.bg/politika_i_ikonomika/bulgaria/2016/07/27/2802122_hakerite_ udarili_bulgarskite_izbori_veroiatno_sa/ (accessed March 10, 2021); *Symantec* (blog), "Dragonfly: Western Energy Sector Targeted by Sophisticated Attack Group," October 20, 2017, https://www.symantec.com/blogs/threat-intelligence/dragon fly-energy-sector-cyber-attacks (accessed March 24, 2021); Andrea Shalal, "Germany Challenges Russia over Alleged Cyberattacks," *Reuters*, May 4, 2017, https://www .reuters.com/article/us-germany-security-cyber-russia/germany-challenges-russia -over-alleged-cyberattacks-idUSKBN1801CA (accessed March 25, 2021); "Merkel Claims Russia behind 2015 Bundestag Hack," *Financial Times*, https://www.ft .com/content/264056c9-a13f-4421–9d35-f1bda82375af (accessed March 25, 2021); National Cybersecurity and Communications Integration Center and Federal Bureau of Investigation, *Grizzly Steppe—Russian Malicious Cyber Activity*, JAR-16–20296A, December 29, 2016, https://www.us-cert.gov/sites/default/files/publications/JAR _16–20296A_GRIZZLY%20STEPPE-2016–1229.pdf (accessed March 25, 2021); Director of National Intelligence, Joint Statement from the Department of Homeland Security and Office of the Director of National Intelligence on Election Security (October 7, 2016); Justin Huggler, "Germany Accuses Russia of Cyber Attack on Ukraine Peace Monitors, as Kremlin Dismisses US Intelligence Claims as a 'Witch Hunt,'" *Telegraph*, January 9, 2017, https://www.telegraph.co.uk/news/2017 /01/09/germany-accuses-russia-cyber-attack-ukraine-peace-monitors-kremlin/ (accessed March 25, 2021); Dragos, *Crashoverride: Analysis of the Threat to Electric Grid Operations*, 2017, https://dragos.com/blog/crashoverride/CrashOverride-01

.pdf (accessed March 26, 2021); Center for Strategic and International Studies, "Significant Cyber Incidents"; World Anti-Doping Agency (WADA), "WADA Confirms Attack by Russian Cyber Espionage Group," September 13, 2016, https://www.wada-ama.org/en/media/news/2016–09/wada-confirms-attack -by-russian-cyber-espionage-group (accessed March 26, 2021); Feike Hacquebord, *Two Years of Pawn Storm: Examining an Increasingly Relevant Threat, Forward-Looking Threat Research (FTR) Team* (Trend Micro, 2017), 5–6, https://documents .trendmicro.com/assets/wp/wp-two-years-of-pawn-storm.pdf (accessed March 26, 2021); "Norway Accuses Group Linked to Russia of Carrying out Cyber-Attack," *Agence France-Presse in Oslo*, February 3, 2017, https://www.theguardian.com/tech nology /2017/feb/03/norway-accuses-group-linked-to-russia-of-carrying-out-cyber -attack (accessed March 17, 2021); Rick Noack, "Cyberattack on French Presidential Front -Runner Bears Russian 'Fingerprints,' Research Group Says," *Washington Post,* April 25, 2017, https://www.washingtonpost.com/news/worldviews/wp/2017 /04/25/cyberattack-on-french-presidential-front-runner-bears-russian-fingerprints -research-group-says/?noredirect=on&utm_term=.fc8acc54ca6e (accessed March 25, 2021); Thessa Lageman, "Russian Hackers Use Dutch Polls as Practice," *Deutsche Welle*, March 10, 2017, https://www.dw.com/en/russian-hackers-use-dutch -polls-as-practice/a-37850898 (accessed March 25, 2021); "Foreign Power Was behind Cyber Attack on Czech Ministry: Senate," *Reuters*, August 13, 2019, https:// www.reuters.com/article/us-czech-security-cyber/foreign-power-was-behind-cyber -attack-on-czech-ministry-senate-idUSKCN1V31DS?il=0 (accessed March 25, 2021); Andrew Liptak, "Russia Was behind the Cyberattack during the Opening Ceremonies for the 2018 Winter Olympics," *Verge*, February 25, 2018, https://www.the verge.com/2018/2/25/17050868/winter-olympics-2018-russia-north-korea-cyber attack-opening-ceremonies (accessed March 25, 2021); "Germany Detects New Cyber Attack by Russian Hacker Group—Spiegel," *Reuters*, November 29, 2018, https://www.reuters.com/article/germany-cyber-russia/germany-detects-new-cyber -attack-by-russian-hacker-group-spiegel-idUSL8N1Y47J5 (accessed March 25, 2021); "UK Exposes Russian Cyber Attacks," *Foreign & Commonwealth Office*, October 4, 2018, https://www.gov.uk/government/news/uk-exposes-russian-cyber -attacks (acessed March 26, 2021); Pavel Polityuk, "Exclusive: Ukraine Says It Sees Surge in Cyber Attacks Targeting Election," *Reuters*, January 25, 2019, https://www .reuters.com/article/us-ukraine-cyber-exclusive/exclusive-ukraine-says-it-sees-surge -in-cyber-attacks-targeting-election-idUSKCN1PJ1KX (accessed March 25, 2021); Aleksi Teivainen, "DoS Attack against Election Results Portal under Investigation in Finland," *Helsinki Times,* April 11, 2019, https://www.helsinkitimes.fi/finland/fin land-news/domestic/16333-dos-attack-against-election-results-portal-under-invest igation-in-finland.html (accessed March 25, 2021); Gerard O'Dwyer, "Finland's Security Agencies Collaborate after Cyber Attacks," *Computer Weekly,* August 29, 2019, https://www.computerweekly.com/news/252469691/Finlands-security-agencies

-collaborate-after-cyber-attacks (accessed March 25, 2021); Robert Muller, "Foreign Power Was behind Cyber Attack on Czech Ministry: Senate," *Reuters*, August 13, 2019, https://www.reuters.com/article/us-czech-security-cyber/foreign-power-was-behind-cyber-attack-on-czech-ministry-senate-idUSKCN1V31DS?il=0 (accessed March 25, 2021); "General Election 2019: Labour Party Hit by Second Cyber-Attack," *BBC News*, November 12, 2019, https://www.bbc.com/news/election-2019–50388879 (accessed March 25, 2021); Ministry of Foreign Affairs of the Republic of Poland, Press Office, "Statement of the Polish MFA on Cyberattacks against Georgia," February 20, 2020, https://www.gov.pl/web/diplomacy/statement-of-the-polish-mfa-on-cyberattacks-against-georgia (accessed March 26, 2021); David E. Sanger and Marc Santora, "U.S. and Allies Blame Russia for Cyberattack on Republic of Georgia," *New York Times*, February 21, 2020, https://www.nytimes.com/2020/02/20/world/europe/georgia-cyberattack-russia.html (accessed March 25, 2021).

25. Some of the consulted literature included: Mark Galeotti, *Putin's Hydra: Inside Russia's Intelligence Services* (European Council on Foreign Relations, May 2016), https://ecfr.eu/publication/putins_hydra_inside_russias_intelligence_services/ (accessed March 25, 2021); Comm. on Foreign Relations, Putin's Asymmetric Assault on Democracy in Russia and Europe: Implications for U.S. National Security, S. Rep. No. 115–21 (January 10, 2018), https://www.foreign.senate.gov/imo/media/doc/FinalRR.pdf (accessed March 26, 2021); Andrey Soldatov and Irina Borogan, *Bitva za Runet* (Fight for Runet), (Moscow: Al'pina Publisher, 2017); Ben Connable, Stephanie Young, Stephanie Pezard, Andrew Radin, Raphael S. Cohen, Katya Migacheva, and James Sladden, *Russia's Hostile Measures: Combating Russian Gray Zone Aggression against NATO in the Contact, Blunt, and Surge Layers of Competition* (Santa Monica, CA: RAND Corporation, 2020), https://www.rand.org/pubs/research_reports/RR2539.html (accessed March 25, 2021).

26. Charles C. Ragin, *The Comparative Method: Moving beyond Qualitative and Quantitative Strategies* (Berkeley, CA: University of California Press, 1987).

27. Ragin, *The Comparative Method*, chapter 6.

28. Christopher Paul, Colin P. Clarke, Beth Grill, and Molly Dunigan, *Paths to Victory: Lessons from Modern Insurgencies* (Santa Monica, CA: RAND Corporation, 2013), 194, https://www.rand.org/pubs/research_reports/RR291z1.html (accessed March 25, 2021).

29. Ragin, *The Comparative Method*, 99.

30. Ragin, *The Comparative Method*, 99.

31. Ragin, *The Comparative Method*, 100.

32. Ragin, *The Comparative Method*, 27–28.

33. For an example see Paul et al., *Paths to Victory*, 219–20.

34. Paul et al., *Paths to Victory*, 195.

35. David Collier, "Understanding Process Tracing," *Political Science and Politics* 44, no. 4 (October 2011): 823; ed. Andrew Bennett and Jeffrey T. Checkel, *Process Tracing;*

From Metaphor to Analytic Tool (British Colombia: Cambridge University Press, November 2014); Hutchins, Cloppert, and Amin, "Intelligence-Driven Computer Network Defense Informed by Analysis of Adversary Campaigns and Intrusion Kill Chains."

36. For a detailed description of the Cyber Kill Chain, refer to Hutchins, Cloppert, and Amin, "Intelligence-Driven Computer Network Defense Informed by Analysis of Adversary Campaigns and Intrusion Kill Chains."

37. See, for example, Comm. on Foreign Relations, Putin's Asymmetric Assault on Democracy; Connable et al., *Russia's Hostile Measures*; Christopher S. Chivvis, "Hybrid War: Russian Contemporary Political Warfare," *Bulletin of the Atomic Scientists* 73, no. 5 (August 2017): 316–21; Keir Giles, "Information Troops—A Russian Cyber Command?" in *2011 3rd International Conference on Cyber Conflict*, ed. C. Czosseck, E. Tyugu, and T. Wingfield (Tallinn, Estonia: NATO Cooperative Cyber Defence Centre of Excellence, 2011); Heather A. Conley, James Mina, Ruslan Stefanov, and Martin Vladimirov, *The Kremlin Playbook: Understanding Russian Influence in Central and Eastern Europe* (Lanham, MD: Rowman & Littlefield, October 13, 2016).

38. *Disinformation: A Primer in Russian Active Measures and Influence Campaigns: Hearings on S. Rep., Before the Select Comm. on Intelligence*, Comey, 9 (March 30, 2017) (statement of Roy Godson), https://www.hsdl.org/?view&did=802222 (accessed March 26, 2021).

39. Department of Defense, Defense Science Board, Task Force on Cyber Deterrence, Final Report (February 2017), 2.

40. Department of Defense, Defense Science Board, Task Force on Cyber Deterrence, Final Report (February 2017), 3.

41. Lilly and Cheravitch, "The Past, Present, and Future of Russia's Cyber Strategy and Forces," 132–33.

42. Ministry of Defense of the Russian Federation, Encyclopedia, s.v. "informatsionnoe protivoborstvo" [information warfare]; Ministry of Defense of the Russian Federation, "Kontseptual'nye vzglyady na deyatel'nost' Vooruzhennykh Sil Rossiyskoy Federatsii v informatsionnom prostranstve" [Conceptual views on the activities of the armed forces of the Russian Federation in the information space], 2011, http://ens.mil.ru/science/publications/more.htm?id=10845074@cmsArticle (accessed March 26, 2021); Gerasimov, "Tsennost' nauki v predvidenii"; Igor' Panarin, *SMI, propaganda i informatsionnyye voyny. Teoriya informatsionnogo protivoborstva* [Mass media, propaganda, and information wars. Information warfare theory] (Moscow: "Pokolenie," 2012), http://propagandahistory.ru/books/Igor-Panarin_SMI—propaganda-i-informatsionnye-voyny/28 (accessed March 24, 2021).

43. North Atlantic Treaty Organization, NATO Glossary of Terms and Definitions (English and French), AAP-06 Edition 2019, at 47, 103, https://www.coemed.org/files/stanags/05_AAP/AAP-06_2019_EF.pdf (accessed March 4, 2021); British Ministry of Defense, Land Warfare Development Center, "Land Operations,"

Army Doctrine Publication AC 71940, updated March 31, 2017, at 8, https://
assets.publishing.service.gov.uk/government/uploads/system/uploads/attachment
_data/file/605298/Army_Field_Manual__AFM__A5_Master_ADP_Interactive_
Gov_Web.pdf (accessed March 26, 2021); Giles, "Information Troops," 46.

44. Martti J. Kari, "Russian Strategic Culture in Cyberspace: Theory of Strategic Culture—
A Tool to Explain Russia's Cyber Threat Perception and Response to Cyber Threats,"
(PhD diss., University of Juvaskyla, 2019); Timothy J. Thomas, *Russian Military
Thought: Concepts and Elements* (McLean, VA: MITRE Corporation, August 2019);
Oscar Jonsson, *The Russian Understanding of War* (Washington, DC: Georgetown
University Press, 2019); Jolanta Darczewska, *Russia's Armed Forces on the Information
War Front: Strategic Documents* (Warsaw, Poland: Centre for Eastern Studies, June
2016); Dmitry (Dima) Adamsky, *Cross-Domain Coercion: The Current Russian Art of
Strategy* (Paris, France: Security Studies Center, November 2015), https://www.ifri
.org/sites/default/files/atoms/files/pp54adamsky.pdf (accessed March 26, 2021); Lilly
and Cheravitch, "The Past, Present, and Future of Russia's Cyber Strategy and Forces."

45. For examples of the former, see Connable et al., *Russia's Hostile Measures*, and Comm.
on Foreign Relations, Putin's Asymmetric Assault on Democracy. For examples of
the latter, see Renée DiResta, Kris Shaffer, Becky Ruppel, David Sullivan, Robert
Matney, Ryan Fox, Jonathan Albright, and Ben Johnson, *The Tactics and Tropes of
the Internet Research Agency* (New Knowledge, November 2018); Philip Howard,
Bharath Ganesh, Dimitra Liotsiou, John Kelly, and Camille François, *The IRA,
Social Media and Political Polarization in the United States, 2012–2018*, (Oxford,
UK: Computational Propaganda Research Project, University of Oxford, 2018).

46. See, for example, MITRE Corporation, "ATT&CK. Getting Started," https://
attack.mitre.org/resources/getting-started/ (accessed March 26, 2021); "Crowd-
Strike's Work with the Democratic National Committee: Setting the Record
Straight," *CrowdStrike* (blog), June 5, 2020, https://www.crowdstrike.com/blog/
bears-midst-intrusion-democratic-national-committee/ (accessed March 25, 2021);
"APT28, Sofacy Playbook Viewer," Unit 42, https://pan-unit42.github.io/play
book_viewer/ (accessed March 26, 2021); FireEye iSIGHT Intelligence, "APT28: At
the Center of the Storm Russia Strategically Evolves Its Cyber Operations," January
11, 2017; National Cybersecurity and Communications Integration Center and
Federal Bureau of Investigation, *Grizzly Steppe—Russian Malicious Cyber Activity*,
JAR-16–20296A, December 29, 2016, https://www.us-cert.gov/sites/default/files
/publications/JAR_16–20296A_GRIZZLY%20STEPPE-2016-1229.pdf (accessed
March 25, 2021); Computer Security Incident Response Team of Thailand, *Threat
Group Cards: A Threat Actor Encyclopedia*, July 8, 2020, https://www.thaicert.or.th
/downloads/files/Threat_Group_Cards_v2.0.pdf (accessed March 28, 2021); Andy
Greenberg, "A Brief History of Russian Hackers' Evolving False Flags," *Wired*,
October 21, 2019, https://www.wired.com/story/russian-hackers-false-flags-iran
-fancy-bear/ (accessed March 25, 2021).

47. Brian Bartholomew and Juan Andrés Guerrero-Saade, "Wave Your False Flags! Deception Tactics Muddying Attribution in Targeted Attacks," *Virus Bulletin* (October 2016): 1–11; John S. Davis II, Benjamin Adam Boudreaux, Jonathan William Welburn, Jair Aguirre, Cordaye Ogletree, Geoffrey McGovern, and Michael S. Chase, *Stateless Attribution: Toward International Accountability in Cyberspace* (Santa Monica, CA: RAND Corporation, 2017), https://www.rand.org/pubs/research_reports/RR 2081.html (accessed March 28, 2021).

48. Michael Daniel (president and chief executive officer of the Cyber Threat Alliance, special assistant to President Barack Obama, and cybersecurity coordinator on the U.S. National Security Council staff from June 2012 to January 2017), in discussion with author, December 29, 2020.

49. See also Florian J. Egloff, "Public Attribution of Cyber Intrusions," *Journal of Cybersecurity* 6, no. 1 (2020): 1–12.

CHAPTER 1. THE ROLE OF CYBER OPERATIONS AND FORCES IN RUSSIA'S UNDERSTANDING OF WARFARE

1. For a detailed discussion on the limitations of Russia's cyber capabilities, see Cheravitch and Lilly, "Russia's Cyber Limitations in Personnel Recruitment and Innovation," 31–59.

2. Konseptsiya vneshnei politiki Rossiiskoi Federatsii [Foreign policy concept of the Russian Federation], *Nezavisimaya Gazeta*, July 1, 2000, http://www.ng.ru/world /2000–07–11/1_concept.html (accessed March 4, 2021); Ministry of Foreign Affairs of the Russian Federation, Konseptsiya vneshnei politiki Rossiiskoi Federatsii, July 15, 2008, http://www.kremlin.ru/acts/news/785 (accessed March 4, 2021); Ministry of Foreign Affairs of the Russian Federation, Konseptsiya vneshnei politiki Rossiiskoi Federatsii, February 18, 2013, http://www.mid.ru/foreign_policy/official _documents/-/asset_publisher/CptICkB6BZ29/content/id/122186 (accessed March 4, 2021); Ministry of Foreign Affairs of the Russian Federation, Konseptsiya vneshnei politiki Rossiiskoi Federatsii, November 30, 2016, http://www.mid.ru/en/foreign_ policy/official_documents/-/asset_publisher/CptICkB6BZ29/content/id/2542248 (accessed March 4, 2021).

3. Konseptsiya vneshnei politiki Rossiiskoi Federatsii, *Nezavisimaya Gazeta*, July 1, 2000.

4. Ministry of Foreign Affairs of the Russian Federation, Konseptsiya vneshnei politiki Rossiiskoi Federatsii, July 15, 2008; Ministry of Foreign Affairs of the Russian Federation, Konseptsiya vneshnei politiki Rossiiskoi Federatsii, February 18, 2013.

5. Ministry of Foreign Affairs of the Russian Federation, Konseptsiya vneshnei politiki Rossiiskoi Federatsii, November 30, 2016.

6. O Strategii natsional'noy bezopasnosti Rossiyskoy Federatsii [On the national security strategy of the Russian Federation], *Rossiyskaya Gazeta*, December 31, 2015, https://rg.ru/2015/12/31/nac-bezopasnost-site-dok.html (accessed March 4, 2021); O Strategii natsional'noy bezopasnosti Rossiyskoy Federatsii do 2020 goda [On the

national security strategy of the Russian Federation until 2020], *Rossiyskaya Gazeta*, May 19, 2009, https://rg.ru/2009/05/19/strategia-dok.html (accessed March 4, 2021).

7. Presidential Administration of the Russian Federation, Ob utverzhdenii voyennoy doktriny Rossiyskoy Federatsii [On the approval of the military doctrine of the Russian Federation], February 5, 2010, http://pravo.gov.ru/proxy/ips/?docbody=& firstDoc=1&lastDoc=1&nd=102065541 (accessed March 4, 2021); Presidential Administration of the Russian Federation, *Voennaya doktrina Rossiiskoi Federatsii* [The military doctrine of the Russian Federation], December 26, 2014, http://krem lin.ru/acts/news/47334 (accessed March 4, 2021).

8. "Putin's Prepared Remarks at 43rd Munich Conference on Security Policy," *Washington Post*, February 12, 2007, http://www.washingtonpost.com/wp-dyn/content /article/2007/02/12/AR2007021200555.html (accessed March 4, 2021).

9. Foreign Ministry of the Russian Federation, Vystupleniye Ministra inostrannykh del Rossii S. V. Lavrova na XV Assambleye Soveta po vneshney i oboronnoy politike [Foreign Minister Sergey Lavrov's speech at the XV Assembly of the Council on Foreign and Defense Policy], March 17, 2007, http://www.mid.ru/web/guest/foreign _policy/news/-/asset_publisher/cKNonkJE02Bw/content/id/379332 (accessed March 21, 2021).

10. Foreign Ministry of the Russian Federation, Interv'yu Ministra inostrannykh del Rossii S. V. Lavrova ital'yanskoy gazete *Libero*, opublikovannoye 30 noyabrya 2017 goda [Russian Foreign Minister Sergey Lavrov's interview with the Italian newspaper *Libero*, November 30, 2017], http://www.mid.ru/web/guest/maps/it/-/asset_pub lisher/y8qQ47DsHQYD/content/id/2971828 (accessed March 4, 2021); Foreign Ministry of the Russian Federation, Vystupleniye Ministra inostrannykh del Rossii S. V. Lavrova na obshchem sobranii chlenov Rossiyskogo soveta po mezhdunarodnym delam, Moskva, 28 noyabrya 2017 goda [Foreign Minister Sergey Lavrov's remarks at the general meeting of members of the Russian International Affairs Council, Moscow, November 28, 2017], http://www.mid.ru/web/guest/meropriyatiya_s _uchastiem_ministra/-/asset_publisher/xK1BhB2bUjd3/content/id/2969147 (accessed March 4, 2021).

11. Charles Bartles, "Getting Gerasimov Right," *Military Review* (January/February 2016): 31–32; "Shoygu rasskazal o zadachakh voysk informatsionnykh operatsiy" [Shoigu spoke about the tasks of the information operation troops, *RIA Novosti*, February 22, 2017, https://ria.ru/20170222/1488617708.html (accessed March 5, 2021).

12. Bilyana Lilly, *Russian Foreign Policy toward Missile Defense: Actors, Motivations, and Influence* (Lanham, MD: Lexington Books, 2014): xix–xxii.

13. O Strategii natsional'noy bezopasnosti Rossiyskoy Federatsii do 2020 goda [On the national security strategy of the Russian Federation until 2020], *Rossiyskaya Gazeta*, May 19, 2009.

14. Presidential Administration of the Russian Federation, O Strategii natsional'noy bezopasnosti Rossiyskoy Federatsii [On the national security strategy of the Russian

Federation], No. 683, December 31, 2015, http://www.kremlin.ru/acts/bank/40391 (accessed March 4, 2021).

15. Presidential Administration of the Russian Federation, Ob utverzhdenii voyennoy doktriny Rossiyskoy Federatsii [On the approval of the military doctrine of the Russian Federation], February 5, 2010.

16. Presidential Administration of the Russian Federation, *Voennaya doktrina Rossiiskoi Federatsii* [The military doctrine of the Russian Federation], December 26, 2014. https://www.offiziere.ch/wp-content/uploads-001/2015/08/Russia-s-2014-Military -Doctrine.pdf

17. Lilly, *Russian Foreign Policy toward Missile Defense*, 179–84, 249–52.

18. "Lavrov: SSHA i NATO provodyat politiku sderzhivaniya v agressivnykh formakh" [Lavrov: The United States and NATO are pursuing a policy of containment in aggressive forms], *RT,* December 10, 2020, https://russian.rt.com/world/news/811 834-lavrov-ssha-nato (accessed March 4, 2021).

19. Valery Gerasimov, "'Tomagavki' na nizkom starte" ["Tomahawks" at a low start], *Voyenno Promyshlennyy Kuryer*, May 3, 2017, https://vpk.name/news/180658_tom agavki_na_nizkom_starte.html (accessed March 4, 2021).

20. "Genshtab zayavil o roste chisla provokatsiy NATO u granits Rossii" [The general staff announced an increase in the number of NATO provocations near Russia's borders], *RIA Novosti,* December 24, 2020, https://ria.ru/20201224/nato-15907 33312.html (accessed March 4, 2021).

21. Senior members of Russia's general staff, in discussion with author, August 2017, Moscow, Russia.

22. Retired lieutenant general, former representative of the Russian Ministry of Defense, in discussion with author, August 2017, Moscow, Russia.

23. Lilly and Cheravitch, "The Past, Present, and Future of Russia's Cyber Strategy and Forces," 131.

24. Lilly and Cheravitch, "The Past, Present, and Future of Russia's Cyber Strategy and Forces," 131; Christopher S. Chivvis, "Hybrid War," 316–21; Lyle J. Morris, Michael J. Mazarr, Jeffrey W. Hornung, Stephanie Pezard, Anika Binnendijk, and Marta Kepe, *Gaining Competitive Advantage in the Gray Zone: Response Options for Coercive Aggression below the Threshold of Major War* (Santa Monica, CA: RAND Corporation, 2019), https://www.rand.org/pubs/research_reports/RR2942.html (accessed March 28, 2021); Mark Galeotti, "I'm Sorry for Creating the 'Gerasimov Doctrine,'" *Foreign Policy* (March 5, 2018), https://foreignpolicy.com/2018/03/05 /im-sorry-for-creating-the-gerasimov-doctrine/ (accessed March 25, 2021); Michael Kofman, "Russian Hybrid Warfare and Other Dark Arts," *War on the Rocks*, March 11, 2016, https://warontherocks.com/2016/03/russian-hybrid-warfare-and-other- dark-arts/ (accessed March 25, 2021).

25. Lilly and Cheravitch, "The Past, Present, and Future of Russia's Cyber Strategy and Forces," 131; Gerasimov, "Tsennost' nauki v predvidenii;" Senior members of Russia's general staff, in discussion with author, August 2017, Moscow, Russia.

26. Academy of Sciences, *Listovki otechestvennoy voyny* [Leaflets from the Patriotic War] (Moscow: U.S.S.R. Academy of Sciences, 1962), cited in Lilly and Cheravitch, "The Past, Present, and Future of Russia's Cyber Strategy and Forces," 131.

27. Oscar Jonsson, *The Russian Understanding of War*, 38–40.

28. K. Shil'bakh and V. Sventsitskiy, *Voennye Razvedki* [Military Intelligence] (Moscow: Military Typography Directorate, 1927), cited in Lilly and Cheravitch, "The Past, Present, and Future of Russia's Cyber Strategy and Forces," 132.

29. Igor Popov and Musa Hamzatov, *Voina budushchego* [War of the future] (Moscow: Kuchkovo Pole, 2016), 229–34; Lilly and Cherativtch, "The Past, Present, and Future of Russia's Cyber Strategy and Forces," 131.

30. S. G. Chekinov and S. A. Bogdanov, "O kharaktere i soderzhanii voyny novogo pokoleniya" [On the nature and content of a new generation of war], *Voyennaya Mysl'*, no. 10 (October 2013): 14–15; Igor Popov and Musa Hamzatov, *Voina budushchego* [War of the future] (Moscow: Kuchkovo Pole, 2016), 229–34; Ministry of Defense of the Russian Federation, Encyclopedia, v.s. "informatsionnoe protivoborstvo" [information warfare]; M. A. Gareev and N. I. Turko, "Voyna: sovremennoye tolkovaniye teorii i realii praktiki" [War: modern interpretation of theory and realities of practice]," *Vestnik Akademii Voyennykh Nauk* 1, no. 58 (2017): 5.

31. S. I. Makarenko, *Informatsionnoye protivoborstvo i radioelektronnaya bor'ba v setetsentricheskikh voynakh nachala XXI veka* [Information confrontation and electronic warfare in network-centric wars at the beginning of the XXI century] (Saint Petersburg: Science-Intensive Technologies, 2017), 2, 275.

32. Gerasimov, "Tsennost' nauki v predvidenii."

33. Gerasimov, "Tsennost' nauki v predvidenii"; Senior members of Russia's general staff in discussion with author, August 2017, Moscow, Russia; Gerasimov 2019.

34. Gerasimov, "Tsennost' nauki v predvidenii"; Valeriy Gerasimov, "Po opytu Sirii" [From the Experience of Syria], *Voyenno Promyshlennyy Kurye*r, March 8, 2016, http://vpk-news.ru/articles/29579 (accessed March 25, 2021); Valeriy Gerasimov, "Generalnyi Shtab i oborona strany" [The General Staff and the defense of the country], *Voyenno Promyshlennyy Kuryer*, February 3, 2014, https://www.vpk-news.ru/articles/18998 (accessed March 25, 2021); Senior members of Russia's general staff in discussion with author, August 2017, Moscow, Russia.

35. Russia's military scholars and Russian doctrinal documents refer to several terms that can be roughly translated as information warfare. These terms include *informatsionnoe protivoborstvo* (information warfare or information confrontation), *informatsionnaya voina* (information war) and *informatsionnaya bor'ba* (information fight, information war, information battle or information struggle). To avoid using multiple terms, "information warfare" will be used for the purposes of this research. Ministry of Defense of the Russian Federation, Encyclopedia, s.v. "Informatsionnoe protivoborstvo" [information warfare]; Defense Ministry of the Russian Federation, "Informatsionnaya voina" [Information war], *Military-Encyclopaedic Dictionary of*

the Ministry of Defense, http://encyclopedia.mil.ru/encyclopedia/dictionary/details .htm?id=5211@morfDictionary (accessed March 4, 2021); V. I. Orlyanskii, "Informatsionnoye oruzhiye i informatsionnaya bor'ba: real'nost' i domysly" [Information weapons and information warfare: reality and speculation], *Voyennaya Mysl'*, no. 1, 68.

36. The United States defines "cyberspace" as a subcomponent of the "information environment," while Russian doctrine treats the two as interchangeable and does not provide a separate definition for cyberspace. Cyberspace, which is a component of the information environment, is defined in U.S. DoD JP 3–12 as "[a] global domain within the information environment consisting of the interdependent network of information technology infrastructures and resident data, including the internet, telecommunications networks, computer systems, and embedded processors and controllers." The same document defines the information environment as "the aggregate of individuals, organizations, and systems that collect, process, disseminate, or act on information." Department of Defense, United States of America, *Joint Publication 3–12 Cyberspace Operations,* June 8, 2018, GL-4, viii, https://www.jcs .mil/Portals/36/Documents/Doctrine/pubs/jp3_12.pdf (accessed March 28, 2021).

37. Ministry of Defense of the Russian Federation, "Kontseptual'nye vzglyady na deyatel'nost' Vooruzhennykh Sil Rossiyskoy Federatsii v informatsionnom prostranstve" [Conceptual views on the activities of the Armed Forces of the Russian Federation in the information space], section 1, 2011, http://ens.mil.ru/science/pub lications/more.htm?id=10845074@cmsArticle (accessed March 26, 2021).

38. Ministry of Defense of the Russian Federation. "Kontseptual'nye vzglyady na deyatel'nost' Vooruzhennykh Sil Rossiyskoy Federatsii v informatsionnom prostranstve," section 1.

39. Psychological war (*psyhologicheskaya bor'ba*) is defined as "active measures in the information-psychological sphere, aimed at changing the behavioral and emotional attitudes of a group of people and individuals on a particular question in a desired direction." I. N. Dylevskiy, V. O. Zapivahin, S. A. Komov, S V. Korotkov, and A. N. Petrunin, "Mezhdunarodnyy rezhim nerasprostraneniya informatsionnogo oruzhiya: utopiya ili real'nost'?" [International regime for the non-proliferation of information weapons: utopia or reality], *Voyennaya Mysl'*, no. 10 (2014): 5.

40. See also K. A. Trotsenko, " Informatsionnoye protivoborstvo v operativno-taktich-eskom zvene upravleniya" [Information confrontation in the operational-tactical control link], *Voyennaya Mysl'*, no. 8 (2016): 20.

41. See also Trotsenko, "Informatsionnoye protivoborstvo v operativno-takticheskom zvene upravleniya," 20.

42. N. A. Molchanov, "Informatsionnyy potentsial zarubezhnykh stran kak istochnik ugroz voyennoy bezopasnosti RF" [Information potential of foreign countries as a source of threats to the military security of the Russian Federation], *Voyennaya Mysl'*, no. 10 (2008): 8.

43. Makarenko, *Informatsionnoye protivoborstvo i radioelektronnaya bor'ba v setetsentrich-eskikh voynakh nachala XXI veka*, 2, 256, 270, 275; Molchanov, "Informatsionnyy potentsial zarubezhnykh stran kak istochnik ugroz voyennoy bezopasnosti RF," 8–9; Gagik Terterov, "Informatsionnyye operatsii: istoriya i sovremennost' [Information operations: history and modernity]," *21st Vek 3*, no. 36 (2015): 40–49.

44. Thomas, *Russian Military Thought: Concepts and Elements*, 8–18.

45. A. A. Kokoshin, Yu. N. Baluyevskiy, and V. Ya. Potapov, "Vliyaniye noveyshikh tendentsiy v razvitii tekhnologiy i sredstv vooruzhennoy bor'by na voyennoye iskusstvo" [The impact of the latest trends in the development of technologies and means of warfare on the art of war], *Vestnik Moskovskogo universiteta* [Bulletin of Moscow University], series 25, Mezhdunarodnyye otnosheniya i mirovaya politika [International Relations and World Politics], no. 4, 2015.

46. A. A. Kokoshin, Yu. N. Baluyevskiy, and V. Ya. Potapov, "Vliyaniye noveyshikh tendentsiy v razvitii tekhnologiy i sredstv vooruzhennoy bor'by na voyennoye iskusstvo."

47. A. A. Kokoshin, Yu. N. Baluyevskiy, and V. Ya. Potapov, "Vliyaniye noveyshikh tendentsiy v razvitii tekhnologiy i sredstv vooruzhennoy bor'by na voyennoye iskusstvo;" Makarenko, *Informatsionnoye protivoborstvo i radioelektronnaya bor'ba v setetsentricheskikh voynakh nachala XXI veka*, 256, 270; Chekinov and Bogdanov, "O kharaktere i soderzhanii voyny novogo pokoleniya," 17.

48. "Shoygu rasskazal o zadachakh voysk informatsionnykh operatsiy" [Shoigu rasskazal o zadachakh voisk informatsionnukh operatsii, *RIA Novosti*, February 22, 2017.

49. Chekinov and Bogdanov, "O kharaktere i soderzhanii voyny novogo pokoleniya," 17, 20.

50. H. I. Sayfetdinov, "Informatsionnoye protivoborstvo v voyennoy sfere" [Information confrontation in the military sphere], *Voyennaya Mysl'*, no. 7 (2014): 38.

51. Makarenko, *Informatsionnoye protivoborstvo i radioelektronnaya bor'ba v setetsentrich-eskikh voynakh nachala XXI veka*, 256, 270.

52. Sayfetdinov, "Informatsionnoye protivoborstvo v voyennoy sfere," 40.

53. Sayfetdinov, "Informatsionnoye protivoborstvo v voyennoy sfere," 41; Ministry of Defense of the Russian Federation, Encyclopedia, s.v. "Informatsionnoe protivoborstvo" [information warfare]; Makarenko, *Informatsionnoye protivoborstvo i radio-elektronnaya bor'ba v setetsentricheskikh voynakh nachala XXI veka*, 2, 253; A. N. Limno and M. F. Krysanov, "Informatsionnoye protivoborstvo i maskirovka voysk" [Information confrontation and masking of troops], *Voyennaya Mysl'* (2013): 74.

54. Chekinov and Bogdanov, "O kharaktere i soderzhanii voyny novogo pokoleniya," 17–18.

55. Chekinov and Bogdanov, "O kharaktere i soderzhanii voyny novogo pokoleniya," 21.

56. Gerasimov, "Po opytu Sirii."

57. Chekinov and Bogdanov, "O kharaktere i soderzhanii voyny novogo pokoleniya," 18–19.

58. A. A. Kokoshin, Yu. N. Baluyevskiy, and V. Ya. Potapov, "Vliyaniye noveyshikh tendentsiy v razvitii tekhnologiy i sredstv vooruzhennoy bor'by na voyennoye iskusstvo."

59. Chekinov and Bogdanov, "O kharaktere i soderzhanii voyny novogo pokoleniya," 19.

60. I. N. Dylevskiy, V. O. Zapivahin, S. A. Komov, S. V. Korotkov, and A. A. Krivchenko, "O dialektike sderzhivaniya i predotvrashcheniya voyennykh konfliktov v informatsionnuyu eru," [On the dialectic of deterring and preventing military conflicts in the information era], *Voyennaya Mysl'*, no. 7 (2016): 8.

61. Molchanov, "Informatsionnyy potentsial zarubezhnykh stran kak istochnik ugroz voyennoy bezopasnosti RF," 6.

62. Sergei Alekseevich Yarkov, "Nevoyennyye sredstva i nevoyennyye mery neytralizatsii voyennykh opasnostey: sushchnostnoye razlichiye i predmetnaya kharakteristika ponyatiy" [Nonmilitary means and nonmilitary measures to neutralize military dangers: essential difference and objective characteristics of the concepts], *Natsional'naya bezopasnost'* [National Security], no. 3 (2017): 114–25; N. N. Bolotov, "Sushchnost' i soderzhaniye ponyatiya 'voyna v informatsionnoy sfere,'" [The essence and content of the concept of "war in the information sphere"], *Vestnik Akademii Voyennykh Nauk* [Bulletin of the Academy of Military Sciences], no. 1, issue 58 (2017): 23.

63. Sayfetdinov, "Informatsionnoye protivoborstvo v voyennoy sfere," 40.

64. See also Sayfetdinov, "Informatsionnoye protivoborstvo v voyennoy sfere," 39; Bolotov, "Sushchnost' i soderzhaniye ponyatiya 'voyna v informatsionnoy sfere,'" 26.

65. Sayfetdinov, "Informatsionnoye protivoborstvo v voyennoy sfere," 40; Gerasimov, "Tsennost' nauki v predvidenii."

66. Sayfetdinov, "Informatsionnoye protivoborstvo v voyennoy sfere," 40.

67. Chekinov and Bogdanov, "O kharaktere i soderzhanii voyny novogo pokoleniya," 17.

68. S. R. Tsyrendorzhiev, "O kolichestvennoy otsenke stepeni voyennoy bezopasnosti" [Quantitative assessment of military security of the state], *Voyennaya Mysl'*, no. 10 (2014): 31.

69. "CrowdStrike's Work with the Democratic National Committee," *CrowdStrike* (blog); Andy Greenberg, *Sandworm: A New Era of Cyberwar and the Hunt for the Kremlin's Most Dangerous Hackers* (New York: Doubleday, 2019). The designations for each cyber threat group are assigned by different cybersecurity companies. For the purposes of this dissertation, the author will use the FireEye/Mandiant convention as the primary reference for APT 28 and APT 29, and Trend Micro's designation for Sandworm. Computer Security Incident Response Team of Thailand, *Threat Group Cards: A Threat Actor Encyclopedia*, 36, 281, 296.

70. According to the General Intelligence and Security Service of the Netherlands (AIVD) infiltrated Russian networks used by the group of hackers known as Cozy Bear. AIVD gained access to the video cameras in the building from which the

group operated and took images of the individuals. AIVD then cross-referenced the images with those of Russian agents and concluded that the group belonged to the SVR. Sean Gallagher, "Candid Camera: Dutch Hacked Russians Hacking DNC, including Security Cameras," *Ars Technica*, January 26, 2018, https://arstechnica .com/information-technology/2018/01/dutch-intelligence-hacked-video-cameras -in-office-of-russians-who-hacked-dnc/ (accessed March 25, 2021); Scott Knight, "The Dukes of Moscow," *VMware Carbon Black*, March 26, 2020, https://www .carbonblack.com/blog/the-dukes-of-moscow/ (accessed March 5, 2021).

71. Computer Security Incident Response Team of Thailand, *Threat Group Cards: A Threat Actor Encyclopedia*, 36, 281, 296.

72. Italy Cohen and Omri Ben Bassat, "Mapping the Connections inside Russia's APT Ecosystem," *Check Point Research*, September 24, 2019, https://research.checkpoint .com/2019/russianaptecosystem/ (accessed March 5, 2021).

73. Joe Cheravitch and Bilyana Lilly, "Russia's Cyber Limitations in Personnel Recruitment and Innovation," 38–39. See chapter 5 on Russia's information warfare campaign against the 2016 U.S. elections.

74. Lilly and Cheravitch, "The Past, Present, and Future of Russia's Cyber Strategy and Forces," 139.

75. Security Council of the Russian Federation, "Sostav Soveta Bezopasnosti Rossiyskoy Federatsii" [Members of the Security Council of the Russian Federation], http:// www.scrf.gov.ru/council/composition/ (accessed March 5, 2021).

76. Galeotti, *Putin's Hydra*, 2, 9; "Wheels Within Wheels: How Mr. Putin Keeps the Country Under Control," *Economist*, October 22, 2016, https://www.economist. com/special-report/2016/10/20/wheels-within-wheels (accessed March 5, 2021).

77. Galeotti, *Putin's Hydra*, 3.

78. Lilly and Cheravitch, "The Past, Present, and Future of Russia's Cyber Strategy and Forces," 139.

79. Lilly and Cheravitch, "The Past, Present, and Future of Russia's Cyber Strategy and Forces," 139.

80. Villalon Antonio, "The Russian ICC (V): FSB," *Securit A(r)TWork*, December 20, 2016, https://www.securityartwork.es/2016/12/20/the-russian-icc-v-fsb/ (accessed March 5, 2021).

81. Government of the Russian Federation, Foreign Intelligence Service, http://govern ment.ru/en/department/112/ (accessed August 26, 2020); "Russia's Three Intelligence Agencies, Explained," *The Moscow Project, Center for American Progress Action Fund*, October 12, 2018, https://themoscowproject.org/explainers/russias-three -intelligence-agencies-explained/ (accessed March 28, 2021).

82. "Expansion of Foreign Intelligence Service HQ (SVR; Former KGB First Main Directorate) Yasenevo, Moscow, Russia 55.584 N, 37.517 E Between 2007 and 2018," *Federation of American Scientists*, updated July 27, 2018, https://fas.org/irp

/eprint/svr-expansion.pdf (accessed March 5, 2021); "Russia's Three Intelligence Agencies, Explained," *The Moscow Project, Center for American Progress Action Fund.*

83. David E. Sanger, Nicole Perlroth, and Julian E. Barnes, "As Understanding of Russian Hacking Grows, So Does Alarm," *New York Times,* January 2, 2021, updated January 5, 2021, https://www.nytimes.com/2021/01/02/us/politics/russian-hacking -government.html (accessed March 5, 2021).

84. *International Security and Estonia 2018* (Estonia: Estonian Foreign Intelligence Service, 2018), 53, https://www.valisluureamet.ee/pdf/raport-2018-ENG-web.pdf (accessed March 5, 2021); Knight, "The Dukes of Moscow"; David E. Sanger et al., "As Understanding of Russian Hacking Grows, So Does Alarm."

85. Computer Security Incident Response Team of Thailand, *Threat Group Cards: A Threat Actor Encyclopedia,* 36.

86. Ministry of Defense of the Russian Federation, "Glavnoye upravleniye General'nogo shtaba Vooruzhennykh Sil Rossiyskoy Federatsii" [Main Directorate of the General Staff of the Armed Forces of the Russian Federation], https://structure.mil.ru/struc ture/ministry_of_defence/details.htm?id=9711@egOrganization (accessed March 5, 2021).

87. Ministry of Defense of the Russian Federation, "Struktura Minoborony Rossii" [Structure of the Russian Defense Ministry], https://structure.mil.ru/structure/ structuremorf.htm (accessed March 5, 2021).

88. Lilly and Cheravitch, "The Past, Present, and Future of Russia's Cyber Strategy and Forces," 140–41.

89. Lilly and Cheravitch, "The Past, Present, and Future of Russia's Cyber Strategy and Forces," 141–44.

90. Anton Troianovski and Ellen Nakashima, "How Russia's Military Intelligence Agency Became the Covert Muscle of Putin's Duels with the West," *Washington Post,* December 28, 2018, https://www.washingtonpost.com/world/europe/how -russias-military-intelligence-agency-became-the-covert-muscle-in-putins-duels -with-the-west/2018/12/27/2736bbe2-fb2d-11e8–8c9a-860ce2a8148f_story.html ?noredirect=on&utm_term=.afbab6c3ba54 (accessed March 25, 2021).

91. United States of America v. Viktor Borisovich Netyksho, Boris Alekseyevich Antonov, Dmitriy Sergeyevich Badin, Ivan Sergeyevich Yerakov, Eleksey Aleksandrovich Morgachev, Nikolay Yuryevich Kozachek, Pavel Vyacheslavovich Yershov, Artem Andreyevich Malyshev, Aleksandr Vladimirovich Osadchuk, Aleksey Aleksan- drovich Potemkin, and Anatoliy Sergeyevich Kovalev, Indictment, 18 U.S.C. 2, 371, 1030, 1028A, 1956 (U.S. District Court for the District of Columbia, July 13, 2018), at 3, https://www.justice.gov/file/1080281/download (accessed March 28, 2021); Troianovski and Nakashima, "How Russia's Military Intelligence Agency Became the Covert Muscle of Putin's Duels with the West."

92. Lilly and Cheravitch, "The Past, Present, and Future of Russia's Cyber Strategy and Forces," 145–46; United States of America v. Viktor Borisovich Netyksho et al.,

Indictment, 18 U.S.C. 2, 371, 1030, 1028A, 1956 (U.S. District Court for the District of Columbia, July 13, 2018), at 3.

93. Troianovski and Nakashima, "How Russia's Military Intelligence Agency Became the Covert Muscle of Putin's Duels with the West."

94. Computer Security Incident Response Team of Thailand, *Threat Group Cards: A Threat Actor Encyclopedia*, 296.

95. Computer Security Incident Response Team of Thailand, *Threat Group Cards: A Threat Actor Encyclopedia*, 296–97. "Who is FANCY BEAR (APT28)?" *Crowd-Strike* (blog), February 12, 2019, https://www.crowdstrike.com/blog/who-is-fancy-bear/ (accessed March 5, 2021).

96. "Who is FANCY BEAR (APT28)?" *CrowdStrike* (blog), February 12, 2019.

97. Computer Security Incident Response Team of Thailand, *Threat Group Cards: A Threat Actor Encyclopedia*, 281.

98. FireEye Threat Intelligence, *Trends in Cyber Threat Activity Targeting Elections, 2016–2019*, January 15, 2020, at 12; Pasi Eronen, "Case: Sandworm," *Cyberwatch, Finland*, 2020, at 17, https://issuu.com/cyberwatchfinland.fi/docs/cyberwatchfin land_q1_issuu/16?fbclid=IwAR1vGPsNdMh5hsUO0md9VSEeOUhAulVVY 6m88Yl25kpiTNIGZsLqkIxAmto (accessed August 26, 2020).

99. Computer Security Incident Response Team of Thailand, *Threat Group Cards: A Threat Actor Encyclopedia*, 281.

100. Daniil Turovskiy, *Vtorzhenie: Kratkaya istoriya Russkikh khakerov* [Invasion: A short history of Russian hackers] (Moscow: Inviduum, 2019), 125–26, 130–39.

101. Daniil Turovskiy, *Vtorzhenie: Kratkaya istoriya Russkikh khakerov* [Invasion: A short history of Russian hackers] (Moscow: Inviduum, 2019), 148.

CHAPTER 2. FRAMEWORKS FOR PREDICTING AND ANALYZING CYBER OPERATIONS IN THE CONTEXT OF INFORMATION WARFARE

1. *Certified Ethical Hacker Complete Guide* (UK: IPSpecialist LTD, September 15, 2018), 30–31; Josh Fruhlinger, "The CIA Triad: Definition, Components and Examples," *CSO Online*, February 10, 2020, https://www.csoonline.com/article/35 19908/the-cia-triad-definition-components-and-examples.html (accessed on March 5, 2021).

2. See chapter 4.

3. Vera Zakem, Paul Saunders, Umida Hashimova, and P. Kathleen Hammerberg, *Mapping Russian Media Network: Media's Role in Russian Foreign Policy and Decision-making* (Arlington, VA: Center for Naval Analysis, January 2018), 21–23. https://www.cna.org/cna_files/pdf/DRM-2017-U-015367–3Rev.pdf (accessed March 9, 2021); Elina Lange-Ionatamišvili, *Analysis of Russia's Information Campaign against Ukraine* (Riga, Latvia: NATO StratCom Centre of Excellence, 2015), 4, 13.

4. Christopher Paul and Miriam Matthews, *The Russian "Firehose of Falsehood" Propaganda Model: Why It Might Work and Options to Counter It* (Santa Monica, CA:

RAND Corporation, 2016), 1. https://www.rand.org/pubs/perspectives/PE198.html (accessed September 08, 2020).

5. Paul and Matthews, *The Russian "Firehose of Falsehood" Propaganda Model*, 1.

6. Lilly, *Russian Foreign Policy Toward Missile Defense: Actors, Motivations, and Influence*, 5–6, 194.

7. Benjamin Elisha Sawe, "What Was the Eastern Bloc?," *World Atlas*, August 8, 2018, https://www.worldatlas.com/articles/what-was-the-eastern-bloc.html (accessed on March 9, 2021); Chivvis, "Hybrid War," 319; Raphael S. Cohen and Andrew Radin, *Russia's Hostile Measures in Europe: Understanding the Threat* (Santa Monica, CA: RAND Corporation, 2019), 68–70, https://www.rand.org/pubs/research_reports /RR1793.html (accessed March 28, 2021).

8. Congressional Research Service, *The Designation of Election Systems as Critical Infrastructure*, September 18, 2019, https://fas.org/sgp/crs/misc/IF10677.pdf (accessed on August 27, 2020).

9. Congressional Research Service, *The Designation of Election Systems as Critical Infrastructure*.

10. Cybersecurity and Infrastructure Security Agency, U.S. Department of Homeland Security, *2020 Election Infrastructure Subsector-Specific Plan. An Annex to the NIPP 2013*, 2020, 4.

11. Kim Zetter, "Top Voting Machine Vendor Admits It Installed Remote-Access Software on Systems Sold to States," *Vice*, July 17, 2018, https://www.vice.com/en_us /article/mb4ezy/top-voting-machine-vendor-admits-it-installed-remote-access-soft ware-on-systems-sold-to-states?wpisrc=nl_cybersecurity202&wpmm=1 (accessed on March 9, 2021).

12. Although the two-level category that this dissertation uses is derived on the basis of Russian literature, some Russian scholars acknowledge that the typology they have applied in their writing is based on Western sources. Therefore, this general typology should not be considered as entirely Russian.

13. N. A. Molchanov, "Informatsionnyy potentsial zarubezhnykh stran kak istochnik ugroz voyennoy bezopasnosti RF," 8.

14. S. Marinin, "Podkhody voyennykh ekspertov SSHA k razrabotke ponyatiynogo apparata v sfere bor'by v kiberprostranstve" [Approaches of U.S. military experts towards the development of concepts in the sphere of warfare in cyberspace], *Zarubezhnoye Voyennoye Obozreniye* [Foreign Military Review], no. 10 (October 2011): 28.

15. For a summary of CHAOS, see Lilly, "Bringing Order Through CHAOS."

16. For an example of the application of machine-learning tools for text analysis to studying defense issues, see Bilyana Lilly and Sale Lilly, "Weaponising Blockchain: Military Applications of Blockchain Technology in the US, China and Russia," *RUSI Journal* 166, no. 3 (March 8, 2021), https://www.tandfonline.com/doi/abs /10.1080/03071847.2021.1886871?journalCode=rusi20 (accessed November 26, 2021).

CHAPTER 3. WEB WAR I

1. Juurvee and Mattiisen, *The Bronze Soldier Crisis of 2007*, 9–10; Heather A. Conley and Theodore P. Gerber, *Russian Soft Power in 21st Century: An Examination of Russian Compatriot Policy in Estonia* (Washington, DC: Center for Strategic and International Studies, September 6, 2011), 3–6, http://www.bearnetwork.ca/wp-content/uploads/2018/02/110826_Conley_RussianSoftPower_Web.pdf (accessed March 28, 2021).

2. Aivars Stranga, "Estonia," *Encyclopedoa Britannica*, February 2, 2021, https://www.britannica.com/place/Estonia (accessed March 9, 2021).

3. "Estonia Seals off Russian Memorial," *BBC News*, April 26, 2007, http://news.bbc.co.uk/2/hi/europe/6597497.stm (accessed March 25, 2021); Conley and Gerber, *Russian Soft Power in 21st Century*, 6.

4. Juurvee and Mattiisen, *The Bronze Soldier Crisis of 2007*, 1.

5. David Mardiste and Olesya Dmitracova, "Estonia Relocates Red Army Statue amid Russia Row," *Reuters*, April 30, 2007, https://uk.reuters.com/article/uk-estonia-russia/estonia-relocates-red-army-statue-amid-russia-row-idUKL3048016020070430 (accessed on March 9, 2021).

6. "Estonia Cancels Russia Talks over Statue," *Associated Press*, May 2, 2007, https://newsok.com/article/3045674/estonia-cancels-russia-talks-over-statue (accessed on March 9, 2021).

7. Juurvee and Mattiisen, *The Bronze Soldier Crisis of 2007*, 14.

8. "Russia's Involvement in the Tallinn Disturbances," *International Center for Defense and Security*, May 11, 2007, https://icds.ee/russias-involvement-in-the-tallinn-disturbances/ (accessed March 9, 2021); Juurvee and Mattiisen, *The Bronze Soldier Crisis of 2007*, iv, 18.

9. Annual Review, 2007, Estonian Security Police, 14, https://www.kapo.ee/sites/default/files/public/content_page/Annual%20Review%202007.pdf (accessed March 28, 2021).

10. Mathias Roth, *Bilateral Disputes between EU Member States and Russia*, CEPS Working Document No. 319, August 2009, at 13, http://aei.pitt.edu/11434/1/1900.pdf (accessed on March 9, 2021).

11. Ruslan Kadrmatov, "Vremennoye pomeshatel'stvo otnosheniy Politicheskiye aktsii protiv Estonii ne nashli podderzhki na Zapade" [Temporary insanity of political actions against Estonia did not find support in the West], *Lenta.ru*, May 3, 2007, https://lenta.ru/articles/2007/05/03/answer/ (accessed March 9, 2021); Juurvee and Mattiisen, *The Bronze Soldier Crisis of 2007*, 30; Roth, *Bilateral Disputes between EU Member States and Russia*, 13.

12. Roth, *Bilateral Disputes between EU Member States and Russia*, 13; René Värk, "The Siege of the Estonian Embassy in Moscow: Protection of a Diplomatic Mission and Its Staff in the Receiving State," *Juridica International*, no. 25 (2008): 149, https://www.juridicainternational.eu/public/pdf/ji_2008_2_144.pdf (accessed March 25, 2021).

13. "'Nashi'" snyali osadu s estonskogo posol'stva" ["Ours" lifted the siege from the Estonian embassy], *Lenta.ru*, May 3, 2007, https://lenta.ru/news/2007/05/03/nashi/ (accessed March 9, 2021).

14. Juurvee and Mattiisen, *The Bronze Soldier Crisis of 2007*, 26; Russia's Involvement in the Tallinn Disturbances," *International Center for Defense and Security*, May 11, 2007.

15. Juurvee and Mattiisen, *The Bronze Soldier Crisis of 2007*, 26.

16. "EU Urges Russia to End Estonia Embassy Blockade," *Deutsche Welle*, May 2, 2007, https://www.dw.com/en/eu-urges-russia-to-end-estonia-embassy-blockade/a-2464370 (accessed March 9, 2021).

17. "US Congress Passes Resolution Supporting Estonia," *Baltic Times*, June 6, 2007, https://www.baltictimes.com/news/articles/18002/ (accessed March 25, 2021).

18. Ministry of Foreign Affairs of the Russian Federation, "O note MID Rossii vnesh-nepoliticheskomu vedomstvu Estonii" [On the note of the Russian Foreign Ministry to the Estonian Foreign Ministry], April 23, 2007, http://www.mid.ru/foreign_policy/rso/-/asset_publisher/0vP3hQoCPRg5/content/id/375656 (accessed March 9, 2021).

19. Ministry of Foreign Affairs of the Russian Federation, "O note MID Rossii vnesh-nepoliticheskomu vedomstvu Estonii," April 23, 2007.

20. "Tallinn Tense after Deadly Riots," *BBC News*, April 28, 2017, http://news.bbc.co.uk/2/hi/europe/6602171.stm (accessed March 9, 2021).

21. Kramer, "Putin Is Said to Compare U.S. Policies to Third Reich."

22. "Alexy II: Estonian Government Disrespect for Soldier Monument Immoral," *Interfax*, May 2, 2007, http://www.interfax-religion.com/?act=news&div=2982 (accessed March 9, 2021).

23. Juurvee and Mattiisen, *The Bronze Soldier Crisis of 2007*, 27.

24. Roth, *Bilateral Disputes between EU Member States and Russia*, 13; "Konflikt Rossii i Estonii stal priobretat' cherty ekonomicheskogo protivostoyaniya i priznaki istoriko-etnicheskogo dissonansa," [The conflict between Russia and Estonia began to acquire features of economic confrontation and signs of historical and ethnic dissonance], *Psikhologia*, May 5, 2007, https://psy.rin.ru/cgi-bin/news.pl?id=124331 (accessed March 25, 2021).

25. "Ssora s Rossiyey obernulas' dlya Estonii ogromnymi poteryami" [The quarrel with Russia turned out to be huge losses for Estonia], *Zagolovki*, November 17, 2007, http://zagolovki.ru/daytheme/estonia/17Nov2007 (accessed March 9, 2021).

26. "Konflikt Rossii i Estonii stal priobretat' cherty ekonomicheskogo protivostoyaniya i priznaki istoriko-etnicheskogo dissonansa" [The conflict between Russia and Estonia began to acquire features of economic confrontation and signs of historical and ethnic dissonance], *Psikhologia*, May 5, 2007.

27. Roth, *Bilateral Disputes between EU Member States and Russia*, 13.

28. Ruslan Kadrmatov, "Vremennoye pomeshatel'stvo otnosheniy Politicheskiye aktsii protiv Estonii ne nashli podderzhki na Zapade" [Temporary insanity of political actions against Estonia did not find support in the West], *Lenta.ru*, May 3, 2007, https://lenta.ru/articles/2007/05/03/answer/ (accessed March 9, 2021).

29. Juurvee and Mattiisen, *The Bronze Soldier Crisis of 2007*, 27; Roth, *Bilateral Disputes between EU Member States and Russia*, 13. http://aei.pitt.edu/11434/1/1900.pdf.

30. Roth, *Bilateral Disputes between EU Member States and Russia*, 13.

31. "Lavrov: rossiyskiye biznesmeny byli vprave sokratit' tranzit cherez Estoniyu posle demontazha Bronzovogo soldata" [Lavrov: Russian businessmen had the right to reduce transit through Estonia after the dismantling of the Bronze Soldier], *Interfax*, April 23, 2009, https://www.interfax.ru/russia/75997 (accessed March 9, 2021).

32. Ian Traynor, "Russia Accused of Unleashing Cyberwar to Disable Estonia," *Guardian*, May 17, 2007, https://www.theguardian.com/world/2007/may/17/topstories 3.russia (accessed March 25, 2021).

33. Rain Ottis, *Analysis of the 2007 Cyber Attacks Against Estonia from the Information Warfare Perspective* (Tallinn, Estonia: NATO Cooperative Cyber Defence Centre of Excellence, 2018), https://ccdcoe.org/uploads/2018/10/Ottis2008_AnalysisOf 2007FromTheInformationWarfarePerspective.pdf (accessed March 25, 2021); Eneken Tikk, Kadri Kaska, and Liis Vihul, *International Cyber Incidents: Legal Considerations* (Tallinn, Estonia: NATO Cooperative Cyber Defence Centre of Excellence, 2010), 18, 20–22.

34. Some analysts contend that the DDoS attacks can be divided into three waves, not four. This research opted to use analyses that group the DDoS attacks into four groups because these analyses were more recent and may be based on an increased amount of available evidence. For documents that group the attacks into three waves, see "Estonia Cyber Attacks 2007" (PowerPoint presentation, Africa Internet Summit, 2011), https://meeting.afrinic.net/afrinic-11/slides/aaf/Estonia_cyber_attacks _2007_latest.pdf (accessed March 25, 2021).

35. Rain Ottis, *Analysis of the 2007 Cyber Attacks Against Estonia from the Information Warfare Perspective*.

36. "The Cyber Raiders Hitting Estonia," *BBC News*, May 17, 2007, http://news.bbc.co .uk/2/hi/europe/6665195.stm (accessed March 9, 2021).

37. Ottis, *Analysis of the 2007 Cyber Attacks against Estonia from the Information Warfare Perspective*.

38. Juurvee and Mattiisen, *The Bronze Soldier Crisis of 2007*, 29.

39. Arthur Bright, "Estonia Accuses Russia of 'Cyberattack,'" *Christian Science Monitor*, May 17, 2007, https://cyber-peace.org/wp-content/uploads/2016/11/Estonia-accuses -Russia-of-cyberattack-CSMonitor.pdf (accessed March 9, 2021); Stephen Herzog, "Revisiting the Estonian Cyber Attacks: Digital Threats and Multinational Responses," *Journal of Strategic Security* 4, no. 2 (2011): 51, 53, 54; Ottis, *Analysis of the 2007 Cyber Attacks against Estonia from the Information Warfare Perspective*.

40. Juurvee and Mattiisen, *The Bronze Soldier Crisis of 2007*, 30. Private citizens, not directly working for the Russian government, publicly admitted their "voluntary" participation in the cyber attacks, which further complicated the ability to attribute the attacks to the Russian government. See, for example, "Komissar dvizheniya 'Nashi' priznalsya v kiber-atakakh protiv Estonii" [Commissioner of the "Nashi" movement admitted to cyber attacks against Estonia], *MassMedia News*, March 12, 2009, https://lenta.ru/news/2009/03/12/confess/ (accessed March 9, 2021).

41. "Estonia Trial of Russia Activists," *BBC News*, January 14, 2008, http://news.bbc.co.uk/2/hi/europe/7187437.stm (accessed March 10, 2021); Michael Lesk, "The New Front Line: Estonia under Cyberassault," *IEEE Security & Privacy*, July/August 2007, https://www.computer.org/csdl/magazine/sp/2007/04/j4076/13rRUwbaqSW (accessed March 10, 2021); Cyrus Farivar, "A Brief Examination of Media Coverage of Cyberattacks (2007–Present)," in *The Virtual Battlefield: Perspective on Cyber Warfare*, ed. Christian Czosseck and Kenneth Geers (Washington, DC: IOS Press, 2009).

42. Urve Eslas, "Confronting Disinfo on TV in Tallinn," *Up North*, January 18, 2018, https://upnorth.eu/confronting-disinfo-tv-tallinn/ (accessed March 10, 2021); Riina Kaljurand, "Estonia's 'Virtual Russian World': The Influence of Russian Media on Estonia's Russian Speakers," *International Center for Defense and Security*, November 13, 2015, https://icds.ee/estonias-virtual-russian-world-the-influence-of-russian-media-on-estonias-russian-speakers/ (accessed March 10, 2021); Aija Krutaine and Andrius Sytas, "Battle of the Airwaves: Baltics Compete with Russia for Hearts and Minds," *Reuters*, February 13, 2015, https://www.reuters.com/article/uk-baltic-russia-propaganda/battle-of-the-airwaves-baltics-compete-with-russia-for-hearts-and-minds-idUKKBN0LH1OG20150213 (accessed March 10, 2021).

43. "Okonchatel'noye resheniye sovetskogo voprosa. Estoniya gotovitsya k perenosu pamyatnikov" [The final solution to the Soviet question. Estonia prepares for the transfer of monuments], *Channel 1*, November 26, 2006, https://www.1tv.ru/news/2006–11–26/214891-okonchatelnoe_reshenie_sovetskogo_voprosa_estoniya_gotovitsya_k_perenosu_pamyatnikov (accessed March 10, 2021); "V Talline razrezan i vyvezen po chastyam pamyatnik Voinu-osvoboditelyu. V besporyadkakh ubit russkoyazychnyy zhitel'" [In Tallinn, a monument to the Liberator Soldier was cut and removed in parts. Russian-speaking resident killed in riots], *Newsru.com*, April 27, 2007, https://www.newsru.com/world/27apr2007/tallin.html (accessed March 10, 2021).

44. Juurvee and Mattiisen, *The Bronze Soldier Crisis of 2007*, 14, 17; "Ukor sovesti. Ne dopustit' demontazh pamyatnika Voinu-osvoboditelyu v Talline" [A reproach of conscience. Prevent the dismantling of the monument to the Liberator Soldier in Tallinn], *Channel 1*, January 27, 2007, https://www.1tv.ru/news/2007–01–24/212715-ukor_sovesti_ne_dopustit_demontazh_pamyatnika_voinu_osvoboditelyu_v_talline (accessed March 10, 2021).

45. "Russia profile—Media," *BBC News*, January 7, 2020, https://www.bbc.com/news /world-europe-17840134 (accessed March 10, 2021).

46. Juurvee and Mattiisen, *The Bronze Soldier Crisis of 2007*, 21.

47. The research downloaded the data for this analysis from the database Integrum. Integrum is available through the Knowledge Services of the RAND Corporation and allows for searches within specific dates and with specific key terms using Boolean algebra. For this analysis, the author performed a search with the following parameters: "Эстони* или Таллин*" from January 27, 2007, to September 18, 2007. The search was performed on June 13, 2019. The examined media included Russian state-sponsored information agencies TASS and Ria Novosti (which as of 2013 was renamed Rossiya Segodnya) and newspapers: *Kommersant, Komsomolskaya Pravda*, and *Izvestiya*. The author wanted to perform a more targeted search on articles from the most-viewed Russian channels in Estonia, namely PBK, NTV, Rossia/ RTA, and RTV, but these are not available via Integrum or other databases that the author had access to. The selected media was chosen because they are known to be state-owned or owned by oligarchs close to the Russian government and reflect a pro-Kremlin position. These media were also available to Estonian audiences who watched such channels in the analyzed period. "Russia profile—Media," *BBC News*, January 7, 2020, https://www.bbc.com/news/world-europe-17840134 (accessed March 10, 2021); Juurvee and Mattiisen, *The Bronze Soldier Crisis of 2007*, 11.

48. Ottis, *Analysis of the 2007 Cyber Attacks against Estonia from the Information Warfare Perspective.*

49. Juurvee and Mattiisen, *The Bronze Soldier Crisis of 2007*, iv, 21.

50. "Estonia Cyber Attacks 2007" (PowerPoint presentation, Africa Internet Summit, 2011).

51. "Estonia Cyber Attacks 2007" (PowerPoint presentation, Africa Internet Summit, 2011).

52. Juurvee and Mattiisen, *The Bronze Soldier Crisis of 2007*, iv.

53. Juurvee and Mattiisen, *The Bronze Soldier Crisis of 2007*, iv.

CHAPTER 4. BLOWING UP ITS OWN TROJAN HORSE IN EUROPE

1. A Russian ambassador called Bulgaria "a kind of Trojan Horse in the EU." Joe Parkinson and Georgi Kantchev, "Document: Russia Uses Rigged Polls, Fake News to Sway Foreign Elections; Bulgarian Officials Say a Former Russian Spy Advised Pro-Moscow Party on How to Manipulate Voters as Part of Kremlin's Effort to Regain Influence in Eastern Europe; a 30-Page Dossier," *Wall Street Journal*, March 23, 2017, https://search.proquest.com/newspapers/document-russia-uses-rigged -polls-fake-news-sway/docview/1880062843/se-2?accountid=25333 (accessed March 10, 2021).

2. See interview with the president of Bulgaria at that time, "Plevneliev: Na izborite 2015 g. imashe moshtna kiberataka" [Plevneliev: In the 2015 elections there was

a powerful cyber attack], *Vesti,* February 13, 2019, https://www.vesti.bg/bulgaria /ruskoto-razuznavane-stoialo-zad-kiberataka-na-izborite-2015-g-6092008 (accessed March 10, 2021); Momchil Milev, "Khakerite, udarili bŭlgarskite izbori, veroyatno sa atakuvali i Klintŭn" [The hackers who hit the Bulgarian elections probably attacked Clinton as well], *Kapital,* July 27, 2016, https://www.capital.bg/politika_i_ikonomika/bulgaria/2016/07/27/2802122_hakerite_udarili_bulgarskite_izbori_veroiatno_sa/ (accessed March 10, 2021); Central Election Commission, *Doklad Otnosno Organizatsiyata i Provezhdaneto na Izbori v Perioda 2015–2017 g.* [Report on the Organization and Conduct of Elections in the Period 2015–2017] (Sofia, Bulgaria, February 6, 2018), 36, https://www.cik.bg/bg/reports (accessed March 10, 2021).

3. Milev, "Khakerite, udarili bŭlgarskite izbori, veroyatno sa atakuvali i Klintŭn."

4. Central Election Commission, *Doklad Otnosno Organizatsiyata i Provezhdaneto na Izbori v Perioda 2015–2017 g.* [Report on the Organization and Conduct of Elections in the Period 2015–2017], 36.

5. Joe Parkinson and Georgi Kantchev, "Document: Russia Uses Rigged Polls, Fake News to Sway Foreign Elections; Bulgarian Officials Say a Former Russian Spy Advised Pro-Moscow Party on How to Manipulate Voters as Part of Kremlin's Effort to Regain Influence in Eastern Europe; a 30-Page Dossier," *Wall Street Journal*, March 23, 2017, https://search.proquest.com/newspapers/document-russia-uses-rigged-polls-fake -news-sway/docview/1880062843/se-2?accountid=25333 (accessed March 10, 2021).

6. Georgi Nikolov, "Beliyat General: Bulgrskata pamet za geroite e neprehodna" [The White General: The Bulgarian memory of the heroes is intransitive], *Duma,* August 6, 2013, https://duma.bg/?go=news&p=detail&nodeId=59833 (accessed March 10, 2021).

7. Dimitar Bechev, *Russia's Influence in Bulgaria* (Brussels, Belgium: New Direction, 2018), 1, 11, https://newdirection.online/2018-publications-pdf/ND-report-Russias InfluenceInBulgaria-preview-lo-res.pdf (accessed March 28, 2021).

8. "Podkpepyame i shte podkpepim novi sanktsii speshty Rysiya, kategopichen Borisov" [We are supporting and will support new sanctions against Russia], *Money.bg*, April 12, 2014, https://money.bg/economics/podkrepyame-i-shte-podkrepim-novi -sanktsii-sreshtu-rusiya-kategorichen-borisov.html (accessed March 10, 2021).

9. Bechev, *Russia's Influence in Bulgaria*, 24–25.

10. Anna Shiryaevskaya and Dina Khrennikova, "Why the World Worries about Russia's Natural Gas Pipeline," *Washington Post,* June 29, 2020, https://www.washington post.com/business/energy/why-the-world-worries-about-russias-natural-gas-pipe line/2020/06/28/3202ec10-b901–11ea-9a1d-d3db1cbe07ce_story.html (accessed March 10, 2021).

11. Darya Korsunskaya, "Putin Drops South Stream Gas Pipeline to EU, Courts Turkey," *Reuters*, December 1, 2014, https://www.reuters.com/article/us-russia-gas-gaz

prom-pipeline-idUSKCN0JF30A20141201 (accessed March 10, 2021); "Reactions after Putin's Announcement on South Stream," *BNT*, December 2, 2014, https://bnt.bg/news/reactions-after-putin%E2%80%99s-announcement-on -south-stream-128513news.html (accessed March 10, 2021); Alexander Andreev, "Fakti i dogadki za 'Yuzhen potok'" [Facts and conjectures about "South Stream"], *Deutsche Welle*, June 13, 2014, https://www.dw.com/bg/%D1%84%D0%B0% D0%BA%D1%82%D0%B8-%D0%B8-%D0%B4%D0%BE%D0% B3%D0%B0%D0%B4%D0%BA%D0%B8-%D0%B7%D0%B0-%D1% 8E%D0%B6%D0%B5%D0%BD-%D0%BF%D0%BE%D1%82%D0%BE%D 0%BA/a-17704205 (accessed March 10, 2021).

12. Bechev, *Russia's Influence in Bulgaria*, 16.

13. "Bŭlgariya otkaza v'zdushen koridor na ruski samoleti za Siriya" [Bulgaria has refused an air corridor for Russian planes to Syria], *BTV Novinite*, September 8, 2015, https://btvnovinite.bg/bulgaria/balgarija-otkaza-vazdushen-dostap-na-ruski -samoleti-za-sirija.html (accessed March 10, 2021).

14. "Nikolaĭ Nenchev: Ima danni, che ruskite samoleti bili natovareni s orŭzhie" [Nikolai Nenchev: There is evidence that Russian planes were loaded with weapons], *Trud*, September 8, 2015, https://trud.bg/article-4970184/ (accessed March 10, 2021).

15. Carol J. Williams, "Russia Says Bulgaria's Refusal of Flyovers to Syria Is a U.S. Plot," *Los Angeles Times*, September 8, 2015, https://www.latimes.com/world/europe /la-fg-russia-syria-us-bulgaria-20150908-story.html (accessed March 10, 2021).

16. Michael Schwirtz, "How a Poisoning in Bulgaria Exposed Russian Assassins in Europe," *New York Times*, December 22, 2019, https://www.nytimes.com /2019/12/22/world/europe/bulgaria-russia-assassination-squad.html?searchResult Position=1 (accessed March 10, 2021).

17. "Importer/Exporter TIV Tables," Stockholm International Peace Research Institute, http://armstrade.sipri.org/armstrade/page/values.php (accessed March 10, 2021).

18. "Khristo Grozev: Malko veroyatno e otravyaneto na Gebrev da e sv'rzano s Dunarit" [Hristo Grozev: It is unlikely that Gebrev's poisoning was related to Dunarit], *24 Chasa*, January 13, 2020, https://www.24chasa.bg/novini/article/8065170 (accessed March 10, 2021); Schwirtz, "How a Poisoning in Bulgaria Exposed Russian Assassins in Europe."

19. See, for example, the Bulgarska Sotsialisticheska Partiya [Bulgarian Socialist Party] official website, Istoriya [History], https://bsp.bg/about/history.html (accessed March 10, 2021).

20. "Evrovizitka: Sergey Stanishev, BSP" [Euro card: Sergey Stanishev, BSP], *BTV Novinite* [BTV News], May 25, 2014, https://btvnovinite.bg/bulgaria/izbori/evrovizitka-ser gei-stanishev-bsp.html (accessed March 10, 2021); Bechev, *Russia's Influence in Bulgaria*, 11.

21. Bechev, *Russia's Influence in Bulgaria*, 16, 24.

22. Dilyana Panaiyotova, "Beli gŭlŭbi pusna kŭm Rusiya BSP protest v Sofiya" [White doves launched a BSP protest against Russia in Sofia], *News.bg*, February 10, 2015, https://news.bg/politics/beli-galabi-pusna-kam-rusiya-bsp-protest-v-sofiya.html (accessed June 26, 2020).

23. Bulgarska Sotsialisticheska Partiya [Bulgarian Socialist Party], "Godishen doklad za deynostta I Godishen finansov otchet na BSP" [Annual activities report and Annual financial report of BSP], official website, https://bsp.bg/documents/publichen_reg ister/godishen_doklad_za_dejnostta_i_godishen_finansov_otchet_na_bsp.html (accessed March 10, 2021).

24. "Elections 2009—Parties, Ataka," *Sofia New Agency*, https://www.novinite.com /elections2009/parties.php?id=1 (accessed March 10, 2021); "Simpatizanti na 'Ataka' otnovo se sŭbrakha na anti natovski protest" [Ataka's supporters gathered again for an anti-NATO protest], *BNT Novini*, March 29, 2015, https://bntnews .bg/bg/a/443835-simpatizanti-na-ataka-otnovo-se-sa-braha-na-anti-natovski-protest (accessed March 10, 2021).

25. Official Website of Attack, "Otcheti" [Financial Reports], http://www.ataka.bg/%d 0%be%d1%82%d1%87%d0%b5%d1%82%d0%b8/ (accessed March 10, 2021).

26. "Wikileaks: Amerikanskite bazi v Bulgaria—'Khlopane na otvorena vrata' ili tajna dogovorka za 'Petrolgeit'?" [WikiLeaks: the American bases in Bulgaria—"Knocking on open door" or a secret agreement for "Petrolgate"?], *Bivol*, May 16, 2011, https://bivol.bg/wlusbasing.html (accessed March 11, 2021).

27. "Valeri Simeonov: Siderov poluchava finansirane ot ruska pravoslavna fondatsiya" [Valeri Simeonov: Siderov receives funding from the Russian Orthodox Foundation], *24 Chasa*, November 30, 2013, https://www.24chasa.bg/novini/article /2504175 (accessed March 10, 2021); "Valeri Simeonov: Ruska fondatsiya naliva pari na Volen Siderov" [Valeri Simeonov: Russian Foundation pours money on Volen Siderov], *Novini BG,* November 30, 2013, https://novini.bg/bylgariya/politika /168682?comment=dislike&page=1 (accessed March 10, 2021).

28. "Wikileaks: Amerikanskite bazi v Bulgaria—'Khlopane na otvorena vrata' ili tajna dogovorka za 'Petrolgeit'?" [WikiLeaks: the American bases in Bulgaria—"Knocking on open door" or a secret agreement for "Petrolgate"?], *Bivol* [Ox].

29. "Siderov v Moskva za rozhdeniya den na Putin" [Siderov in Moscow for Putin's birthday], *Vesti* [News], October 8, 2012, https://www.vesti.bg/bulgaria/politika /siderov-v-moskva-za-rozhdeniia-den-na-putin-5188831 (accessed March 11, 2021).

30. "Emiliyan Gebrev razkri koy spored nego stoi zad otravyaneto mu" [Emilian Gebrev revealed who he thinks is behind his poisoning], *Novini BG*, February 19, 2019, https://novini.bg/bylgariya/kriminalno/525041 (accessed March 11, 2021); "Tsatsarov: Gebrev e otroven s insektitsid, nyama danni za 'Novichok'" [Tsatsarov: Gebrev was poisoned with insecticide, no data for "Novichok"], *Dnevnik*, February 11, 2019, https://www.pan.bg/?page=view_article&section_id=64&article_id =464308 (accessed March 11, 2021); Schwirtz, "How a Poisoning in Bulgaria

Exposed Russian Assassins in Europe"; "Emiliyan Gebrev otroven ot treti ruski agent, zapodozryan po sluchaya 'Skripal'" [Emilian Gebrev poisoned by a third Russian agent suspected in the "Skripal" case], *News BG*, February 8, 2019, https://news.bg/bulgaria/emiliyan-gebrev-otroven-ot-treti-ruski-agent-zapodozryan-po-sluchaya-skripal.html (accessed March 11, 2021).

31. Schwirtz, "How a Poisoning in Bulgaria Exposed Russian Assassins in Europe."

32. "Khristo Grozev: Malko veroyatno e otravyaneto na Gebrev da e sv'rzano s Dunarit" [Hristo Grozev: It is unlikely that Gebrev's poisoning was related to Dunarit], *24 Chasa*; Schwirtz, "How a Poisoning in Bulgaria Exposed Russian Assassins in Europe."

33. "Vzrivove na zavodi v Bŭlgariya ot 2000 g. Nasam," [Explosions of factories in Bulgaria since 2000], March 21, 2015, *Vesti* [News], https://www.vesti.bg/bulgaria/incidenti/vzrivove-na-zavodi-v-bylgariia-ot-2000-g.-nasam-6033381 (accessed March 11, 2021); Tatyana Baksberg, "Koy e vinoven za tragediyata v 'Arsenal'?" [Who is to blame for the tragedy at "Arsenal"?], April 26, 2016, *Deutsche Welle*, https://www.dw.com/bg/%D0%BA%D0%BE%D0%B9-%D0%B5-%D0%B2%D0%B8%D0%BD%D0%BE%D0%B2%D0%B5%D0%BD-%D0%B7%D0%B0-%D1%82%D1%80%D0%B0%D0%B3%D0%B5%D0%B4%D0%B8%D1%8F%D1%82%D0%B0-%D0%B2-%D0%B0%D1%80%D1%81%D0%B5%D0%BD%D0%B0%D0%BB/a-19214824 (accessed March 11, 2021).

34. "Boyko Noev podozira ruski sabotazh vuv vzrivovete vuv 'VMZ Sopot'" [Boyko Noev suspects Russian sabotage in explosions at VMZ Sopot], *Mediapool*, February 24, 2019, https://www.mediapool.bg/boiko-noev-podozira-ruski-sabotazh-vav-vzrivovete-vav-vmz-sopot-news290282.html (accessed March 11, 2021); VMZ official website, "Dobre doshli vuv 'Vazovski Mashinostroitelni Zavodi' EAD" [Welcome to "Vazov Machine-Building Factories" EAD], http://vmz.bg/ (accessed March 11, 2021).

35. Dilyana Gaytandzhieva, "Kak bŭlgarskoto orŭzhie stiga do teroristite v Siriya" [How Bulgarian weapons reach terrorists in Syria], *Trud* [Labor], April 21, 2017, https://trud.bg/%D0%BA%D0%B0%D0%BA-%D0%B1%D1%8A%D0%BB%D0%B3%D0%B0%D1%80%D1%81%D0%BA%D0%BE%D1%82%D0%BE-%D0%BE%D1%80%D1%8A%D0%B6%D0%B8%D0%B5-%D1%81%D1%82%D0%B8%D0%B3%D0%B0-%D0%B4%D0%BE-%D1%82%D0%B5%D1%80%D0%BE%D1%80/ (accessed March 11, 2021); Senior researcher, in discussion with author, February 18, 2021.

36. "Versiya sabotazh za vzrivovete v Iganovo" [Sabotage version of the explosions in Iganovo], *BNT*, April 14, 2015, https://bntnews.bg/bg/a/458713-versiya-sabotazh-za-vzrivovete-v-iganovo (accessed March 11, 2021).

37. "Boyko Noev podozira ruski sabotazh vuv vzrivovete vuv 'VMZ Sopot,'" [Boyko Noev suspects Russian sabotage in explosions at VMZ Sopot], *Mediapool*.

38. "Amerikanets zagina, a chetirima sa raneni pri nov vzriv na polygon na VMZ Sopot," [An American was killed and four were injured in another explosion at the VMZ

Sopot test site], June 6, 2015, Mediapol.bg, https://www.mediapool.bg/amerika nets-zagina-a-chetirima-sa-raneni-pri-nov-vzriv-na-poligon-na-vmz-sopot-news 235039.html (accessed March 11, 2021); Senior researcher, in discussion with author, February 18, 2021; "US Embassy Confirms Death of One American in Bulgaria Grenade Accident," *Guardian,* June 6, 2015, https://www.theguardian.com/world /2015/jun/06/bulgaria-american-killed-in-grenade-launcher-accident (accessed March 11, 2021).

39. Milev, "Khakerite, udarili bŭlgarskite izbori, veroyatno sa atakuvali i Klintŭn."
40. The DDoS attacks commenced at 9:30 a.m. on election day—October 25, 2015— and originated from seven to eleven different points abroad. CEC's website received 530 million requests within ten hours. Mariya Manolova and Momchil Milev, "Da 'khaknesh' izborite. Kiberatakata v denya na mestniya vot ne probi publichnata IT-infrastruktura, no pripomni, che da se pesti ot onlaĭn-sigurnost e vse po-khazartno" [To "hack" the election. The cyberattack on the day of the local vote did not break the public IT infrastructure, but reminded that saving from online security is increasingly gambling], *Kapital,* October 30, 2015, https://www.capital.bg/politika_i_ ikonomika/bulgaria/2015/10/30/2639773_da_haknesh_izborite/ (accessed March 11, 2021); "Masirana khakerska ataka sreshtu dŭrzhavni saĭtove v izborniya den (obnovena)" [Massive hacker attack on government sites on election day (updated)], *Kapital,* October 25, 2016, https://www.capital.bg/politika_i_ikonomika/bulgaria /mestni_izbori2015/2015/10/25/2636035_masirana_hakerska_ataka_sreshtu _durjavni_saitove_v/ (accessed March 11, 2021).
41. Milev, "Khakerite, udarili bŭlgarskite izbori, veroyatno sa atakuvali i Klintŭn."
42. Directorate General for Civil Registration and Administrative Services [Glavna direktsiya grazhdanska registratsiya i administrativno obsluzhvane], official website, https://www.grao.bg/ (accessed March 11, 2021).
43. "Masirana khakerska ataka sreshtu dŭrzhavni saĭtove v izborniya den (obnovena)" [Massive hacker attack on government sites on election day (updated)], *Kapital.*
44. "Masirana khakerska ataka sreshtu dŭrzhavni saĭtove v izborniya den (obnovena)" [Massive hacker attack on government sites on election day (updated)], *Kapital.*
45. Manolova and Milev, "Da 'khaknesh' izborite."
46. Milev, "Khakerite, udarili bŭlgarskite izbori, veroyatno sa atakuvali i Klintŭn."
47. Interview with the president of Bulgaria at that time, "Plevneliev: Na izborite 2015 g. imashe moshtna kiberataka" [Plevneliev: in the 2015 elections there was a powerful cyber attack], *Vesti,* February 13, 2019.
48. Dimitar Vatsov and Milena Iakimova, "Co-opting Discontent: Russian Propaganda in the Bulgarian Media," *Eurozone,* October 18, 2017, https://www.stopfake.org/en/co -opting-discontent-russian-propaganda-in-the-bulgarian-media/ (accessed March 11, 2021); Bechev, *Russia's Influence in Bulgaria,* 22.
49. Bechev, *Russia's Influence in Bulgaria,* 22.
50. Bechev, *Russia's Influence in Bulgaria,* 22, https://newdirection.online/2018-publica tions-pdf/ND-report-RussiasInfluenceInBulgaria-preview-lo-res.pdf; "How Russia

Infiltrates the Media Landscape of the Black Sea Region," *Euromaidan Press,* September 14, 2018, http://euromaidanpress.com/2018/09/14/how-russia-infiltrates -media-of-the-black-sea-region/ (accessed March 11, 2021).

51. Bechev, *Russia's Influence in Bulgaria*, 22.

52. Ruslan Stefanov and Martin Vladimirov, *The Kremlin Playbook in Southeast Europe: Economic Influence and Sharp Power* (Sofia, Bulgaria: Center for the Study of Democracy, 2020), 85, https://csd.bg/fileadmin/user_upload/publications_library/files/2020 _12/KREMLIN_PLAYBOOK_3_WEB_NEW.pdf (accessed March 11, 2021).

53. Bechev, *Russia's Influence in Bulgaria*, 22.

54. Bechev, *Russia's Influence in Bulgaria*, 22.

55. "Ruskoto vliyanie i zavladyavaneto na mediite v stranite ot Chernomorskiya region" [Russian influence and the conquest of the media in the countries of the Black Sea region], Center for the Study of Democracy, February 21, 2018, https://csd.bg/bg /events/event/ruskoto-vlijanie-i-zavladjavaneto-na-mediite-v-stranite-ot-cherno morskija-region/ (accessed March 11, 2021).

56. Bechev, *Russia's Influence in Bulgaria*, 23.

57. *Anti-Democratic Propaganda in Bulgaria. Bulgaria and Russian Propaganda* (Sofia, Bulgaria: Human and Social Studies Foundation, 2017), 2, https://hssfoundation .org/wp-content/uploads/2017/04/SUMMARY_Bulgaria-and-Russian-propagan dal_EN.pdf (accessed March 28, 2021).

58. The analysis was performed on December 16, 2020, and January 31, 2021, using data available on the website https://bg.rbth.com/.

59. Although there is no proven connection between the poisoning attempts on Emilian Gebrev and the DDoS attacks, which would indicate that both sets of activities were conducted with a common objective and, hence, can be categorized as belonging to a single information warfare campaign, this analysis includes them in the operation and discusses their potential relations in the next section.

60. The analysis was performed on January 13 and January 31, 2021, using data available on the website https://trud.bg/.

61. Bechev, *Russia's Influence in Bulgaria*, 23; Senior researcher, in discussion with author, February 18, 2021.

62. This conclusion pertains only to articles that mention GERB or BSP in their titles. Labor may have published negative articles about individual candidates from GERB without mentioning their party affiliation, but this analysis did not include such articles. "Tsvetan Tsvetanov v selo Zvŭnartsi: GERB uvazhava vsichki etnosi i raboti za vsichki khora" [Tsvetan Tsvetanov in the village of Zvanartsi: GERB respects all ethnic groups and works for all people], *Trud,* October 9, 2015, https://trud.bg /article-5036262/ (accessed March 11, 2021); "Mikov v Kostinbrod: Za BSP i kandidatite ĭ obrazovanieto e osnoven prioritet" [Mikov in Kostinbrod: For the BSP and its candidates, education is a top priority], *Trud,* October 9, 2015, https://trud .bg/article-5035458/ (accessed March 11, 2021).

63. "BSP: Stolichna obshtina prakhosva parite na sofiyantsi" [BSP: Municipality Sofia is wasting the money of Sofia residents], *Trud,* October 12, 2015, https://trud.bg /article-5041933/ (accessed March 11, 2021); "Tsvetanov v Dŭlgopol: GERB poe otgovornost v mnogo gradove na stranata i rezultatite sa nalitse" [Tsvetanov in Dalgopol: GERB has taken responsibility in many cities of the country and the results are there], *Trud,* October 13, 2015, https://trud.bg/article-5043484/ (accessed March 11, 2021).

64. "Mikhail Mikov: BSP shte iska kasirane na izborite v reditsa naseleni mesta" [Mihail Mikov: BSP will ask for the cancellation of the elections in a number of settlements], *Trud,* October 29, 2015, https://trud.bg/article-5081364/ (accessed March 11, 2021); "Stolichniyat lider na BSP Kaloyan Pargov vnese zhalbata za kasirane na izborite za kmet i sŭvetnitsi v Sofiya" [Sofia BSP leader Kaloyan Pargov files complaint over cancellation of mayoral and councilor elections in Sofia], *Trud,* November 4, 2015, https://trud.bg/article-5092282/ (accessed March 11, 2021); Boris Popivanov, "Iskrite mezhdu GERB i RB sa izgodni i za dvete partii" [The sparks between GERB and RB are beneficial for both parties], *Trud* [Labor], November 5, 2015, https://trud.bg/article-5092621/ (accessed March 11, 2021); "Plamen Nunev: Kandidatite za kmetove na GERB spechelikha v chetiri ot osemte obshtinski tsentŭra na Rusenska oblast" [Plamen Nunev: The candidates for mayors of GERB won in four of the eight municipal centers of Ruse region], *Trud,* November 27, 2015, https://trud.bg/article-5075999/ (accessed March 11, 2021).

65. Zdravka Andonova, "Rŭkovodstvoto na BSP gotovo da podade ostavka. Mikov ostava lider" [The BSP leadership is ready to resign. Mikov remains the leader], *Trud* [Labor], November 11, 2015, https://trud.bg/article-5087526/ (accessed March 11, 2021); "Plamen Nunev: Kandidatite za kmetove na GERB spechelikha v chetiri ot osemte obshtinski tsentŭra na Rusenska oblast" [Plamen Nunev: The candidates for mayors of GERB won in four of the eight municipal centers of Ruse region], *Trud,* October 27, 2015, https://trud.bg/article-5075999/ (accessed March 11, 2021).

66. *Anti-Democratic Propaganda in Bulgaria. Bulgaria and Russian Propaganda* (Sofia, Bulgaria: Human and Social Studies Foundation, 2017), 5.

67. Andrew E. Kramer, "How Russia Recruited Elite Hackers for Its Cyberwar," *New York Times,* December 29, 2016, https://www.nytimes.com/2016/12/29/world /europe/how-russia-recruited-elite-hackers-for-its-cyberwar.html (accessed February 17, 2021).

68. The author collected the data on February 3 and February 4, 2021, from *Trud*'s official website https://trud.bg/.

69. "Bulgaria's Parliament Rejects Call against EU Sanctions on Russia," *Sofia Globe,* March 4, 2020, https://sofiaglobe.com/2020/03/04/bulgarias-parliament-rejects-call -against-eu-sanctions-on-russia/ (accessed March 25, 2021); Bechev, *Russia's Influence in Bulgaria,* 15–16.

70. After 2016, the officially reported value of Bulgarian arms exports dropped by 50 percent or more. If this was a reflection of Russian pressure, given the decline in exports that occurred more than a year after the activities discussed in this chapter, this pressure was likely applied through Russian activities after the period examined in this chapter. "Importer/Exporter TIV Tables," Stockholm International Peace Research Institute.

CHAPTER 5. THE 2016 AND 2020 U.S. PRESIDENTIAL ELECTIONS, OR WHY THE DEVIL WEARS GUCCI, NOT PRADA

1. The author chose this title because it combines a reference to Guccifer 2.0 and the movie *The Devil Wears Prada*. In the case of Russia's interference in the 2016 U.S. elections, it is more accurate to suggest that the devil wears Gucci, not Prada.

2. Director of National Intelligence, Joint Statement from the Department of Homeland Security and Office of the Director of National Intelligence on Election Security (October 7, 2016).

3. Select Comm. on Intelligence, Russian Active Measures Campaigns and Interference in the 2016 U.S. Election, Volume 5: Counterintelligence Threats and Vulnerabilities, S. Rep. No. 116-XX, at v (August 18, 2020), https://www.intelligence .senate.gov/sites/default/files/documents/report_volume5.pdf (accessed March 24, 2021); Select Comm. on Intelligence, Russian Active Measures Campaigns and Interference in the 2016 U.S. Election, Volume 2: Russia's Use of Social Media with Additional Views, S. Rep. No. 116-XX, at 5; Michael McFaul, foreword to *Securing American Elections: Prescriptions for Enhancing the Integrity and Independence of the 2020 U.S. Presidential Election and Beyond* (Stanford University, June 2019), iii; Tim Starks, Laurens Cerulus, and Mark Scott, "Russia's Manipulation of Twitter Was Far Vaster Than Believed," *Politico,* June 5, 2019, https://www.polit ico.com/ story/2019/06/05/study-russia-cybersecurity-twitter-1353543 (accessed March 11, 2021).

4. Some of the key documents and analyses produced on this case that this research consulted includes indictments by the Department of Justice, a joint CIA, NSA, and FBI assessment, five volumes on Russian election interference released by the Senate Intellience Committee and two papers by social media experts: Office of the Director of National Intelligence, *Background to "Assessing Russian Activities and Intentions in Recent US Elections": The Analytic Process and Cyber Incident Attribution,* January 6, 2017; United States of America v. Internet Research Agency LLC A/K/A Mediasintez LLC A/K/A Glavset LLC A/K/A Mixinfo LLC A/K/A Azimut LLC A/K/A Novinfo LLC, Concord Management and Consulting LLC, Concord Catering, Yevgeniy Viktorovich Prigozhin, Mikhail Ivanovich Bystrov, Mikhail Leonidovich Burchik A/K/A Mikhail Abramov, Aleksandra Yuryevna Krylova, Anna Vladislavovna Bogacheva, Sergey Pavlovich Polozov, Maria Anatolyevna Bovda

A/K/A Maria Anatolyevna Belyaeva, Robert Sergeyevich Bovda, Dzheykhun Nasimi Ogl Aslanov A/K/A Jayhoon Aslanov A/K/A Jay Aslanov, Vadim Vladimirovich Podkopaev, Gleb Igorevich Vasilchenko, Irina Viktorovna Kaverzin, and Vladimir Venkov, Indictment, 18 U.S.C. sections 2, 371, 1349, 1028A (U.S. District Court for the District of Columbia, February 16, 2018), https://www.justice.gov/opa/press -release/file/1035562/download (accessed March 28, 2021); United States of America v. Viktor Borisovich Netyksho, Boris Alekseyevich Antonov, Dmitriy Sergeyevich Badin, Ivan Sergeyevich Yerakov, Eleksey Aleksandrovich Morgachev, Nikolay Yur-yevich Kozachek, Pavel Vyacheslavovich Yershov, Artem Andreyevich Malyshev, Aleksandr Vladimirovich Osadchuk, Aleksey Aleksandrovich Potemkin, and Ana-toliy Sergeyevich Kovalev, Indictment, 18 U.S.C. sections 2, 371, 1030, 1028A, 1956 (U.S. District Court for the District of Columbia, July 13, 2018); United States of America v. Elena Alekseevna Khusyaynova, Indictment, 1:18-MJ-464 (U.S. District Court for the Eastern District of Virginia, September 28, 2018), https://www.justice.gov/usao-edva/press-release/file/1102591/download (ac-cessed March 28, 2021); U.S. Department of Justice, Report on the Investigation into Russian Interference in the 2016 Presidential Election, Volume I of II, Special Counsel Robert S. Mueller, III, Washington, D.C., March 2019, https://fm.cnbc .com/applications/cnbc.com/resources/editorialfiles/2019/04/18/muellerreport.pdf (accessed March 28, 2021); DiResta et al., *The Tactics and Tropes of the Internet Research Agency*; Howard et al., *The IRA, Social Media, and Political Polarization in the United States, 2012–2018*, 2018; Select Comm. on Intelligence, Russian Active Measures Campaigns and Interference in the 2016 U.S. Election, Volume 1: Russian Efforts against Election Infrastructure with Additional Views, S. Rep. No. 116-XX (July 2019), https://www.intelligence.senate.gov/sites/default/files/documents/Report _Volume1.pdf (accessed March 26, 2021); Select Comm. on Intelligence, Russian Active Measures Campaigns and Interference in the 2016 U.S. Election, Volume 2: Russia's Use of Social Media with Additional Views, S. Rep. No. 116-XX; Select Comm. on Intelligence, Russian Active Measures Campaigns and Interference in the 2016 U.S. Election, Volume 3: U.S. Government Response to Russian Activ-ities, S. Rep. No. 116-XX, https://www.intelligence.senate.gov/sites/default/files /documents/Report_Volume3.pdf (accessed March 26, 2021); Select Comm. on Intelligence, Russian Active Measures Campaigns and Interference in the 2016 U.S. Election, Volume 4: Review of the Intelligence Community Assessment, S. Rep. No. 116-XX, https://www.intelligence.senate.gov/sites/default/files/documents /Report_Volume4.pdf (accessed March 26, 2021); Select Comm. on Intelligence, Russian Active Measures Campaigns and Interference in the 2016 U.S. Election, Volume 5: Counterintelligence Threats and Vulnerabilities, S. Rep. No. 116-XX (August 18, 2020).

5. Office of the Director of National Intelligence, *Background to "Assessing Russian Activities and Intentions in Recent US Elections": The Analytic Process and Cyber Incident*

Attribution, January 6, 2017, at ii; Select Comm. on Intelligence, Russian Active Measures Campaigns and Interference in the 2016 U.S. Election, Volume 2: Russia's Use of Social Media with Additional Views, S. Rep. No. 116-XX, at 4.

6. National Intelligence Council, *Foreign Threats to the 2020 US Federal Elections*, March 10, 2021, at i, 2, https://int.nyt.com/data/documenttools/2021-intelligence -community-election-interference-assessment/abd0346ebdd93e1e/full.pdf (accessed July 5, 2021).

7. Doug Mallouk, "Russian Hack of 2016 Elections Didn't Happen," *Baltimore Sun,* April 29, 2019, https://www.baltimoresun.com/opinion/readers-respond/bs-ed-rr -russian-hack-elections-letter-20190429-story.html (accessed March 11, 2021); "CrowdStrike's Work with the Democratic National Committee," *CrowdStrike* (blog).

8. "CrowdStrike's Work with the Democratic National Committee," *CrowdStrike* (blog); Office of the Director of National Intelligence, *Background to "Assessing Russian Activities and Intentions in Recent US Elections": The Analytic Process and Cyber Incident Attribution*, January 6, 2017; Select Comm. on Intelligence, Russian Active Measures Campaigns and Interference in the 2016 U.S. Election, Volume 5: Counterintelligence Threats and Vulnerabilities, S. Rep. No. 116-XX, at 48–49 (August 18, 2020); David E. Sanger and Matthew Rosenberg, "From the Start, Trump Has Muddied a Clear Message: Putin Interfered," *New York Times*, July 18, 2018, https://www.nytimes.com/2018/07/18/world/europe/trump-intelli gence-russian-election-meddling-.html (accessed March 25, 2021).

9. "Watch: Fiona Hill's Full Opening Statement—Trump's First Impeachment Hear- ings," *PBS*, November 21, 2019, video, 5:00–5:40, https://www.youtube.com/watch ?v=L5gmpdtbWB0 (accessed March 11, 2021).

10. One of the most detailed investigations on Russia's interference in the 2016 U.S. presidential elections was conducted by the Senate Intelligence Committee. Volume 5 of the committee's investigation results focused on counterintelligence threats and vulnerabilities. Despite the thorough investigation outlined in the 966-page report and the multiple ties and engagements between the Trump campaign and individ- uals affiliated with the Russian government, the committee found no evidence to substantiate the allegation that Donald Trump or his campaign colluded with the Russian government. Select Comm. on Intelligence, Russian Active Measures Cam- paigns and Interference in the 2016 U.S. Election, Volume 5: Counterintelligence Threats and Vulnerabilities, S. Rep. No. 116-XX, at 941 (August 18, 2020). Like- wise, Robert Mueller's detailed investigation into the issue of potential collusion also concluded that there was insufficient evidence to issue charges of coordination or conspiracy between the Russian government and the Trump campaign. U.S. Department of Justice, Report on the Investigation into Russian Interference in the 2016 Presidential Election, Volume I of II, at 1–2.

11. Cory Welt, Ukraine: Background, Conflict with Russia, and U.S. Policy (Wash- ington, DC: Congressional Research Service, April 29, 2020), 44, https://fas.org/

sgp/crs/row/R45008.pdf (accessed March 11, 2021); Steven Pifer, "Five Years after Crimea's Illegal Annexation, the Issue Is No Closer to Resolution," *Order from Chaos,* March 18, 2019, https://www.brookings.edu/blog/order-from-chaos/2019/03/18/five-years-after-crimeas-illegal-annexation-the-issue-is-no-closer-to-resolution/ (accessed March 11, 2021).

12. "G7 Leaders Reject Russia's Return after Trump Summit Invite," *BBC News,* June 2, 2020, https://www.bbc.com/news/world-us-canada-52885178 (accessed March 11, 2021); "NATO-Russia Council," North Atlantic Treaty Organization, March 23, 2020, https://www.nato.int/cps/en/natohq/topics_50091.htm (accessed March 11, 2021); Welt, *Ukraine: Background, Conflict with Russia, and U.S. Policy,* 44.

13. Carol E. Lee, "Obama Criticizes Russia over Syria Strikes," *Wall Street Journal,* October 2, 2015, https://www.wsj.com/articles/obama-criticizes-russia-over-syria-strikes-1443820003 (accessed March 11, 2021).

14. "Obama: Putin Defending Assad 'Out of Weakness,'" October 2, 2015, *Wall Street Journal,* https://www.wsj.com/video/obama-putin-defending-assad-out-of-weakness/ABA21763–7F7E-4EB5–8E5B-C85016016541.html (accessed March 11, 2021).

15. Office of the Director of National Intelligence, *Background to "Assessing Russian Activities and Intentions in Recent US Elections": The Analytic Process and Cyber Incident Attribution,* January 6, 2017, at 1.

16. "Key Quotes from Congress' Hearing on Russia and the U.S. Election," *Reuters,* March 20, 2017, https://www.reuters.com/article/us-usa-trump-russia-factbox-id USKBN16R229 (accessed March 11, 2021).

17. Tom Blackwell, "The Top Four Reasons Vladimir Putin Might Have a Grudge against Hillary Clinton," *National Post,* December 16, 2016, https://nationalpost.com/news/world/the-top-four-reasons-vladimir-putin-might-have-a-grudge-against-hillary-clinton/ (accesssed March 11, 2021).

18. Michael McFaul and Bronte Kass, "Understanding Putin's Intentions and Actions in the 2016 U.S. Presidential Election," in *Securing American Elections: Prescriptions for Enhancing the Integrity and Independence of the 2020 U.S. Presidential Election and Beyond,* ed. Michael McFaul (Stanford University, June 2019), 3; Blackwell, "The Top Four Reasons Vladimir Putin Might Have a Grudge against Hillary Clinton."

19. Office of the Director of National Intelligence, *Background to "Assessing Russian Activities and Intentions in Recent US Elections": The Analytic Process and Cyber Incident Attribution,* January 6, 2017, at 1.

20. McFaul and Kass, "Understanding Putin's Intentions and Actions in the 2016 U.S. Presidential Election," 4.

21. Emma Burrows, "'Pro-Kremlin Youth Groups' Could Be behind DNC Hack," *Deutsche Welle,* July 27, 2016, https://www.dw.com/en/pro-kremlin-youth-groups-could-be-behind-dnc-hack/a-19430216 (accessed March 11, 2021).

22. Senior representative of the Embassy of the Russian Federation in Washington, DC, in discussion with author, April 2015, Washington, DC.

23. Office of the Director of National Intelligence, *Background to "Assessing Russian Activities and Intentions in Recent US Elections": The Analytic Process and Cyber Incident Attribution*, January 6, 2017, at ii; McFaul and Kass, "Understanding Putin's Intentions and Actions in the 2016 U.S. Presidential Election," 3.

24. Select Comm. on Intelligence, Russian Active Measures Campaigns and Interference in the 2016 U.S. Election, Volume 5: Counterintelligence Threats and Vulnerabilities, S. Rep. No. 116-XX, at viii–ix, 259–463, 647–62 (August 18, 2020).

25. Select Comm. on Intelligence, Russian Active Measures Campaigns and Interference in the 2016 U.S. Election, Volume 5: Counterintelligence Threats and Vulnerabilities, S. Rep. No. 116-XX, at 301–4 (August 18, 2020).

26. McFaul and Kass, "Understanding Putin's Intentions and Actions in the 2016 U.S. Presidential Election," 4.

27. Office of the Director of National Intelligence, *Background to "Assessing Russian Activities and Intentions in Recent US Elections": The Analytic Process and Cyber Incident Attribution*, January 6, 2017, at ii, iii; Select Comm. on Intelligence, Russian Active Measures Campaigns and Interference in the 2016 U.S. Election, Volume 5: Counterintelligence Threats and Vulnerabilities, S. Rep. No. 116-XX, at viii (August 18, 2020).

28. Select Comm. on Intelligence, Russian Active Measures Campaigns and Interference in the 2016 U.S. Election, Volume 2: Russia's Use of Social Media with Additional Views, S. Rep. No. 116-XX, at 5; United States of America v. Internet Research Agency LLC et al., Indictment, at 6–7.

29. United States of America v. Internet Research Agency LLC et al., Indictment, at 2–3; Select Comm. on Intelligence, Russian Active Measures Campaigns and Interference in the 2016 U.S. Election, Volume 2: Russia's Use of Social Media with Additional Views, S. Rep. No. 116-XX, at 3. Some of the earliest accounts about the IRA come from investigative journalists, particularly Shaun Walker's article "Salutin' Putin" and Adrian Chen's "The Agency." Shaun Walker, "Salutin' Putin: Inside a Russian Troll House," *Guardian*, April 2, 2015; Adrian Chen, "The Agency," *New York Times*, June 2, 2015.

30. United States of America v. Elena Alekseevna Khusyaynova, Indictment, 1:18-MJ-464 (U.S. District Court for the Eastern District of Virginia, September 28, 2018), at 4; United States of America v. Internet Research Agency LLC et al., Indictment, at 5–6.

31. United States of America v. Internet Research Agency et al., Indictment, at 5–7.

32. United States of America v. Elena Alekseevna Khusyaynova, Indictment, 1:18-MJ-464 (U.S. District Court for the Eastern District of Virginia, September 28, 2018), at 13; United States of America v. Internet Research Agency LLC et al., Indictment, at 6; U.S. Department of Justice, Report on the Investigation into Russian Interference in the 2016 Presidential Election, Volume I of II, at 14.

33. United States of America v. Internet Research Agency LLC et al., Indictment, at 6.

34. United States of America v. Internet Research Agency LLC et al., Indictment, at 8–9.

35. United States of America v. Internet Research Agency LLC et al., Indictment, at 13.

36. United States of America v. Internet Research Agency LLC et al., Indictment, at 15–17.

37. Select Comm. on Intelligence, Russian Active Measures Campaigns and Interference in the 2016 U.S. Election, Volume 2: Russia's Use of Social Media with Additional Views, S. Rep. No. 116-XX, at 16–17.

38. Select Comm. on Intelligence, Russian Active Measures Campaigns and Interference in the 2016 U.S. Election, Volume 2: Russia's Use of Social Media with Additional Views, S. Rep. No. 116-XX, at 16; United States of America v. Internet Research Agency LLC et al., Indictment, at 6.

39. For example, see *Social Media Influence in the 2016 US Election: Hearings on S. Rep., Before the Select Comm. on Intelligence*, 115th Cong. 25–26 (November 1, 2017) (statement by Sean J. Edgett, general counsel, Twitter), https://www.govinfo .gov/content/pkg/CHRG-115shrg27398/pdf/CHRG-115shrg27398.pdf (accessed March 28, 2021); DiResta et al., *The Tactics and Tropes of the Internet Research Agency*, 13, 66, 92; Howard et al., *The IRA, Social Media, and Political Polarization in the United States*, 3, 39.

40. United States of America v. Internet Research Agency LLC et al., Indictment, at 17.

41. United States of America v. Internet Research Agency LLC et al., Indictment, at 14.

42. Select Comm. on Intelligence, Russian Active Measures Campaigns and Interference in the 2016 U.S. Election, Volume 2: Russia's Use of Social Media with Additional Views, S. Rep. No. 116-XX, at 6.

43. Select Comm. on Intelligence, Russian Active Measures Campaigns and Interference in the 2016 U.S. Election, Volume 2: Russia's Use of Social Media with Additional Views, S. Rep. No. 116-XX, at 6.

44. United States of America v. Internet Research Agency LLC et al., Indictment, at 14, 17; Select Comm. on Intelligence, Russian Active Measures Campaigns and Interference in the 2016 U.S. Election, Volume 2: Russia's Use of Social Media with Additional Views, S. Rep. No. 116-XX, at 6, 33, 45, 47.

45. Select Comm. on Intelligence, Russian Active Measures Campaigns and Interference in the 2016 U.S. Election, Volume 2: Russia's Use of Social Media with Additional Views, S. Rep. No. 116-XX, at 6–7.

46. Select Comm. on Intelligence, Russian Active Measures Campaigns and Interference in the 2016 U.S. Election, Volume 2: Russia's Use of Social Media with Additional Views, S. Rep. No. 116-XX, at 35.

47. Select Comm. on Intelligence, Russian Active Measures Campaigns and Interference in the 2016 U.S. Election, Volume 2: Russia's Use of Social Media with Additional Views, S. Rep. No. 116-XX, at 32.

48. Nicholas Confessore and Daisuke Wakabayashi, "How Russia Harvested American Rage to Reshape U.S. Politics," *New York Times*, October 9, 2017, https://nytimes

.com/2017/10/09/technology/russia-election-facebook-ads-rage.html (accessed March 25, 2021).

49. *Social Media Influence in the 2016 US Election: Hearings on S. Rep., Before the Select Comm. on Intelligence*, 115th Cong. 12–13 (November 1, 2017) (statement by Colin Stretch, vice president and general counsel, Facebook), https://www.govinfo.gov /content/pkg/CHRG-115shrg27398/pdf/CHRG-115shrg27398.pdf (accessed March 28, 2021).

50. United States of America v. Internet Research Agency LLC et al., Indictment, at 15.

51. Eugene Kiely and Lori Robertson, "Kushner Distorts Scope of Russia Interference," *Factcheck*, April 24, 2019, https://www.factcheck.org/2019/04/kushner-distorts -scope-of-russia-interference/?platform=hootsuite (accessed March 12, 2021); U.S. Department of Justice, Report on the Investigation into Russian Interference in the 2016 Presidential Election, Volume I of II, at 51–60.

52. Impressions is a common metric that identifies the number of times a piece of content has been on screen. *Social Media Influence in the 2016 US Election: Hearings on S. Rep., Before the Select Comm. on Intelligence*, 115th Cong. 25–26 (November 1, 2017) (statement by Sean J. Edgett, general counsel, Twitter); "Frequently Asked Questions," Facebook, https://www.facebook.com/business/help/675615 482516035 (accessed February 16, 2021).

53. "Update on Twitter's Review of the 2016 US Election," *Twitter Public Policy Blog*, January 19, 2018, https://blog.twitter.com/en_us/topics/company/2018/2016-elec tion-update.html (accessed March 12, 2021).

54. Select Comm. on Intelligence, Russian Active Measures Campaigns and Interference in the 2016 U.S. Election, Volume 2: Russia's Use of Social Media with Additional Views, S. Rep. No. 116-XX, at 50.

55. Engagement on Instagram refers to the sum of all comments and likes "per post, divided by the number of followers." Andrew Roach, "Instagram Engagement: What It Is and How to Improve It," *Oberlo*, October 7, 2020, https://www.oberlo .com/blog/instagram-engagement-improve (accessed March 12, 2021); Select Comm. on Intelligence, Russian Active Measures Campaigns and Interference in the 2016 U.S. Election, Volume 2: Russia's Use of Social Media with Additional Views, S. Rep. No. 116-XX, at 48.

56. Select Comm. on Intelligence, Russian Active Measures Campaigns and Interference in the 2016 U.S. Election, Volume 2: Russia's Use of Social Media with Additional Views, S. Rep. No. 116-XX, at 48.

57. United States of America v. Internet Research Agency LLC et al., Indictment, at 14, 19.

58. Select Comm. on Intelligence, Russian Active Measures Campaigns and Interference in the 2016 U.S. Election, Volume 2: Russia's Use of Social Media with Additional Views, S. Rep. No. 116-XX, at 7.

59. United States of America v. Internet Research Agency LLC et al., Indictment, at 19.

60. Nate Persily and Alex Stamos, "Regulating Online Political Advertising by Foreign Governments and Nationals," in *Securing American Elections: Prescriptions for Enhancing the Integrity and Independence of the 2020 U.S. Presidential Election and Beyond,* ed. Michael McFaul (Stanford University, June 2019), 28. The IRA staff and its affiliates conducted these operations under concealed identities using fictitious personas, without registering as foreign agents with the U.S. Justice Department and without reporting expenditures to the U.S. Federal Election Commission as legal protocol dictates. To finance the advertisements, the IRA staff used Russian bank accounts registered under fake U.S. names and also used PayPal accounts. United States of America v. Internet Research Agency LLC et al., Indictment, at 19.

61. *Social Media Influence in the 2016 US Election: Hearings on S. Rep., Before the Select Comm. on Intelligence,* 115th Cong. 12–13 (November 1, 2017) (statement by Colin Stretch, vice president and general counsel, Facebook); Select Comm. on Intelligence, Russian Active Measures Campaigns and Interference in the 2016 U.S. Election, Volume 2: Russia's Use of Social Media with Additional Views, S. Rep. No. 116-XX, at 7. When purchasing the ads, Russia seemed to have exploited a legislative loophole in the 2002 Bipartisan Campaign Reform Act, which demands that any actor discloses campaign ad purchases and bans foreign nationals from such practices. However, the act's definition of "electioneering communications" does not cover social media platforms such as Facebook and Twitter. See Lawrence Norden and Ian Vandewalker, "This Bill Would Help Stop Russia from Buying Online Election Ads," *Slate,* October 19, 2017, http://slate.com/articles/technology/future_tense/2017/10/the_honest_ads_act_would_help_stop_online_election_meddling_from_foreign.html (accessed March 25, 2021).

62. Kevin Poulsen, Spencer Ackerman, and Ben Collins, "Russia's Facebook Fake News Could Have Reached 70 Million Americans," Daily Beast, August 8, 2017, https://www.thedailybeast.com/russias-facebook-fake-news-could-have-reached-70-million-americans (accessed of March 14 2021).

63. United States of America v. Internet Research Agency LLC et al., Indictment, at 21–22; Select Comm. on Intelligence, Russian Active Measures Campaigns and Interference in the 2016 U.S. Election, Volume 2: Russia's Use of Social Media with Additional Views, S. Rep. No. 116-XX, at 37, 47.

64. United States of America v. Internet Research Agency LLC et al., Indictment, at 22.

65. United States of America v. Internet Research Agency LLC et al., Indictment, at 23.

66. United States of America v. Internet Research Agency LLC et al., Indictment, at 23.

67. McFaul and Kass, "Understanding Putin's Intentions and Actions in the 2016 U.S. Presidential Election," 10.

68. Hannah Levintova, "Russian Journalists Just Published a Bombshell Investigation about a Kremlin-Linked 'Troll Factory,'" *Mother Jones,* October 18, 2017, https://www.motherjones.com/politics/2017/10/russian-journalists-just-published-a-bombshell-investigation-about-a-kremlin-linked-troll-factory/ (accessed March 15, 2021).

69. Select Comm. on Intelligence, Russian Active Measures Campaigns and Interference in the 2016 U.S. Election, Volume 5: Counterintelligence Threats and Vulnerabilities, S. Rep. No. 116-XX, at 170–1 (August 18, 2020); United States of America v. Viktor Borisovich Netyksho et al., Indictment.

70. Robert McMillan and Jennifer Valentin-Devries, "Russian Hackers Show Cybersecurity Limits: The Suspected Attempts by the Kremlin to Influence the U.S. Election Highlight the Risks of Mundane Attacks and Information Warfare," *Wall Street Journal*, November 1, 2016.

71. "Microsoft Says Russian Hackers Exploiting Flaw in Windows System," *Radio Free Europe*, November 2, 2016, https://www.rferl.org/a/microsfot-warns-russian-hackers-exploiting-flaw-windows-10-operating-system/28089791.html?utm_source=Sailthru&utm_medium=email&utm_campaign=Early%20Bird%20Brief%2011.02.2016&utm_term=Editorial%20-%20Military%20-%20Early%20Bird%20Brief (accessed March 15, 2021).

72. FireEye iSight Intelligence, *APT28: At the Center of the Storm*, 5; Select Comm. on Intelligence, Russian Active Measures Campaigns and Interference in the 2016 U.S. Election, Volume 5: Counterintelligence Threats and Vulnerabilities, S. Rep. No. 116-XX, at 171 (August 18, 2020).

73. United States of America v. Viktor Borisovich Netyksho et al., Indictment, at 1–3; National Cybersecurity and Communications Integration Center and Federal Bureau of Investigation, *Grizzly Steppe*, 2; "CrowdStrike's Work with the Democratic National Committee," *CrowdStrike* (blog).

74. National Cybersecurity and Communications Integration Center and Federal Bureau of Investigation, *Grizzly Steppe*, 2.

75. United States of America v. Viktor Borisovich Netyksho et al., Indictment, at 2.

76. Lipton et al., "The Perfect Weapon: How Russian Cyberpower Invaded the U.S."

77. Select Comm. on Intelligence, Russian Active Measures Campaigns and Interference in the 2016 U.S. Election, Volume 5: Counterintelligence Threats and Vulnerabilities, S. Rep. No. 116-XX, at 171 (August 18, 2020).

78. "CrowdStrike's Work with the Democratic National Committee," *CrowdStrike* (blog); Andy Greenberg, "Hack Brief: Russia's Breach of the DNC Is about More Than Trump's Dirt," *Wired*, June 14, 2016, https://www.wired.com/2016/06/hack-brief-russias-breach-dnc-trumps-dirt/ (accessed March 21, 2021); "Naming without Shaming," *Economist*, October 29, 2016, https://www.economist.com/node/21709312/print (accessed March 25, 2021); "Microsoft Says Russian Hackers Exploiting Flaw in Windows System," *Radio Free Europe*, November 2, 2016.

79. United States of America v. Viktor Borisovich Netyksho et al., Indictment, at 2.

80. Select Comm. on Intelligence, Russian Active Measures Campaigns and Interference in the 2016 U.S. Election, Volume 1: Russian Efforts against Election Infrastructure with Additional Views, S. Rep. No. 116-XX, at 6, 8 (July 2019).

81. United States of America v. Viktor Borisovich Netyksho et al., Indictment, at 25, 26.

82. Wesley Bruer and Evan Perez, "Officials: Hackers Breach Election Systems in Illinois, Arizona," *CNN*, August 30, 2016, www.cnn.com/2016/08/29/politics/hackers -breach-illinois-arizona-election-systems/ (accessed March 15, 2021).

83. Select Comm. on Intelligence, Russian Active Measures Campaigns and Interference in the 2016 U.S. Election, Volume 1: Russian Efforts against Election Infrastructure with Additional Views, S. Rep. No. 116-XX, at 6, 22 (July 2019); Bruer and Perez, "Officials: Hackers Breach Election Systems in Illinois, Arizona."

84. Select Comm. on Intelligence, Russian Active Measures Campaigns and Interference in the 2016 U.S. Election, Volume 1: Russian Efforts against Election Infrastructure with Additional Views, S. Rep. No. 116-XX, at 3, 5 (July 2019).

85. Matthew Rosenberg, Nicole Perlroth, and David E. Sanger, "'Chaos Is the Point': Russian Hackers and Trolls Grow Stealthier in 2020," *New York Times*, January 10, 2020, https://www.nytimes.com/2020/01/10/us/politics/russia-hacking-disinform ation-election.html?action=click&module=Top%20Stories&pgtype=Homepage (accessed March 15, 2021); United States of America v. Viktor Borisovich Netyksho et al., Indictment, at 25.

86. McFaul and Kass, "Understanding Putin's Intentions and Actions in the 2016 U.S. Presidential Election," 13.

87. Office of the Director of National Intelligence, *Background to "Assessing Russian Activities and Intentions in Recent US Elections": The Analytic Process and Cyber Incident Attribution*, January 6, 2017, at ii.

88. "CrowdStrike's Work with the Democratic National Committee," *CrowdStrike* (blog).

89. "CrowdStrike's Work with the Democratic National Committee," *CrowdStrike* (blog).

90. Select Comm. on Intelligence, Russian Active Measures Campaigns and Interference in the 2016 U.S. Election, Volume 5: Counterintelligence Threats and Vulnerabilities, S. Rep. No. 116-XX, at 171 (August 18, 2020); Patrick Tucker, "How Putin Weaponized Wikileaks to Influence the Election of an American President," Defense One, July 24, 2016, http://www.defenseone.com/technology/2016/07/how-putin-weap onized-wikileaks-influence-election-american-president/130163/ (accessed March 15, 2021); Jason Koebler, "'Guccifer 2.0' Claims Responsibility for DNC Hack, Releases Docs to Prove It," *Motherboard*, June 15, 2016, https://motherboard.vice .com/read/guccifer-20-claims-responsibility-for-dnc-hack-releases-documents (accessed March 15, 2021); Office of the Director of National Intelligence, *Background to "Assessing Russian Activities and Intentions in Recent US Elections": The Analytic Process and Cyber Incident Attribution*, January 6, 2017, at ii.

91. Tim Starks, "Obama Administration Accuses Russian Government of Election-year Hacking," *Politico*, October 8, 2016, http://www.politico.com/story/2016/10/obama -administration-accuses-russian-government-of-election-year-hacking-229296 (accessed March 15, 2021); Director of National Intelligence, Joint Statement from the Department of Homeland Security and Office of the Director of National Intelligence on Election Security (October 7, 2016).

92. Office of the Director of National Intelligence, *Background to "Assessing Russian Activities and Intentions in Recent US Elections": The Analytic Process and Cyber Incident Attribution*, January 6, 2017, at ii.

93. Select Comm. on Intelligence, Russian Active Measures Campaigns and Interference in the 2016 U.S. Election, Volume 4: Review of the Intelligence Community Assessment, S. Rep. No. 116-XX, at 6–7.

94. Sanger et al., "From the Start, Trump Has Muddied a Clear Message: Putin Interfered."

95. United States of America v. Viktor Borisovich Netyksho et al., Indictment, at 5, 13–17; Select Comm. on Intelligence, Russian Active Measures Campaigns and Interference in the 2016 U.S. Election, Volume 5: Counterintelligence Threats and Vulnerabilities, S. Rep. No. 116-XX, at 170–1 (August 18, 2020); Benjamin Jensen, Brandon Valeriano, and Ryan Maness, "Fancy Bears and Digital Trolls: Cyber Strategy with a Russian Twist," *Journal of Strategic Studies* 42, no. 2 (2019): 11; McFaul and Kass, "Understanding Putin's Intentions and Actions in the 2016 U.S. Presidential Election," 7–8.

96. "Guccifer 2.0 DNC's Servers Hacked by a Lone Hacker," *Guccifer 2.0*, June 15, 2016, https://guccifer2.wordpress.com/2016/06/15/dnc/ (accessed March 15, 2021); Lipton, Sanger, and Shanedec, "The Perfect Weapon."

97. Lipton, Sanger, and Shanedec, "The Perfect Weapon."

98. Select Comm. on Intelligence, Russian Active Measures Campaigns and Interference in the 2016 U.S. Election, Volume 5: Counterintelligence Threats and Vulnerabilities, S. Rep. No. 116-XX, at 201–15 (August 18, 2020).

99. Select Comm. on Intelligence, Russian Active Measures Campaigns and Interference in the 2016 U.S. Election, Volume 5: Counterintelligence Threats and Vulnerabilities, S. Rep. No. 116-XX, at 212 (August 18, 2020).

100. McFaul and Kass, "Understanding Putin's Intentions and Actions in the 2016 U.S. Presidential Election," 7–8; Director of National Intelligence, Joint Statement from the Department of Homeland Security and Office of the Director of National Intelligence on Election Security (October 7, 2016); Select Comm. on Intelligence, Russian Active Measures Campaigns and Interference in the 2016 U.S. Election, Volume 5: Counterintelligence Threats and Vulnerabilities, S. Rep. No. 116-XX, at 213 (August 18, 2020).

101. FireEye iSight Intelligence, *APT28: At the Center of the Storm*, 5; Lipton, Sanger, and Shanedec, "The Perfect Weapon"; "Following the Links from Russian Hackers to the U.S. Election," *New York Times*, January 6, 2016, https://www.nytimes.com/interactive/2016/07/27/us/politics/trail-of-dnc-emails-russia-hacking.html (accessed March 15, 2021).

102. FireEye iSight Intelligence, *APT28: At the Center of the Storm*, 5; Select Comm. on Intelligence, Russian Active Measures Campaigns and Interference in the 2016 U.S. Election, Volume 5: Counterintelligence Threats and Vulnerabilities, S. Rep. No. 116-XX, at 177 (August 18, 2020).

103. Lipton, Sanger, and Shanedec, "The Perfect Weapon."

104. Such articles include: "Friendly Journos and Bankers, Attacks on Bernie and Trump: Part 3 of Podesta Emails," *RT*, October 11, 2016, https://www.rt.com/usa /362358-wikileaks-third-podesta-emails/ (accessed March 15, 2021); "Julian Assange Special: Do Wikileaks Have the Email That Will Put Hillary Clinton in Prison? (E376)," *RT*, August 6, 2016, https://www.rt.com/shows/going-under ground/354847-wikileaks-dnc-leaks-russia/ (accessed March 15, 2021); "Guccifer 2.0 Reveals Clinton Expenses, Clues on Identity and Slams Presidential Hopefuls," *RT*, July 1, 2016, https://www.rt.com/usa/349193-guccifer-clinton-expenses/ (accessed March 15, 2021); "Hacker 'Guccifer 2.0' Publishes DNC Campaign Docs with Strategies for Defending Clinton," *RT*, June 21, 2016, https://www.rt.com/usa/34 7681-guccifer-clinton-dnc-defense/ (accessed March 15, 2021); "'Guccifer 2.0' Releases Hacked DNC Docs Revealing Mega Donors, Clinton Collusion," *RT*, June 16, 2016, https://www.rt.com/usa/347005-dnc-hack-donors-collusion/ (accessed March 15, 2021); see also section "Pro-Kremlin Media Coverage" in this chapter.

105. "Following the Links from Russian Hackers to the U.S. Election," *New York Times*.

106. Select Comm. on Intelligence, Russian Active Measures Campaigns and Interference in the 2016 U.S. Election, Volume 5: Counterintelligence Threats and Vulnerabilities, S. Rep. No. 116-XX, at vii (August 18, 2020).

107. McFaul and Kass, "Understanding Putin's Intentions and Actions in the 2016 U.S. Presidential Election," 8.

108. Lipton et al., "The Perfect Weapon: How Russian Cyberpower Invaded the U.S."

109. McFaul and Kass, "Understanding Putin's Intentions and Actions in the 2016 U.S. Presidential Election," 8.

110. Eric Lipton and Scott Shane, "Democratic House Candidates Were Also Targets of Russian Hacking," *New York Times*, December 13, 2016, https://www.nytimes.com /2016/12/13/us/politics/house-democrats-hacking-dccc.html (accessed March 25, 2021).

111. Office of the Director of National Intelligence, *Background to "Assessing Russian Activities and Intentions in Recent US Elections": The Analytic Process and Cyber Incident Attribution*, January 6, 2017, at 3–4; McFaul and Kass, "Understanding Putin's Intentions and Actions in the 2016 U.S. Presidential Election," 8; Robert D. Blackwill and Philip H. Gordon, *Containing Russia: How to Respond to Moscow's Intervention in U.S. Democracy and Growing Geopolitical Challenge* (New York: Council on Foreign Relations, January 2018), Special Report No. 80, 3, 7, https://cfrd8-files .cfr.org/sites/default/files/report_pdf/CSR80_BlackwillGordon_ContainingRussia .pdf (accessed March 28, 2021); Persily and Stamos, "Regulating Online Political Advertising by Foreign Governments and Nationals," 36.

112. Office of the Director of National Intelligence, *Background to "Assessing Russian Activities and Intentions in Recent US Elections": The Analytic Process and Cyber Incident Attribution*, January 6, 2017, at 3, 9.

113. Zakem et al., *Mapping Russian Media Network*, 38.
114. Office of the Director of National Intelligence, *Background to "Assessing Russian Activities and Intentions in Recent US Elections": The Analytic Process and Cyber Incident Attribution*, January 6, 2017, at 3.
115. The process and algorithms that social media companies use to identify the IRA accounts and activities are also usually not made public, and due to the inability to subject these methods to scrutiny, it is not possible to evaluate the comprehensiveness and accuracy of IRA's presence beyond the data provided by the platforms. This constitutes another potential data limitation.
116. The research does not include analysis of *RT* data because data for the period under examination was not available online or through the Knowledge Services of the RAND Corporation as of September 11, 2020.
117. The article references in this analysis were accessed through the official website of *Sputnik News*, sputniknews.com, on September 11, 2020, and September 12, 2020. The author performed separate searches for materials containing the keywords "Hillary" and "Trump" because the search engine did not recognize boolean logic connectors (such as *and* and *or*), which precluded the ability to collect all material during one search only. Furthermore, when multiple keywords are written in the search engine, the website identifies only all materials that contain *all* key words. Therefore, to solve the issue of double counting in the searches separately containing "Hillary" and containing "Trump," the author performed a third manual search for "Hillary Trump." The author then subtracted the combined number of articles from the individual "Hillary" and "Trump" searches from the third search of combined articles ("Hillary Trump") to remove double counting. The author used the keyword "Hillary" rather than "Clinton" to avoid articles that discuss Bill Clinton only. To identify the number of articles related to the leaked documents through WikiLeaks, the author performed a search with the keywords "WikiLeaks" and "Hillary." As this latest search identified all articles that contained both words, the author examined the results as a subsection of the total coverage referencing Hillary Clinton and Donald Trump.
118. Select Comm. on Intelligence, Russian Active Measures Campaigns and Interference in the 2016 U.S. Election, Volume 2: Russia's Use of Social Media with Additional Views, S. Rep. No. 116-XX, at 42.
119. See, for example, "WikiLeaks Releases over 8,000 New Democratic National Committee Emails," *Sputnik International*, November 7, 2016, https://sputniknews.com/us/201611071047130918-wikileaks-releases-thousands-dnc-emails/ (accessed March 15, 2021); "Coming Soon: Julian Assange Teases Juicy Release of Scandalous Clinton Emails," *Sputnik International*, September 7, 2016, https://sputniknews.com/politics/201609071045070527-assange-hannity-email-tease/ (accessed March 15, 2021); "FBI Chief Announces No Change in July Ruling on Clinton Email Probe," *Sputnik International*, November 6, 2016, https://sputniknews.com

/politics/201611061047127724-FBI-says-no-change-clinton-ruling/ (accessed March 15, 2021); "Clinton Health Charity Failed to Disclose $225Mln in Government Donations," *Sputnik International*, September 6, 2016, https://sputniknews.com/us/201609061045028210-us-clinton-charity-donation/ (accessed March 15, 2021).

120. "Clinton and Abedin Are Parts of Long-Term US Policy to Back Extremists," *Sputnik International*, November 7, 2016, https://sputniknews.com/analysis/2016 11071047134864-clinton-extremists-support/ (accessed March 15, 2021).

121. "Hillary Clinton Thanks Participants of Anti-Trump Women's March on Washington," *Sputnik International*, January 21, 2017, https://sputniknews.com/us/2017 01211049867469-hillary-clinton-women-march/ (accessed March 15, 2021); "'Peaceful Protest' Continues into Evening in Portland after Trump Inauguration," *Sputnik International*, January 21, 2017, https://sputniknews.com/us/201701211049848 411-portland-trump-peaceful-protest/ (accessed March 15, 2021); "Ads Offer Protesters $2500 to Disrupt Trump Inauguration," *Sputnik International*, January 17, 2017, https://sputniknews.com/us/201701171049697952-ads-offering-thousands -protest-trump/ (accessed March 15, 2021); "Cher, Scarlett Johansson, Katy Perry to March Against Trump in Washington, DC," *Sputnik International*, January 10, 2017, https://sputniknews.com/us/201701101049458383-katy-perry-cher-celeb rities-protest-trump/ (accessed March 15, 2021); "US Voter Fraud Probe Not to Focus Solely on 2016 Election—White House," *Sputnik International*, January 25, 2017, https://sputniknews.com/us/201701251050009062-us-voter-fraud/ (accessed March 15, 2021); "US Senator John McCain Attends a News Conference at the Benjamin Franklin Library in Mexico City, Mexico, December 20, 2016. Senator McCain Says He Is Unaware of Any Evidence of Illegal Voting," *Sputnik International*, January 25, 2017, https://sputniknews.com/us/201701 251050001526-mccain-trump-illegal-voting/ (accessed March 15, 2021); "Trump Asks for 2016 Presidential Election Voter Fraud Probe," *Sputnik International*, January 25, 2017, https://sputniknews.com/us/201701251049992301-trump -voters-probe-fraud/ (accessed March 15, 2021); "Trump's Dangerous New 'Voter Fraud' Lies," *Sputnik International*, January 25, 2017, https://sputniknews.com /radio_the_bradcast/201701251050024100-trump-voter-fraud/ (accessed March 15, 2021); "Hillary Clinton Email Probe Ongoing—US House Oversight Chairman," *Sputnik International*, January 26, 2017, https://sputniknews.com/us/2017 01261050042478-clinton-probe-email-chairman/ (accessed March 15, 2021); "Chaffetz Shakes Clinton's Hand, Vows to Continue Email Investigation," *Sputnik International*, January 20, 2017, https://sputniknews.com/us/2017012010 49843190-chaffetz-shakes-clinton-hand-investigation/ (accessed March 15, 2021); "Clinton Is 'Guilty as Hell': Trump Returns to His Campaign Rhetoric," *Sputnik International*, January 13, 2017, https://sputniknews.com/us/201701131049566 759-trump-clinton-guilty-as-hell/ (accessed March 15, 2021).

122. "CrowdStrike's Work with the Democratic National Committee," *CrowdStrike* (blog).

123. Galeotti, *Putin's Hydra*; "CrowdStrike's Work with the Democratic National Committee," *CrowdStrike* (blog).

124. Select Comm. on Intelligence, Russian Active Measures Campaigns and Interference in the 2016 U.S. Election, Volume 1: Russian Efforts against Election Infrastructure with Additional Views, Minority Views of Senator Wyden, S. Rep. No. 116-XX, at 3–4 (July 2019).

125. Robert D. Blackwill and Philip H. Gordon, *Containing Russia: How to Respond to Moscow's Intervention in U.S. Democracy and Growing Geopolitical Challenge*, 3.

126. Paola Chavez, Veronica Stracqualursi, and Adam Kelsey, "Democratic National Convention 2016: Everything You Need to Know," *ABC News*, July 23, 2016, https://abcnews.go.com/Politics/democratic-national-convention-2016/story?id=40781224 (accessed March 15, 2021); Max Boot, "Time to Get Real about Russia Cyber War: Max Boot," *USA Today*, October 12, 2016, https://www.usatoday.com/story/opinion/2016/10/12/russia-podesta-emails-hackers-cyber-warfare-max-boot/91940364/ (accessed March 15, 2021); Select Comm. on Intelligence, Russian Active Measures Campaigns and Interference in the 2016 U.S. Election, Volume 5: Counterintelligence Threats and Vulnerabilities, S. Rep. No. 116-XX, at 212 (August 18, 2020).

127. Select Comm. on Intelligence, Russian Active Measures Campaigns and Interference in the 2016 U.S. Election, Volume 3: U.S. Government Response to Russian Activities, S. Rep. No. 116-XX, at 3.

128. Select Comm. on Intelligence, Russian Active Measures Campaigns and Interference in the 2016 U.S. Election, Volume 3: U.S. Government Response to Russian Activities, S. Rep. No. 116-XX, at 25.

129. William M. Arkin, Ken Dilanian, and Cynthia McFadden, "What Obama Said to Putin on the Red Phone about the Election Hack," *NBC News,* December 19, 2016, https://www.nbcnews.com/news/us-news/what-obama-said-putin-red-phone-about-election-hack-n697116 (accessed March 25, 2021); Select Comm. on Intelligence, Russian Active Measures Campaigns and Interference in the 2016 U.S. Election, Volume 3: U.S. Government Response to Russian Activities, S. Rep. No. 116-XX, at 26.

130. Select Comm. on Intelligence, Russian Active Measures Campaigns and Interference in the 2016 U.S. Election, Volume 5: Counterintelligence Threats and Vulnerabilities, S. Rep. No. 116-XX, at vii (August 18, 2020).

131. William M. Arkin, Ken Dilanian, and Cynthia McFadden, "What Obama Said to Putin on the Red Phone about the Election Hack," *NBC News,* December 19, 2016, https://www.nbcnews.com/news/us-news/what-obama-said-putin-red-phone-about-election-hack-n697116 (accessed March 15, 2021); Select Comm. on Intelligence, Russian Active Measures Campaigns and Interference in the 2016 U.S. Election,

Volume 3: U.S. Government Response to Russian Activities, S. Rep. No. 116-XX, at 27–28.

132. Select Comm. on Intelligence, Russian Active Measures Campaigns and Interference in the 2016 U.S. Election, Volume 3: U.S. Government Response to Russian Activities, S. Rep. No. 116-XX, at 3.

133. Daniel, discussion, December 29, 2020.

134. Daniel, discussion, December 29, 2020.

135. Daniel, discussion, December 29, 2020.

136. Select Comm. on Intelligence, Russian Active Measures Campaigns and Interference in the 2016 U.S. Election, Volume 3: U.S. Government Response to Russian Activities, S. Rep. No. 116-XX, at 37–39.

137. CISA and EAC Develop Risk Profile Tool for Election Officials, September 2, 2020, https://www.cisa.gov/news/2020/09/02/cisa-eac-develop-risk-profile-tool-election-officials (accessed March 15, 2021); Select Comm. on Intelligence, Russian Active Measures Campaigns and Interference in the 2016 U.S. Election, Volume 1: Russian Efforts against Election Infrastructure with Additional Views, S. Rep. No. 116-XX, at 4 (July 2019).

138. Persily and Stamos, "Regulating Online Political Advertising by Foreign Governments and Nationals," 27–34; Alex Stamos, Sergey Sanovich, Andrew Grotto, and Allison Berke, "Combatting State-Sponsored Disinformation Campaigns from State-aligned Actors," in *Securing American Elections: Prescriptions for Enhancing the Integrity and Independence of the 2020 U.S. Presidential Election and Beyond*, ed. Michael McFaul (Stanford University, June 2019), 43–52.

CHAPTER 6. PHISHING IN NORWAY'S NETS IN 2016

1. The author respectfully adopts the phrase from Anke Schmidt's section "When Russia's Sputniks Crashed and Burned in the Nordic Countries" and applauds Schmidt for the spot-on metaphor. Anke Schmidt-Felzmann, "More Than 'Just' Disinformation. Russia's Information Operations in the Nordic Region," in *Information Warfare. New Security Challenge for Europe*, ed. Tomas Cizik (Bratislava, Slovkia: Centre for European and North Atlantic Affairs, April 2017), 53.

2. "Norway Institutions 'Targeted by Russia-linked Hackers,'" *BBC News*, February 3, 2017, https://www.bbc.com/news/world-europe-38859491 (accessed March 15, 2021).

3. Anke Schmidt-Felzmann, "More Than 'Just' Disinformation," 34.

4. *Annual Threat Assessment 2015* (Norway: Norwegian Police Security Service, 2015), 15, https://www.pst.no/globalassets/artikler/trusselvurderinger/annual-threat-assessment-2015.pdf (accessed March 28, 2021).

5. "Norway Accuses Group Linked to Russia of Carrying out Cyber-Attack," *Agence France-Presse in Oslo*, February 3, 2017, https://www.theguardian.com/technology/2017/feb/03/norway-accuses-group-linked-to-russia-of-carrying-out-cyber-attack (accessed March 17, 2021).

6. "Putin's Stance on Ukraine Supported by Minority of Nations," *Bloomberg*, March 14, 2014, bloomberg.com/graphics/infographics/countries-react-to-russian-interven tion-in-crimea.html (accessed March 15, 2021); Anke Schmidt-Felzmann, "More Than 'Just' Disinformation," 35.

7. Natalia Golysheva, "Ukraine Crisis Spells Arctic Freeze in Russia-Norway Ties," *BBC News*, October 4, 2014, https://www.bbc.com/news/world-europe-29465312 (accessed March 15, 2021).

8. Anke Schmidt-Felzmann, "More Than 'Just' Disinformation," 40–41.

9. Golysheva, "Ukraine Crisis Spells Arctic Freeze in Russia-Norway Ties"; Tim Whewell, "Has the Kremlin Been Meddling with Its Arctic Friends?" *BBC News*, November 12, 2015, https://www.bbc.com/news/magazine-34789927 (accessed March 15, 2021); Kjetil Bjørkmann, "The Impact from the Russian Import-Ban (2014–) on the Norwegian Seafood Industry: When an Export-Dependent Indus-try Face Spill-Over Effects from Geopolitical Conflicts" (master's thesis, University of Oslo, 2016), (accessed March 15, 2021).

10. "Norway Institutions 'Targeted by Russia-Linked Hackers,'" *BBC News*.

11. "Major Russian Naval Force Sails to North Sea Past Norway," *BBC News*, October 18, 2016, https://www.bbc.com/news/world-europe-37694137 (accessed March 15, 2021).

12. "US Troops to Be Stationed in Norway in Break with Tradition," *BBC News*, Octo-ber 25, 2016, https://www.bbc.com/news/world-europe-37761376 (accessed March 15, 2021).

13. *Focus 2020: The Norwegian Intelligence Service's Assessment of Current Security Chal-lenges* (Norway: Norwegian Intelligence Service, 2020), 69–70; Thomas Nilsen, "Russian Influence Operations Work to Fuel Disagreements between North and South in Norway, Says Report," *Independent Barents Observer*, February 11, 2020, https://www.arctictoday.com/russian-influence-operations-work-to-fuel-disagree-ments-between-north-and-south-in-norway-says-report/ (accessed March 15, 2021).

14. Niels Nagelhus Schia and Lars Gjesvik, "Hacking Democracy: Managing Influence Campaigns and Disinformation in the Digital Age," *Journal of Cyber Policy* 5, no. 3 (2020): 419; Anke Schmidt-Felzmann, "More Than 'Just' Disinformation," 56.

15. The author would like to express her deepest gratitude to Bernt Tore Bratane for conducting valuable research on this topic in Norwegian and for contributing to understanding the scope of the reported breaches. "Norway Accuses Group Linked to Russia of Carrying out Cyber-Attack," *Agence France-Presse in Oslo*; "Norway Insti-tutions 'Targeted by Russia-Linked Hackers,'" *BBC News*; Doug G. Wave, "Norway Says Russians Hacked Defense, Security Agencies," *UPI*, February 3, 2017, https://www.upi.com/Top_News/World-News/2017/02/03/Norway-says-Rus sians-hacked-defense-security-agencies/5121486150733/ (accessed March 17, 2021); Thomas Nilsen, "Norway's PST Says Russian Intelligence Targets Individu-als," *Barents Observer*, February 3, 2017, https://thebarentsobserver.com/en/security

/2017/02/norways-pst-says-russian-intelligence-targets-individuals (accessed March 17, 2021).

16. Norwegian Labor Party (Arbeiderparteit), *Party Manifesto 2017–2021: Everyone Participates*, 94–95, https://res.cloudinary.com/arbeiderpartiet/image/upload/v1/ievv_filestore/f9d8039b230240f3aedb79ad7620543a0a8dd04c769c4600832e b7a354801839 (accessed March 17, 2021).

17. "Jens Stoltenberg, NATO Secretary General," North Atlantic Treaty Organization, 2014, https://www.nato.int/cps/en/natohq/who_is_who_49999.htm (accessed March 28, 2021).

18. "Norway Accuses Group Linked to Russia of Carrying out Cyber-Attack," *Agence France-Presse in Oslo*; "Norway Institutions 'Targeted by Russia-Linked Hackers,'" *BBC News*, https://www.bbc.com/news/world-europe-38859491; Wave, "Norway Says Russians Hacked Defense, Security Agencies."

19. "Norway Accuses Group Linked to Russia of Carrying out Cyber-Attack," *Agence France-Presse in Oslo*.

20. "Norway Accuses Group Linked to Russia of Carrying out Cyber-Attack," *Agence France-Presse in Oslo*.

21. "Norway's Labour Party Was Hacked by Russia: Report," *NTB/The Local*, February 3, 2017, https://www.thelocal.no/20170203/norways-labour-party-was-hacked-by -russia-report (accessed March 17, 2021); "Norway Accuses Group Linked to Russia of Carrying out Cyber-Attack," *Agence France-Presse in Oslo*.

22. *Focus 2017: The Norwegian Intelligence Service's Assessment of Current Security Challenges* (Norway: Norwegian Intelligence Service, 2017), 34, https://www.forsvaret .no/aktuelt-og-presse/publikasjoner/fokus/Fokus%202017%20english.pdf/_/at tachment/inline/c5af8e37–1897–47d9-b1b9–44a9a646d78b:6fd3d3056a6ee63c fe521ab912e7736db91203f2/Fokus%202017%20english.pdf (accessed March 17, 2021).

23. *Annual Threat Assessment 2015* (Norway: Norwegian Police Security Service, 2015), 16; *National Threat Assessment 2016* (Norway: Norwegian Police Security Service, 2016), 6–7, https://www.pst.no/globalassets/artikler/trusselvurderinger/threat-assess ment-2016.pdf (accessed March 17, 2021).

24. Anke Schmidt-Felzmann, "More Than 'Just' Disinformation," 53; Edward Deverell, Charlotte Wagnsson, and Eva-Karin Olsson, "Destruct, Direct and Suppress: Sputnik Narratives on the Nordic Countries," *Journal of International Communication* 27, no. 1 (2020): 14–16.

25. Another reason analysts offered as an explanation for the closing of *Sputnik Norway* was economic conditions. Comm. on Foreign Relations, Putin's Asymmetric Assault on Democracy, 109; Anke Schmidt-Felzmann, "More Than 'Just' Disinformation," 53–55.

26. The author obtained the analyzed data by examining all articles containing the word "Norway" in the period between June 22, 2016, and March 21, 2017, and

available through the online website of *Sputnik International News,* https://sputnik news.com/. The author collected the data on January 21, 2021.

27. Comm. on Foreign Relations, Putin's Asymmetric Assault on Democracy, 109.

28. *Focus 2020: The Norwegian Intelligence Service's Assessment of Current Security Challenges* (Norway: Norwegian Intelligence Service, 2020), 69.

29. Anke Schmidt-Felzmann, "More Than 'Just' Disinformation," 46–47.

30. Nilsen, "Russian Influence Operations Work to Fuel Disagreements between North and South in Norway, Says Report;" Comm. on Foreign Relations, Putin's Asymmetric Assault on Democracy, 110; Nilsen, "Norway's PST Says Russian Intelligence Targets Individuals."

31. Anke Schmidt-Felzmann, "More Than 'Just' Disinformation," 49–50; Nilsen, "Russian Influence Operations Work to Fuel Disagreements between North and South in Norway, Says Report."

32. Kjetil Bjørkmann, "The Impact from the Russian Import-Ban (2014–) on the Norwegian Seafood Industry: When an Export-Dependent Industry Face Spill-Over Effects from Geopolitical Conflicts," 52.

33. Comm. on Foreign Relations, Putin's Asymmetric Assault on Democracy, 109.

34. *Focus 2020: The Norwegian Intelligence Service's Assessment of Current Security Challenges* (Norway: Norwegian Intelligence Service, 2020), 69.

CHAPTER 7. HOW THE TINY BALKAN NATION OF MONTENEGRO WITHSTOOD A RUSSIAN-SPONSORED COUP

1. Estimates indicate that between 50 percent and 60 percent of Montenegro's population at the time supported NATO membership. Christo Grozev, "Balkan Gambit: Part 2. The Montenegro Zugzwang," *Bellingcat,* March 25, 2017, https://www.bell ingcat.com/news/uk-and-europe/2017/03/25/balkan-gambit-part-2-montenegro -zugzwang/ (accessed March 17, 2021).

2. *Russian Interference in European Elections, Russia and Montenegro: Hearings on S. Rep., Before the Select Comm. on Intelligence* (June 28, 2017) (statement of Vesko Garčević, ambassador of Montenegro), 11, https://www.intelligence.senate.gov/sites /default/files/documents/sfr-vgarcevic-062817b.pdf (accessed March 28, 2021).

3. Dusica Tomovic, "Pro-Russian Montenegrins Publish New Anti-Western Media," *Balkan Insight,* October 18, 2017, https://balkaninsight.com/2017/10/18/pro-russian -montenegrins-publish-new-anti-western-media-10–17–2017/ (accessed March 17, 2021).

4. Also see *The Attempted Coup in Montenegro and Malign Russian Influence in Europe: Hearings on S. Rep., Before the Comm. on Armed Services* (July 13, 2017) (statement of Janusz Bugajski, senior fellow, Center for European Policy Analysis), at 10–14, https://www.govinfo.gov/content/pkg/CHRG-115shrg34738/html/CHRG-115 shrg34738.htm (accessed March 28, 2021).

5. *Russian Interference in European Elections, Russia and Montenegro: Hearings on S. Rep., Before the Select Comm. on Intelligence* (June 28, 2017) (statement of Vesko Garčević, ambassador of Montenegro), 2.

6. *Russian Interference in European Elections, Russia and Montenegro: Hearings on S. Rep., Before the Select Comm. on Intelligence* (June 28, 2017) (statement of Vesko Garčević, ambassador of Montenegro), 2. Ben Farmer, "Russia Plotted to Overthrow Montenegro's Government by Assassinating Prime Minister Milo Djukanovic Last Year, According to Senior Whitehall Sources," *Telegraph*, February 18, 2017, https://advance.lexis.com/api/document?collection=news&id=urn:contentItem:5MX7-PPR1-F021-63J7-00000-00&context=1516831 (accessed March 17, 2021).

7. Comm. on Foreign Relations, Putin's Asymmetric Assault on Democracy, 79; Bechev, *The 2016 Coup Attempt in Montenegro: Is Russia's Balkans Footprint Expanding?* 9.

8. Comm. on Foreign Relations, Putin's Asymmetric Assault on Democracy, 79.

9. *Russian Interference in European Elections, Russia and Montenegro: Hearings on S. Rep., Before the Select Comm. on Intelligence* (June 28, 2017) (statement of Vesko Garčević, Ambassador of Montenegro), 5.

10. Tomovic, "Pro-Russian Montenegrins Publish New Anti-Western Media."

11. *Assessing Russia's Economic Footprint in Montenegro,* Center for the Study of Democracy, Policy Brief No. 73, January 2018, 6–7, https://csd.bg/fileadmin/user_upload/publications_library/files/2018_01/CSD_Policy_Brief_73_Montenegro.pdf (accessed March 17, 2021).

12. *Russian Interference in European Elections, Russia and Montenegro: Hearings on S. Rep., Before the Select Comm. on Intelligence* (June 28, 2017) (statement of Vesko Garčević, ambassador of Montenegro), 2; Comm. on Foreign Relations, Putin's Asymmetric Assault on Democracy, 78.

13. "Relations with Montenegro (Archived)," North Atlantic Treaty Organization, December 14, 2017, https://www.nato.int/cps/en/natohq/topics_49736.htm (March 17, 2021); Comm. on Foreign Relations, Putin's Asymmetric Assault on Democracy, 78.

14. "Kremlin Says NATO Expansion to East Will Lead to Retaliation from Russia," *Reuters,* December 2, 2015, https://www.reuters.com/article/us-kremlin-nato-expansion-idUSKBN0TL0V720151202 (March 17, 2021).

15. The Ministry of Foreign Affairs of the Russian Federation, "Comment by the Information and Press Department on invitation for Montenegro to start talks on joining NATO," December 2, 2015, https://www.mid.ru/en_GB/foreign_policy/rso/-/asset_publisher/0vP3hQoCPRg5/content/id/1963259 (accessed March 17, 2021).

16. Grozev, "Balkan Gambit: Part 2."

17. Comm. on Foreign Relations, Putin's Asymmetric Assault on Democracy, 78; *Russian Interference in European Elections, Russia and Montenegro: Hearings on S. Rep., Before the Select Comm. on Intelligence* (June 28, 2017) (statement of Vesko Garčević, Ambassador of Montenegro), 6https://www.intelligence.senate.gov/sites/default/files/documents/sfr-vgarcevic-062817b.pdf; Farmer, "Russia Plotted to Overthrow

Montenegro's Government by Assassinating Prime Minister Milo Djukanovic Last Year, According to Senior Whitehall Sources"; Ken Dilanian, Josh Meyer, Cynthia McFadden, William M. Arkin, and Robert Windrem, "Exclusive: White House Readies to Fight Election Day Cyber Mayhem," *NBC News*, November 3, 2016, https://www.nbcnews.com/news/us-news/white-house-readies-fight-election-day -cyber-mayhem-n677636 (accessed March 17, 2021).

18. Comm. on Foreign Relations, Putin's Asymmetric Assault on Democracy, 78.

19. Ruslan Stefanov and Martin Vladimirov, *The Kremlin Playbook in Southeast Europe: Economic Influence and Sharp Power* (Sofia, Bulgaria: Center for the Study of Democracy, 2020), 77.

20. *Russian Interference in European Elections, Russia and Montenegro: Hearings on S. Rep., Before the Select Comm. on Intelligence* (June 28, 2017) (statement of Vesko Garčević, ambassador of Montenegro), 5; Joe Parkinson and Georgi Kantchev, "Document: Russia Uses Rigged Polls, Fake News to Sway Foreign Elections; Bulgarian Officials Say a Former Russian Spy Advised Pro-Moscow Party on How to Manipulate Voters as Part of Kremlin's Effort to Regain Influence in Eastern Europe; a 30-Page Dossier," *Wall Street Journal*, March 23, 2017, https://search.proquest.com/news papers/document-russia-uses-rigged-polls-fake-news-sway/docview/1880062843 /se-2?accountid=25333 (accessed March 10, 2021).

21. *Russian Interference in European Elections, Russia and Montenegro: Hearings on S. Rep., Before the Select Comm. on Intelligence* (June 28, 2017) (statement of Vesko Garčević, Ambassador of Montenegro), 5.

22. Comm. on Foreign Relations, Putin's Asymmetric Assault on Democracy, 78.

23. "Montenegro Coup Suspect Linked to Russian-Backed Ultranationalist Organization," *Bellingcat*, April 25, 2017, https://www.bellingcat.com/news/uk-and-europe /2017/04/25/montenegro-coup-suspect-linked-russian-backed-ultranationalist -organisation/ (accessed March 17, 2021).

24. *Russian Interference in European Elections, Russia and Montenegro: Hearings on S. Rep., Before the Select Comm. on Intelligence* (June 28, 2017) (statement of Vesko Garčević, ambassador of Montenegro), 3; *The Attempted Coup in Montenegro and Malign Russian Influence in Europe: Hearings on S. Rep., Before the Comm. on Armed Services* (July 13, 2017) (statement of Damon Wilson, executive vice president, the Atlantic Council), https://www.govinfo.gov/content/pkg/CHRG-115shrg34738/html/CHRG -115shrg34738.htm (accessed March 28, 2021).

25. *Russian Interference in European Elections, Russia and Montenegro: Hearings on S. Rep., Before the Select Comm. on Intelligence* (June 28, 2017) (statement of Vesko Garčević, ambassador of Montenegro), 4; Organization for Security and Co-operation in Europe, Office for Democratic Institutions and Human Rights, Montenegro Parliamentary Elections 2016, *OSCE/ODIHR Election Observation Mission Final Report* (Warsaw, Poland, January 25, 2017), 4, https://www.osce.org/files/f/docu ments/3/d/295511. pdf (accessed March 28, 2021).

26. Dimitar Bechev, *The 2016 Coup Attempt in Montenegro: Is Russia's Balkans Footprint Expanding?* (Philadelphia, PA: Foreign Policy Research Institute, April 2018), 9, https://www.fpri.org/article/2018/04/the-2016-coup-attempt-in-montenegro-is-russias-balkans-footprint-expanding/ (accessed March 28, 2021).

27. Bechev, *The 2016 Coup Attempt in Montenegro: Is Russia's Balkans Footprint Expanding?* 9.

28. *The Attempted Coup in Montenegro and Malign Russian Influence in Europe: Hearings on S. Rep., Before the Comm. on Armed Services* (July 13, 2017) (statement of Nebojsa Kaludjerovic, ambassador of Montenegro to the United States), at 1–9, https://www.govinfo.gov/content/pkg/CHRG-115shrg34738/html/CHRG-115shrg34738.htm (accessed March 28, 2021); *The Attempted Coup in Montenegro and Malign Russian Influence in Europe: Hearings on S. Rep., Before the Comm. on Armed Services* (July 13, 2017) (statement of Janusz Bugajski, senior fellow, Center for European Policy Analysis), at 10–14; Farmer, "Russia Plotted to Overthrow Montenegro's Government by Assassinating Prime Minister Milo Djukanovic Last Year, According to Senior Whitehall Sources"; Organization for Security and Co-operation in Europe, Office for Democratic Institutions and Human Rights, Montenegro Parliamentary Elections 2016, *OSCE/ODIHR Election Observation Mission Final Report* (Warsaw, Poland, January 25, 2017), 4.

29. Christo, "Balkan Gambit: Part 2"; Ben Farmer, "Reconstruction: The Full Incredible Story behind Russia's Deadly Plot to Stop Montenegro Embracing the West," *Telegraph*, February 18, 2017, https://advance.lexis.com/api/document?collection=news&id=urn:contentItem:5MXF-VFW1-F021–61G1–00000–00&context=1516831 (accessed March 25, 2021); *The Attempted Coup in Montenegro and Malign Russian Influence in Europe: Hearings on S. Rep., Before the Comm. on Armed Services* (July 13, 2017) (statement of Damon Wilson, executive vice president, the Atlantic Council).

30. Farmer, "Reconstruction: The Full Incredible Story behind Russia's Deadly Plot to Stop Montenegro Embracing the West."

31. Bechev, *The 2016 Coup Attempt in Montenegro: Is Russia's Balkans Footprint Expanding?* 10.

32. Stevo Vasiljevic, "Russians, Opposition Figures Sentenced over Role in 2016 Montenegro Coup Attempt," *Reuters*, May 9, 2019, https://www.reuters.com/article/us-montenegro-court/russians-opposition-figures-sentenced-over-role-in-2016-montenegro-coup-attempt-idUSKCN1SF144 (accessed March 17, 2021).

33. "Montenegro Overturns Coup Verdict for Two Russians, 11 Others," *Aljazeera*, February 5, 2021, https://www.aljazeera.com/news/2021/2/5/montenegro-overturns-coup-verdict-for-2-russians-11-others (accessed April 2, 2021).

34. "Russian Import Ban on EU Products," European Commission, https://ec.europa.eu/food/safety/international_affairs/eu_russia/russian_import_ban_eu_products_en (accessed March 19, 2021); "Russia Bans Agricultural Imports from West in

Tit-for-Tat Sanctions Move," *Guardian,* August 6, 2014, https://www.theguardian
.com/world/2014/aug/06/russia-bans-imports-eu-us-sanctions (accessed March
17, 2021).

35. "Montenegro Approves Nato Membership as Russia Protests," *BBC News,* April
28, 2017, https://www.bbc.com/news/world-europe-39738238 (accessed March
17, 2021); *Assessing Russia's Economic Footprint in Montenegro,* Center for the Study
of Democracy, Policy Brief No. 73, January 2018, at 7, https://csd.bg/fileadmin
/user_upload/publications_library/files/2018_01/CSD_Policy_Brief_73_Monte
negro.pdf (accessed March 28, 2021).

36. *Assessing Russia's Economic Footprint in Montenegro,* Center for the Study of Democracy, 7.

37. The main election administration bodies in Montenegro are three election commis-
sions: the state election commission, municipal election commissions, and polling
boards. The Montenegro Ministry of the Interior maintais the country's electoral
register. For a description of the main bodies responsible for conducting elections in
Montenegro, please refer to Organization for Security and Co-operation in Europe,
Office for Democratic Institutions and Human Rights, Montenegro Parliamentary
Elections 2016, *OSCE/ODIHR Election Observation Mission Final Report* (Warsaw,
Poland, January 25, 2017), 1–2, 6–8.

38. *Russian Interference in European Elections, Russia and Montenegro: Hearings on S. Rep.,
Before the Select Comm. on Intelligence* (June 28, 2017) (statement by of Vesko
Garčević, ambassador of Montenegro), 11; "Web Portal of the Government of Montenegro Exposed to DDoS Attacks," *CIRT,* October 19, 2016, www.cirt.me/en/news
/167139/Web-portal-of-the-Government-of-Montenegro-exposed-to-DDoS-attacks
.html (accessed March 17, 2021).

39. Dusica Tomovic and Maja Zivanovic, "Russia's Fancy Bear Hacks Its Way into Montenegro," *Balkan Insight,* March 5, 2018, https://balkaninsight.com/2018/03/05/
russia-s-fancy-bear-hacks-its-way-into-montenegro-03–01–2018/ (accessed March
17, 2021).

40. *Bearing Witness: Uncovering the Logic behind Russian Military Cyber Operations* (Booz
Allen Hamilton: 2020), 12.

41. Some of Montenegro's election administration bodies can be joined by authorized
political party representatives, and it is possible that some cyber operations that
occurred in 2007 targeted representatives that had participated or would participate
in administering elections in Montenegro. Due to lack of specific information on
the individuals targeted in the cyber operations in 2007, attribution, and data on
whether these individuals were targeted because of their past or future roles in the
conduct of elections, this chapter does not include such cases in the analysis. For
more information on Montenegro's election administration, please refer to Organization for Security and Co-operation in Europe, Office for Democratic Institutions
and Human Rights, Montenegro Parliamentary Elections 2016, *OSCE/ODIHR
Election Observation Mission Final Report* (Warsaw, Poland, January 25, 2017), 6–8.

42. In addition to DDoS attacks, four days after the elections, a phishing campaign was launched against Montenegro's parliament. Trend Micro attributed the campaign to GRU's APT 28. The government of Montenegro considered this campaign less serious than the operations four days prior because the former cyber operation appeared to be "a blind shot" and did not target confidential data. In 2007, Montenegro was routinely a target of sophisticated and serious cyber intrusions as the country approached its official NATO accession date. These operations included a phishing campaign launched in January 2017 against members of the Montenegro government and Defense Ministry. FireEye, ESET, and Trend Micro attributed the phishing campaign to APT 28. Another episode of cyber intrusions against Montenegro's government started on February 15, 2017, and intensified over the course of the following days. The Montenegrin government assessed these attacks to be more intense that the cyber attacks in October 2016. These cyber attacks targeted websites of state institutions and the government and media. Dusica Tomovic and Maja Zivanovic, "Russia's Fancy Bear Hacks its Way into Montenegro," *Balkan Insight*, March 5, 2018, http://www.balkaninsight.com/en/article/russia-s-fancy-bear-hacks-its-way -into-montenegro-03–01–2018 (accessed March 17, 2021); Eduard Kovacs, "Russian Hackers Target Montenegro as Country Joins NATO," *Security Week*, June 7, 2017, https://www.securityweek.com/russian-hackers-target-montenegro-country -joins-nato (accessed March 17, 2021); Government of Montenegro, "Web Portal of Government of Montenegro and Several Other Web Sites Were under Enhanced Cyberattacks," February 17, 2017, http://www.gov.me/en/News/169508/Web-portal -of-Government-of-Montenegro-and-several-other-web-sites-were-under-enhanced -cyberattacks.html (accessed March 17, 2021).

43. *Russian Interference in European Elections, Russia and Montenegro: Hearings on S. Rep., Before the Select Comm. on Intelligence* (June 28, 2017) (statement of Vesko Garčević, ambassador of Montenegro), 2; Comm. on Foreign Relations, Putin's Asymmetric Assault on Democracy, 78; Tomovic, "Pro-Russian Montenegrins Publish New Anti-Western Media."

44. *Russian Interference in European Elections, Russia and Montenegro: Hearings on S. Rep., Before the Select Comm. on Intelligence* (June 28, 2017) (statement of Vesko Garčević, ambassador of Montenegro), 3.

45. Dilanian et al., "Exclusive: White House Readies to Fight Election Day Cyber Mayhem."

46. "Milo organizuje dijasporu i plaća 250 evra glas" [Milo organizes the diaspora and pays 250 euros a vote], *Sputnik Srbija*, October 11, 2016, https://rs.sputniknews. com/regioni/201610111108433460-dps-djukanovic-dijaspora-glasovi-placenje / (accessed March 19, 2021); "Vreme je da Milo ode u političko čistilište" [It is time for Milo to go to political purgatory], *Sputnik Srbija*, October 13, 2016, https:// rs.sputniknews.com/intervju/201610131108467555-Vreme-je-da-Milo-ode-u-pol iticko-cistiliste/ (accessed March 19, 2021); "Crna Gora: Milovi aktivisti prave

haos—pritiskaju glasače, vode evidenciju . . ." [Montenegro: Milo's activists are creating chaos—pressuring voters, keeping records . . .], *Sputnik Srbija*, October 16, 2016, https://rs.sputniknews.com/regioni/201610161108500337-izbori-crna-gora-malverzacije-1/ (accessed March 19, 2021).

47. "Orilo se iz 10.000 grla: 'Milo lopove'" [It was shouted from 10,000 heads: "Milo thieves"] (video), *Sputnik Srbija*, September 28, 2016, https://rs.sputniknews.com/regioni/201609281108282745-crna-gora-milo-opozicija-protest/ (accessed March 19, 2021); "Vladajuća crnogorska partija najavila osnivanje fonda koji već postoji" [The ruling Montenegrin party announced the establishment of a fund that already exists], *Sputnik Srbija*, October 9, 2016, https://rs.sputniknews.com/regioni/2016 10091108414860-Vladajuca-crnogorska-partija-najavila-Fond-koji-vec-postoji/ (accessed March 19, 2021).

48. "Duma: Izbori pokazali da se veliki broj Crnogoraca protivi ulasku u NATO" [Duma: The elections showed that a large number of Montenegrins oppose joining NATO], *Sputnik Srbija*, October 17, 2016, https://rs.sputniknews.com/rusija/201610171108510916-crna-gora-izbori-nato-rusija-/ (accessed March 19, 2021).

49. "Medojević: DPS je jedina teroristička organizacija" [Medojevic: DPS is the only terrorist organization] (video), *Sputnik Srbija*, October 26, 2016, https://rs.sputniknews.com/regioni/201610261108630768-Medojevic-video-poruka/ (accessed March 19, 2021).

50. "Crnogorski izbori ličili na državni udar" [The Montenegrin elections looked like a coup], *Sputnik Srbija*, October 17, 2016, https://rs.sputniknews.com/regioni/2016 10171108514218-knezevic-izbori-intervju1/ (accessed March 19, 2021).

51. "DF: Najvažnije je detronizovati Đukanovića" [DF: The most important thing is to dethrone Djukanovic], *Sputnik Srbija*, October 19, 2016, https://rs.sputniknews.com/intervju/201610191108540942-df-detronizovati-djukanovic/ (accessed March 19, 2021); "DF: Lopovska banda DPS uvodi otvorenu diktaturu u Crnoj Gori" [DF: The thieving gang DPS is introducing an open dictatorship in Montenegro], *Sputnik Srbija*, October 30, 2016, https://rs.sputniknews.com/regioni/20161030 1108669110-df-saopstenje-izbori-rezultati/ (accessed March 19, 2021).

52. Comm. on Foreign Relations, Putin's Asymmetric Assault on Democracy, 79.

53. "Relations with Montenegro (Archived)," North Atlantic Treaty Organization, December 14, 2017, https://www.nato.int/cps/en/natohq/topics_49736.htm (accessed March 28, 2021).

54. *Russian Interference in European Elections, Russia and Montenegro: Hearings on S. Rep., Before the Select Comm. on Intelligence* (June 28, 2017) (statement of Vesko Garčević, ambassador of Montenegro), 3–4.

55. *Assessing Russia's Economic Footprint in Montenegro,* Center for the Study of Democracy, 1, 5.

56. *Russian Interference in European Elections, Russia and Montenegro: Hearings on S. Rep., Before the Select Comm. on Intelligence* (June 28, 2017) (statement of Vesko Garčević, ambassador of Montenegro), 3–4.

CHAPTER 8. TRYING TO TRUMP EN MARCHE!

1. The political party of then French presidential candidate Emmanuel Macron, against which the Russian government launched a series of cyber operations, is called La Republique En Marche! which is translated as "the Republic Onward!" En Marche, Le Movement [The Movement], https://en-marche.fr/le-mouvement (accessed March 19, 2021).

2. See for example Jean-Baptiste Jeangene Vilmer, *The "Macron Leaks" Operation: A Post-Mortem* (Washington, DC: Atlantic Council, June 2019), v, https://www .atlanticcouncil.org/wp-content/uploads/2019/06/The_Macron_Leaks_Opera tion-A_Post-Mortem.pdf (accessed March 28, 2021).

3. "France Condemns Putin's Crimea Annexation, Mulls Sanctions," *RFI*, March 18, 2014, https://www.rfi.fr/en/france/20140318-france-condemns-putins-annexaton -crimea-mulls-sanctions (accessed March 19, 2021).

4. "Hollande: Russia Is a Partner, Not a Threat," *Radio Free Europe Radio Liberty*, July 8, 2016, https://www.rferl.org/a/hollande-russia-is-a-partner-not-a-threat/27847690 .html (accessed March 19, 2021).

5. Sale Lilly and Bilyana Lilly, "Punish Russia and Revolutionize NATO's Navy," *Real Clear Defense*, August 4, 2014, https://www.realcleardefense.com/articles/2014 /08/05/punish_russia__revolutionize_natos_navy_107343.html (accessed March 19, 2021).

6. Pierre Tran, "Mistral Dispute with Russia Settled, France Eyes Exports," *Defense News*, August 9, 2015, https://www.defensenews.com/naval/2015/08/09/mistral-dis pute-with-russia-settled-france-eyes-exports/ (accessed March 19, 2021); Matthew Dalton, "France to Sell Two Mistral Warships to Egypt," *Washington Post*, September 23, 2015, https://www.wsj.com/articles/france-to-sell-mistral-warships-to -egypt-1443009701 (accessed March 19, 2021).

7. "France Rules Out Easing Russia Sanctions before Progress on Ukraine Made," *French Press Agency*, June 6, 2018, https://www.dailysabah.com/europe/2018/06/06/ france-rules-out-easing-russia-sanctions-before-progress-on-ukraine-made (accessed March 19, 2021).

8. "Merkel and Hollande Support Sanction Extensions against Russia," *Deutsche Welle*, December 13, 2016, https://p.dw.com/p/2UCY9 (accessed March 19, 2021).

9. European Commission, "Russian Import Ban on EU Products;" Jennifer Rankin, "Russia Bans Agricultural Imports from West in Tit-for-Tat Sanctions Move," *Guardian*, August 6, 2014, https://www.theguardian.com/world/2014/aug/06/russia -bans-imports-eu-us-sanctions (accessed March 19, 2021).

10. Vivienne Walk, "Why France's Marine Le Pen Is Doubling Down on Russia Support," *Time*, January 9, 2017, http://time.com/4627780/russia-national-front-marine -le-pen-putin/ (accessed March 19, 2021).

11. Andrew Rettman, "Illicit Russian Billions Pose Threat to EU Democracy," *EUobserver*, April 21, 2017, https://euobserver.com/foreign/137631 (accessed March 19, 2021).

12. Anne-Claude Martin, "National Front's Russian Loans Cause Uproar in European Parliament," *Euractiv*, December 4, 2014, updated December 7, 2014, https://www .euractiv.com/section/europe-s-east/news/national-front-s-russian-loans-cause-up roar-in-european-parliament/ (accessed March 19, 2021); Walk, "Why France's Marine Le Pen Is Doubling Down on Russia Support."

13. Andrew Rettman, "Illicit Russian Billions Pose Threat to EU Democracy," *EUob-server*, April 21, 2017, https://euobserver.com/foreign/137631 (accessed March 19, 2021).

14. Anne-Claude Martin, "National Front's Russian Loans Cause Uproar in European Parliament," *Euractiv*, December 4, 2014, updated December 7, 2014, https://www .euractiv.com/section/europe-s-east/news/national-front-s-russian-loans-cause-uproar -in-european-parliament/ (accessed March 19, 2021).

15. Walk, "Why France's Marine Le Pen Is Doubling Down on Russia Support."

16. "Emmanuel Macron est le seul candidat à proposer une politique étrangère digne de la France" [Emmanuel Macron is the only candidate to propose a foreign policy worthy of France], *Huffington Post*, March 4, 2017, https://www.huffingtonpost.fr /nicolas-tenzer/emmanuel-macron-est-le-seul-candidat-a-proposer-une-politique -et_a_22022672/ (accessed March 19, 2021).

17. Association of Accredited Public Policy Advocates to the European Union, Associa-tion Dialogue Franco-Russe (French-Russian Dialogue), February 11, 2015, http:// www.aalep.eu/association-dialogue-franco-russe-french-russian-dialogue (accessed March 19, 2021); Dialogue Franco Russe, "Qui Sommes Nous" [Who we are], 2021, https://dialoguefrancorusse.com/fr/association.html (accessed March 19, 2021).

18. Natalya Kanevskaya, "How the Kremlin Wields Its Soft Power in France," *Radio Free Europe/Radio Liberty*, June 24, 2014, https://www.rferl.org/a/russia-soft-power -france/25433946.html (accessed March 19, 2021).

19. Antoine Blua, "Russia Unveils Cultural, Orthodox Jewel on the Seine," *Radio Free Europe/Radio Liberty*, October 17, 2016, https://www.rferl.org/a/russia-paris-ortho dox-cathedral-cultural-center-to-open/28058923.html (accessed March 19, 2021).

20. United States of America v. Yuriy Sergeyevich Andrienko, Sergey Vladimirovich Detistov, Pavel Valeryevich Frolov, Anatoliy Sergeyevich Kovalev, Artem Valeryevich Ochichenko, and Petr Nikolayevich Pliskin, Indictment, Count One, Conspiracy to Commit an Offense Against the United States, No. 20–316 (U.S. District Court Western District of Pennsylvania, October 15, 2020), at 3, https://www.justice.gov/ opa/press-release/file/1328521/download (accessed March 29, 2021).

21. Mehdi Chebil, "France Takes Steps to Prevent an Election Hack Attack," *France 24*, January 14, 2017, https://www.france24.com/en/20170114-france-vulnerable -cyber-attacks-hacking-presidential-elections (accessed March 19, 2021); Lizzie Dearden, "Emmanuel Macron Hacked Emails: French Media Ordered by Electoral Commission Not to Publish Content of Messages," *Independent*, May 6, 2017, https://www.independent.co.uk/news/world/europe/emmanuel-macron-email -hack-leaks-election-marine-le-pen-russia-media-ordered-not-publish-commis

sion-a7721111.html (accessed March 19, 2021); Hacquebord, *Two Years of Pawn Storm*, 13.

22. Rick Noack, "Report: Hack of French Candidate Has Russian Link," *Washington Post*, April 26, 2017, https://search.proquest.com/docview/1891675252?accountid =25333 (accessed March 14, 2019).

23. United States of America v. Yuriy Sergeyevich Andrienko et al., at 15.

24. Vilmer, *The "Macron Leaks" Operation: A Post-Mortem*, 11.

25. Noack, "Report: Hack of French Candidate Has Russian Link."

26. Vilmer, *The "Macron Leaks" Operation: A Post-Mortem*, 21; Adam Nossiter, David E. Sanger, and Nicole Perlroth, "Hackers Came, but the French Were Prepared," *New York Times*, May 9, 2017, https://www.nytimes.com/2017/05/09/world/europe /hackers-came-but-the-french-were-prepared.html (accessed March 19, 2021).

27. Vilmer, *The "Macron Leaks" Operation: A Post-Mortem*, 6–7.

28. Vilmer, *The "Macron Leaks" Operation: A Post-Mortem*, 6.

29. Vilmer, *The "Macron Leaks" Operation: A Post-Mortem*, 6.

30. Vilmer, *The "Macron Leaks" Operation: A Post-Mortem*, 8.

31. Joseph Menn, "Exclusive: Russia Used Facebook to Try to Spy on Macron Campaign—Sources," *Reuters*, July 26, 2017, https://www.reuters.com/article/us-cyber -france-facebook-spies-exclusive/exclusive-russia-used-facebook-to-try-to-spy-on -macron-campaign-sources-idUSKBN1AC0EI (accessed March 19, 2021).

32. Vilmer, *The "Macron Leaks" Operation: A Post-Mortem*, 6–7.

33. Vilmer, *The "Macron Leaks" Operation: A Post-Mortem*, 9–10.

34. Vilmer, *The "Macron Leaks" Operation: A Post-Mortem*, 12–14.

35. Andy Kroll, "John Podesta Is Ready to Talk about Pizzagate," *Rolling Stone*, December 9, 2018, https://www.rollingstone.com/politics/politics-features/john-podesta-pizza gate-766489/ (accessed March 5, 2021); Vilmer, *The "Macron Leaks" Operation: A Post-Mortem*, 12–13.

36. Vilmer, *The "Macron Leaks" Operation: A Post-Mortem*, 12–13.

37. Vilmer, *The "Macron Leaks" Operation: A Post-Mortem*, v.

38. "Number of Monthly Active Twitter Users Worldwide from 1st Quarter 2010 to 1st Quarter 2019," *Statista 2021*, https://www.statista.com/statistics/282087/number -of-monthly-active-twitter-users/ (accessed March 19, 2021); Vilmer, *The "Macron Leaks" Operation: A Post-Mortem*, 13.

39. Vilmer, *The "Macron Leaks" Operation: A Post-Mortem*, 14.

40. James Titcomb, "WikiLeaks Releases Thousands of Hacked Macron Campaign Emails," *Telegraph*, July 31, 2017, https://www.telegraph.co.uk/news/2017/07/31/ wikileaks-releases-thousands-hacked-macron-campaign-emails/ (accessed March 19, 2021).

41. See the sections on pro-Kremlin media coverage in this chapter and the chapter on Russia's interference in the 2016 U.S. elections.

42. Vilmer, *The "Macron Leaks" Operation: A Post-Mortem*, 19.

43. Vilmer, *The "Macron Leaks" Operation: A Post-Mortem*, 19–20.

44. Vilmer, *The "Macron Leaks" Operation: A Post-Mortem*, 20.

45. Nossiter et al., "Hackers Came, but the French Were Prepared"; Vilmer, *The "Macron Leaks" Operation: A Post-Mortem*, 21.

46. Vilmer, *The "Macron Leaks" Operation: A Post-Mortem*, 23.

47. Vilmer, *The "Macron Leaks" Operation: A Post-Mortem*, 18, 25.

48. United States of America v. Yuriy Sergeyevich Andrienko et al., at 16.

49. James McAuley "French President Macron Blasts Russian State-Owned Media as 'Propaganda,'" *Washington Post*, May 29, 2017, https://www.washingtonpost.com /world/europe/french-president-macron-blasts-russian-state-run-media-as-pro paganda/2017/05/29/4e758308–4479–11e7–8de1-cec59a9bf4b1_story.html (accessed March 19, 2021).

50. Nicole Perlroth, "Russian Hackers Who Targeted Clinton Appear to Attack France's Macron," *New York Times*, April 24, 2017, https://www.nytimes.com/2017/04/24 /world/europe/macron-russian-hacking.html (accessed March 19, 2021).

51. Ben Nimmo, "Frankly Unfair? Fact-Checking *Sputnik France*'s Claim That It Is Reporting the French Election Fairly," *Medium*, February 11, 2017, https://medium .com/dfrlab/frankly-unfair-3a43f4347dfe (accessed March 19, 2021).

52. Vilmer, *The "Macron Leaks" Operation: A Post-Mortem*, 4.

53. "D'où les rumeurs sur Macron proviennent-elles en réalité?" [Where do the Macron rumors actually come from?], *Sputnik France*, February 17, 2017, https://fr.sputnik news.com/france/201702171030136506-macron-rumeurs-medias/ (accessed March 19, 2021).

54. "Côte-d'Or: plusieurs centaines de bulletins Marine Le Pen volés" [Côte-d'Or: several hundred stolen Marine Le Pen bulletins], *Sputnik France*, May 7, 2017, https:// fr.sputniknews.com/france/201705071031275987-buletins-vol-mlp/ (accessed March 19, 2021).

55. "Témoin à Sputnik: 'Dans les trois enveloppes le bulletin Le Pen est déchiré'" [Witness to Sputnik: "In the three envelopes the Le Pen bulletin is torn"], *Sputnik France*, May 7, 2017, https://fr.sputniknews.com/france/201705071031279598-vote -france-bulletins-dechires/ (accessed March 19, 2021).

56. "Présidentielle: l'abstention finale devrait être un record depuis près d'un demi-siècle" [Presidential: final abstention should be a record for almost half a century], *Sputnik France*, May 7, 2017, https://fr.sputniknews.com/france/20170507103 1278753-election-abstention-record-estimations/ (accessed March 19, 2021); "Présidentielle: participation de 65,30% à 17h, en baisse par rapport au 1er tour" [Presidential: 65.30 percent participation at 5 p.m., down from the 1st round], *Sputnik France*, May 7, 2017, https://fr.sputniknews.com/france/20170507103 1276506-presidentielle-participation-17h/ (accessed March 19, 2021); "Macron élu par seulement 44% des inscrits" [Macron elected by only 44 percent of those registered], *Sputnik France*, May 8, 2017, https://fr.sputniknews.com/france

/201705081031293191-france-election-macron/ (accessed March 19, 2021); "Echauffourées à Paris: 141 interpellations et 9 gardes à vue" [Scuffles in Paris: 141 arrests and 9 police custody], *Sputnik France*, May 8, 2017, https://fr.sputniknews.com/france/201705081031291604-paris-manifestation-interpellation/ (accessed March 19, 2021); "Manif à Paris: violents clashs et correspondante de Sputnik agressée par la police" [Demonstration in Paris: violent clashes and Sputnik correspondent attacked by the police], *Sputnik France*, May 9, 2017, https://fr.sputnik news.com/france/201705081031295670-manifestation-regression-sociale-paris / (accessed March 19, 2021); "Violents accrochages à Paris: la police passe à tabac des manifestants et des journalists" [Violent clashes in Paris: police beat protesters and journalists], *Sputnik France*, May 8, 2017, https://fr.sputniknews.com/france/2 01705081031296310-france-paris-accrochages/ (accessed March 19, 2021).

57. "Vice-Président LR: Macron est 'un Président élu sans envie ni enthousiasme'" [Vice-President LR: Macron is "an elected President without envy or enthusiasm"], *Sputnik France*, May 7, 2017, https://fr.sputniknews.com/france/2017050710312 85367-macron-president-elu-commentaire/ (accessed March 19, 2021).

58. "Nigel Farage La France a choisi 'cinq ans d'échec de plus,' selon Farage" [Nigel Farage France has chosen "five more years of failure," according to Farage], *Sputnik France*, May 8, 2017, https://fr.sputniknews.com/international/20170508103 1294281-macron-election-farage/ (accessed March 19, 2021).

59. "Les félicitations continuent d'affluer suite à la victoire de Macron" [Congratulations keep pouring in following Macron's victory], *Sputnik France*, May 8, 2017, https://fr.sputniknews.com/international/201705081031300998-felicitation-ma cron-personnalites-politiques/ (accessed March 19, 2021). To be fair, some articles contained positive information about Macron. For example, in one article, *Sputnik France* adjudicated that Macron won the "handshake battle" in his first meeting with U.S. president Trump, who is known for his firm and long handshake. "Score 1 à 0: Macron remporte la 'bataille des poignées de main' contre Trump" [Score 1 to 0: Macron wins "handshake battle" against Trump] (video), *Sputnik France*, May 25, 2017, https://fr.sputniknews.com/international/201705251031537841-macron -trump-poignee-main/ (accessed March 19, 2021).

60. Mehdi Chebil, "France Takes Steps to Prevent an Election Hack Attack," *France 24*, January 14, 2017, https://www.france24.com/en/20170114-france-vulnerable-cyber -attacks-hacking-presidential-elections (accessed March 19, 2021).

61. Adam Nossiter, David E. Sanger, and Nicole Perlroth, "Hackers Came, but the French Were Prepared," *New York Times*, May 9, 2017 (accessed March 19, 2021); Rachel Donadio, "Why the Macron Hacking Attack Landed with a Thud in France," *New York Times*, May 8, 2017, https://www.nytimes.com/2017/05/08/ world/europe/macron-hacking-attack-france.html (accessed March 19, 2021).

62. "Emmanuel Macron's Campaign Team Bans Russian News Outlets from Events," *Guardian*, April 27, 2017, https://www.theguardian.com/world/2017/apr/27/russia -emmanuel-macron-banned-news-outlets-discrimination (accessed March 19, 2021).

63. Dana Priest and Michael Birnbaum, "Europe Has Been Working to Expose Russian Meddling for Years," *Washington Post*, June 25, 2017, https://www.washingtonpost .com/world/europe/europe-has-been-working-to-expose-russian-meddling-for -years/2017/06/25/e42dcece-4a09–11e7–9669–250d0b15f83b_story.html (accessed March 19, 2021); Jessica Davies, "Le Monde Identifies 600 Unreliable Websites in Fake-News Crackdown," *Digiday*, January 25, 2017, https://digiday.com/uk/le -monde-identifies-600-unreliable-websites-fake-news-crackdown/ (accessed March 19, 2021).

64. "French Prosecutors Investigate Hacking of Macron Campaign," *Reuters,* May 9, 2017, https://www.reuters.com/article/us-france-election-cyber/french-prosecutors -investigate-hacking-of-macron-campaign-idUSKBN18525X (accessed March 19, 2021).

65. Vilmer, *The "Macron Leaks" Operation: A Post-Mortem*, 26–28.

CHAPTER 9. THE HACK OF THE BUNDESTAG AND AIDING AFD

1. AfD or Alternative for Germany is an extreme right-wing German party that won the third largest share of seats in the German parliament during the 2017 German elections that this chapter examines. Melissa Eddy, "Alternative for Germany: Who Are They, and What Do They Want?" *New York Times*, September 25, 2017, https://www.nytimes.com/2017/09/25/world/europe/germany-election-afd.html (accessed March 20, 2021).

2. Federal Returning Officer, "Election Date: 19th German Bundestag to Be Elected on 24 September 2017," January 25, 2017, https://www.bundeswahlleiter.de/en /mitteilungen/bundestagswahl-2017/20170125-wahltermin.html (accessed March 20, 2021); Janosch Delcker, "Germany Fears Russia Stole Information to Disrupt Election: Fears of Hacking Has German Lawmakers Worried Ahead of September's Ballot," *Politico*, March 20, 2017, https://www.politico.eu/article/hacked-inform ation-bomb-under-germanys-election/ (accessed March 20, 2021); Griff Witte, "As Germans Prepare to Vote, a Mystery Grows: Where Are the Russians?" *Washington Post,* September 10, 2017, https://www.washingtonpost.com/world/as-germans-pre pare-to-vote-a-mystery-grows-where-are-the-russians/2017/09/10/07d47f54–9257 –11e7–8482–8dc9a7af29f9_story.html (accessed March 19, 2021); Herpig, *Cyber Operations: Defending Political IT-Infrastructures*, 6–7.

3. Catherine Stupp, "Germany Seeks EU Sanctions for 2015 Cyberattack on Its Parliament," *Investors Hub*, June 11, 2020, advance.lexis.com/api/document?collection =news&id=urn:contentItem:603V-X2R1-F07F-800J-00000–00&context=15 16831 (accessed June 11, 2020).

4. Patrick Beuth, Kai Biermann, Martin Klingst, and Holger Stark, "Merkel and the Fancy Bear," *ZEIT Online*, May 12, 2017, https://www.zeit.de/digital/2017–05/ cyberattack-bundestag-angela-merkel-fancy-bear-hacker-russia (accessed June 18, 2020); Stupp, "Germany Seeks EU Sanctions for 2015 Cyberattack on Its Parliament."

5. Stupp, "Germany Seeks EU Sanctions for 2015 Cyberattack on Its Parliament"; Zdravko Ljuba, "German Chancellor Confirms Russian Cyberattack from 2015," *Organized Crime and Corruption Reporting Project*, May 18, 2020, https://www. occrp.org/en/daily/12359-german-chancellor-confirms-russian-cyberattack -from-2015 (accessed March 20, 2021).

6. Patrick Donahue and Ilya Arkhipov, "In Tense Encounter, Merkel Tells Putin Sanctions Must Remain," *Bloomberg*, May 2, 2017, https://www.bloomberg.com/news/ articles/2017–05–02/merkel-tells-putin-russia-sanctions-will-have-to-remain -for-now (accessed March 20, 2021).

7. European Commission, "Russian Import Ban on EU Products"; Jennifer Rankin, "Russia Bans Agricultural Imports from West in Tit-for-Tat Sanctions Move," *Guardian*, August 6, 2014, https://www.theguardian.com/world/2014/aug/06/rus sia-bans-imports-eu-us-sanctions (accessed March 20, 2021).

8. Constanze Stelzenmüller, "The Impact of Russian Interference on Germany's 2017 Elections," Testimony, *Brookings Institution*, June 28, 2017, https://www.brookings .edu/testimonies/the-impact-of-russian-interference-on-germanys-2017-elections/ (accessed March 20, 2021).

9. Patrick Donahue and Ilya Arkhipov, "In Tense Encounter, Merkel Tells Putin Sanctions Must Remain," *Bloomberg*, May 2, 2017, https://www.bloomberg.com/news /articles/2017–05–02/merkel-tells-putin-russia-sanctions-will-have-to-remain-for -now (accessed March 20, 2021).

10. FireEye iSight Intelligence, *APT28: At the Center of the Storm*, 4; Delcker, "Germany Fears Russia Stole Information to Disrupt Election."

11. Comm. on Foreign Relations, Putin's Asymmetric Assault on Democracy, 128–29; Stelzenmüller, "The Impact of Russian Interference on Germany's 2017 Elections."

12. Melanie Amann and Pavel Lokshin, "German Populists Forge Ties with Russia," *Spiegel Online*, April 27, 2016, https://www.spiegel.de/international/germany/german -populists-forge-deeper-ties-with-russia-a-1089562.html (accessed March 31, 2021).

13. Simon Shuster, "How Russian Voters Fueled the Rise of Germany's Far-Right," *TIME*, September 25, 2017, https://time.com/4955503/germany-elections-2017-far -right-russia-angela-merkel/ (accessed March 31, 2021).

14. Shuster, "How Russian Voters Fueled the Rise of Germany's Far-Right"; "Head of the AfD Frauke Petry Meets with Russian Officials in Moscow," *Deutsche Welle*, February 20, 2017, https://www.dw.com/en/head-of-the-afd-frauke-petry-meets -with-russian-officials-in-moscow/a-37643188 (accessed March 21, 2021).

15. Shuster, "How Russian Voters Fueled the Rise of Germany's Far-Right"; "Head of the AfD Frauke Petry Meets with Russian Officials in Moscow," *Deutsche Welle*.

16. Melanie Amann and Pavel Lokshin, "German Populists Forge Ties with Russia," *Spiegel International*, April 27, 2016, https://www.spiegel.de/international/germany/ german-populists-forge-deeper-ties-with-russia-a-1089562.html (accessed March 21, 2021).

17. Andrew Rettman, "Illicit Russian Billions Pose Threat to EU Democracy," *EUob-server*, April 21, 2017, https://euobserver.com/foreign/137631 (accessed March 21, 2021).

18. Stelzenmüller, "The Impact of Russian Interference on Germany's 2017 Elections."

19. Andrea Shala, "Germany Challenges Russia over Alleged Cyberattacks," *Reuters,* May 4, 2017, https://www.reuters.com/article/us-germany-security-cyber-russia /germany-challenges-russia-over-alleged-cyberattacks-idUSKBN1801CA (accessed March 21, 2021).

20. Delcker, "Germany Fears Russia Stole Information to Disrupt Election."

21. Patrick Beuth, Kai Biermann, Martin Klingst, and Holger Stark, "Merkel and the Fancy Bear," *ZEIT Online*, May 12, 2017, https://www.zeit.de/digital/2017–05/ cyberattack-bundestag-angela-merkel-fancy-bear-hacker-russia (accessed March 21, 2021).

22. Beuth et al., "Merkel and the Fancy Bear."

23. Beuth et al., "Merkel and the Fancy Bear."

24. Delcker, "Germany Fears Russia Stole Information to Disrupt Election."

25. Shalal, "Germany Challenges Russia over Alleged Cyberattacks."

26. For more information, please refer to the chapters on the 2016 U.S. elections and the 2017 French elections in this book. Michael Schwirtz, "German Election Mystery: Why No Russian Meddling?" *New York Times,* September 21, 2017, https:// www.nytimes.com/2017/09/21/world/europe/german-election-russia.html (accessed March 21, 2021).

27. Stelzenmüller, "The Impact of Russian Interference on Germany's 2017 Elections."

28. FireEye iSight Intelligence, *APT28: At the Center of the Storm,* 4.

29. Delcker, "Germany Fears Russia Stole Information to Disrupt Election"; Witte, "As Germans Prepare to Vote, a Mystery Grows"; Herpig, *Cyber Operations: Defending Political IT-Infrastructures,* 7.

30. Herpig, *Cyber Operations: Defending Political IT-Infrastructures,* 5.

31. Jeffrey Mankoff, "Russian Influence Operations in Germany and Their Effect," *Center for Strategic and International Studies,* February 3, 2020, https://www.csis. org/analysis/russian-influence-operations-germany-and-their-effect (accessed March 21, 2021).

32. To perform the analysis, the author accessed *Sputnik Deuscheland*'s official website https://de.sputniknews.com on December 11, 2020.

33. "Bundestagswahl: Sieg für AfD und Merkel—gut oder schlecht für Russland?" [Bundestag election: victory for AfD and Merkel—good or bad for Russia?], *Sputnik Deutschland,* September 24, 2017, https://de.sputniknews.com/kommentare /20170924317574980-bundestagswahl-sieg-fuer-afd-und-merkel-gut-oder-sch lecht-fuer-russland/ (accessed December 11, 2020).

34. "Wahlergebnis Zeichen der Gesellschaftlichen Spaltung Kommentar" [Election result signs of social division comment], *Sputnik Deutschland,* September 28, 2017,

https://de.sputniknews.com/kommentare/20170928317626301-wahlergebnis
-zeichen-der-gesellschaftlichen-spaltung-kommentar/ (accessed December 11, 2020);
"Merkel CDU Abrechnung Kritik" [Merkel CDU accounting criticism], *Sputnik Deutschland,* October 22, 2017, https://de.sputniknews.com/politik/2017
1022317976720-merkel-cdu-abrechnung-kritik/ (accessed December 11, 2020).

35. See Jörg Michael Dostal, "The German Federal Election of 2017: How the Wedge Issue of Refugees and Migration Took the Shine off Chancellor Merkel and Transformed the Party System," *The Political Quarterly* 88, no. 4 (October/December 2017): 589–602.

36. Dostal, "The German Federal Election of 2017," 589–602; Andrea Grunau and Mara Bierbach, "Immigrant voters in German federal election could prove influential," *Deutsche Welle,* September 7, 2017, https://www.dw.com/en/immigrant-voters
-in-german-federal-election-could-prove-influential/a-40387375 (accessed March 21, 2021).

37. *Sputnik Deuscheland*'s official website, https://de.sputniknews.com, was not accessible as of February 2, 2021.

38. Official website of *Sputnik International,* https://sputniknews.com/ (accessed February 2, 2021).

39. "#ElectionWatch: Russian Botnet Boosts German Far-Right Posts," *Medium,* September 21, 2017, https://medium.com/dfrlab/german-election-russian-botnet
-boosts-far-right-posts-45f170bc2321 (accessed March 21, 2021).

40. Andrea Shalal and Eric Auchard, "German Election Campaign Largely Unaffected by Fake News or Bots," *Reuters,* September 22, 2017, https://www.reuters.com/
article/us-germany-election-fake/german-election-campaign-largely-unaffected-by
-fake-news-or-bots-idUSKCN1BX258 (accessed March 21, 2021); Henk Van Ess and Jane Lytvynenko, "This Russian Hacker Says His Twitter Bots Are Spreading Messages to Help Germany's Far Right Party in the Election," *BuzzFeed,* September 24, 2017, https://www.buzzfeednews.com/article/henkvaness/these-russian
-hackers-say-theyre-using-twitter-bots-to-help (accessed March 21, 2021); Schwirtz, "German Election Mystery."

41. Henk Van Ess and Jane Lytvynenko, "This Russian Hacker Says His Twitter Bots Are Spreading Messages to Help Germany's Far Right Party in the Election," *BuzzFeed,* September 24, 2017, https://www.buzzfeednews.com/article/henkvaness/these
-russian-hackers-say-theyre-using-twitter-bots-to-help (accessed March 21, 2021).

42. Stefan Meister, "The 'Lisa Case': Germany as a Target of Russian Disinformation," *NATO Review,* July 25, 2016, https://www.nato.int/docu/review/articles/2016
/07/25/the-lisa-case-germany-as-a-target-of-russian-disinformation/index.html
(accessed March 21, 2021); Damien McGuinness, "Russia Steps into Berlin 'Rape' Storm Claiming German Cover-Up," *BBC News,* January 27, 2016, https://www
.bbc.com/news/blogs-eu-35413134 (accessed March 21, 2021); "Lavrov Accuses German Authorities of Covering Up," *NTV,* January 26, 2016, https://www.n-tv.de

/mediathek/videos/politik/Lawrow-wirft-deutschen-Behoerden-Vertuschung
-vor-article16857771.html (accessed March 21, 2021).

43. Meister, "The 'Lisa Case'"; McGuinness, "Russia Steps into Berlin 'Rape' Storm
    Claiming German Cover-Up"; "Lavrov Accuses German Authorities of Covering
    Up," *NTV*, January 26, 2016, https://www.n-tv.de/mediathek/videos/politik/Law
    row-wirft-deutschen-Behoerden-Vertuschung-vor-article16857771.html (accessed
    March 21, 2021).

44. Shuster, "How Russian Voters Fueled the Rise of Germany's Far-Right."

45. Shuster, "How Russian Voters Fueled the Rise of Germany's Far-Right."

46. Dostal, "The German Federal Election of 2017," 589–602; Andrea Grunau and
    Mara Bierbach, "Immigrant Voters in German Federal Election Could Prove Influ-
    ential," *Deutsche Welle,* September 7, 2017, https://www.dw.com/en/immigrant
    -voters-in-german-federal-election-could-prove-influential/a-40387375 (accessed
    December 14, 2020).

47. Beuth et al., "Merkel and the Fancy Bear."

48. Beuth et al., "Merkel and the Fancy Bear."

49. Beuth et al., "Merkel and the Fancy Bear."

50. Stelzenmüller, "The Impact of Russian Interference on Germany's 2017 Elections."

51. Comm. on Foreign Relations, Putin's Asymmetric Assault on Democracy, 131.

52. Stelzenmüller, "The Impact of Russian Interference on Germany's 2017 Elections."

53. Schwirtz, "German Election Mystery."

54. Schwirtz, "German Election Mystery."

55. Stelzenmüller, "The Impact of Russian Interference on Germany's 2017 Elections";
    Herpig, *Cyber Operations: Defending Political IT-Infrastructures,* 8.

56. Stelzenmüller, "The Impact of Russian Interference on Germany's 2017 Elections."

57. Schwirtz, "German Election Mystery."

58. Comm. on Foreign Relations, Putin's Asymmetric Assault on Democracy, 130.

59. Comm. on Foreign Relations, Putin's Asymmetric Assault on Democracy, 131.

60. Schwirtz, "German Election Mystery."

61. Comm. on Foreign Relations, Putin's Asymmetric Assault on Democracy, 131.

62. Stupp, "Germany Seeks EU Sanctions for 2015 Cyberattack on Its Parliament."

CHAPTER 10. CROSS-COUNTRY ANALYSIS AND EFFECTIVENESS OF RUSSIA'S CYBER OPERATIONS AND INFORMATION WARFARE CAMPAIGNS

1. Lilly, *Russian Foreign Policy toward Missile Defense: Actors, Motivations, and Influence,*
   5–6, 194.

2. The author has developed several detailed project proposals based on a robust combination of methodologies that can assess the relative effect of Russia's various activities and can facilitate the prioritization of threats that Russia's information warfare
   components pose to the population of different NATO states. For more information,
   contact the author.

3. Joe Cheravitch (former analyst at the RAND Corporation), in discussion with author, April 2, 2021; Lilly, *Russian Foreign Policy toward Missile Defense: Actors, Motivations, and Influence*, 23–27.

4. Cheravitch, in discussion with author.

5. Cheravitch and Lilly, "Russia's Cyber Limitations in Personnel Recruitment and Innovation," 39–47.

CHAPTER 11. POLICY RECOMMENDATIONS FOR DEFENDING AGAINST RUSSIA'S INFORMATION WARFARE ACTIVITIES

1. See, for example, Michael McFaul, ed., *Securing American Elections: Prescriptions for Enhancing the Integrity and Independence of the 2020 U.S. Presidential Election and Beyond* (Stanford University, June 2019); Paul M. Nakasone and Michael Sulmeyer, "How to Compete in Cyberspace: Cyber Command's New Approach," Foreign Affairs, August 25, 2020, https://www.foreignaffairs.com/articles/united -states/2020–08–25/cybersecurity (accessed March 22, 2021); Sean Lyngaas, "Cyber Command's Midterm Election Work Included Trips to Ukraine, Montenegro, and North Macedonia," CyberScoop, March 14, 2019, https://www.cyberscoop.com /cyber-command-midterm-elections-ukraine-montenegro-and-north-macedonia /(accessed March 22, 2021).

2. For the value of this data and how it could be used to enhance network defenses, see Bilyana Lilly, Adam S. Moore, Quentin E. Hodgson, and Daniel Weishoff, *RAND's Scalable Warning and Resilience Model (SWARM): Enhancing Defenders' Predictive Power in Cyberspace* (Santa Monica, CA: RAND Corporation, 2021).

3. The group Anonymous Poland has been suspected of having connections with a Russian state actor who used the group to leak information that could be a part of an information warfare campaign. See "Anonymous Poland—Not Your Typical Hacktivist Group," Digital Shadows Analyst Team, October 28, 2016, https://www .digitalshadows.com/blog-and-research/anonymous-poland-not-your-typical-hack tivist-group/ (accessed March 22, 2021). The message of Anonymous Bulgaria closely reflects positions of the Russian government. See Anonymous Bulgaria, https:// anonybulgaria.wordpress.com/ (accessed March 22, 2021).

4. Svetlana Sharenkova, "Svetlana Sharenkova: Na prav pŭt ste, g-n prezident!" [Svetlana Sharenkova: You are on the right track, Mr. President!], *Epicenter*, April 6, 2017, http://epicenter.bg/article/Svetlana-Sharenkova—Na-prav-pat-ste—g-n-prezident -/124686/11/33 (accessed March 22, 2021).

5. Open Campaign, https://www.opencampaign.com/ (accessed March 30, 2021).

6. "Senate Report Reveals NRA Was 'Foreign Asset' to Russia Ahead of 2016," *NPR*, September 27, 2019, https://www.npr.org/2019/09/27/765037952/senate-report -reveals-nra-was-foreign-asset-to-russia-ahead-of-2016 (accessed April 1, 2021).

7. For a holistic list of recommendations on reducing the probability and effects of significant cyber incidents, see Angus King and Mike Gallagher, *Cyberspace Solarium*

Report (Cyberspace Solarium Commission, March 2020), https://www.solarium
.gov/report (accessed March 22, 2021)

8. U.S. Election Assistance Commission (EAC), https://www.eac.gov/ (accessed March
30, 2021).

9. "What We Do," Defending Digital Campaigns, https://www.defendcampaigns.org/
(accessed March 30, 2021).

10. "What We Do," Defending Digital Campaigns, https://www.defendcampaigns.org/
(accessed March 30, 2021).

11. "2020 Election Impact," *Defending Digital Campaigns*, https://static1.squarespace
.com/static/5d9b44c17da4145c6cac8acf/t/5ffe9aa17a9d6a20d53967bf/16105
21271096/2020-Election-Impact.pdf (accessed March 30, 2021).

12. Daniel, discussion, December 29, 2020.

13. Daniel, discussion, December 29, 2020.

14. Ari Chasnoff, "Election Integrity Partnership Releases Final Report on Mis- and
Disinformation in 2020 U.S. Election," Stanford Internet Observatory Cyber Policy
Center, https://cyber.fsi.stanford.edu/io/news/election-integrity-partnership-releases
-final-report-mis-and-disinformation-2020-us-election (accessed March 22, 2021);
Chloe Colliver, Peter Pomerantsev, Anne Applebaum, and Jonathan Birdwell,
"Smearing Sweden: International Influence Campaigns in the 2018 Swedish Election," Swedish Civil Contingencies Agency (MSB), November 2018, https://www
.isdglobal.org/wp-content/uploads/2018/11/Smearing-Sweden.pdf (accessed March
22, 2021); "Pillars of Russia's Disinformation and Propaganda Ecosystem," Global
Engagement Center, U.S. Department of State, August 2020, https://www.state.gov
/wp-content/uploads/2020/08/Pillars-of-Russia%E2%80%99s-Disinformation
-and-Propaganda-Ecosystem_08–04–20.pdf (accessed March 22, 2021).

15. Ellen Nakashima (national security reporter of the *Washington Post*), in discussion
with author, March 30, 2021; Joe Pompeo, "'Connect the Dots': Marty Baron Warns
Washington Post Staff about Covering Hacked Materials," *Vanity Fair*, September 23,
2020, https://www.vanityfair.com/news/2020/09/marty-baron-warns-wapo-staff
-about-covering-hacked-materials (accessed April 1, 2021).

16. Nakashima, discussion.

17. "Montenegro Overturns Coup Verdict for Two Russians, 11 Others," *Aljazeera*, February 5, 2021, https://www.aljazeera.com/news/2021/2/5/montenegro-overturns
-coup-verdict-for-2-russians-11-others (accessed April 2, 2021).

SELECTED BIBLIOGRAPHY

24 Chasa. "Khristo Grozev: Malko veroyatno e otravyaneto na Gebrev da e sv'rzano s Dunarit" [Hristo Grozev: It is unlikely that Gebrev's poisoning was related to Dunarit]. January 13, 2020. https://www.24chasa.bg/novini/article/8065170 (accessed March 10, 2021).

24 Chasa. "Valeri Simeonov: Siderov poluchava finansirane ot ruska pravoslavna fondatsiya" [Valeri Simeonov: Siderov receives funding from the Russian Orthodox Foundation]. November 30, 2013. https://www.24chasa.bg/novini/article/2504175 (accessed March 10, 2021).

Adamsky, Dmitry (Dima). *Cross-Domain Coercion: The Current Russian Art of Strategy*. Paris, France: Security Studies Center, November 2015. https://www.ifri.org/sites/default/files/atoms/files/pp54adamsky.pdf (accessed March 26, 2021).

AFP. "Russian 'Spies' Accused of Trying to Hack MH17 Inquiry." October 23, 2015. https://tribune.com.pk/story/978152/russian-spies-accused-of-trying-to-hack-mh17-inquiry/ (accessed March 24, 2021).

Africa Internet Summit. "Estonia Cyber Attacks 2007." PowerPoint presentation, 2011. https://meeting.afrinic.net/afrinic-11/slides/aaf/Estonia_cyber_attacks_2007_latest.pdf (accessed March 25, 2021).

Agence France-Presse in Oslo. "Norway Accuses Group Linked to Russia of Carrying out Cyber-Attack." February 3, 2017. https://www.theguardian.com/technology/2017/feb/03/norway-accuses-group-linked-to-russia-of-carrying-out-cyber-attack (accessed March 17, 2021).

Aljazeera. "Montenegro Overturns Coup Verdict for Two Russians, 11 Others." February 5, 2021. https://www.aljazeera.com/news/2021/2/5/montenegro-overturns-coup-verdict-for-2-russians-11-others (accessed April 2, 2021).

Amann, Melanie, and Pavel Lokshin. "German Populists Forge Ties with Russia." *Spiegel Online*. April 27, 2016. https://www.spiegel.de/international/germany/german-populists-forge-deeper-ties-with-russia-a-1089562.html (accessed March 31, 2021).

Andonova, Zdravka. "Rŭkovodstvoto na BSP gotovo da podade ostavka. Mikov ostava lider" [The BSP leadership is ready to resign. Mikov remains the leader]. *Trud*. November 11, 2015. https://trud.bg/article-5087526/ (accessed March 11, 2021).

Andreev, Alexander. "Fakti i dogadki za 'Yuzhen potok'" [Facts and conjectures about "South Stream"]. *Deutsche Welle*. June 13, 2014. https://www.dw.com/bg/%D1% 84%D0%B0%D0%BA%D1%82%D0%B8-%D0%B8-%D0%B4%D0% BE%D0%B3%D0%B0%D0%B4%D0%BA%D0%B8-%D0%B7%D0%B0-% D1%8E%D0%B6%D0%B5%D0%BD-%D0%BF%D0%BE%D1%82%D0%B E%D0%BA/a-17704205 (accessed March 10, 2021).

Anonymous Bulgaria. Official website. https://anonybulgaria.wordpress.com/ (accessed March 22, 2021).

Anti-Democratic Propaganda in Bulgaria. Bulgaria and Russian Propaganda. Sofia, Bulgaria: Human and Social Studies Foundation, 2017. https://hssfoundation.org/wp-content /uploads/2017/04/SUMMARY_Bulgaria-and-Russian-propagandal_EN.pdf (accessed March 28, 2021).

Antonio, Villalon. "The Russian ICC (V): FSB." *Securit A(r)TWork*. December 20, 2016. https://www.securityartwork.es/2016/12/20/the-russian-icc-v-fsb/ (accessed March 5, 2021).

Arkin, William M., Ken Dilanian, and Cynthia McFadden. "What Obama Said to Putin on the Red Phone about the Election Hack." *NBC News*. December 19, 2016. https:// www.nbcnews.com/news/us-news/what-obama-said-putin-red-phone-about-election -hack-n697116 (accessed March 25, 2021).

Associated Press. "Estonia Cancels Russia Talks over Statue." May 2, 2007. https://newsok .com/article/3045674/estonia-cancels-russia-talks-over-statue (accessed March 9, 2021).

Association of Accredited Public Policy Advocates to the European Union. "Association Dialogue Franco-Russe (French-Russian Dialogue)." February 11, 2015. http://www .aalep.eu/association-dialogue-franco-russe-french-russian-dialogue (accessed March 19, 2021).

Baksberg, Tatyana. "Koy e vinoven za tragediyata v 'Arsenal'?" [Who is to blame for the tragedy at "Arsenal"?]. April 26, 2016. *Deutsche Welle*. https://www.dw.com/bg/%D0 %BA%D0%BE%D0%B9-%D0%B5-%D0%B2%D0%B8%D0%BD% D0%BE%D0%B2%D0%B5%D0%BD-%D0%B7%D0%B0-%D1%82%D1% 80%D0%B0%D0%B3%D0%B5%D0%B4%D0%B8%D1%8F%D1%82%D0 %B0-%D0%B2-%D0%B0%D1%80%D1%81%D0%B5%D0%BD%D0%B0% D0%BB/a-19214824 (accessed March 11, 2021).

Baltic Times. "US Congress Passes Resolution Supporting Estonia." June 6, 2007. https:// www.baltictimes.com/news/articles/18002/ (accessed March 25, 2021).

Bartholomew, Brian, and Juan Andrés Guerrero-Saade. "Wave Your False Flags! Deception Tactics Muddying Attribution in Targeted Attacks." *Virus Bulletin* (October 2016): 1–11.

Bartles, Charles. "Getting Gerasimov Right." *Military Review* (January/February 2016): 31–32.

BBC News. "Estonia Seals Off Russian Memorial." April 26, 2007. http://news.bbc.co .uk/2/hi/europe/6597497.stm (accessed March 25, 2021).

BBC News. "Estonia Trial of Russia Activists." January 14, 2008. http://news.bbc.co.uk/2 /hi/europe/7187437.stm (accessed March 10, 2021).

BBC News. "G7 Leaders Reject Russia's Return after Trump Summit Invite." June 2, 2020. https://www.bbc.com/news/world-us-canada-52885178 (accessed March 11, 2021).

BBC News. "General Election 2019: Labour Party Hit by Second Cyber-Attack." November 12, 2019. https://www.bbc.com/news/election-2019–50388879 (accessed March 25, 2021).

BBC News. "Major Russian Naval Force Sails to North Sea Past Norway." October 18, 2016. https://www.bbc.com/news/world-europe-37694137 (accessed March 15, 2021).

BBC News. "Montenegro Approves NATO Membership as Russia Protests." April 28, 2017. https://www.bbc.com/news/world-europe-39738238 (accessed March 17, 2021).

BBC News. "Norway Institutions 'Targeted by Russia-linked Hackers.'" February 3, 2017. https://www.bbc.com/news/world-europe-38859491 (accessed March 15, 2021).

BBC News. "Russia Profile—Media." January 7, 2020. https://www.bbc.com/news/world -europe-17840134 (accessed March 10, 2021).

BBC News. "Tallinn Tense after Deadly Riots." April 28, 2017. http://news.bbc.co.uk/2/ hi/europe/6602171.stm (accessed March 9, 2021).

BBC News. "The Cyber Raiders Hitting Estonia." May 17, 2007. http://news.bbc.co .uk/2/hi/europe/6665195.stm (accessed March 9, 2021).

BBC News. "US Troops to Be Stationed in Norway in Break with Tradition." October 25, 2016. https://www.bbc.com/news/world-europe-37761376 (accessed March 15, 2021).

Bechev, Dimitar. *Russia's Influence in Bulgaria*. Brussels, Belgium: New Direction, 2018. https://newdirection.online/2018-publications-pdf/ND-report-RussiasInfluence InBulgaria-preview-lo-res.pdf (accessed March 28, 2021).

Bechev, Dimitar. *The 2016 Coup Attempt in Montenegro: Is Russia's Balkans Footprint Expanding?* Philadelphia, PA: Foreign Policy Research Institute, April 2018. https:// www.fpri.org/article/2018/04/the-2016-coup-attempt-in-montenegro-is-russias-bal kans-footprint-expanding/ (accessed March 28, 2021).

Bellingcat. "Montenegro Coup Suspect Linked to Russian-Backed 'Ultranationalist' Organization." April 25, 2017. https://www.bellingcat.com/news/uk-and-europe/2017/04 /25/montenegro-coup-suspect-linked-russian-backed-ultranationalist-organisation/ (accessed March 17, 2021).

Bennett, Andrew, and Jeffrey T. Checkel, eds. *Process Tracing: From Metaphor to Analytic Tool*. British Colombia: Cambridge University Press, November 2014.

Beuth, Patrick, Kai Biermann, Martin Klingst, and Holger Stark. "Merkel and the Fancy Bear." *ZEIT Online*. May 12, 2017. https://www.zeit.de/digital/2017–05/cyberattack -bundestag-angela-merkel-fancy-bear-hacker-russia (accessed March 21, 2021).

Bivol. "Wikileaks: Amerikanskite bazi v Bulgaria—'Khlopane na otvorena vrata' ili tajna dogovorka za 'Petrolgeit'?" [WikiLeaks: The American bases in Bulgaria—"Knocking on open door" or a secret agreement for "Petrolgate"?]. May 16, 2011. https://bivol .bg/wlusbasing.html (accessed March 11, 2021).

Bjørkmann, Kjetil. "The Impact from the Russian Import-Ban (2014–) on the Norwegian Seafood Industry: When an Export-Dependent Industry Face Spill-Over Effects from Geopolitical Conflicts" (master's thesis, University of Oslo, 2016) (accessed March 15, 2021).

Blackwell, Tom. "The Top Four Reasons Vladimir Putin Might Have a Grudge against Hillary Clinton." *National Post.* December 16, 2016. https://nationalpost.com/news /world/the-top-four-reasons-vladimir-putin-might-have-a-grudge-against-hillary -clinton/ (accesssed March 11, 2021).

Blackwill, Robert D., and Philip H. Gordon. *Containing Russia: How to Respond to Moscow's Intervention in U.S. Democracy and Growing Geopolitical Challenge.* New York: Council on Foreign Relations, January 2018. Special Report No. 80, at 3, 7. https://cfrd8-files .cfr.org/sites/default/files/report_pdf/CSR80_BlackwillGordon_ContainingRussia .pdf (accessed March 28, 2021).

Bloomberg. "Putin's Stance on Ukraine Supported by Minority of Nations." March 14, 2014. bloomberg.com/graphics/infographics/countries-react-to-russian-intervention -in-crimea.html (accessed March 15, 2021).

Blua, Antoine. "Russia Unveils Cultural, Orthodox Jewel on the Seine." *Radio Free Europe/ Radio Liberty.* October 17, 2016. https://www.rferl.org/a/russia-paris-orthodox-cathe dral-cultural-center-to-open/28058923.html (accessed March 19, 2021).

BNT. "Simpatizanti na 'Ataka' otnovo se sŭbrakha na anti natovski protest" ["Ataka" supporters gathered again for an anti-NATO protest]. March 29, 2015. https://bntnews. bg/bg/a/443835-simpatizanti-na-ataka-otnovo-se-sa-braha-na-anti-natovski-protest (accessed March 10, 2021).

BNT. "Reactions after Putin's Announcement on South Stream." December 2, 2014. https://bnt.bg/news/reactions-after-putin%E2%80%99s-announcement-on-south- stream-128513news.html (accessed March 10, 2021).

BNT. "Versiya sabotazh za vzrivovete v Iganovo" [Sabotage version of the explosions in Iganovo]. April 14, 2015. https://bntnews.bg/bg/a/458713-versiya-sabotazh-za-vzri vovete-v-iganovo (accessed March 11, 2021).

Bolotov, N. N. "Sushchnost' i soderzhaniye ponyatiya 'voyna v informatsionnoy sfere,'" [The essence and content of the concept of "war in the information sphere"]. *Vestnik Akademii Voyennykh Nauk* [Bulletin of the Academy of Military Sciences] 1, no. 58 (2017): 22–28.

Boot, Max. "Time to Get Real about Russia Cyber War: Max Boot." *USA Today.* October 12, 2016. https://www.usatoday.com/story/opinion/2016/10/12/russia-podesta -emails-hackers-cyber-warfare-max-boot/91940364/ (accessed March 15, 2021).

Booz Allen Hamilton. *Bearing Witness: Uncovering the Logic behind Russian Military Cyber Operations*. 2020. https://www.boozallen.com/c/insight/publication/the-logic-behind -russian-military-cyber-operations.html (accessed November 27, 2021).

Bright, Arthur. "Estonia Accuses Russia of 'Cyberattack.'" *Christian Science Monitor*. May 17, 2007. https://cyber-peace.org/wp-content/uploads/2016/11/Estonia-accuses -Russia-of-cyberattack-CSMonitor.pdf (accessed March 9, 2021).

British Ministry of Defense, Land Warfare Development Center. "Land Operations." Army Doctrine Publication AC 71940. Updated March 31, 2017. https://assets. publishing.service.gov.uk/government/uploads/system/uploads/attachment_data /file/605298/Army_Field_Manual__AFM__A5_Master_ADP_Interactive_Gov_ Web.pdf (accessed March 26, 2021).

Bruer, Wesley, and Evan Perez. "Officials: Hackers Breach Election Systems in Illinois, Arizona." *CNN*. August 30, 2016. www.cnn.com/2016/08/29/politics/hack-ers-breach-illinois-arizona-election-systems/ (accessed March 15, 2021).

BTV Novinite. "Bŭlgariya otkaza v'zdushen koridor na ruski samoleti za Siriya" [Bulgaria has refused an air corridor for Russian planes to Syria]. September 8, 2015. https:// btvnovinite.bg/bulgaria/balgarija-otkaza-vazdushen-dostap-na-ruski-samoleti-za -sirija.html (accessed March 10, 2021).

BTV Novinite. "Evrovizitka: Sergey Stanishev, BSP" [Euro card: Sergey Stanishev, BSP]. May 25, 2014. https://btvnovinite.bg/bulgaria/izbori/evrovizitka-sergei-stanishev -bsp.html (accessed March 10, 2021).

Bulgarska Sotsialisticheska Partiya [Bulgarian Socialist Party]. Official website. "Godishen doklad za deynostta I Godishen finansov otchet na BSP" [Annual activities report and Annual financial report of BSP]. https://bsp.bg/documents/publichen_register/ godishen_doklad_za_dejnostta_i_godishen_finansov_otchet_na_bsp.html (accessed March 10, 2021).

Bulgarska Sotsialisticheska Partiya [Bulgarian Socialist Party]. Official website. "Istoriya" [History]. https://bsp.bg/about/history.html (accessed March 10, 2021).

Burrows, Emma. "'Pro-Kremlin Youth Groups' Could Be behind DNC Hack." *Deutsche Welle*. July 27, 2016. https://www.dw.com/en/pro-kremlin-youth-groups-could-be -behind-dnc-hack/a-19430216 (accessed March 11, 2021).

Business.com. "The Best DDoS Protection Services of 2020: How to Choose a DDoS Protection Service." Updated February 7, 2018. https://www.business.com/categories /best-ddos-protection-services/ (accessed March 26, 2021).

Carnegie Endowment for International Peace. "Appendix: A Review of Past Cyber Incidents Involving Financial Institutions." http://carnegieendowment.org/files/Carnegie _Cyber_Financial_Data_white_paper_appendix.pdf (accessed March 26, 2021).

Center for Long-Term Cybersecurity and Microsoft. *Digital Accountability: Designing Futures for Cyber Attack Attribution, Background Document*. Berkeley, CA: July 17, 2018.

Center for Strategic and International Studies. "Russian Foreign Policy: Research and Analysis Regarding All Aspects of Russia's Foreign Policy." Updated July 15, 2019.

https://www.csis.org/programs/russia-and-eurasia-program/archives/russian-for
eign-policy (accessed March 26, 2021).

Center for Strategic and International Studies. "Significant Cyber Incidents." https://
www.csis.org/programs/cybersecurity-and-governance/technology-policy-program
/other-projects-cybersecurity (accessed April 2, 2021).

Center for the Study of Democracy. "Ruskoto vliyanie i zavladyavaneto na mediite v stranite
ot Chernomorskiya region" [Russian influence and the conquest of the media in
the countries of the Black Sea region]. February 21, 2018. https://csd.bg/bg/events/
event/ruskoto-vlijanie-i-zavladjavaneto-na-mediite-v-stranite-ot-chernomorskija
-region/ (accessed March 11, 2021).

Center for the Study of Democracy. *Assessing Russia's Economic Footprint in Montenegro.*
Policy Brief No. 73. January 2018. https://csd.bg/fileadmin/user_upload/public
ations_library/files/2018_01/CSD_Policy_Brief_73_Montenegro.pdf (accessed March
17, 2021).

Center for the Study of Democracy. *Assessing Russia's Economic Footprint in Montenegro.*
Policy Brief No. 73. January 2018. https://csd.bg/fileadmin/user_upload/publications
_library/files/2018_01/CSD_Policy_Brief_73_Montenegro.pdf (accessed March 28,
2021).

Central Election Commission. *Doklad Otnosno Organizatsiyata i Provezhdaneto na Izbori
v Perioda 2015–2017 g.* [Report on the Organization and Conduct of Elections in
the Period 2015–2017]. Sofia, Bulgaria, February 6, 2018. https://www.cik.bg/bg/
reports (accessed March 10, 2021).

Channel 1. "Okonchatel'noye resheniye sovetskogo voprosa. Estoniya gotovitsya k perenosu
pamyatnikov" [The final solution to the Soviet question. Estonia prepares for the
transfer of monuments]. November 26, 2006. https://www.1tv.ru/news/2006–11
–26/214891-okonchatelnoe_reshenie_sovetskogo_voprosa_estoniya_gotovitsya_k
_perenosu_pamyatnikov (accessed March 10, 2021).

Channel 1. "Ukor sovesti. Ne dopustit' demontazh pamyatnika Voinu-osvoboditelyu v
Talline" [A reproach of conscience. Prevent the dismantling of the monument to the
Liberator Soldier in Tallinn]. January 27, 2007. https://www.1tv.ru/news/2007–01
–24/212715-ukor_sovesti_ne_dopustit_demontazh_pamyatnika_voinu_osvo
boditelyu_v_talline (accessed March 10, 2021).

Chasnoff, Ari. "Election Integrity Partnership Releases Final Report on Mis- and Disinformation in 2020 U.S. Election." Stanford Internet Observatory Cyber Policy
Center. https://cyber.fsi.stanford.edu/io/news/election-integrity-partnership-releases
-final-report-mis-and-disinformation-2020-us-election (accessed March 22, 2021).

Chavez, Paola, Veronica Stracqualursi, and Adam Kelsey. "Democratic National Convention 2016: Everything You Need to Know." *ABC News.* July 23, 2016. https://
abcnews.go.com/Politics/democratic-national-convention-2016/story?id=40781224
(accessed March 15, 2021).

Chebil, Mehdi. "France Takes Steps to Prevent an Election Hack Attack." *France 24.* January 14, 2017. https://www.france24.com/en/20170114-france-vulnerable-cyber -attacks-hacking-presidential-elections (accessed March 19, 2021).

Chekinov, S. G., and S. A. Bogdanov. "O kharaktere i soderzhanii voyny novogo pokole niya" [On the nature and content of a new generation of war]. *Voyennaya Mysl'*, no. 10 (October 2013).

Chen, Adrian. "The Agency." *New York Times.* June 2, 2015.

Cheravitch, Joe, and Bilyana Lilly. "Russia's Cyber Limitations in Personnel Recruitment and Innovation, Their Potential Impact on Future Operations, and How NATO and Its Members Can Respond." In *Cyber Threats and NATO 2030: Horizon Scanning and Analysis*, edited by A. Ertan, K. Floyd, P. Pernik, and T. Stevens, 31–59. Tallinn, Estonia: NATO Cooperative Cyber Defence Centre of Excellence, 2020.

Chivvis, Christopher S. "Hybrid War: Russian Contemporary Political Warfare." *Bulletin of the Atomic Scientists* 73, no. 5 (August 2017).

CIRT. "Web Portal of the Government of Montenegro Exposed to DDoS Attacks." October 19, 2016. www.cirt.me/en/news/167139/Web-portal-of-the-Government-of -Montenegro-exposed-to-DDoS-attacks.html (accessed March 17, 2021).

Cohen, Italy, and Omri Ben Bassat. "Mapping the Connections inside Russia's APT Ecosystem." *Check Point Research.* September 24, 2019, https://research.checkpoint .com/2019/russianaptecosystem/ (accessed March 5, 2021).

Cohen, Raphael S., and Andrew Radin. *Russia's Hostile Measures in Europe: Understanding the Threat.* Santa Monica, CA: RAND Corporation, 2019. https://www.rand.org /pubs/research_reports/RR1793.html (accessed March 28, 2021).

Collier, David. "Understanding Process Tracing." *Political Science and Politics* 44, no. 4 (October 2011).

Colliver, Chloe, Peter Pomerantsev, Anne Applebaum, and Jonathan Birdwell. "Smearing Sweden: International Influence Campaigns in the 2018 Swedish Election." Swedish Civil Contingencies Agency (MSB). November 2018. https://www.isdglobal.org/wp -content/uploads/2018/11/Smearing-Sweden.pdf (accessed March 22, 2021).

Comm. on Foreign Relations, Putin's Asymmetric Assault on Democracy in Russia and Europe: Implications for U.S. National Security, S. Rep. No. 115–21 (January 10, 2018). https://www.foreign.senate.gov/imo/media/doc/FinalRR.pdf (accessed March 26, 2021).

Computer Security Incident Response Team of Thailand. *Threat Group Cards: A Threat Actor Encyclopedia.* July 8, 2020. https://www.thaicert.or.th/downloads/files/Threat _Group_Cards_v2.0.pdf (accessed March 28, 2021).

Confessore, Nicholas, and Daisuke Wakabayashi. "How Russia Harvested American Rage to Reshape U.S. Politics." *New York Times.* October 9, 2017. https://nytimes. com/2017/10/09/technology/russia-election-facebook-ads-rage.html (accessed March 25, 2021).

Congressional Research Service. *The Designation of Election Systems as Critical Infrastructure.* September 18, 2019. https://fas.org/sgp/crs/misc/IF10677.pdf (accessed on August 27, 2020).

Congressional Task Force on Election Security, Final Report. January 2018. https://homeland.house.gov/imo/media/doc/TFESReport.pdf (accessed March 26, 2021).

Conley, Heather A., and Theodore P. Gerber. *Russian Soft Power in 21st Century: An Examination of Russian Compatriot Policy in Estonia.* Washington, DC: Center for Strategic and International Studies, September 6, 2011. http://www.bearnetwork.ca/wp-content/uploads/2018/02/110826_Conley_RussianSoftPower_Web.pdf (accessed March 28, 2021).

Conley, Heather A., James Mina, Ruslan Stefanov, and Martin Vladimirov. *The Kremlin Playbook: Understanding Russian Influence in Central and Eastern Europe.* Lanham, MD: Rowman & Littlefield, October 13, 2016.

Connable, Ben, Stephanie Young, Stephanie Pezard, Andrew Radin, Raphael S. Cohen, Katya Migacheva, and James Sladden. *Russia's Hostile Measures: Combating Russian Gray Zone Aggression Against NATO in the Contact, Blunt, and Surge Layers of Competition.* Santa Monica, CA: RAND Corporation, 2020. https://www.rand.org/pubs/research_reports/RR2539.html (accessed March 25, 2021).

Council on Foreign Relations. "Cyber Operations Tracker." https://www.cfr.org/interactive/cyber-operations/search?keys=russia (accessed March 26, 2021).

Croft, Adrian, and Peter Apps. "NATO Websites Hit in Cyber Attack Linked to Crimea Tension." *Reuters.* March 15, 2014. https://www.reuters.com/article/us-ukraine-nato/nato-websites-hit-in-cyber-attack-linked-to-crimea-tension-idUSBREA2E0T320140316 (accessed March 24, 2021).

CrowdStrike (blog). "CrowdStrike's Work with the Democratic National Committee: Setting the Record Straight." June 5, 2020. https://www.crowdstrike.com/blog/bears-midst-intrusion-democratic-national-committee/ (accessed March 25, 2021).

CrowdStrike (blog). "Who is FANCY BEAR (APT28)?" February 12, 2019. https://www.crowdstrike.com/blog/who-is-fancy-bear/ (accessed March 5, 2021).

Cybersecurity and Infrastructure Security Agency, U.S. Department of Homeland Security. *2020 Election Infrastructure Subsector-Specific Plan. An Annex to the NIPP 2013.* 2020.

Cybersecurity and Infrastructure Security Agency, U.S. Department of Homeland Security. "CISA and EAC Develop Risk Profile Tool for Election Officials." September 2, 2020. https://www.cisa.gov/news/2020/09/02/cisa-eac-develop-risk-profile-tool-election-officials (accessed March 15, 2021).

Dalton, Matthew. "France to Sell Two Mistral Warships to Egypt." *Washington Post.* September 23, 2015. https://www.wsj.com/articles/france-to-sell-mistral-warships-to-egypt-1443009701 (accessed March 19, 2021).

Darczewska, Jolanta, *Russia's Armed Forces on the Information War Front: Strategic Documents.* Warsaw, Poland: Centre for Eastern Studies, June 2016.

Davies, Jessica. "Le Monde Identifies 600 Unreliable Websites in Fake-News Crackdown." *Digiday*. January 25, 2017. https://digiday.com/uk/le-monde-identifies-600 -unreliable-websites-fake-news-crackdown/ (accessed March 19, 2021).

Davis, John S. II, Benjamin Adam Boudreaux, Jonathan William Welburn, Jair Aguirre, Cordaye Ogletree, Geoffrey McGovern, and Michael S. Chase. *Stateless Attribution: Toward International Accountability in Cyberspace*. Santa Monica, CA: RAND Corporation, 2017. https://www.rand.org/pubs/research_reports/RR2081.html (accessed March 28, 2021).

Dearden, Lizzie. "Emmanuel Macron Hacked Emails: French Media Ordered by Electoral Commission Not to Publish Content of Messages." *Independent*. May 6, 2017. https://www.independent.co.uk/news/world/europe/emmanuel-macron-email -hack-leaks-election-marine-le-pen-russia-media-ordered-not-publish-commission -a7721111.html (accessed March 19, 2021).

Defending Digital Campaigns. "2020 Election Impact." https://static1.squarespace.com /static/5d9b44c17da4145c6cac8acf/t/5ffe9aa17a9d6a20d53967bf/16105212 71096/2020-Election-Impact.pdf (accessed March 30, 2021).

Defending Digital Campaigns. "What We Do." https://www.defendcampaigns.org/ (accessed March 30, 2021).

Delcker, Janosch. "Germany Fears Russia Stole Information to Disrupt Election: Fears of Hacking as German Lawmakers Worried ahead of September's Ballot." *Politico*. March 20, 2017. https://www.politico.eu/article/hacked-information-bomb-under -germanys-election/ (accessed March 20, 2021).

Department of Defense, Defense Science Board, Task Force on Cyber Deterrence, *Final Report*. (February 2017).

Department of Defense, United States of America. *Joint Publication 3–12 Cyberspace Operations*. June 8, 2018. https://www.jcs.mil/Portals/36/Documents/Doctrine/pubs/jp3 _12.pdf (accessed March 28, 2021).

Deutsche Welle. "EU Urges Russia to End Estonia Embassy Blockade." May 2, 2007. https:// www.dw.com/en/eu-urges-russia-to-end-estonia-embassy-blockade/a-2464370 (accessed March 9, 2021).

Deutsche Welle. "Head of the AfD Frauke Petry Meets with Russian Officials in Moscow." February 20, 2017. https://www.dw.com/en/head-of-the-afd-frauke-petry-meets -with-russian-officials-in-moscow/a-37643188 (accessed March 21, 2021).

Deutsche Welle. "Merkel and Hollande Support Sanction Extensions against Russia." December 13, 2016. https://p.dw.com/p/2UCY9 (accessed March 19, 2021).

Deverell, Edward, Charlotte Wagnsson, and Eva-Karin Olsson. "Destruct, Direct and Suppress: Sputnik Narratives on the Nordic Countries." *Journal of International Communication* 27, no. 1 (2020): 15–37.

Dialogue Franco Russe. "Qui Sommes Nous" [Who we are]. 2021. https://dialoguefran- corusse.com/fr/association.html (accessed March 19, 2021).

Digital Shadows Analyst Team. "Anonymous Poland—Not Your Typical Hacktivist Group." October 28, 2016. https://www.digitalshadows.com/blog-and-research/anonymous-poland-not-your-typical-hacktivist-group/ (accessed March 22, 2021).

Dilanian, Ken, Josh Meyer, Cynthia McFadden, William M. Arkin, and Robert Windrem. "Exclusive: White House Readies to Fight Election Day Cyber Mayhem." *NBC News.* November 3, 2016. https://www.nbcnews.com/news/us-news/white-house-readies-fight-election-day-cyber-mayhem-n677636 (accessed March 17, 2021).

Director of National Intelligence, Joint Statement from the Department of Homeland Security and Office of the Director of National Intelligence on Election Security, October 7, 2016. https://www.dhs.gov/news/2016/10/07/joint-statement-department-homeland-security-and-office-director-national (accessed March 26, 2021).

Directorate General for Civil Registration and Administrative Services [Glavna direktsiya "Grazhdanska registratsiya i administrativno obsluzhvane"]. Official website. https://www.grao.bg/ (accessed March 11, 2021).

DiResta, Renée, Kris Shaffer, Becky Ruppel, David Sullivan, Robert Matney, Ryan Fox, Jonathan Albright, and Ben Johnson. *The Tactics and Tropes of the Internet Research Agency.* New Knowledge, November 2018.

Disinformation: A Primer in Russian Active Measures and Influence Campaigns: Hearings on S. Rep., Before the Select Comm. on Intelligence, Comey (March 30, 2017) (statement of Roy Godson). https://www.hsdl.org/?view&did=802222 (accessed March 26, 2021).

Dnevnik. "Tsatsarov: Gebrev e otroven s insektitsid, nyama danni za 'Novichok.'" [Tsatsarov: Gebrev was poisoned with insecticide, no data for "Novichok"]. February 11, 2019. https://www.pan.bg/?page=view_article&section_id=64&article_id=464308 (accessed March 11, 2021).

Donadio, Rachel. "Why the Macron Hacking Attack Landed with a Thud in France." *New York Times.* May 8, 2017. https://www.nytimes.com/2017/05/08/world/europe/macron-hacking-attack-france.html (accessed March 19, 2021).

Donahue, Patrick, and Ilya Arkhipov. "In Tense Encounter, Merkel Tells Putin Sanctions Must Remain." *Bloomberg.* May 2, 2017. https://www.bloomberg.com/news/articles/2017–05–02/merkel-tells-putin-russia-sanctions-will-have-to-remain-for-now (accessed March 20, 2021).

Dostal, Jörg Michael. "The German Federal Election of 2017: How the Wedge Issue of Refugees and Migration Took the Shine off Chancellor Merkel and Transformed the Party System." *The Political Quarterly* 88, no. 4 (October/December 2017): 589–602.

Dragos. *Crashoverride: Analysis of the Threat to Electric Grid Operations.* 2017. https://dragos.com/blog/crashoverride/CrashOverride-01.pdf (accessed March 26, 2021).

Dylevskiy, I. N., V. O. Zapivahin, S. A. Komov, S V. Korotkov, and A. N. Petrunin. "Mezhdunarodnyy rezhim nerasprostraneniya informatsionnogo oruzhiya: utopiya ili real'nost'? [International regime for the non-proliferation of information weapons: utopia or reality]." *Voyennaya Mysl',* no. 10 (2014).

Dylevskiy, I. N., V. O. Zapivahin, S. A. Komov, S. V. Korotkov, A. A. Krivchenko. "O dialektike sderzhivaniya i predotvrashcheniya voyennykh konfliktov v informatsionnuyu eru" [On the dialectic of deterring and preventing military conflicts in the information era]. *Voyennaya Mysl'*, no. 7 (2016).

Economist. "Naming without Shaming." October 29, 2016. https://www.economist.com /node/21709312/print (accessed March 25, 2021).

Economist. "Wheels within Wheels: How Mr. Putin Keeps the Country Under Control." October 22, 2016. https://www.economist.com/special-report/2016/10/20/wheels -within-wheels (accessed March 5, 2021).

Eddy, Melissa. "Alternative for Germany: Who Are They, and What Do They Want?" *New York Times*. September 25, 2017. https://www.nytimes.com/2017/09/25/world /europe/germany-election-afd.html (accessed March 20, 2021).

Egloff, Florian J. "Public Attribution of Cyber Intrusions." *Journal of Cybersecurity* 6, no. 1 (2020): 1–12.

Encyclopedoa Britannica. s.v. "Estonia." February 2, 2021. https://www.britannica.com/ place/Estonia (accessed March 9, 2021).

En Marche, Le Movement [The movement]. https://en-marche.fr/le-mouvement (accessed March 19, 2021).

Eronen, Pasi. "Case: Sandworm." *Cyberwatch, Finland.* 2020. https://issuu.com/cyber watchfinland.fi/docs/cyberwatchfinland_q1_issuu/16?fbclid=IwAR1vGPsNdMh5hs UO0md9VSEeOUhAulVVY6m88Yl25kpiTNIGZsLqkIxAmto (accessed August 26, 2020).

Eslas, Urve. "Confronting Disinfo on TV in Tallinn." *Up North*. January 18, 2018. https://upnorth.eu/confronting-disinfo-tv-tallinn/ (accessed March 10, 2021).

Espiner, Tom. "Georgia Accuses Russia of Coordinated Cyberattack." *CNet*. August 11, 2008. https://www.cnet.com/news/georgia-accuses-russia-of-coordinated-cyberattack/ (accessed March 24, 2021).

Ess, Henk Van, and Jane Lytvynenko. "This Russian Hacker Says His Twitter Bots Are Spreading Messages to Help Germany's Far Right Party in the Election." *BuzzFeed*. September 24, 2017. https://www.buzzfeednews.com/article/henkvaness/these-rus sian-hackers-say-theyre-using-twitter-bots-to-help (accessed March 21, 2021).

Estonian Foreign Intelligence Service. *International Security and Estonia 2018*. Estonia: 2018. https://www.valisluureamet.ee/pdf/raport-2018-ENG-web.pdf (accessed March 5, 2021).

Estonian Security Police. *Annual Review, 2007*. Estonia. https://www.kapo.ee/sites/default /files/public/content_page/Annual%20Review%202007.pdf (accessed March 28, 2021).

Euromaidan Press. "How Russia Infiltrates the Media Landscape of the Black Sea Region." September 14, 2018. http://euromaidanpress.com/2018/09/14/how-russia-infiltrates -media-of-the-black-sea-region/ (accessed March 11, 2021).

Euronews. "Russian Hackers Blamed for TV5 Cyber Attack." June 10, 2015. https:// www.youtube.com/watch?v=KuDzqYUwygc (accessed March 24, 2021).

European Commission. "Russian Import Ban on EU Products." https://ec.europa.eu /food/safety/international_affairs/eu_russia/russian_import_ban_eu_products_en (accessed March 19, 2021).

Facebook. "Frequently Asked Questions." https://www.facebook.com/business/help /675615482516035 (accessed February 16, 2021).

Farivar, Cyrus. "A Brief Examination of Media Coverage of Cyberattacks (2007–Present)." In *The Virtual Battlefield: Perspective on Cyber Warfare*, edited by Christian Czosseck and Kenneth Geers. Washington, DC: IOS Press, 2009.

Farmer, Ben. "Reconstruction: The Full Incredible Story behind Russia's Deadly Plot to Stop Montenegro Embracing the West." *Telegraph*. February 18, 2017. https://advance .lexis.com/api/document?collection=news&id=urn:contentItem:5MXF-VFW1-F02 1–61G1–00000–00&context=1516831 (accessed March 25, 2021).

Farmer, Ben. "Russia Plotted to Overthrow Montenegro's Government by Assassinating Prime Minister Milo Djukanovic Last Year, according to Senior Whitehall Sources." *Telegraph*. February 18, 2017. https://advance.lexis.com/api/document?collection=news &id=urn:contentItem:5MX7-PPR1-F021–63J7–00000–00&context=1516831 (accessed March 17, 2021).

Federal Returning Officer. "Election Date: 19th German Bundestag to be Elected on 24 September 2017." January 25, 2017. https://www.bundeswahlleiter.de/en/mitteilun gen/bundestagswahl-2017/20170125-wahltermin.html (accessed March 20, 2021).

Federation of American Scientists. "Expansion of Foreign Intelligence Service HQ (SVR; Former KGB First Main Directorate) Yasenevo, Moscow, Russia 55.584 N, 37.517 E Between 2007 and 2018." Version of 2018–07–27. https://fas.org/irp/eprint/svr -expansion.pdf (accessed March 5, 2021).

Financial Times. "Merkel Claims Russia behind 2015 Bundestag Hack." https://www.ft .com/content/264056c9-a13f-4421–9d35-f1bda82375af (accessed March 25, 2021).

Finland Times. "Russian Turla behind Foreign Ministry Hacking." January 14, 2016. http://www.finlandtimes.fi/national/2016/01/14/24215/Russian-Turla-behind -foreign-ministry-hacking (accessed March 24, 2021).

FireEye iSight Intelligence. *APT28: A Window into Russia's Cyber Espionage Operations? Special Report*. 2014. https://www.fireeye.com/content/dam/fireeye-www/global/en /current-threats/pdfs/rpt-apt28.pdf (accessed March 26, 2021).

FireEye iSight Intelligence. *APT28: At the Center of the Storm Russia Strategically Evolves Its Cyber Operations*. January 11, 2017.

FireEye Threat Intelligence. *Trends in Cyber Threat Activity Targeting Elections, 2016– 2019*. January 15, 2020.

Foreign and Commonwealth Office. "UK Exposes Russian Cyber Attacks." October 4, 2018. https://www.gov.uk/government/news/uk-exposes-russian-cyber-attacks (accessed March 26, 2021).

Foreign Ministry of the Russian Federation. Interv'yu Ministra inostrannykh del Rossii S. V. Lavrova ital'yanskoy gazete *Libero*, opublikovannoye 30 noyabrya 2017 goda

[Russian Foreign Minister Sergey Lavrov's interview with the Italian newspaper *Libero*, published on November 30, 2017]. November 30, 2017. http://www.mid.ru/web /guest/maps/it/-/asset_publisher/y8qQ47DsHQYD/content/id/2971828 (accessed March 4, 2021).

Foreign Ministry of the Russian Federation. Vystupleniye Ministra inostrannykh del Rossii S. V. Lavrova na XV Assambleye Soveta po vneshney i oboronnoy politike [Foreign Minister Sergey Lavrov's speech at the XV Assembly of the Council on Foreign and Defense Policy]. March 17, 2007. http://www.mid.ru/web/guest/foreign_policy/news /-/asset_publisher/cKNonkJE02Bw/content/id/379332 (accessed March 21, 2021).

Foreign Ministry of the Russian Federation. Vystupleniye Ministra inostrannykh del Rossii S. V. Lavrova na obshchem sobranii chlenov Rossiyskogo soveta po mezhdunarodnym delam, Moskva, 28 noyabrya 2017 goda [Foreign Minister Sergey Lavrov's remarks at the general meeting of members of the Russian International Affairs Council, Moscow, November 28, 2017]. November 28, 2017. http://www.mid.ru/web/guest /meropriyatiya_s_uchastiem_ministra/-/asset_publisher/xK1BhB2bUjd3/content /id/2969147 (accessed March 4, 2021).

French Press Agency. "France Rules out Easing Russia Sanctions before Progress on Ukraine Made." June 6, 2018. https://www.dailysabah.com/europe/2018/06/06/france-rules -out-easing-russia-sanctions-before-progress-on-ukraine-made (accessed March 19, 2021).

Fruhlinger, Josh. "The CIA Triad: Definition, Components and Examples." *CSO Online*. February 10, 2020. https://www.csoonline.com/article/3519908/the-cia-triad-defini tion-components-and-examples.html (accessed on March 5, 2021).

Galeotti, Mark. "I'm Sorry for Creating the 'Gerasimov Doctrine.'" *Foreign Policy*. March 5, 2018. https://foreignpolicy.com/2018/03/05/im-sorry-for-creating-the-gerasimov -doctrine/ (accessed March 25, 2021).

Galeotti, Mark. *Putin's Hydra: Inside Russia's Intelligence Services*. European Council on Foreign Relations, May 2016. https://ecfr.eu/publication/putins_hydra_inside_russias _intelligence_services/ (as of March 25, 2021).

Gallagher, Sean. "Candid Camera: Dutch Hacked Russians Hacking DNC, including Security Cameras." *Ars Technica*. January 26, 2018. https://arstechnica.com/informa tion-technology/2018/01/dutch-intelligence-hacked-video-cameras-in-office-of-rus sians-who-hacked-dnc/ (as of March 25, 2021).

Gareev, M. A., and N. I. Turko. "Voyna: sovremennoye tolkovaniye teorii i realii praktiki" [War: modern interpretation of theory and realities of practice]. *Vestnik Akademii Voyennykh Nauk* 1, no. 58 (2017): 4–10.

Gaytandzhieva, Dilyana. "Kak bŭlgarskoto orŭzhie stiga do teroristite v Siriya" [How Bulgarian weapons reach terrorists in Syria]. *Trud* [Labor]. April 21, 2017. https://trud .bg/%D0%BA%D0%B0%D0%BA-%D0%B1%D1%8A%D0%BB%D0%B3% D0%B0%D1%80%D1%81%D0%BA%D0%BE%D1%82%D0%BE-%D 0%BE%D1%80%D1%8A%D0%B6%D0%B8%D0%B5-%D1%81%D1

%82%D0%B8%D0%B3%D0%B0-%D0%B4%D0%BE-%D1%82%D0%
B5%D1%80%D0%BE%D1%80/ (accessed March 11, 2021).

Gerasimov, Valeriy. "Generalnyi Shtab i oborona strany" [The General Staff and the defense of the country]. *Voyenno Promyshlennyy Kuryer*. February 3, 2014. https://www.vpk-news .ru/articles/18998 (accessed March 25, 2021).

Gerasimov, Valeriy. "Po opytu Sirii." [From the experience of Syria]. *Voyenno Promyshlennyy Kuryer*. March 8, 2016. http://vpk-news.ru/articles/29579 (accessed March 25, 2021).

Gerasimov, Valeriy. "'Tomagavki' na nizkom starte" ["Tomahawks" at a low start]. *Voyenno Promyshlennyy Kuryer*. May 3, 2017. https://vpk.name/news/180658_tomagavki_na _nizkom_starte.html (accessed March 4, 2021).

Gerasimov, Valeriy. "Tsennost' nauki v predvidenii" [The value of science is in foresight]. *Voyenno Promyshlennyy Kuryer*. February 26, 2013. http://vpk-news.ru/articles/14632 (accessed March 24, 2021).

Giles, Keir. "Information Troops—a Russian Cyber Command?" In *2011 3rd International Conference on Cyber Conflict*, edited by C. Czosseck, E. Tyugu, and T. Wingfield. Tallinn, Estonia: NATO Cooperative Cyber Defence Centre of Excellence, 2011.

Global Engagement Center. "Pillars of Russia's Disinformation and Propaganda Ecosystem." August 2020. U.S. Department of State. https://www.state.gov/wp-content /uploads/2020/08/Pillars-of-Russia%E2%80%99s-Disinformation-and-Propaganda -Ecosystem_08–04–20.pdf. (accessed March 22, 2021).

Golysheva, Natalia. "Ukraine Crisis Spells Arctic Freeze in Russia-Norway Ties." *BBC News*. October 4, 2014. https://www.bbc.com/news/world-europe-29465312 (accessed March 15, 2021).

Government of Montenegro. "Web Portal of Government of Montenegro and Several Other Web Sites Were under Enhanced Cyberattacks." February 17, 2017. http://www.gov .me/en/News/169508/Web-portal-of-Government-of-Montenegro-and-several-other -web-sites-were-under-enhanced-cyberattacks.html (accessed March 17, 2021).

Government of the Russian Federation, Foreign Intelligence Service. http://government .ru/en/department/112/ (accessed August 26, 2020).

Greenberg, Andy. "A Brief History of Russian Hackers' Evolving False Flags." *Wired*. October 21, 2019. https://www.wired.com/story/russian-hackers-false-flags-iran-fancy -bear/ (accessed March 25, 2021).

Greenberg, Andy. "Hack Brief: Russia's Breach of the DNC Is about More Than Trump's Dirt." *Wired*. June 14, 2016. https://www.wired.com/2016/06/hack-brief-russias -breach-dnc-trumps-dirt/ (accessed March 21, 2021).

Greenberg, Andy. *Sandworm: A New Era of Cyberwar and the Hunt for the Kremlin's Most Dangerous Hackers*. New York: Doubleday, 2019.

Grotto, Andrew. "Deconstructing Cyber Attribution: A Proposed Framework and Lexicon." *IEEE Security & Privacy* 18, no. 1 (January/February 2020): 12–20.

Grozev, Christo. "Balkan Gambit: Part 2. The Montenegro Zugzwang." *Bellingcat*. March 25, 2017. https://www.bellingcat.com/news/uk-and-europe/2017/03/25/balkan-gambit -part-2-montenegro-zugzwang/ (accessed March 17, 2021).

Grunau, Andrea, and Mara Bierbach. "Immigrant voters in German federal election could prove influential." *Deutsche Welle*. September 7, 2017. https://www.dw.com/en /immigrant-voters-in-german-federal-election-could-prove-influential/a-40387375 (accessed March 21, 2021).

Guardian. "Emmanuel Macron's Campaign Team Bans Russian News Outlets from Events." April 27, 2017. https://www.theguardian.com/world/2017/apr/27/russia -emmanuel-macron-banned-news-outlets-discrimination (accessed March 19, 2021).

Guardian. "Russia Bans Agricultural Imports from West in Tit-for-Tat Sanctions Move." August 6, 2014. https://www.theguardian.com/world/2014/aug/06/russia-bans -imports-eu-us-sanctions (accessed March 17, 2021).

Guardian. "US Embassy Confirms Death of One American in Bulgaria Grenade Accident." June 6, 2015. https://www.theguardian.com/world/2015/jun/06/bulgaria -american-killed-in-grenade-launcher-accident (accessed March 11, 2021).

Guccifer 2.0. "Guccifer 2.0 DNC's Servers Hacked by a Lone Hacker." June 15, 2016. https://guccifer2.wordpress.com/2016/06/15/dnc/ (accessed March 15, 2021).

Hacquebord, Feike. *Two Years of Pawn Storm: Examining an Increasingly Relevant Threat, Forward-Looking Threat Research (FTR) Team*. Trend Micro, 2017. https://documents .trendmicro.com/assets/wp/wp-two-years-of-pawn-storm.pdf (accessed March 26, 2021).

Herpig, Sven. *Cyber Operations: Defending Political IT-Infrastructures*. Berlin, Germany: Stiftung Neue Verantwortung, June 2017.

Herzog, Stephen. "Revisiting the Estonian Cyber Attacks: Digital Threats and Multinational Responses." *Journal of Strategic Security* 4, no. 2 (2011): 49–60.

Howard, Philip, Bharath Ganesh, Dimitra Liotsiou, John Kelly, and Camille François. *The IRA, Social Media, and Political Polarization in the United States, 2012–2018*. Oxford, United Kingdom: Computational Propaganda Research Project, University of Oxford, 2018.

Huffington Post. "Emmanuel Macron est le seul candidat à proposer une politique étrangère digne de la France" [Emmanuel Macron is the only candidate to propose a foreign policy worthy of France]. March 4, 2017. https://www.huffingtonpost.fr /nicolas-tenzer/emmanuel-macron-est-le-seul-candidat-a-proposer-une-politique -et_a_22022672/ (accessed March 19, 2021).

Huggler, Justin. "Germany Accuses Russia of Cyber Attack on Ukraine Peace Monitors, as Kremlin Dismisses US Intelligence Claims as a 'Witch Hunt.'" *Telegraph*. January 9, 2017. https://www.telegraph.co.uk/news/2017/01/09/germany-accuses-russia -cyber-attack-ukraine-peace-monitors-kremlin/ (accessed March 25, 2021).

Hutchins, Eric M., Michael J. Cloppert, and Rohan M. Amin. "Intelligence-Driven Computer Network Defense Informed by Analysis of Adversary Campaigns and Intrusion Kill Chains." *Leading Issues in Information Confrontation & Security Research* 1, no. 1 (2011): 7–8. https://www.lockheedmartin.com/content/dam/lockheed-martin /rms/documents/cyber/LM-White-Paper-Intel-Driven-Defense.pdf (as of March 24, 2021).

Interfax. "Alexy II: Estonian Government Disrespect for Soldier Monument Immoral." May 2, 2007. http://www.interfax-religion.com/?act=news&div=2982 (accessed March 9, 2021).

Interfax. "Lavrov: rossiyskiye biznesmeny byli vprave sokratit' tranzit cherez Estoniyu posle demontazha Bronzovogo soldata" [Lavrov: Russian businessmen had the right to reduce transit through Estonia after the dismantling of the Bronze Soldier]. April 23, 2009. https://www.interfax.ru/russia/75997 (accessed March 9, 2021).

International Center for Defense and Security. "Russia's Involvement in the Tallinn Disturbances." May 11, 2007. https://icds.ee/russias-involvement-in-the-tallinn-distur bances/ (accessed March 9, 2021).

IPSpecialist LTD. *Certified Ethical Hacker Complete Guide.* United Kingdom: September 15, 2018.

Jensen, Benjamin, Brandon Valeriano, and Ryan Maness. "Fancy Bears and Digital Trolls: Cyber Strategy with a Russian Twist." *Journal of Strategic Studies* 42, no. 2 (2019).

Jonsson, Oscar. *The Russian Understanding of War.* Washington, DC: Georgetown University Press, 2019.

Juurvee, Ivo, and Mariita Mattiisen. *The Bronze Soldier Crisis of 2007: Revisiting an Early Case of Hybrid Conflict.* Tallinn, Estonia: International Centre for Defence and Security, August 2020.

Kadrmatov, Ruslan. "Vremennoye pomeshatel'stvo otnosheniy Politicheskiye aktsii protiv Estonii ne nashli podderzhki na Zapade" [Temporary insanity of political actions against Estonia did not find support in the West]. *Lenta.ru.* May 3, 2007. https:// lenta.ru/articles/2007/05/03/answer/ (accessed March 9, 2021).

Kaljurand, Riina. "Estonia's 'Virtual Russian World'; The Influence of Russian Media on Estonia's Russian Speakers." International Center for Defense and Security. November 13, 2015. https://icds.ee/estonias-virtual-russian-world-the-influence-of -russian-media-on-estonias-russian-speakers/ (accessed March 10, 2021).

Kanevskaya, Natalya. "How the Kremlin Wields Its Soft Power in France." *Radio Free Europe/Radio Liberty.* June 24, 2014. https://www.rferl.org/a/russia-soft-power -france/25433946.html (accessed March 19, 2021).

Kapital. "Masirana khakerska ataka sreshtu dǔrzhavni saĭtove v izborniya den (obnovena), [Massive hacker attack on government sites on election day (updated)]. October 25, 2016. https://www.capital.bg/politika_i_ikonomika/bulgaria/mestni_izbori2015 /2015/10/25/2636035_masirana_hakerska_ataka_sreshtu_durjavni_saitove_v/ (accessed March 11, 2021).

Kari, Martti J. "Russian Strategic Culture in Cyberspace: Theory of Strategic Culture—A Tool to Explain Russia's Cyber Threat Perception and Response to Cyber Threats." PhD diss., University of Juvaskyla, Faculty of Information Technology, 2019.

Kiely, Eugene, and Lori Robertson. "Kushner Distorts Scope of Russia Interference." Factcheck. April 24, 2019. https://www.factcheck.org/2019/04/kushner-distorts -scope-of-russia-interference/?platform=hootsuite (accessed March 12, 2021).

King, Angus, and Mike Gallagher. *Cyberspace Solarium Report.* Cyberspace Solarium Commission. March 2020. https://www.solarium.gov/report (accessed March 22, 2021).

Knight, Scott. "The Dukes of Moscow." *VMware Carbon Black.* March 26, 2020. https://www.carbonblack.com/blog/the-dukes-of-moscow/ (accessed March 5, 2021).

Koebler, Jason. "'Guccifer 2.0' Claims Responsibility for DNC Hack, Releases Docs to Prove It." *Motherboard.* June 15, 2016. https://motherboard.vice.com/read/guccifer-20-claims-responsibility-for-dnc-hack-releases-documents (accessed March 15, 2021).

Kofman, Michael. "Russian Hybrid Warfare and Other Dark Arts." *War on the Rocks.* March 11, 2016. https://warontherocks.com/2016/03/russian-hybrid-warfare-and-other-dark-arts/ (accessed March 25, 2021).

Kokoshin, A. A., Yu. N. Baluyevskiy, and V. Ya. Potapov. "Vliyaniye noveyshikh tendentsiy v razvitii tekhnologiy i sredstv vooruzhennoy bor'by na voyennoye iskusstvo" [The impact of the latest trends in the development of technologies and means of warfare on the art of war]. *Vestnik Moskovskogo universiteta* [Bulletin of Moscow University], series 25: Mezhdunarodnyye otnosheniya i mirovaya politika [International Relations and World Politics], No. 4, 2015.

Korsunskaya, Darya. "Putin Drops South Stream Gas Pipeline to EU, Courts Turkey." *Reuters.* December 1, 2014. https://www.reuters.com/article/us-russia-gas-gazprom-pipeline-idUSKCN0JF30A20141201 (accessed March 10, 2021).

Kovacs, Eduard. "Russian Hackers Target Montenegro as Country Joins NATO." *Security Week.* June 07, 2017. https://www.securityweek.com/russian-hackers-target-montenegro-country-joins-nato (accessed March 17, 2021).

Kozlowski, Andrzej. "Comparative Analysis of Cyberattacks on Estonia, Georgia, and Kyrgyzstan." *European Scientific Journal February* 3 (2014): 240–41.

Kramer, Andrew E. "How Russia Recruited Elite Hackers for Its Cyberwar." *New York Times.* December 29, 2016. https://www.nytimes.com/2016/12/29/world/europe/how-russia-recruited-elite-hackers-for-its-cyberwar.html (accessed February 17, 2021).

Kroll, Andy. "John Podesta Is Ready to Talk about Pizzagate." *Rolling Stone.* December 9, 2018. https://www.rollingstone.com/politics/politics-features/john-podesta-pizzagate-766489/ (accessed March 5, 2021).

Krutaine, Aija, and Andrius Sytas. "Battle of the Airwaves: Baltics Compete with Russia for Hearts and Minds." *Reuters.* February 13, 2015. https://www.reuters.com/article/uk-baltic-russia-propaganda/battle-of-the-airwaves-baltics-compete-with-russia-for-hearts-and-minds-idUKKBN0LH1OG20150213 (accessed March 10, 2021).

Lageman, Thessa. "Russian Hackers Use Dutch Polls as Practice." *Deutsche Welle.* March 10, 2017. https://www.dw.com/en/russian-hackers-use-dutch-polls-as-practice/a-37850898 (accessed March 25, 2021).

Lange-Ionatamišvili, Elina. *Analysis of Russia's Information Campaign against Ukraine.* Riga, Latvia: NATO StratCom Centre of Excellence, 2015.

Lee, Carol E. "Obama Criticizes Russia over Syria Strikes." *Wall Street Journal.* October 2, 2015. https://www.wsj.com/articles/obama-criticizes-russia-over-syria-strikes-14438 20003 (accessed March 11, 2021).

Lenta.ru. "'Nashi' snyali osadu s estonskogo posol'stva" ["Ours" lifted the siege from the Estonian Embassy]. May 3, 2007. https://lenta.ru/news/2007/05/03/nashi/ (accessed March 9, 2021).

Lesk, Michael. "The New Front Line: Estonia under Cyberassault." *IEEE Security & Privacy* (July/August 2007). https://www.computer.org/csdl/magazine/sp/2007/04/ j4076/13rRUwbaqSW (accessed March 10, 2021).

Levintova, Hannah. "Russian Journalists Just Published a Bombshell Investigation about a Kremlin-Linked 'Troll Factory.'" *Mother Jones.* October 18, 2017. https:// www .motherjones.com/politics/2017/10/russian-journalists-just-published-a-bomb shell-investigation-about-a-kremlin-linked-troll-factory/ (accessed March 15, 2021).

Leyden, John. "Russian Spy Agencies Linked to Georgian Cyber-Attacks. Follow the Bear Prints." *Register.* March 23, 2009. https://www.theregister.co.uk/2009/03/23/georgia _russia_cyberwar_analysis/ (accessed March 24, 2021).

Lilly, Bilyana. "Bringing Order through CHAOS: A Framework for Understanding Russian Cyber Operations and Disinformation during the 2020 U.S. Elections and Beyond." *CyberWire.* November 2, 2020. https://www.thecyberwire.com/stories /572863ea3b074fc3867caa362c6bef5a/bringing-order-through-chaos-a-framework-for-understanding-russian-cyber-operations-and-disinformation-during-the-2020-us-elections-and-beyond (accessed March 24, 2021).

Lilly, Bilyana. *Russian Foreign Policy Toward Missile Defense: Actors, Motivations, and Influence.* Lanham, MD: Lexington Books, 2014.

Lilly, Bilyana, and Joe Cheravitch. "The Past, Present, and Future of Russia's Cyber Strategy and Forces." In *20/20 Vision: The Next Decade,* edited by T. Jančárková, L. Lindström, M. Signoretti, I. Tolga, and G. Visky. Tallinn. Estonia: 12th International Conference on Cyber Conflict, NATO Cooperative Cyber Defence Centre of Excellence, 2020. https://ccdcoe.org/uploads/2020/05/CyCon_2020_8_Lilly_Cheravitch .pdf (accessed March 25, 2021).

Lilly, Bilyana, and Sale Lilly. "Weaponising Blockchain: Military Applications of Blockchain Technology in the US, China, and Russia." *RUSI Journal* 165, no. 7 (March 8, 2021). https://rusi.org/publication/rusi-journal/weaponising-blockchain-military -applications-blockchain-technology-us-china?fbclid=IwAR3WpyP8FXHF1z560i 34AUdanYgWNI_J_c7ZTCWp8j6XilXtKYRbuJjHnVc (accessed March 9, 2021).

Lilly, Bilyana, Adam S. Moore, Quentin E. Hodgson, and Daniel Weishoff. *RAND's Scalable Warning and Resilience Model (SWARM): Enhancing Defenders' Predictive Power in Cyberspace.* Santa Monica, CA: RAND Corporation, 2021.

Lilly, Sale, and Bilyana Lilly. "Punish Russia and Revolutionize NATO's Navy." *Real Clear Defense.* August 4, 2014. https://www.realcleardefense.com/articles/2014/08/05/ punish_russia__revolutionize_natos_navy_107343.html (accessed March 19, 2021).

Limno, A. N., and M. F. Krysanov. "Informatsionnoye protivoborstvo i maskirovka voysk" [Information confrontation and masking of troops]. *Voyennaya Mysl'* (2013): 70–74.

Liptak, Andrew. "Russia Was behind the Cyberattack during the Opening Ceremonies for the 2018 Winter Olympics." *Verge*. February 25, 2018. https://www.theverge .com/2018/2/25/17050868/winter-olympics-2018-russia-north-korea-cyber attack-opening-ceremonies (accessed March 25, 2021).

Lipton, Eric, David E. Sanger, and Scott Shanedec. "The Perfect Weapon: How Russian Cyberpower Invaded the U.S." *New York Times*. December 13, 2016. https://www .nytimes.com/2016/12/13/us/politics/russia-hack-election-dnc.html (accessed March 21, 2021).

Lipton, Eric, and Scott Shane. "Democratic House Candidates Were also Targets of Russian Hacking." *New York Times*. December 13, 2016. https://www.nytimes.com /2016/12/13/us/politics/house-democrats-hacking-dccc.html (accessed March 25, 2021).

Ljuba, Zdravko. "German Chancellor Confirms Russian Cyberattack from 2015." *Organized Crime and Corruption Reporting Project*. May 18, 2020. https://www.occrp.org /en/daily/12359-german-chancellor-confirms-russian-cyberattack-from-2015 (accessed March 20, 2021).

Lyngaas, Sean. "Cyber Command's Midterm Election Work included Trips to Ukraine, Montenegro, and North Macedonia." *CyberScoop*. March 14, 2019. https://www .cyberscoop.com/cyber-command-midterm-elections-ukraine-montenegro-and -north-macedonia/ (accessed March 22, 2021).

Makarenko, S. I. *Informatsionnoye protivoborstvo i radioelektronnaya bor'ba v setetsentrich-eskikh voynakh nachala XXI veka* [Information confrontation and electronic warfare in network-centric wars at the beginning of the XXI century]. Saint Petersburg: Science-intensive technologies, 2017.

Mallouk, Doug. "Russian Hack of 2016 Elections Didn't Happen." *Baltimore Sun*. April 29, 2019. https://www.baltimoresun.com/opinion/readers-respond/bs-ed-rr-russian -hack-elections-letter-20190429-story.html (accessed March 11, 2021).

Mankoff, Jeffrey. "Russian Influence Operations in Germany and Their Effect." *Center for Strategic and International Studies*. February 3, 2020. https://www.csis.org/analysis /russian-influence-operations-germany-and-their-effect (accessed March 21, 2021).

Manolova, Mariya, and Momchil Milev. "Da 'khaknesh' izborite. Kiberatakata v denya na mestniya vot ne probi publichnata IT-infrastruktura, no pripomni, che da se pesti ot onlaiïn-sigurnost e vse po-khazartno" [To "hack" the election. The cyberattack on the day of the local vote did not break the public IT infrastructure, but reminded that saving from online security is increasingly gambling]. *Kapital*. October 30, 2015. https://www.capital.bg/politika_i_ikonomika/bulgaria/2015/10/30/2639773_da _haknesh_izborite/ (accessed March 11, 2021).

Mardiste, David, and Olesya Dmitracova. "Estonia Relocates Red Army Statue amid Russia Row." *Reuters*. April 30, 2007. https://uk.reuters.com/article/uk-estonia-russia

/estonia-relocates-red-army-statue-amid-russia-row-idUKL3048016020070430 (accessed on March 9, 2021).

Marinin, S. "Podkhody voyennykh ekspertov SSHA k razrabotke ponyatiynogo apparata v sfere bor'by v kiberprostranstve" [Approaches of U.S. military experts toward the development of concepts in the sphere of warfare in cyberspace]. *Zarubezhnoye Voyennoye Obozreniye* [Foreign Military Review], no. 10 (October 2011).

Markoff, John. "Before the Gunfire, Cyberattacks." *New York Times.* August 12, 2008. https://www.nytimes.com/2008/08/13/technology/13cyber.html (accessed March 24, 2021).

Martin, Anne-Claude. "National Front's Russian Loans Cause Uproar in European Parliament." *Euractiv.* December 4, 2014. Updated December 7, 2014. https://www.euractiv.com/section/europe-s-east/news/national-front-s-russian-loans-cause-uproar-in-european-parliament/ (accessed March 19, 2021).

MassMedia News. "Komissar dvizheniya 'Nashi' priznalsya v kiber-atakakh protiv Estonii" [Commissioner of the "Nashi" movement admitted to cyber attacks against Estonia]. March 12, 2009. https://lenta.ru/news/2009/03/12/confess/ (accessed March 9, 2021).

McAuley, James. "French President Macron Blasts Russian State-Owned Media as 'Propaganda.'" *Washington Post.* May 29, 2017. https://www.washingtonpost.com/world/europe/french-president-macron-blasts-russian-state-run-media-as-propaganda/2017/05/29/4e758308–4479–11e7–8de1-cec59a9bf4b1_story.html (accessed March 19, 2021).

McFaul, Michael, ed. *Securing American Elections: Prescriptions for Enhancing the Integrity and Independence of the 2020 U.S. Presidential Election and Beyond.* Stanford, CA: Stanford University, June 2019.

McGuinness, Damien. "Russia Steps into Berlin 'Rape' Storm Claiming German Cover-Up," *BBC News.* January 27, 2016. https://www.bbc.com/news/blogs-eu-35413134 (accessed March 21, 2021).

McMillan, Robert, and Jennifer Valentin-Devries. "Russian Hacks Show Cybersecurity Limits: The Suspected Attempts by the Kremlin to Influence the U.S. Election Highlight the Risks of Mundane Attacks and Information Warfare." *Wall Street Journal.* November 1, 2016.

Mediapol.bg. "Amerikanets zagina, a chetirima sa raneni pri nov vzriv na poligon na VMZ Sopot" [An American was killed and four were injured in another explosion at the VMZ Sopot test site]. June 6, 2015. https://www.mediapool.bg/amerikanets-zagina-a-chetirima-sa-raneni-pri-nov-vzriv-na-poligon-na-vmz-sopot-news235039.html (accessed March 11, 2021).

Mediapool. "Boyko Noev podozira ruski sabotazh vuv vzrivovete vuv VMZ Sopot" [Boyko Noev suspects Russian sabotage in explosions at VMZ Sopot]. February 24, 2019. https://www.mediapool.bg/boiko-noev-podozira-ruski-sabotazh-vav-vzrivovete-vav-vmz-sopot-news290282.html (accessed March 11, 2021).

Medium. "#ElectionWatch: Russian Botnet Boosts German Far-Right Posts." September 21, 2017. https://medium.com/dfrlab/german-election-russian-botnet-boosts-far-right -posts-45f170bc2321 (accessed March 21, 2021).

Meister, Stefan. "The 'Lisa Case': Germany as a Target of Russian Disinformation." *NATO Review.* July 25, 2016. https://www.nato.int/docu/review/articles/2016/07/25 /the-lisa-case-germany-as-a-target-of-russian-disinformation/index.html (accessed March 21, 2021).

Menn, Joseph. "Exclusive: Russia Used Facebook to Try to Spy on Macron Campaign— Sources." *Reuters.* July 26, 2017. https://www.reuters.com/article/us-cyber-france-face book-spies-exclusive/exclusive-russia-used-facebook-to-try-to-spy-on-macron-cam paign-sources-idUSKBN1AC0EI (accessed March 19, 2021).

Milev, Momchil. "Khakerite, udarili bŭlgarskite izbori, veroyatno sa atakuvali i Klintŭn" [The hackers who hit the Bulgarian elections probably attacked Clinton as well]. *Kapital.* July 27, 2016. https://www.capital.bg/politika_i_ikonomika/bulgaria/2016 /07/27/2802122_hakerite_udarili_bulgarskite_izbori_veroiatno_sa/ (accessed March 10, 2021).

Ministry of Defense of the Russian Federation. "Glavnoye upravleniye General'nogo shtaba Vooruzhennykh Sil Rossiyskoy Federatsii" [Main Directorate of the General Staff of the Armed Forces of the Russian Federation]. https://structure.mil.ru/structure /ministry_of_defence/details.htm?id=9711@egOrganization (accessed March 5, 2021).

Ministry of Defense of the Russian Federation. "Kontseptual'nye vzglyady na deyatel'-nost' Vooruzhennykh Sil Rossiyskoy Federatsii v informatsionnom prostranstve" [Conceptual views on the activities of the armed forces of the Russian Federation in the information space]. 2011. http://ens.mil.ru/science/publications/more.htm?id =10845074@cmsArticle (accessed March 26, 2021).

Ministry of Defense of the Russian Federation. "Struktura Minoborony Rossii" [Struc-ture of the Russian Defense Ministry]. https://structure.mil.ru/structure/structure morf.htm (accessed March 5, 2021).

Ministry of Defense of the Russian Federation, Encyclopedia, s.v. "Informatsionnoe pro-tivoborstvo" [information warfare]. http://encyclopedia.mil.ru/encyclopedia/dictionary /details.htm?id=5221@morfDictionary (accessed March 26, 2021).

Ministry of Defense of the Russian Federation, s.v. "Informatsionnaya voina" [Informa-tion war]. *Military-Encyclopaedic Dictionary of the Ministry of Defense.* http://ency clopedia.mil.ru/encyclopedia/dictionary/details.htm?id=5211@morfDictionary (accessed March 4, 2021).

Ministry of Foreign Affairs of the Republic of Poland, Press Office. "Statement of the Polish MFA on Cyberattacks against Georgia." February 20, 2020. https://www.gov .pl/web/diplomacy/statement-of-the-polish-mfa-on-cyberattacks-against-georgia (accessed March 26, 2021).

Ministry of Foreign Affairs of the Russian Federation. "Comment by the Information and Press Department on invitation for Montenegro to start talks on joining NATO."

December 2, 2015. https://www.mid.ru/en_GB/foreign_policy/rso/-/asset_publisher /0vP3hQoCPRg5/content/id/1963259 (accessed March 17, 2021).

Ministry of Foreign Affairs of the Russian Federation. "O note MID Rossii vneshnepoliticheskomu vedomstvu Estonii" [On the note of the Russian Foreign Ministry to the Estonian Foreign Ministry]. April 23, 2007. http://www.mid.ru/foreign_policy/rso/-/asset_publisher/0vP3hQoCPRg5/content/id/375656 (accessed March 9, 2021).

Ministry of Foreign Affairs of the Russian Federation. Konseptsiya vneshnei politiki Rossiiskoi Federatsii [Foreign policy concept of the Russian Federation]. July 15, 2008. http://www.kremlin.ru/acts/news/785 (accessed March 4, 2021).

Ministry of Foreign Affairs of the Russian Federation. Konseptsiya vneshnei politiki Rossiiskoi Federatsii [Foreign policy concept of the Russian Federation]. February 18, 2013. http://www.mid.ru/foreign_policy/official_documents/-/asset_publisher/CptICkB6BZ29/content/id/122186 (accessed March 4, 2021).

Ministry of Foreign Affairs of the Russian Federation. Konseptsiya vneshnei politiki Rossiiskoi Federatsii [Foreign policy concept of the Russian Federation]. November 30, 2016. http://www.mid.ru/en/foreign_policy/official_documents/-/asset_publisher/CptICkB6BZ29/content/id/2542248 (accessed March 4, 2021).

MITRE Corporation. "ATT&CK. Getting Started." https://attack.mitre.org/resources /getting-started/ (accessed March 26, 2021).

Molchanov, N. A. "Informatsionnyy potentsial zarubezhnykh stran kak istochnik ugroz voyennoy bezopasnosti RF" [Information potential of foreign countries as a source of threats to the military security of the Russian Federation]. *Voyennaya Mysl'*, no. 10 (2008).

Money.bg. "Podкpepyame i shte podкpepim novi sanкtsii speshty Rysiya, кategopichen Borisov" [We are supporting and will support new sanctions against Russia]. April 12, 2014. https://money.bg/economics/podkrepyame-i-shte-podkrepim-novi-sanktsii -sreshtu-rusiya-kategorichen-borisov.html (accessed March 10, 2021).

Morris, Lyle J., Michael J. Mazarr, Jeffrey W. Hornung, Stephanie Pezard, Anika Binnendijk, and Marta Kepe. *Gaining Competitive Advantage in the Gray Zone: Response Options for Coercive Aggression below the Threshold of Major War.* Santa Monica, CA: RAND Corporation, 2019. https://www.rand.org/pubs/research_reports/RR2942.html (accessed March 28, 2021).

Muller, Robert. "Foreign Power Was behind Cyber Attack on Czech Ministry: Senate." *Reuters.* August 13, 2019. https://www.reuters.com/article/us-czech-security-cyber /foreign-power-was-behind-cyber-attack-on-czech-ministry-senate-idUSKCN 1V31DS?il=0 (accessed March 25, 2021).

Nakashima, Ellen. "New Details Emerge about 2014 Russian Hack of the State Department: It Was 'Hand to Hand Combat.'" *Washington Post.* April 3, 2017. https://www .washingtonpost.com/world/national-security/new-details-emerge-about-2014 -russian-hack-of-the-state-department-it-was-hand-to-hand-combat/2017/04/03 /d89168e0–124c-11e7–833c-503e1f6394c9_story.html?utm_term=.9d6cc3a7c930 (accessed March 24, 2021).

Nakasone, Paul M., and Michael Sulmeyer. "How to Compete in Cyberspace: Cyber Command's New Approach." August 25, 2020. *Foreign Affairs*. https://www.foreignaffairs.com/articles/united-states/2020–08–25/cybersecurity (accessed March 22, 2021).

National Cybersecurity and Communications Integration Center and Federal Bureau of Investigation. *Grizzly Steppe—Russian Malicious Cyber Activity*, JAR-16–20296A, December 29, 2016. https://www.us-cert.gov/sites/default/files/publications/JAR_16–20296A_GRIZZLY%20STEPPE-2016–1229.pdf (accessed March 25, 2021).

NATO Review. "Cyber—The Good, the Bad, and the Bug-Free: The History of Cyber Attacks—A Timeline." https://www.nato.int/docu/review/2013/cyber/timeline/en/index.htm (accessed March 26, 2021).

New York Times. "Following the Links from Russian Hackers to the U.S. Election." January 6, 2016. https://www.nytimes.com/interactive/2016/07/27/us/politics/trail-of-dnc-emails-russia-hacking.html (accessed March 15, 2021).

News BG. "Emiliyan Gebrev otroven ot treti ruski agent, zapodozryan po sluchaya 'Skripal'" [Emilian Gebrev poisoned by a third Russian agent suspected in the "Skripal" case]. February 8, 2019. https://news.bg/bulgaria/emiliyan-gebrev-otroven-ot-treti-ruski-agent-zapodozryan-po-sluchaya-skripal.html (accessed March 11, 2021).

Newsru.com. "V Talline razrezan i vyvezen po chastyam pamyatnik Voinu-osvoboditelyu. V besporyadkakh ubit russkoyazychnyy zhitel" [In Tallinn, a monument to the Liberator Soldier was cut and removed in parts. Russian-speaking resident killed in riots]. April 27, 2007. https://www.newsru.com/world/27apr2007/tallin.html (accessed March 10, 2021).

Nezavisimaya Gazeta. Konseptsiya vneshnei politiki Rossiiskoi Federatsii [Foreign Policy Concept of the Russian Federation]. July 1, 2000. http://www.ng.ru/world/2000–07–11/1_concept.html (accessed March 4, 2021).

Nikolov, Georgi. "Beliyat General: Bulgrskata pamet za geroite e neprehodna" [The White General: The Bulgarian memory of the heroes is intransitive]. *Duma*. August 6, 2013. https://duma.bg/?go=news&p=detail&nodeId=59833 (accessed March 10, 2021).

Nilsen, Thomas. "Norway's PST Says Russian Intelligence Targets Individuals." *Barents Observer*. February 3, 2017. https://thebarentsobserver.com/en/security/2017/02/norways-pst-says-russian-intelligence-targets-individuals (accessed March 17, 2021).

Nilsen, Thomas. "Russian Influence Operations Work to Fuel Disagreements between North and South in Norway, Says Report." *Independent Barents Observer*. February 11, 2020. https://www.arctictoday.com/russian-influence-operations-work-to-fuel-disagreements-between-north-and-south-in-norway-says-report/ (accessed March 15, 2021).

Nimmo, Ben. "Frankly Unfair? Fact-Checking *Sputnik France*'s Claim That It Is Reporting the French Election Fairly." *Medium*. February 11, 2017. https://medium.com/dfrlab/frankly-unfair-3a43f4347dfe (accessed March 19, 2021).

Noack, Rick. "Cyberattack on French Presidential Front-Runner Bears Russian 'Finger-prints,' Research Group Says." *Washington Post*. April 25, 2017. https://www.washingtonpost.com/news/worldviews/wp/2017/04/25/cyberattack-on-french-presidential-front-runner-bears-russian-fingerprints-research-group-says/?noredirect=on&utm_term=.fc8acc54ca6e (accessed March 25, 2021).

Noack, Rick. "Report: Hack of French Candidate Has Russian Link." *Washington Post*. April 26, 2017. https://search.proquest.com/docview/1891675252?accountid=25333 (accessed March 14, 2019).

Norden, Lawrence, and Ian Vandewalker. "This Bill Would Help Stop Russia from Buying Online Election Ads." *Slate*. October 19, 2017. http://slate.com/articles/technology/future_tense/2017/10/the_honest_ads_act_would_help_stop_online_election_meddling_from_foreign.html (accessed March 25, 2021).

North Atlantic Treaty Organization. "Jens Stoltenberg, NATO Secretary General." 2014. https://www.nato.int/cps/en/natohq/who_is_who_49999.htm (accessed March 28, 2021).

North Atlantic Treaty Organization. NATO Glossary of Terms and Definitions (English and French). AAP-06 Edition 2019, at 47, 103. https://www.coemed.org/files/stanags/05_AAP/AAP-06_2019_EF.pdf (accessed March 4, 2021).

North Atlantic Treaty Organization. "NATO-Russia Council." March 23, 2020. https://www.nato.int/cps/en/natohq/topics_50091.htm (accessed March 11, 2021);

North Atlantic Treaty Organization. "Relations with Montenegro (Archived)." December 14, 2017. https://www.nato.int/cps/en/natohq/topics_49736.htm (March 17, 2021).

Norwegian Intelligence Service. *Focus 2017: The Norwegian Intelligence Service's Assessment of Current Security Challenges*. Norway: 2017. https://www.forsvaret.no/aktuelt-og-presse/publikasjoner/fokus/Fokus%202017%20english.pdf/_/attachment/inline/c5af8e37–1897–47d9-b1b9–44a9a646d78b:6fd3d3056a6ee63cfe521a b912e7736db91203f2/Fokus%202017%20english.pdf (accessed March 17, 2021).

Norwegian Intelligence Service. *Focus 2020: The Norwegian Intelligence Service's Assessment of Current Security Challenges*. Norway: 2020.

Norwegian Labor Party (Arbeiderpartiet). *Party Manifesto 2017–2021: Everyone participates*. https://res.cloudinary.com/arbeiderpartiet/image/upload/v1/ievv_filestore/f9d 8039b230240f3aedb79ad7620543a0a8dd04c769c4600832eb7a354801839 (accessed March 17, 2021).

Norwegian Police Security Service. *Annual Threat Assessment 2015*. Norway: 2015. https://www.pst.no/globalassets/artikler/trusselvurderinger/annual-threat-assessment-2015.pdf (accessed March 28, 2021).

Norwegian Police Security Service. *National Threat Assessment 2016*. Norway: 2016. https://www.pst.no/globalassets/artikler/trusselvurderinger/threat-assessment-2016.pdf (accessed March 17, 2021).

Nossiter, Adam, David E. Sanger, and Nicole Perlroth. "Hackers Came, but the French Were Prepared." *New York Times*. May 9, 2017. https://www.nytimes.com/2017/05

/09/world/europe/hackers-came-but-the-french-were-prepared.html (accessed March 19, 2021).

Novini BG. "Emiliyan Gebrev razkri koy spored nego stoi zad otravyaneto mu" [Emilian Gebrev revealed who he thinks is behind his poisoning]. February 19, 2019. https://novini.bg/bylgariya/kriminalno/525041 (accessed March 11, 2021);

Novini BG. "Valeri Simeonov: Ruska fondatsiya naliva pari na Volen Siderov" [Valeri Simeonov: Russian Foundation pours money on Volen Siderov]. November 30, 2013. https://novini.bg/bylgariya/politika/168682?comment=dislike&page=1 (accessed March 10, 2021).

NPR. "Senate Report Reveals NRA Was 'Foreign Asset' to Russia ahead of 2016." September 27, 2019. https://www.npr.org/2019/09/27/765037952/senate-report-reveals-nra-was-foreign-asset-to-russia-ahead-of-2016 (accessed April 1, 2021).

NTB/The Local. "Norway's Labour Party Was Hacked by Russia: Report." February 3, 2017. https://www.thelocal.no/20170203/norways-labour-party-was-hacked-by-russia-report (accessed March 17, 2021).

NTV. "Lavrov Accuses German Authorities of Covering Up." January 26, 2016. https://www.n-tv.de/mediathek/videos/politik/Lawrow-wirft-deutschen-Behoerden-Vertuschung-vor-article16857771.html (accessed March 21, 2021).

O'Dwyer, Gerard. "Finland's Security Agencies Collaborate after Cyber Attacks." *Computer Weekly.* August 29, 2019. https://www.computerweekly.com/news/252469691/Finlands-security-agencies-collaborate-after-cyber-attacks (accessed March 25, 2021).

Office of the Director of National Intelligence. *Background to "Assessing Russian Activities and Intentions in Recent US Elections": The Analytic Process and Cyber Incident Attribution.* January 6, 2017. https://dni.gov/files/documents/ICA_2017_01.pdf (accessed March 26, 2021).

Official Website of Attack. "Otcheti" [Financial Reports]. http://www.ataka.bg/%d0%be%d1%82%d1%87%d0%b5%d1%82%d0%b8/ (accessed March 10, 2021).

Open Campaign. https://www.opencampaign.com/ (accessed March 30, 2021).

Organization for Security and Co-operation in Europe, Office for Democratic Institutions and Human Rights, Montenegro Parliamentary Elections 2016. *OSCE/ODIHR Election Observation Mission Final Report.* Warsaw, Poland, January 25, 2017. https://www.osce.org/files/f/documents/3/d/295511.pdf (accessed March 28, 2021).

Orlyanskii, V. I. "Informatsionnoye oruzhiye i informatsionnaya bor'ba: real'nost' i domysly" [Information weapons and information warfare: reality and speculation]. *Voyennaya Mysl'*, no. 1.

Ottis, Rain. *Analysis of the 2007 Cyber Attacks against Estonia from the Information Warfare Perspective.* Tallinn, Estonia: NATO Cooperative Cyber Defence Centre of Excellence, 2018. https://ccdcoe.org/uploads/2018/10/Ottis2008_AnalysisOf2007FromTheInformationWarfarePerspective.pdf (accessed March 25, 2021).

Pakharenko, Glib. "Cyber Operations at Maidan: A First-Hand Account." In *Cyber War in Perspective: Russian Aggression against Ukraine*, edited by Kenneth Geers. Tallinn, Estonia: NATO Cooperative Cyber Defense Center of Excellence, 2015.

Panaiyotova, Dilyana. "Beli gŭlŭbi pusna kŭm Rusiya BSP protest v Sofiya" [White doves launched a BSP protest against Russia in Sofia]. *News.bg.* February 10, 2015. https://news.bg/politics/beli-galabi-pusna-kam-rusiya-bsp-protest-v-sofiya.html (accessed June 26, 2020).

Panarin, Igor'. *SMI, propaganda i informatsionnyye voyny. Teoriya informatsionnogo protivoborstva* [Mass Media, Propaganda, and Information Wars. Information warfare theory]. Moscow: "Pokolenie," 2012. http://propagandahistory.ru/books/Igor-Panarin_SMI—propaganda-i-informatsionnye-voyny/28 (as of March 24, 2021).

Parkinson, Joe, and Georgi Kantchev. "Document: Russia Uses Rigged Polls, Fake News to Sway Foreign Elections; Bulgarian Officials Say a Former Russian Spy Advised Pro-Moscow Party on How to Manipulate Voters as Part of Kremlin's Effort to Regain Influence in Eastern Europe; a 30-Page Dossier." *Wall Street Journal.* March 23, 2017. https://search.proquest.com/newspapers/document-russia-uses-rigged-polls-fake-news-sway/docview/1880062843/se-2?accountid=25333 (accessed March 10, 2021).

Paul, Christopher, and Miriam Matthews. *The Russian "Firehose of Falsehood" Propaganda Model: Why It Might Work and Options to Counter It.* Santa Monica, CA: RAND Corporation, 2016. https://www.rand.org/pubs/perspectives/PE198.html (accessed September 08, 2020).

Paul, Christopher, Colin P. Clarke, Beth Grill, and Molly Dunigan. *Paths to Victory: Lessons from Modern Insurgencies.* Santa Monica, CA: RAND Corporation, 2013. https://www.rand.org/pubs/research_reports/RR291z1.html (as of March 25, 2021).

PBS. "Watch: Fiona Hill's Full Opening Statement—Trump's First Impeachment Hearings," November 21, 2019. Video, 5:00–5:40. https://www.youtube.com/watch?v=L5gmpdtbWB0 (accessed March 11, 2021).

Perez, Evan, and Shimon Prokupecz. "Sources: State Dept. Hack the 'Worst Ever.'" *CNN.* March 10, 2015. https://www.cnn.com/2015/03/10/politics/state-department-hack-worst-ever/ (accessed March 24, 2021).

Perlroth, Nicole. "Russian Hackers Who Targeted Clinton Appear to Attack France's Macron." *New York Times.* April 24, 2017. https://www.nytimes.com/2017/04/24/world/europe/macron-russian-hacking.html (accessed March 19, 2021).

Persily, Nate, and Alex Stamos. "Regulating Online Political Advertising by Foreign Governments and Nationals." In *Securing American Elections: Prescriptions for Enhancing the Integrity and Independence of the 2020 U.S. Presidential Election and Beyond,* edited by Michael McFaul. Stanford, CA: Stanford University, June 2019.

Pifer, Steven. "Five Years after Crimea's Illegal Annexation, the Issue Is No Closer to Resolution." *Order from Chaos.* March 18, 2019. https://www.brookings.edu/blog/order-from-chaos/2019/03/18/five-years-after-crimeas-illegal-annexation-the-issue-is-no-closer-to-resolution/ (accessed March 11, 2021).

Polityuk, Pavel. "Exclusive: Ukraine Says It Sees Surge in Cyber Attacks Targeting Election." *Reuters.* January 25, 2019. https://www.reuters.com/article/us-ukraine-cyber-exclusive/exclusive-ukraine-says-it-sees-surge-in-cyber-attacks-targeting-election-idUSKCN1PJ1KX (accessed March 25, 2021).

Pompeo, Joe. "'Connect the Dots': Marty Baron Warns *Washington Post* Staff about Covering Hacked Materials." *Vanity Fair.* September 23, 2020. https://www.vanityfair.com/news/2020/09/marty-baron-warns-wapo-staff-about-covering-hacked-materials (accessed April 1, 2021).

Popivanov, Boris. "Iskrite mezhdu GERB i RB sa izgodni i za dvete partii" [The sparks between GERB and RB are beneficial for both parties]. *Trud.* November 5, 2015. https://trud.bg/article-5092621/ (accessed March 11, 2021).

Popov, Igor, and Musa Hamzatov. *Voina budushchego* [War of the future]. Moscow: Kuchkovo Pole, 2016.

Poulsen, Kevin, Spencer Ackerman, and Ben Collins. "Russia's Facebook Fake News Could Have Reached 70 Million Americans." *Daily Beast.* August 8, 2017. https://www.thedailybeast.com/russias-facebook-fake-news-could-have-reached-70-million-americans (accessed of March 14 2021).

Presidential Administration of the Russian Federation. Ob utverzhdenii voyennoy doktriny Rossiyskoy Federatsii [On the approval of the military doctrine of the Russian Federation]. February 5, 2010. http://pravo.gov.ru/proxy/ips/?docbody=&firstDoc=1&lastDoc=1&nd=102065541 (accessed March 4, 2021).

Presidential Administration of the Russian Federation. O Strategii natsional'noy bezopasnosti Rossiyskoy Federatsii [On the national security strategy of the Russian Federation], No. 683. December 31, 2015. http://www.kremlin.ru/acts/bank/40391 (accessed March 4, 2021).

Presidential Administration of the Russian Federation. *Voennaya doktrina Rossiiskoi Federatsii* [The military doctrine of the Russian Federation]. December 26, 2014. http://kremlin.ru/acts/news/47334 (accessed March 4, 2021).

Priest, Dana, and Michael Birnbaum. "Europe Has Been Working to Expose Russian Meddling for Years." *Washington Post.* June 25, 2017. https://www.washingtonpost.com/world/europe/europe-has-been-working-to-expose-russian-meddling-for-years/2017/06/25/e42dcece-4a09-11e7-9669-250d0b15f83b_story.html (accessed March 19, 2021);

Psikhologia. "Konflikt Rossii i Estonii stal priobretat' cherty ekonomicheskogo protivostoyaniya i priznaki istoriko-etnicheskogo dissonansa" [The conflict between Russia and Estonia began to acquire features of economic confrontation and signs of historical and ethnic dissonance]. May 5, 2007. https://psy.rin.ru/cgi-bin/news.pl?id=124331 (accessed March 25, 2021).

Radio Free Europe. "Microsoft Says Russian Hackers Exploiting Flaw in Windows System." November 2, 2016. https://www.rferl.org/a/microsfot-warns-russian-hackers-exploiting-flaw-windows-10-operating-system/28089791.html?utm_source=Sailthru&utm_medium=email&utm_campaign=Early%20Bird%20Brief%2011.02.2016&utm_term=Editorial%20-%20Military%20-%20Early%20Bird%20Brief (accessed March 15, 2021).

Radio Free Europe Radio Liberty. "Hollande: Russia Is a Partner, Not a Threat." July 8, 2016. https://www.rferl.org/a/hollande-russia-is-a-partner-not-a-threat/27847690.html (accessed March 19, 2021).

Ragin, Charles C. *The Comparative Method: Moving Beyond Qualitative and Quantitative Strategies.* Berkeley, CA: University of California Press, 1987.

Rankin, Jennifer. "Russia Bans Agricultural Imports from West in Tit-for-Tat Sanctions Move." *Guardian.* August 6, 2014. https://www.theguardian.com/world/2014/aug /06/russia-bans-imports-eu-us-sanctions (accessed March 20, 2021).

Rettman, Andrew. "Illicit Russian Billions Pose Threat to EU Democracy." *EUobserver.* April 21, 2017. https://euobserver.com/foreign/137631 (accessed March 19, 2021).

Reuters. "Foreign Power Was Behind Cyber Attack on Czech Ministry: Senate." August 13, 2019. https://www.reuters.com/article/us-czech-security-cyber/foreign-power-was -behind-cyber-attack-on-czech-ministry-senate-idUSKCN1V31DS?il=0 (accessed March 25, 2021).

Reuters. "French Prosecutors Investigate Hacking of Macron Campaign." May 9, 2017. https://www.reuters.com/article/us-france-election-cyber/french-prosecutors-invest igate-hacking-of-macron-campaign-idUSKBN18525X (accessed March 19, 2021).

Reuters. "Germany Detects New Cyber Attack by Russian Hacker Group—Spiegel." November 29, 2018. https://www.reuters.com/article/germany-cyber-russia/germany -detects-new-cyber-attack-by-russian-hacker-group-spiegel-idUSL8N1Y47J5 (accessed March 25, 2021).

Reuters. "'Key Quotes from Congress' Hearing on Russia and the U.S. Election." March 20, 2017. https://www.reuters.com/article/us-usa-trump-russia-factbox-idUSKBN 16R229 (accessed March 11, 2021).

Reuters. "Kremlin Says NATO Expansion to East Will Lead to Retaliation from Russia." December 2, 2015. https://www.reuters.com/article/us-kremlin-nato-expansion-id USKBN0TL0V720151202 (March 17, 2021).

RFI. "France Condemns Putin's Crimea Annexation, Mulls Sanctions." March 18, 2014. https://www.rfi.fr/en/france/20140318-france-condemns-putins-annexaton-crimea -mulls-sanctions (accessed March 19, 2021).

RIA Novosti. "Genshtab zayavil o roste chisla provokatsiy NATO u granits Rossii" [The General Staff announced an increase in the number of NATO provocations near Russia's borders]. December 24, 2020. https://ria.ru/20201224/nato-1590733312. html (accessed March 4, 2021).

RIA Novosti. "Shoygu rasskazal o zadachakh voysk informatsionnykh operatsiy" [Shoigu spoke about the tasks of the information operation troops." February 22, 2017. https://ria.ru/20170222/1488617708.html (acessed March 5, 2021).

Roach, Andrew. "Instagram Engagement: What It Is and How to Improve It." *Oberlo.* October 7, 2020. https://www.oberlo.com/blog/instagram-engagement-improve (accessed March 12, 2021).

Rosenberg, Matthew, Nicole Perlroth, David E. Sanger. "'Chaos Is the Point': Russian Hackers and Trolls Grow Stealthier in 2020." *New York Times.* January 10, 2020. https://www.nytimes.com/2020/01/10/us/politics/russia-hacking-disinformation -election.html?action=click&module=Top%20Stories&pgtype=Homepage (accessed March 15, 2021).

Rossiyskaya Gazeta. O Strategii natsional'noy bezopasnosti Rossiyskoy Federatsii do 2020 goda [On the national security strategy of the Russian Federation until 2020]. May 19, 2009. https://rg.ru/2009/05/19/strategia-dok.html (accessed March 4, 2021).

Rossiyskaya Gazeta. O Strategii natsional'noy bezopasnosti Rossiyskoy Federatsii [On the national security strategy of the Russian Federation], no. 683. December 31, 2015. https://rg.ru/2015/12/31/nac-bezopasnost-site-dok.html (accessed March 4, 2021).

Roth, Mathias. *Bilateral Disputes between EU Member States and Russia.* CEPS Working Document, No. 319. August 2009, 13. http://aei.pitt.edu/11434/1/1900.pdf (accessed March 9, 2021).

RT. "Friendly Journos and Bankers, Attacks on Bernie and Trump: Part 3 of Podesta Emails." October 11, 2016. https://www.rt.com/usa/362358-wikileaks-third-podesta -emails/ (accessed March 15, 2021).

RT. "'Guccifer 2.0' Releases Hacked DNC Docs Revealing Mega Donors, Clinton Collusion." June 16, 2016. https://www.rt.com/usa/347005-dnc-hack-donors-collusion/ (accessed March 15, 2021).

RT. "Guccifer 2.0 Reveals Clinton Expenses, Clues on Identity and Slams Presidential Hopefuls." July 1, 2016. https://www.rt.com/usa/349193-guccifer-clinton-expenses/ (accessed March 15, 2021).

RT. "Hacker 'Guccifer 2.0' Publishes DNC Campaign Docs with Strategies for Defending Clinton." June 21, 2016. https://www.rt.com/usa/347681-guccifer-clinton-dnc -defense/ (accessed March 15, 2021).

RT. "Julian Assange Special: Do Wikileaks Have the Email That Will Put Hillary Clinton in Prison? (E376)." August 6, 2016. https://www.rt.com/shows/going-underground /354847-wikileaks-dnc-leaks-russia/ (accessed March 15, 2021).

RT. "Lavrov: SSHA i NATO provodyat politiku sderzhivaniya v agressivnykh formakh" [Lavrov: the United States and NATO are pursuing a policy of containment in aggressive forms]. December 10, 2020. https://russian.rt.com/world/news/811834-lavrov -ssha-nato (accessed March 4, 2021).

Russian Interference in European Elections, Russia and Montenegro: Hearings on S. Rep., Before the Select Comm. on Intelligence (June 28, 2017) (statement of Vesko Garčević, ambassador of Montenegro). https://www.intelligence.senate.gov/sites/default/files/docu ments/sfr-vgarcevic-062817b.pdf (accessed March 28, 2021).

Sanger, David E., and Marc Santora. "U.S. and Allies Blame Russia for Cyberattack on Republic of Georgia." *New York Times.* February 21, 2020. https://www.nytimes. com/2020/02/20/world/europe/georgia-cyberattack-russia.html (accessed March 25, 2021).

Sanger, David E., and Matthew Rosenberg. "From the Start, Trump Has Muddied a Clear Message: Putin Interfered." *New York Times*. July 18, 2018. https://www.nytimes.com/2018/07/18/world/europe/trump-intelligence-russian-election-meddling-.html (accessed March 25, 2021).

Sanger, David E., Nicole Perlroth, and Julian E. Barnes. "As Understanding of Russian Hacking Grows, So Does Alarm." *New York Times*. January 2, 2021. Updated January 5, 2021. https://www.nytimes.com/2021/01/02/us/politics/russian-hacking-government.html (accessed March 5, 2021).

Sawe, Benjamin Elisha. "What Was the Eastern Bloc?" *World Atlas*. August 8, 2018. https://www.worldatlas.com/articles/what-was-the-eastern-bloc.html (accessed on March 9, 2021).

Sayfetdinov, H. I. "Informatsionnoye protivoborstvo v voyennoy sfere" [Information confrontation in the military sphere]. *Voyennaya Mysl'*, no. 7 (2014): 38–41.

Schia, Niels Nagelhus, and Lars Gjesvik. "Hacking Democracy: Managing Influence Campaigns and Disinformation in the Digital Age." *Journal of Cyber Policy* 5, no. 3 (2020): 413–28.

Schmidt-Felzmann, Anke. "More Than 'Just' Disinformation. Russia's Information Operations in the Nordic Region." In *Information Warfare. New Security Challenge for Europe*, edited by Tomas Cizik. Bratislava, Slovakia: Centre for European and North Atlantic Affairs, April 2017.

Schwartz, Matthew. "French Officials Detail 'Fancy Bear' Hack of TV5Monde." *Bank Info Security*. June 12, 2017. https://www.bankinfosecurity.com/french-officials-detail-fancy-bear-hack-tv5monde-a-9983 (accessed March 24, 2021).

Schwarzenegger, Arnold. "Governor Schwarzenegger's Message Following This Week's Attack on the Capitol." *YouTube*. January 10, 2021. Video, 0:46. https://youtu.be/x_P-0I6sAck (accessed February 17, 2021).

Schwirtz, Michael. "German Election Mystery: Why No Russian Meddling?" *New York Times*. September 21, 2017. https://www.nytimes.com/2017/09/21/world/europe/german-election-russia.html (accessed March 21, 2021).

Schwirtz, Michael. "How a Poisoning in Bulgaria Exposed Russian Assassins in Europe." *New York Times*. December 22, 2019. https://www.nytimes.com/2019/12/22/world/europe/bulgaria-russia-assassination-squad.html?searchResultPosition=1 (accessed March 10, 2021).

Security Council of the Russian Federation. "Sostav Soveta Bezopasnosti Rossiyskoy Federatsii" [Members of the Security Council of the Russian Federation]. http://www.scrf.gov.ru/council/composition/ (accessed March 5, 2021).

Select Comm. on Intelligence, Russian Active Measures Campaigns and Interference in the 2016 U.S. Election, Volume 1: Russian Efforts against Election Infrastructure with Additional Views, S. Rep. No. 116–XX (July 2019). https://www.intelligence.senate.gov/sites/default/files/documents/Report_Volume1.pdf (accessed March 26, 2021).

Select Comm. on Intelligence, Russian Active Measures Campaigns and Interference in the 2016 U.S. Election, Volume 2: Russia's Use of Social Media With Additional Views, S. Rep. No. 116–XX. https://www.intelligence.senate.gov/sites/default/files/documents/Report_Volume2.pdf (accessed Mach 26, 2021).

Select Comm. on Intelligence, Russian Active Measures Campaigns and Interference in the 2016 U.S. Election, Volume 3: U.S. Government Response to Russian Activities, S. Rep. No. 116–XX. https://www.intelligence.senate.gov/sites/default/files/documents/Report_Volume3.pdf (accessed March 26, 2021).

Select Comm. on Intelligence, Russian Active Measures Campaigns and Interference in the 2016 U.S. Election, Volume 4: Review of the Intelligence Community Assessment, S. Rep. No. 116–XX. https://www.intelligence.senate.gov/sites/default/files/documents/Report_Volume4.pdf (accessed March 26, 2021).

Select Comm. on Intelligence, Russian Active Measures Campaigns and Interference in the 2016 U.S. Election, Volume 5: Counterintelligence Threats and Vulnerabilities, S. Rep. No. 116–XX (August 18, 2020). https://www.intelligence.senate.gov/sites/default/files/documents/report_volume5.pdf (accessed March 24, 2021).

Shalal, Andrea. "Germany Challenges Russia over Alleged Cyberattacks." *Reuters*. May 4, 2017. https://www.reuters.com/article/us-germany-security-cyber-russia/germany-challenges-russia-over-alleged-cyberattacks-idUSKBN1801CA (accessed March 25, 2021).

Shalal, Andrea, and Eric Auchard. "German Election Campaign Largely Unaffected by Fake News or Bots." *Reuters*. September 22, 2017. https://www.reuters.com/article/us-germany-election-fake/german-election-campaign-largely-unaffected-by-fake-news-or-bots-idUSKCN1BX258 (accessed March 21, 2021).

Sharenkova, Svetlana. "Svetlana Sharenkova: Na prav pŭt ste, g-n prezident!" [Svetlana Sharenkova: You are on the right track, Mr. President!]. *Epicenter*. April 6, 2017. http://epicenter.bg/article/Svetlana-Sharenkova—Na-prav-pat-ste—g-n-prezident-/124686/11/33 (accessed March 22, 2021).

Shil'bakh, K., and V. Sventsitskiy. *Voennye Razvedki* [Military intelligence]. Moscow: Military Typography Directorate, 1927. Cited in Lilly and Cheravitch. "The Past, Present, and Future of Russia's Cyber Strategy and Forces," 2020.

Shiryaevskaya, Anna, and Dina Khrennikova. "Why the World Worries about Russia's Natural Gas Pipeline." *Washington Post*. June 29, 2020. https://www.washingtonpost.com/business/energy/why-the-world-worries-about-russias-natural-gas-pipeline/2020/06/28/3202ec10-b901–11ea-9a1d-d3db1cbe07ce_story.html (accessed March 10, 2021).

Shuster, Simon. "How Russian Voters Fueled the Rise of Germany's Far-Right." *TIME*. September 25, 2017. https://time.com/4955503/germany-elections-2017-far-right-russia-angela-merkel/ (accessed March 31, 2021).

Social Media Influence in the 2016 US Election: Hearings on S. Rep., Before the Select Comm. on Intelligence, 115th Cong. (November 1, 2017) (statement by Sean J. Edgett, general counsel, Twitter). https://www.govinfo.gov/content/pkg/CHRG-115shrg27398 /pdf /CHRG-115shrg27398.pdf (accessed March 28, 2021).

Social Media Influence in the 2016 US Election: Hearings on S. Rep., Before the Select Comm. on Intelligence, 115th Cong. (November 1, 2017) (statement by Colin Stretch, vice president and general counsel, Facebook). https://www.govinfo.gov/content/pkg /CHRG-115shrg27398/pdf/CHRG-115shrg27398.pdf (accessed March 28, 2021).

Sofia Globe. "Bulgaria's Parliament Rejects Call against EU Sanctions on Russia." March 4, 2020. https://sofiaglobe.com/2020/03/04/bulgarias-parliament-rejects-call-against -eu-sanctions-on-russia/ (accessed March 25, 2021).

Sofia News Agency. "Elections 2009—Parties, Ataka." https://www.novinite.com/elections 2009/parties.php?id=1 (accessed March 10, 2021).

Soldatov, Andrey, and Irina Borogan. *Bitva za Runet* [Fight for Runet]. Moscow: Al'pina Publisher, 2017.

Sputnik Deutschland. "Bundestagswahl: Sieg für AfD und Merkel—gut oder schlecht für Russland?" [Bundestag election: victory for AfD and Merkel—good or bad for Russia?]. September 24, 2017. https://de.sputniknews.com/kommentare/2017092 4317574980-bundestagswahl-sieg-fuer-afd-und-merkel-gut-oder-schlecht-fuer-russ land/ (accessed December 11, 2020).

Sputnik Deutschland. "Merkel CDU Abrechnung Kritik" [Merkel CDU accounting criticism]. October 22, 2017. https://de.sputniknews.com/politik/20171022317976720 -merkel-cdu-abrechnung-kritik/ (accessed December 11, 2020).

Sputnik Deutschland. "Wahlergebnis Zeichen der Gesellschaftlichen Spaltung Kommentar" [Election result signs of social division comment]. September 28, 2017. https://de.sputniknews.com/kommentare/20170928317626301-wahlergebnis -zeichen-der-gesellschaftlichen-spaltung-kommentar/ (accessed December 11, 2020).

Sputnik France. "Côte-d'Or: plusieurs centaines de bulletins Marine Le Pen volés" [Côte-d'Or: several hundred stolen Marine Le Pen bulletins]. May 7, 2017. https://fr .sputniknews.com/france/201705071031275987-buletins-vol-mlp/ (accessed March 19, 2021).

Sputnik France. "D'où les rumeurs sur Macron proviennent-elles en réalité?" [Where do the Macron rumors actually come from?]. February 17, 2017. https://fr.sputniknews. com/france/201702171030136506-macron-rumeurs-medias/ (accessed March 19, 2021).

Sputnik France. "Echauffourées à Paris: 141 interpellations et 9 gardes à vue" [Scuffles in Paris: 141 arrests and 9 police custody]. May 8, 2017. https://fr.sputniknews.com/ france/201705081031291604-paris-manifestation-interpellation/ (accessed March 19, 2021).

Sputnik France. "Les félicitations continuent d'affluer suite à la victoire de Macron" [Congratulations keep pouring in following Macron's victory]. May 8, 2017. https://fr .sputniknews.com/international/201705081031300998-felicitation-macron-per sonnalites-politiques/ (accessed March 19, 2021).

Sputnik France. "Macron élu par seulement 44% des inscrits" [Macron elected by only 44% of those registered]. May 8, 2017. https://fr.sputniknews.com/france/2017 05081031293191-france-election-macron/ (accessed March 19, 2021).

Sputnik France. "Manif à Paris: violents clashs et correspondante de Sputnik agressée par la police" [Demonstration in Paris: violent clashes and Sputnik correspondent attacked by the police]. May 9, 2017. https://fr.sputniknews.com/france/201705 081031295670-manifestation-regression-sociale-paris/ (accessed March 19, 2021).

Sputnik France. "Nigel FarageLa France a choisi 'cinq ans d'échec de plus', selon Farage" [Nigel Farage France has chosen "five more years of failure," according to Farage]. May 8, 2017. https://fr.sputniknews.com/international/201705081031294281-macron -election-farage/ (accessed March 19, 2021).

Sputnik France. "Présidentielle: l'abstention finale devrait être un record depuis près d'un demi-siècle" [Presidential: final abstention should be a record for almost half a century]. May 7, 2017. https://fr.sputniknews.com/france/201705071031278753-election -abstention-record-estimations/ (accessed March 19, 2021).

Sputnik France. "Présidentielle: participation de 65,30% à 17h, en baisse par rapport au 1er tour" [Presidential: 65.30% participation at 5 p.m., down from the 1st round]. May 7, 2017. https://fr.sputniknews.com/france/201705071031276506-presidentielle -participation-17h/ (accessed March 19, 2021).

Sputnik France. "Score 1 à 0: Macron remporte la 'bataille des poignées de main' contre Trump (Vidéo)" [Score 1 to 0: Macron wins 'handshake battle' against Trump (Video)]. May 25, 2017. https://fr.sputniknews.com/international/20170525103 1537841-macron-trump-poignee-main/ (accessed March 19, 2021).

Sputnik France. "Témoin à Sputnik: 'Dans les trois enveloppes le bulletin Le Pen est déchiré'" [Witness to Sputnik: "In the three envelopes the Le Pen bulletin is torn"]. May 7, 2017. https://fr.sputniknews.com/france/201705071031279598-vote-france -bulletins-dechires/ (accessed March 19, 2021).

Sputnik France. "Vice-Président LR: Macron est 'un Président élu sans envie ni enthousi-asme'" [Vice-President LR: Macron is "an elected President without envy or enthu-siasm"]. May 7, 2017. https://fr.sputniknews.com/france/201705071031285367 -macron-president-elu-commentaire/ (accessed March 19, 2021).

Sputnik France. "Violents accrochages à Paris: la police passe à tabac des manifestants et des journalists" [Violent clashes in Paris: police beat protesters and journalists]. May 8, 2017. https://fr.sputniknews.com/france/201705081031296310-france-paris -accrochages/ (accessed March 19, 2021).

Sputnik International. "Ads Offer Protesters $2500 to Disrupt Trump Inauguration." Jan-uary 17, 2017. https://sputniknews.com/us/201701171049697952-ads-offering-thousands-protest-trump/ (accessed March 15, 2021).

Sputnik International. "Chaffetz Shakes Clinton's Hand, Vows to Continue Email Investi-gation." January 20, 2017. https://sputniknews.com/us/201701201049843190-chaf fetz-shakes-clinton-hand-investigation/ (accessed March 15, 2021).

Sputnik International. "Cher, Scarlett Johansson, Katy Perry to March against Trump in Washington DC." January 10, 2017. https://sputniknews.com/us/2017011010 49458383-katy-perry-cher-celebrities-protest-trump/ (accessed March 15, 2021).

Sputnik International. "Clinton and Abedin Are Parts of Long-Term US Policy to Back Extremists." November 7, 2016. https://sputniknews.com/analysis/20161107 1047134864-clinton-extremists-support/ (accessed March 15, 2021).

Sputnik International. "Clinton Health Charity Failed to Disclose $225Mln in Government Donations." September 6, 2016. https://sputniknews.com/us/2016090610 45028210-us-clinton-charity-donation/ (accessed March 15, 2021).

Sputnik International. "Clinton Is 'Guilty as Hell': Trump Returns to His Campaign Rhetoric." January 13, 2017. https://sputniknews.com/us/201701131049566759 -trump-clinton-guilty-as-hell/ (accessed March 15, 2021).

Sputnik International. "Coming Soon: Julian Assange Teases Juicy Release of Scandalous Clinton Emails." September 7, 2016. https://sputniknews.com/politics/201609 071045070527-assange-hannity-email-tease/ (accessed March 15, 2021).

Sputnik International. "FBI Chief Announces No Change in July Ruling on Clinton Email Probe." November 6, 2016. https://sputniknews.com/politics/20161106 1047127724-FBI-says-no-change-clinton-ruling/ (accessed March 15, 2021).

Sputnik International. "Hillary Clinton Email Probe Ongoing—US House Oversight Chairman." January 26, 2017. https://sputniknews.com/us/201701261050042478 -clinton-probe-email-chairman/ (accessed March 15, 2021).

Sputnik International. "Hillary Clinton Thanks Participants of Anti-Trump Women's March on Washington." January 21, 2017. https://sputniknews.com/us/20170121 1049867469-hillary-clinton-women-march/ (accessed March 15, 2021).

Sputnik International. "'Peaceful Protest' Continues into Evening in Portland after Trump Inauguration." January 21, 2017. https://sputniknews.com/us/201701211049848411 -portland-trump-peaceful-protest/ (accessed March 15, 2021).

Sputnik International. "Trump Asks for 2016 Presidential Election Voter Fraud Probe." January 25, 2017. https://sputniknews.com/us/201701251049992301-trump-voters -probe-fraud/ (accessed March 15, 2021).

Sputnik International. "Trump's Dangerous New 'Voter Fraud' Lies." January 25, 2017. https://sputniknews.com/radio_the_bradcast/201701251050024100-trump-voter -fraud/ (accessed March 15, 2021).

Sputnik International. "US Senator John McCain Attends a News Conference at the Benjamin Franklin Library in Mexico City, Mexico, December 20, 2016. Senator McCain Says He Is Unaware of Any Evidence of Illegal Voting." January 25, 2017. https://sputniknews.com/us/201701251050001526-mccain-trump-illegal-voting/ (accessed March 15, 2021).

Sputnik International. "US Voter Fraud Probe Not to Focus Solely on 2016 Election—White House." January 25, 2017. https://sputniknews.com/us/20170125105000 9062-us-voter-fraud/ (accessed March 15, 2021).

Sputnik International. "WikiLeaks Releases Over 8,000 New Democratic National Committee Emails." November 7, 2016. https://sputniknews.com/us/20161107 1047130918-wikileaks-releases-thousands-dnc-emails/ (accessed March 15, 2021).

Sputnik Srbija. "Crna Gora: Milovi aktivisti prave haos—pritiskaju glasače, vode evidenciju . . ." [Montenegro: Milo's activists are creating chaos—pressuring voters, keeping records . . .]. October 16, 2016. https://rs.sputniknews.com/regioni/2016 10161108500337-izbori-crna-gora-malverzacije-1/ (accessed March 19, 2021).

Sputnik Srbija. "Crnogorski izbori ličili na državni udar" [The Montenegrin elections looked like a coup]. October 17, 2016. https://rs.sputniknews.com/regioni/2016 10171108514218-knezevic-izbori-intervju1/ (accessed March 19, 2021).

Sputnik Srbija. "DF: Lopovska banda DPS uvodi otvorenu diktaturu u Crnoj Gori" [DF: The thieving gang DPS is introducing an open dictatorship in Montenegro]. October 30, 2016. https://rs.sputniknews.com/regioni/201610301108669110-df-saop stenje-izbori-rezultati/ (accessed March 19, 2021).

Sputnik Srbija. "DF: Najvažnije je detronizovati Đukanovića" [DF: The most important thing is to dethrone Djukanovic]. October 19, 2016. https://rs.sputniknews.com/ intervju/201610191108540942-df-detronizovati-djukanovic/ (accessed March 19, 2021).

Sputnik Srbija. "Duma: Izbori pokazali da se veliki broj Crnogoraca protivi ulasku u NATO" [Duma: The elections showed that a large number of Montenegrins oppose joining NATO]. October 17, 2016. https://rs.sputniknews.com/rusija/2016 10171108510916-crna-gora-izbori-nato-rusija-/ (accessed March 19, 2021).

Sputnik Srbija. "Medojevićć: DPS je jedina teroristička organizacija (video)" [Medojevic: DPS is the only terrorist organization (video)]. October 26, 2016. https://rs.sputnik news.com/regioni/201610261108630768-Medojevic-video-poruka/ (accessed March 19, 2021).

Sputnik Srbija. "Milo organizuje dijasporu i plaća 250 evra glas" [Milo organizes the diaspora and pays 250 euros a vote]. October 11, 2016. https://rs.sputniknews.com/ regioni/201610111108433460-dps-djukanovic-dijaspora-glasovi-placenje/ (accessed March 19, 2021).

Sputnik Srbija. "Orilo se iz 10.000 grla: 'Milo lopove' (video)" [It was shouted from 10,000 heads: "Milo thieves" (video)]. September 28, 2016. https://rs.sputniknews .com/regioni/201609281108282745-crna-gora-milo-opozicija-protest/ (accessed March 19, 2021).

Sputnik Srbija. "Vladajuća crnogorska partija najavila osnivanje fonda koji već postoji" [The ruling Montenegrin party announced the establishment of a fund that already exists]. October 9, 2016. https://rs.sputniknews.com/regioni/20161009 1108414860-Vladajuca-crnogorska-partija-najavila-Fond-koji-vec-postoji/ (accessed March 19, 2021).

Sputnik Srbija. "Vreme je da Milo ode u političko čistilište" [It is time for Milo to go to political purgatory]. October 13, 2016. https://rs.sputniknews.com/intervju/20

1610131108467555-Vreme-je-da-Milo-ode-u-politicko-cistiliste/ (accessed March 19, 2021).

Starks, Tim. "Obama Administration Accuses Russian Government of Election-Year Hacking," *Politico*. October 8, 2016. http://www.politico.com/story/2016/10/obama -administration-accuses-russian-government-of-election-year-hacking-229296 (accessed March 15, 2021).

Starks, Tim, Laurens Cerulus, and Mark Scott. "Russia's Manipulation of Twitter Was Far Vaster Than Believed." *Politico*. June 5, 2019, https://www.politico.com/story/2019 /06/05/study-russia-cybersecurity-twitter-1353543 (accessed March 11, 2021).

Statista 2021. "Number of Monthly Active Twitter Users Worldwide from 1st Quarter 2010 to 1st Quarter 2019." https://www.statista.com/statistics/282087/number-of -monthly-active-twitter-users/ (accessed March 19, 2021).

Stefanov, Ruslan, and Martin Vladimirov. *The Kremlin Playbook in Southeast Europe: Economic Influence and Sharp Power*. Sofia, Bulgaria: Center for the Study of Democracy, 2020. https://csd.bg/fileadmin/user_upload/publications_library/files/2020_12/ KREMLIN_PLAYBOOK_3_WEB_NEW.pdf (accessed March 11, 2021).

Stefanov, Ruslan, and Martin Vladimirov. *The Kremlin Playbook in Southeast Europe: Economic Influence and Sharp Power*. Sofia, Bulgaria: Center for the Study of Democracy, 2020.

Stelzenmüller, Constanze. "The Impact of Russian Interference on Germany's 2017 Elections." Testimony. *Brookings Institution*, June 28, 2017. https://www.brookings.edu /testimonies/the-impact-of-russian-interference-on-germanys-2017-elections/ (accessed March 20, 2021).

Stockholm International Peace Research Institute. "Importer/Exporter TIV Tables." http://armstrade.sipri.org/armstrade/page/values.php (accessed March 10, 2021).

Strom, Blake E., Andy Applebaum, Douglas P. Miller, Kathryn C. Nickels, Adam G. Pennington, and Cody B. Thomas. "MITRE ATT&CK Design and Philosophy." July 2018. https://www.mitre.org/sites/default/files/publications/pr-18–0944–11 -mitre-attack-design-and-philosophy.pdf (accessed March 24, 2021).

Stupp, Catherine. "Germany Seeks EU Sanctions for 2015 Cyberattack on Its Parliament." *Investors Hub*. June 11, 2020. advance.lexis.com/api/document?collection =news&id=urn:contentItem:603V-X2R1-F07F-800J-00000–00&context=1516831 (accessed June 11, 2020).

Symantec (blog). "Dragonfly: Western Energy Sector Targeted by Sophisticated Attack Group." October 20, 2017. https://www.symantec.com/blogs/threat-intelligence/ dragonfly-energy-sector-cyber-attacks (accessed March 24, 2021).

Teivainen, Aleksi. "DoS Attack against Election Results Portal under Investigation in Finland." *Helsinki Times*. April 11, 2019. https://www.helsinkitimes.fi/finland/finland -news/domestic/16333-dos-attack-against-election-results-portal-under-investiga tion-in-finland.html (accessed March 25, 2021).

Terterov, Gagik. "Informatsionnyye operatsii: istoriya i sovremennost" [Information operations: history and modernity]. *21st Vek* 3, no. 36 (2015): 40–49.

The Attempted Coup in Montenegro and Malign Russian Influence in Europe: Hearings on S. Rep., Before the Comm. on Armed Services (July 13, 2017) (statement of Janusz Bugajski, senior fellow, Center for European Policy Analysis). https://www.govinfo.gov/content/pkg/CHRG-115shrg34738/html/CHRG-115shrg34738.htm (accessed March 28, 2021).

The Attempted Coup in Montenegro and Malign Russian Influence in Europe: Hearings on S. Rep., Before the Comm. on Armed Services (July 13, 2017) (statement of Nebojsa Kaludjerovic, ambassador of Montenegro to the United States). https://www.govinfo.gov/content/pkg/CHRG-115shrg34738/html/CHRG-115shrg34738.htm (accessed Mach 28, 2021).

The Attempted Coup in Montenegro and Malign Russian Influence in Europe: Hearings on S. Rep., Before the Comm. on Armed Services (July 13, 2017) (statement of Damon Wilson, executive vice president, the Atlantic Council). https://www.govinfo.gov/content/pkg/CHRG-115shrg34738/html/CHRG-115shrg34738.htm (accessed March 28, 2021).

The Moscow Project. "Russia's Three Intelligence Agencies, Explained." *Center for American Progress Action Fund.* October 12, 2018. https://themoscowproject.org/explainers/russias-three-intelligence-agencies-explained/ (accessed March 28, 2021).

Thomas, Timothy J. *Russian Military Thought: Concepts and Elements.* McLean, VA: MITRE Corporation, August 2019.

Tikk, Eneken, Kadri Kaska, and Liis Vihul. *"International Cyber Incidents: Legal Considerations."* Tallinn, Estonia: NATO Cooperative Cyber Defence Centre of Excellence, 2010.

Titcomb, James. "WikiLeaks Releases Thousands of Hacked Macron Campaign Emails." *Telegraph.* July 31, 2017. https://www.telegraph.co.uk/news/2017/07/31/wikileaks-releases-thousands-hacked-macron-campaign-emails/ (accessed March 19, 2021).

Tomovic, Dusica. "Pro-Russian Montenegrins Publish New Anti-Western Media." *Balkan Insight.* October 18, 2017. https://balkaninsight.com/2017/10/18/pro-russian-montenegrins-publish-new-anti-western-media-10–17–2017/ (accessed March 17, 2021).

Tomovic, Dusica, and Maja Zivanovic. "Russia's Fancy Bear Hacks Its Way into Montenegro." *Balkan Insight.* March 5, 2018. https://balkaninsight.com/2018/03/05/russia-s-fancy-bear-hacks-its-way-into-montenegro-03–01–2018/ (accessed March 17, 2021).

Tran, Pierre. "Mistral Dispute with Russia Settled, France Eyes Exports." *Defense News.* August 9, 2015. https://www.defensenews.com/naval/2015/08/09/mistral-dispute-with-russia-settled-france-eyes-exports/ (accessed March 19, 2021).

Traynor, Ian. "Russia Accused of Unleashing Cyberwar to Disable Estonia." *Guardian.* May 17, 2007. https://www.theguardian.com/world/2007/may/17/topstories3.russia (accessed March 25, 2021).

Troianovski, Anton, and Ellen Nakashima. "How Russia's Military Intelligence Agency Became the Covert Muscle of Putin's Duels with the West." *Washington Post.* December 28, 2018. https://www.washingtonpost.com/world/europe/how-russias-military

-intelligence-agency-became-the-covert-muscle-in-putins-duels-with-the-west /2018/12/27/2736bbe2-fb2d-11e8–8c9a-860ce2a8148f_story.html?noredirect=on &utm_term=.afbab6c3ba54 (as of March 25, 2021).

Trotsenko, K. A. "Informatsionnoye protivoborstvo v operativno-takticheskom zvene upravleniya" [Information confrontation in the operational-tactical control link]. *Voyennaya Mysl'*, no. 8 (2016): 20–25.

Trud. "BSP: Stolichna obshtina prakhosva parite na sofiyantsi" [BSP: Municipality Sofia is wasting the money of Sofia residents]. October 12, 2015. https://trud.bg/article -5041933/ (accessed March 11, 2021).

Trud. "Mikhail Mikov: BSP shte iska kasirane na izborite v reditsa naseleni mesta" [Mihail Mikov: BSP will ask for the cancellation of the elections in a number of settlements]. October 29, 2015. https://trud.bg/article-5081364/ (accessed March 11, 2021).

Trud. "Mikov v Kostinbrod: Za BSP i kandidatiteĭobrazovanieto e osnoven prioritet" [Mikov in Kostinbrod: For the BSP and its candidates, education is a top priority]. October 9, 2015. https://trud.bg/article-5035458/ (accessed March 11, 2021).

Trud. "Nikolaĭ Nenchev: Ima danni, che ruskite samoleti bili natovareni s orŭzhie" [Nikolai Nenchev: There is evidence that Russian planes were loaded with weapons]. September 8, 2015. https://trud.bg/article-4970184/ (accessed March 10, 2021).

Trud. "Plamen Nunev: Kandidatite za kmetove na GERB spechelikha v chetiri ot osemte obshtinski tsentŭra na Rusenska oblast" [Plamen Nunev: The candidates for mayors of GERB won in four of the eight municipal centers of Ruse region]. November 27, 2015. https://trud.bg/article-5075999/ (accessed March 11, 2021).

Trud. "Stolichniyat lider na BSP Kaloyan Pargov vnese zhalbata za kasirane na izborite za kmet i sŭvetnitsi v Sofiya" [Sofia BSP leader Kaloyan Pargov files complaint over cancellation of mayoral and councilor elections in Sofia]. November 4, 2015. https:// trud.bg/article-5092282/ (accessed March 11, 2021).

Trud. "Tsvetan Tsvetanov v selo Zvŭnartsi: GERB uvazhava vsichki etnosi i raboti za vsichki khora" [Tsvetan Tsvetanov in the village of Zvanartsi: GERB respects all ethnic groups and works for all people]. October 9, 2015. https://trud.bg/article-5036262/ (accessed March 11, 2021).

Trud. "Tsvetanov v Dŭlgopol: GERB poe otgovornost v mnogo gradove na stranata i rezultatite sa nalitse" [Tsvetanov in Dalgopol: GERB has taken responsibility in many cities of the country and the results are there]. October 13, 2015. https://trud .bg/article-5043484/ (accessed March 11, 2021).

Tsyrendorzhiev, S. R. "O kolichestvennoy otsenke stepeni voyennoy bezopasnosti" [Quantitative assessment of military security of the state]. *Voyennaya Mysl'*, no. 10 (2014).

Tucker, Patrick. "How Putin Weaponized Wikileaks to Influence the Election of an American President." Defense One, July 24, 2016. http://www.defenseone.com/ technology/2016/07/how-putin-weaponized-wikileaks-influence-election-ameri-can-president/130163/ (accessed March 15, 2021).

Turovskiy, Daniil. *Vtorzhenie: Kratkaya istoriya Russkikh khakerov* [Invasion: A short history of Russian hackers]. Moscow: Inviduum, 2019.

Twitter Public Policy Blog. "Update on Twitter's Review of the 2016 US Election." January 19, 2018. https://blog.twitter.com/en_us/topics/company/2018/2016-election-update.html (accessed March 12, 2021).

U.S. Department of Justice, Report on the Investigation into Russian Interference in the 2016 Presidential Election, Volume I of II, Special Counsel Robert S. Mueller, III, Washington D.C., March 2019. https://fm.cnbc.com/applications/cnbc.com/resources/editorialfiles/2019/04/18/muellerreport.pdf (accessed March 28, 2021).

U.S. Election Assistance Commission (EAC). https://www.eac.gov/ (accessed March 30, 2021).

Unit 42. "APT28, Sofacy Playbook Viewer." https://pan-unit42.github.io/playbook_viewer/ (accessed March 26, 2021).

United States of America v. Elena Alekseevna Khusyaynova, Indictment, 1:18-MJ-464 (U.S. District Court for the Eastern District of Virginia, September 28, 2018). https://www.justice.gov/usao-edva/press-release/file/1102591/download (accessed March 28, 2021).

United States of America v. Internet Research Agency LLC A/K/A Mediasintez LLC A/K/A Glavset LLC A/K/A Mixinfo LLC A/K/A Azimut LLC A/K/A Novinfo LLC, Concord Management and Consulting LLC, Concord Catering, Yevgeniy Viktorovich Prigozhon, Mikhail Ivanovich Bystrov, Mikhail Leonidovich Burchik A/K/A Mikhail Abramov, Aleksandra Yuryevna Krylova, Anna Vladislavovna Bogacheva, Sergey Pavlovich Polozov, Maria Anatolyevna Bovda A/K/A Maria Anatolyevna Belyaeva, Robert Sergeyevich Bovda, Dzheykhun Nasimi Ogl Aslanov A/K/A Jayhoon Aslanov A/K/A Jay Aslanov, Vadim Vladimirovich Podkopaev, Gleb Igorevich Vasilchenko, Irina Viktorovna Kaverzin, and Vladimir Venkov, Indictment, 18 U.S.C. sections 2, 371, 1349, 1028A (U.S. District Court for the District of Columbia, February 16, 2018). https://www.justice.gov/opa/press-release/file/1035562/download (accessed March 28, 2021);

United States of America v. Viktor Borisovich Netyksho, Boris Alekseyevich Antonov, Dmitriy Sergeyevich Badin, Ivan Sergeyevich Yerakov, Eleksey Aleksandrovich Morgachev, Nikolay Yuryevich Kozachek, Pavel Vyacheslavovich Yershov, Artem Andreyevich Malyshev, Aleksandr Vladimirovich Osadchuk, Aleksey Aleksandrovich Potemkin, and Anatoliy Sergeyevich Kovalev, Indictment, 18 U.S.C. sections 2, 371, 1030, 1028A, 1956 (U.S. District Court for the District of Columbia, July 13, 2018). https://www.justice.gov/file/1080281/download (accessed March 28, 2021).

United States of America v. Yuriy Sergeyevich Andrienko, Sergey Vladimirovich Detistov, Pavel Valeryevich Frolov, Anatoliy Sergeyevich Kovalev, Artem Valeryevich Ochichenko, and Petr Nikolayevich Pliskin, Indictment, Count One, Conspiracy to Commit an Offense Against the United States, No. 20–316 (U.S. District Court Western District of Pennsylvania, October 15, 2020), at 3. https://www.justice.gov/opa/press-release/file/1328521/download (accessed March 29, 2021).

Värk, René. "The Siege of the Estonian Embassy in Moscow: Protection of a Diplomatic Mission and Its Staff in the Receiving State." *Juridica International*, no. 25 (2008). https://www.juridicainternational.eu/public/pdf/ji_2008_2_144.pdf (accessed March 25, 2021).

Vasiljevic, Stevo. "Russians, Opposition Figures Sentenced over Role in 2016 Montenegro Coup Attempt." *Reuters*. May 9, 2019. https://www.reuters.com/article/us-montenegro-court/russians-opposition-figures-sentenced-over-role-in-2016-montenegro-coup-attempt-idUSKCN1SF144 (accessed March 17, 2021).

Vatsov, Dimitar, and Milena Iakimova. "Co-opting Discontent: Russian Propaganda in the Bulgarian Media." *Eurozone*. October 18, 2017. https://www.stopfake.org/en/co-opting-discontent-russian-propaganda-in-the-bulgarian-media/ (accessed March 11, 2021).

Vesoulis, Abby. "States Are Trying to Stop Election Meddling. But the Real Risk is Public Confidence." *Time*. March 5, 2019. https://time.com/5543649/2020-elections-voter-security-states/ (accessed March 24, 2021).

Vesti. "Siderov v Moskva za rozhdeniya den na Putin" [Siderov in Moscow for Putin's birthday]. October 8, 2012. https://www.vesti.bg/bulgaria/politika/siderov-v-moskva-za-rozhdeniia-den-na-putin-5188831 (accessed March 11, 2021).

Vesti. "Plevneliev: Na izborite 2015 g. imashe moshtna kiberataka" [Plevneliev: in the 2015 elections there was a powerful cyber attack]. February 13, 2019. https://www.vesti.bg/bulgaria/ruskoto-razuznavane-stoialo-zad-kiberataka-na-izborite-2015-g-6092008 (accessed March 10, 2021).

Vesti. "Vzrivove na zavodi v Bŭlgariya ot 2000 g. Nasam," [Explosions of factories in Bulgaria since 2000]. March 21, 2015. https://www.vesti.bg/bulgaria/incidenti/vzrivove-na-zavodi-v-bylgariia-ot-2000-g.-nasam-6033381 (accessed March 11, 2021);

Vilmer, Jean-Baptiste Jeangene. The *"Macron Leaks" Operation: A Post-Mortem*. Washington, DC: Atlantic Council, June 2019. https://www.atlanticcouncil.org/wp-content/uploads/2019/06/The_Macron_Leaks_Operation-A_Post-Mortem.pdf (accessed March 28, 2021).

VMZ, official website. "Dobre doshli vuv 'Vazovski Mashinostroitelni Zavodi' EAD" [Welcome to "Vazov Machine-Building Factories" EAD]. http://vmz.bg/ (accessed March 11, 2021).

Walk, Vivienne. "Why France's Marine Le Pen Is Doubling Down on Russia Support." *Time*. January 9, 2017. http://time.com/4627780/russia-national-front-marine-le-pen-putin/ (accessed March 19, 2021).

Walker, Shaun. "Salutin' Putin: Inside a Russian Troll House." *Guardian*. April 2, 2015.

Wall Street Journal. "Obama: Putin Defending Assad 'Out of Weakness.'" October 2, 2015. https://www.wsj.com/video/obama-putin-defending-assad-out-of-weakness/ABA21763–7F7E-4EB5–8E5B-C85016016541.html (accessed March 11, 2021).

Washington Post. "Putin's Prepared Remarks at 43rd Munich Conference on Security Policy." February 12, 2007. http://www.washingtonpost.com/wp-dyn/content/article/2007/02/12/AR2007021200555.html (accessed March 4, 2021).

Wave, Doug G. "Norway Says Russians Hacked Defense, Security Agencies." *UPI.* February 3, 2017. https://www.upi.com/Top_News/World-News/2017/02/03/Norway-says-Russians-hacked-defense-security-agencies/5121486150733/ (accessed March 17, 2021).

Welt, Cory. *Ukraine: Background, Conflict with Russia, and U.S. Policy.* Washington, DC: Congressional Research Service, April 29, 2020. https://fas.org/sgp/crs/row/R45008.pdf (accessed March 11, 2021).

Whewell, Tim. "Has the Kremlin Been Meddling with Its Arctic Friends?" *BBC News.* November 12, 2015. https://www.bbc.com/news/magazine-34789927 (accessed March 15, 2021).

Williams, Carol J. "Russia Says Bulgaria's Refusal of Flyovers to Syria Is a U.S. Plot." *Los Angeles Times.* September 8, 2015. https://www.latimes.com/world/europe/la-fg-russia-syria-us-bulgaria-20150908-story.html (accessed March 10, 2021).

Witte, Griff. "As Germans Prepare to Vote, a Mystery Grows: Where Are the Russians?" *Washington Post.* September 10, 2017. https://www.washingtonpost.com/world/as-germans-prepare-to-vote-a-mystery-grows-where-are-the-russians/2017/09/10/07d47f54-9257-11e7-8482-8dc9a7af29f9_story.html (accessed March 19, 2021).

World Anti-Doping Agency (WADA). "WADA Confirms Attack by Russian Cyber Espionage Group." September 13, 2016. https://www.wada-ama.org/en/media/news/2016-09/wada-confirms-attack-by-russian-cyber-espionage-group (accessed March 26, 2021).

Yarkov, Sergei Alekseevich. "Nevoyennyye sredstva i nevoyennyye mery neytralizatsii voyennykh opasnostey: sushchnostnoye razlichiye i predmetnaya kharakteristika ponyatiy" [Nonmilitary means and non-military measures to neutralize military dangers: essential difference and objective characteristics of the concepts]. *Natsional'naya bezopasnost'* [National Security], no. 3 (2017).

Yle. "Russian Group behind 2013 Foreign Ministry Hack." January 13, 2016. https://yle.fi/uutiset/osasto/news/russian_group_behind_2013_foreign_ministry_hack/8591548 (accessed March 24, 2021).

Zagolovki. "Ssora s Rossiyey obernulas' dlya Estonii ogromnymi poteryami" [The quarrel with Russia turned out to be huge losses for Estonia]. November 17, 2007. http://zagolovki.ru/daytheme/estonia/17Nov2007 (accessed March 9, 2021).

Zakem, Vera, Paul Saunders, Umida Hashimova, and P. Kathleen Hammerberg. *Mapping Russian Media Network: Media's Role in Russian Foreign Policy and Decision-Making.* Arlington, VA: Center for Naval Analysis, January 2018. https://www.cna.org/cna_files/pdf/DRM-2017-U-015367-3Rev.pdf (accessed March 9, 2021).

Zetter, Kim. "Top Voting Machine Vendor Admits It Installed Remote-Access Software on Systems Sold to States." *Vice.* July 17, 2018. https://www.vice.com/en_us/article/mb4ezy/top-voting-machine-vendor-admits-it-installed-remote-access-software-on-systems-sold-to-states?wpisrc=nl_cybersecurity202&wpmm=1 (accessed on March 9, 2021).

INDEX

ABOUT THE AUTHOR

Denounced by the Russian Ministry of Foreign Affairs, **Dr. Bilyana Lilly** has managed projects on ransomware, cyber threat intelligence, AI, disinformation, and information warfare. She is now a geopolitical risk lead at the Krebs Stamos Group and previously worked as a cyber manager at Deloitte and as a cyber expert for the RAND Corporation. Dr. Lilly has spoken at DefCon, CyCon, the Executive Women's Forum, and the Warsaw Security Forum. She is the author of more than a dozen peer-reviewed publications and has been cited in the *Wall Street Journal, Foreign Policy*, and ZDNet.

The Naval Institute Press is the book-publishing arm of the U.S. Naval Institute, a private, nonprofit, membership society for sea service professionals and others who share an interest in naval and maritime affairs. Established in 1873 at the U.S. Naval Academy in Annapolis, Maryland, where its offices remain today, the Naval Institute has members worldwide.

Members of the Naval Institute support the education programs of the society and receive the influential monthly magazine *Proceedings* or the colorful bimonthly magazine N*aval History* and discounts on fine nautical prints and on ship and aircraft photos. They also have access to the transcripts of the Institute's Oral History Program and get discounted admission to any of the Institute-sponsored seminars offered around the country.

The Naval Institute's book-publishing program, begun in 1898 with basic guides to naval practices, has broadened its scope to include books of more general interest. Now the Naval Institute Press publishes about seventy titles each year, ranging from how-to books on boating and navigation to battle histories, biographies, ship and aircraft guides, and novels. Institute members receive significant discounts on the Press' more than eight hundred books in print.

Full-time students are eligible for special half-price membership rates. Life memberships are also available.

For more information about Naval Institute Press books that are currently available, visit www.usni.org/press/books. To learn about joining the U.S. Naval Institute, please write to:

Member Services
U.S. NAVAL INSTITUTE
291 Wood Road
Annapolis, MD 21402-5034
Telephone: (800) 233-8764
Fax: (410) 571-1703
Web address: www.usni.org